Declarations of
Stock Car Independents

ALSO BY
PERRY ALLEN WOOD

*Silent Speedways of the Carolinas: The Grand National
Histories of 29 Former Tracks* (McFarland, 2007)

Declarations of Stock Car Independents

Interviews with Twelve Racers of the 1950s, 1960s and 1970s

PERRY ALLEN WOOD
Foreword by Jeff Gilder

McFarland & Company, Inc., Publishers
Jefferson, North Carolina, and London

All photographs were provided by the author unless otherwise credited.

LIBRARY OF CONGRESS CATALOGUING-IN-PUBLICATION DATA

Wood, Perry Allen, 1952–
　　Declarations of stock car independents : interviews with twelve racers of the 1950s, 1960s and 1970s / Perry Allen Wood ; foreword by Jeff Gilder.
　　　　p.　cm.
　　Includes bibliographical references and index.

ISBN 978-0-7864-4764-0
softcover : 50# alkaline paper ♾

　1. Stock car drivers — United States — Interviews.
　2. Stock car drivers — United States — Biography.
　3. Stock car racing — United States — History.
　4. NASCAR (Association) — History.　I. Title.
GV1032.A1W75　2010
796.720922 — dc22　　　　　　　　　　　　　　　2010038796
[B]

British Library cataloguing data are available

© 2010 Perry Allen Wood. All rights reserved

No part of this book may be reproduced or transmitted in any form or by any means, electronic or mechanical, including photocopying or recording, or by any information storage and retrieval system, without permission in writing from the publisher.

Front cover: With the '65 Dodge showing the battle scars of three seasons, James Hylton is eager to go at Trenton, New Jersey, on July 9, 1967. He started sixth and finished tenth (photograph courtesy James Hylton)

Manufactured in the United States of America

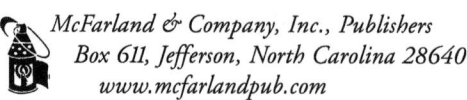

McFarland & Company, Inc., Publishers
Box 611, Jefferson, North Carolina 28640
www.mcfarlandpub.com

To three wise men. Dr. Eric L. Cole, our family physician who made me get a physical before refilling a simple prescription and found an imbalance of bodily humors. Dr. Clifton L. Williams, Jr., who identified the demon growing inside me. And Dr. Gerald W. Hull who cut it out. Thank you, gentlemen. You saved my life.

Also to the memory of one brave woman, Angala Tarlton. She fought the demon for two-and-a-half years with extraordinary courage and was an inspiration to all who knew her.

Table of Contents

Acknowledgments ix

Foreword by Jeff Gilder 1

Preface 3

Introduction 5

1. Johnny Allen — *Spectacular Speedster*	9
2. Tommy Irwin — *Tough Tommy*	30
3. Curtis Crider — *Crawfish*	48
4. Elmo Henderson — *The Lone Pioneer*	66
5. Reb Wickersham — *The Flying Rebel*	83
6. Paul Lewis — *Gentleman Teacher*	104
7. Gene Hobby — *The Racing Marine*	126
8. Jimmy Helms — *The Dreamer*	143
9. Joe Frasson — *Jackhandle Joe*	160
10. Raymond Williams — *Captain America*	182
11. D.K. Ulrich — *The Wild Westerner*	203
12. James Hylton — *Ageless Wonder*	222

Bibliography 245

Index 247

Acknowledgments

My interviews with these great race drivers will live among the most cherished memories of my life. They are heroes one and all. But heroes have their shortcomings and some of these gentlemen had one in common. For this book and me, the one that mattered was the fact that most of them did not keep a photographic record of their careers. The comment heard frequently was that it never occurred to them to take nor have pictures taken while they raced as Grand National drivers. They had loads of photos at one time, but loaned, misplaced, or lost them over the decades. Some of these drivers had many, most had a few, and one had none. I personally took hundreds from the late sixties through 1982 and used many here. However, I had to scratch and scrounge for some of these. In an effort to provide the best documentation possible, purchasing photographs at considerable expense was absolutely necessary. Most are perfect, some are less than that, and a few are of marginal quality at best. Of those I say this, if a picture is worth a thousand words, some of these are worth less than 500. But I figured that a rough view along with the driver's description of an event is better than none at all. In some instances, there may just not be a better record.

Therefore, I would like to thank the following benevolent individuals for their much needed and appreciated photographic contributions: Jack Walker of Myrtle Beach, South Carolina, who approached me first and generously contributed many shots from his website, www.raceplace.zoomshare.com, having previously obtained the cooperation of his contributors, Pete Peterson, Buzz Mims, and Marty Little; stock car racing's legendary historian, Greg L. Fielden of Myrtle Beach, South Carolina, who offered use of the photographs in his four volumes of *Forty Years of Stock Car Racing*, which are the scriptures of the sport; Jeff Droke, noted wrestler, actor, and sound engineer from Memphis, Tennessee, who serves as a longtime crewman for James Hylton and maintains his website, www.jameshylton.com; Tim Allen of Spartanburg, South Carolina, who offered dozens of photos for use; and educator Steve Jeffords of Spartanburg and his one dramatic moment-of-impact shot. At least one of the images is a screen shot captured online from YouTube footage of which the provenance is unclear. In the event I am contacted by the rights holder of a particular photograph, I will eagerly provide the proper credit.

Foreword by Jeff Gilder

This book is an idea I'm glad the author pursued. It is an overdue perspective of our sport that has been overlooked by many. Being "factory-backed" during the formative years of racing was much more of an advantage then than it is today. The stories of the non-factory-backed race drivers and their crews who competed during those early years of NASCAR are a very important piece in the puzzle that forms racing history. Their participation produced popular story lines "back in the day" and provides more insight into history, now that we have had sixty years to consider them. The better funded factory-backed drivers took away most of the wins, but not all of them. They certainly received most of the fame. How much of the credit for NASCAR's success do the factory-backed drivers deserve? They deserve much of the credit, but certainly not all of it.

When one takes the time to thoroughly study stock car racing history, it becomes apparent those independents may have played a bigger role than even they realize. Many spent everything they could muster to pay for an experience that may, and did in some cases, cost them their lives, all for the thrill of being there. The question that persists: What would racing history be without them? The answer is obvious; stock car racing history, specifically NASCAR history, would be much shorter. Am I suggesting NASCAR might not be the force it has grown to be today without them? You do the math: Would you have paid to watch a race with seven to ten cars competing? Would you give a driver who wins a race of ten competitors the same credit as one who won a race of thirty? Would you pay today to see the same? Would that type of racing attract the big money marketing advances that we have seen develop? I don't think so.

"You can't outrun money" is a well known truism in the racing world that didn't stop lesser funded drivers from expending any effort to compete with teams that had the latest technology. That technology not only enabled the factory teams to develop parts that were not available to the average racer, it included the power of knowledge that comes from having factory engineers researching and feeding their teams results. It included personnel trained to do specific tasks for the team and therefore an advantageous element of time. That element of time is crucial! Time, a factor of available manpower, may have been the biggest advantage of all. Independent drivers, on the other hand, in most cases built their cars, prepared their cars, drove the tow vehicle to the tracks for testing and to the races, drove in the race, and then returned home in time to begin the process all over. And by the way, they had to find the dollars to support all this from smaller pools afforded the factory teams. Looking at just how one-sided the competition was from the resource perspective makes the accomplishments of the independent race drivers even more remarkable. But they were there week in and week out working harder, racing smarter, and doing more with less.

Racing smarter? What does that mean? That means driving the car just hard enough and finishing well enough to cover expenses, without risking breaking something or blowing an expensive engine. That reminds me of a story Jabe Thomas tells regarding racing smart to survive. His son, Ronnie (who later became the 1978 Winston Cup Rookie of the Year) told him his school buddies wanted to know why his daddy never won. Jabe decided to show Ronnie what he could do and charged to the front during a race at Richmond against some tough competition only to blow the engine in the process. Some of these guys would even coordinate their pit stops in a manner that would allow them to use the tires that were taken off a factory team car in a previous stop. Are you getting the picture? These are just a few examples of the kinds of sacrifices the independents made to compete in a sport that may very well have failed to get off the ground without them.

After reading this book, go back through the records and take note of how well many of the independents raced in a sport that was clearly tougher for them than the factory backed teams. Consider the win Paul Lewis accomplished in 1966 in Maryville, Tennessee, against a field of the best. Think about how long some of these guys survived racing against the odds. This book is an inside look at the real-life accounts of real racing heroes. This doesn't take anything away from the great factory-backed drivers of days gone by. But I think the independent race drivers who competed against them deserve credit for their critical place in racing history. Thank you, Perry Allen Wood, for making it possible for their stories to be told.

Jeff Gilder is a former race driver who, in 2008, founded RacersReunion.com to unite former drivers with fans, an idea initiated fifteen years earlier by his former crew chief, Paul Lewis. In 2009 he founded the Racers Reunion Memory Lane Hall of Fame, recognizing the grass roots of auto racing.

Preface

The first product of my second life as an author was *Silent Speedways of the Carolinas*, a book very well received by auto racing history enthusiasts around the country. When attending book signings, school and library presentations, and racing-related events, I was asked one question more than any other. What will you write about next? I always shrugged it off because I never really set out to write the first one, let alone a second. Since it took nearly five years to produce *Silent Speedways*, I never considered having enough free time to do it again.

Quizzed often enough about writing another book, I started entertaining the idea. What else could I write about? The first book was relatively easy because I was practically self-sufficient. I researched, found, and visited the old speedways myself. I took the pictures and wrote the text. So I thought along the lines of an auto racing biography. My hometown of Spartanburg is still heavily populated with living stock car racing history.

In September 2007, I was in Hillsborough, North Carolina, at the remains of the Occoneechee Speedway, a venue featured prominently in *Silent Speedways*. There was a celebration of the old track featuring dozens of well-known figures in stock car racing history. Many of their racecars were there on a perfect autumn weekend. Tens of thousands of auto enthusiasts were on hand, too, soaking up the rich history of the sport. I had a booth set up to sell *Silent Speedways* and met folks eager to purchase it. An older gentleman wearing bib overalls picked up my book and asked if he might be in it. I asked his name, to which he replied "Bobby Keck." I excitedly told him that he sure was and I had seen him crash in Spartanburg in 1963. He chuckled as I checked the index explaining that he was included on six different pages, which pleased him. He asked how much my book cost, I told him, and then felt badly that he might not be able to afford it. Before I felt too badly, Mr. Keck whipped out a wad of bills from one of his many pockets and peeled off the required price without diminishing the size of his roll very much at all. I had one of my books set aside for the autographs of only those individuals indexed therein. Bobby Keck bought his copy and was the first to sign my personal edition.

I sold all nine copies of *Silent Speedways* by 10:00 A.M., an hour after the start of the event and six hours before it ended. So I wandered the grounds and met many racing heroes or their family members, such as Cotton Owens, Neil Castles, Jimmy Massey, Gene Hobby, Rex White, and Bill Blair, Jr., Sybil Scott (Wendell's daughter), Frances Flock (Tim's widow), Pam Roberts (Fireball's daughter), Margaret Sue Turner Wright (Curtis Turner's daughter), and others. Gene Hobby was chosen to announce over the public address system, "Gentlemen, start your engines!" beginning the festivities and getting those dozens of old racecars, street rods, and customized classics fired up. I listened to Neil Castles discuss making his entrance onto the Hollywood scene and Gene Hobby recount his horrendous flips down the homestretch right there at Hillsborough in 1965. I met many wonderful people and heard stories from one of the sport's great untapped resources, the independent racecar drivers.

Fast forward to another event; Sam Ard Day at Alex Beam's Memory Lane Museum in Mooresville, North Carolina, on a snowy January Saturday in 2008. I sold more books, gave Sam the money, and heard exciting tales from "Little Bud" Moore, Tom Pistone, Ted Musgrave, Bobby Allison, Dave Marcis, Paul Lewis, and others. Then it hit me. Forget writing one racer's biography; instead, tell stories of the independents, those lightly funded field-fillers who did it the hard way. There are scores of them who would otherwise never have their stories told. Theirs are tales of hardship and humor, despair and delight, pain and pleasure, and failure and fulfillment. Rarely were they stories of victory.

With deep appreciation I present the personal recollections of 12 of these wonderful racers of yesterday, most never before published, that we might understand a time lost forever. It is to the dozen drivers included here and others not appearing to which we race fans owe a debt of gratitude we can never repay. They raced, struggled, endured, and died pursuing their dreams — and their stories need to be told.

Introduction

In·de·pen·dent
Noun
1: A person not subject to control by others;
2: A person not affiliated with a larger controlling unit;
3: A person not requiring or relying on something else.

As stock car racers from the early 1950s to early 1980s, the independents were a breed alone. While greatly in the majority, they had other names, such as "field-fillers," "back-markers," or the dreaded "also-rans." Occasionally, they ran up front and on very rare outings they won. The independents frequently finished in the top five and usually battled into the top ten. They were youngsters just getting started, old-timers racing out their careers, and obscure devotees trying to make their mark.

Just what was an independent and where did they go? In short, in 1951 a shrewd and skilled Daytona Beach mechanic and racer named Marshall Teague secured factory sponsorship for his bottom-heavy Hudson Hornets and became what is generally regarded as the first stock car racing team backed by a Detroit auto manufacturer. Marshall won often as did his teammate Herb Thomas. Their Fabulous Hudson Hornets mostly roared out of a garage ruled over by Henry "Smokey" Yunick in Daytona Beach. Teague's financial equals at the time were team owners with deep pockets not having factory support like Marshall and his "Teaguemobiles." Among those financially gifted sportsmen was Raymond Parks, an ex-moonshiner who actually predates Teague's Hudson deal with his Parks' Novelty Machine Company–sponsored, Red Vogt–wrenched Oldsmobiles of 1949 Strictly Stock champion Red Byron.

Then on August 12, 1951, a watershed event in stock car racing history took place at the Michigan State Fairgrounds in Detroit for that city's 250th anniversary. The Motor City 250 was held and the American automotive world was there in force. An astounding 15 different marques took to the mile of dirt with Tommy Thompson's Chrysler edging Bud Moore's Joe Eubanks–driven Hudson for the win. Later, wealthy team owners like Ernest Woods, Ted Chester, Frank Christian, Walt Chapman, and the incredible Carl Kiekhaefer arrived on the scene. Mr. K. never owned up to having factory help from Mopar, but his Chryslers, Dodges, and occasional Fords totally dominated the stock car world. In NASCAR, it was mostly Tim Flock and Buck Baker winning on southern tracks seemingly at will in 1955 and 1956 and Frank Mundy, Tony Bettenhausen, and Norm Nelson up north in the AAA.

After Kiekhaefer left, 1957 saw an all-out Detroit assault on NASCAR's Grand National Division with Ford, Mercury, Chevrolet, Pontiac, Oldsmobile, and to a lesser extent Plymouth jumping in with checkbooks blazing. Forms of this factory-backing continue to this day. Through the years there have been interruptions in Detroit's support for various reasons, like bad publicity on safety and squabbling over rules. None of the factories have remained committed the entire time. However, you can bet that they always had their collective wet fingers in the air to keep tabs on which way the winds of public opinion were blowing as it pertained to stock car racing. All the while, parts and engineering flowed out of the factories' back doors and money was dealt under the table. After 1971 with the arrival of The Winston Cup, live television coverage, and increasing corporate sponsorships like STP, Coca-Cola, Dow Chemicals, Purolator, Holly Farms, Gatorade, Anheuser-Busch, and many others helped defray the ever rising costs of fielding a racecar.

As of this writing in 2010, the trend is totally to the multi-car teams. In fact, NASCAR drew the line at an owner having more than four teams. However, Raymond Parks often raced more than one car, as did Ernest Woods, Bud Moore, Ted Chester, and many others. By 1955, Carl Kiekhaefer perfected it coast-to-coast and border-to border in NASCAR and AAA, fielding three- and four-car teams at the same time in the south and the north. These days an independent is thought of as an organization with only one team, such as owner-driver Robby Gordon's Jim Beam Toyota or the once mighty Wood Brothers solo Ford mostly with Bill Elliott. There are other teams starting and struggling along that will not survive. Staggering sums of money are required just to enter a Sprint Cup race and still not even qualify. And if in 2009 an owner is not able to afford multiple teams à la Hendrick, Roush, Gibbs, Childress, Penske, and the others, that owner is surely doomed to failure.

Dario Franchitti won the 2007 Indianapolis 500 with glamorous actress wife Ashley Judd splashing barefoot down pit road toward Victory Lane in the rain to meet him, a fabulous racing image for all times. In 2008, that Indy Racing League champion was thought a sure-fire NASCAR success, but was in and out of a top-notch Ganassi Dodge before the season reached halfway in July. Why? No sponsor ... no money ... no racing. The point is, it is tough now to race without cash and always has been. This book deals with independents from the fifties to the seventies, which is mostly the Grand National period of NASCAR's history. Some raced a little longer. One still does.

So who are the independents and what did they do? These gentlemen are to this day the framework of stock car racing. This book concentrates on those independents who started their careers prior to 1971, by which time the big money came from RJ Reynolds, the schedule was slashed, and the dirt tracks were erased from the series. Very, very few racers can claim that they were never an independent. But one who can is Richard Petty. Every time he saddled up, Richard was in equipment as good as and usually better than anyone else's in the field. With his brother Maurice and their dad Lee, he was possibly the only driver who competed consistently in a first line racecar and who raced for any appreciable length of time. Pearson, Yarborough, the Allisons, the Bakers, Lorenzen, Turner, Jarrett, and scores of others at one time or another climbed into something less than the best.

Independents plied their trade mostly during those early years when to race required not much more than having a fairly stock racecar, a helmet, and a great deal of courage. Independents had little funding, only second-hand or inferior equipment, little support by outsiders, and usually another job to hold down away from the track. They had a distinct dilemma as they raced with caution to preserve the machinery, but had to go hard to attract the eye of the Detroit suits and beat the others of their ilk. Their pride dictated that they race and race hard because it is what they risked all to do.

The independents traveled different paths away from the tracks, too. Money drivers dined in nice restaurants, stayed in the clean motels, and arrived just in time to buckle up. Simultaneously, the independents often ate cold bologna sandwiches, slept in their cars or passed out under them from exhaustion, and rose with the sun to start the cycle all over again.

The risks were not the same for the independents as it was for the factory boys either. It was multiplied. The money men confidently raced top equipment hard, fast, and up front with the full attention of the fans and press. The independents labored mid-pack and worse, in mostly unreliable, second-class racecars that were usually constructed of hand-me-down and rebuilt parts. Even as they raced as hard as they could, they had to be aware of fast-closing leaders that seemed to lap them much too regularly. As with the rest of the car, the safety features were also strained with age and there was a constant worry of catastrophic failure at high speeds. A worn right ball joint breaking going into a turn on a lightning-fast dirt track like Hillsborough could easily end with sheet time or worse for the driver. It was not just on dirt, though. These brave souls went head-to-head with the factory teams at Daytona, Darlington, Talladega, Charlotte, Atlanta, Bridgehampton, and blacktop everywhere. It had to be strange for Ned Jarrett to dive past Wendell Scott driving Ned's old car, which still sported one of Ned's old sponsors, although that sponsor was no longer funding the car. Parts that a factory team would change after every race might never get replaced by an independent until after its failure caused a crash. The late, great champion Benny Parsons once said that he drove cars that he "wouldn't get out of the electric chair to drive." Were the independents as courageous as the money drivers? Yes, if not much more so.

These wonderful independents fall into four categories, which are not populated equally. This book includes examples of all four. The first, vastly larger than the others, is the independents never having sufficient funding and never sniffing victory. Whether it was their equipment or luck, they just never came particularly close to winning. They all had enough skill to win. Maybe they just could not race often enough. Anyway, these men never were runner ups, but had fine finishes of which to be very proud. The second group finished second at least once. Many even had a big break in a top ride. There are fewer of these than the previous group, and if not for a lack of good fortune at the right time, they could have easily tasted the sweet nectar of first. There are quite a few bridesmaids and some were left at the altar more than once. The third and even smaller category is that of the independents who looked Detroit's chosen few in the eyes and snatched the checkered flag from them, proving they had what it takes. This is a pretty exclusive club. Truth is, anybody who ever won a Grand National race at all is in a very exclusive club, whether you won 200 times or once. But for an independent to win is a substantial feat. These drivers also had occasional factory seat time, too. The fourth and final category is that of the independents who raced the large majority of their career as such, but sat in some fine Detroit iron, bringing home first place hardware more than once. This is an extremely close-knit fraternity with fewer members than you have fingers on one hand, and the thumb is not a finger.

The independents sharing their declarations here were chosen very carefully by several factors. The most obvious criterion is if the driver appears likely to have any interesting stories to tell. They all do, but does his longevity, number of races, finishes, or participation in one or more particularly noteworthy events warrant inclusion? If so, he must also be willing to be interviewed. Finally, after putting it all on paper, is it interesting enough to appeal to the book-reading public? These twelve independents passed those tests easily. These anecdotes offer an appreciation for and understanding of the trials and tribulations endured by those brave warriors who fought on a shoestring mostly in the background of stock car racing history. All interviews were taped in person when possible, or over the phone. Some drivers were very close by and one was 2,800 miles away.

The independents are rightfully very spirited. Go to a gathering of racers at an event like that at Occoneechee Speedway. They proudly walk among men they were rarely ever able to beat. Now they are absolute equals laughing and sharing their stories, signing autographs, and adored by fans who appreciate what they did no matter where they finished. It is abundantly clear that the money men of yesterday are unanimous in their admiration and respect of the independents. These men did what they did without one single spotter, without soft walls, without HANS devices, without a big block of Styrofoam in the right side door to absorb shock, without full-face helmets, without pit road speed limits, without a vast weekly television audience, without a substantial purse, and without a top-notch car and crew to see them to Victory Lane. The factory drivers got most of the ink, glory, and money, but the independents made the race *a race*. The starting fields would have been pretty small without these warriors. So listen to their tales of struggle, pain, despair, hope, exhilaration, hilarity, and triumph. Miracles were rarely possible for independents, but miracles often come in strange packages. Now the spotlight is theirs to tell you how it was when money and luck were in short supply, but hope and courage were in abundance riding shotgun with them from race to race in the shadows of the sport.

1

Johnny Allen

Spectacular Speedster

Johnny Allen was born September 17, 1934, in Los Angeles, California. He served in the U.S. Navy and mustered out in Corpus Christi, Texas, before his 21st birthday in 1955. Johnny decided to pursue a love of auto racing that had been incubating for years. After gaining some paved short-track experience in Corpus Christi and Houston, Johnny took his savings, teamed with one Spook Crawford who had sold his Kaiser racecars, purchased a Plymouth, and headed to the nearest NASCAR race they could find. And what a race they found! Johnny Allen raced in 173 Grand Nationals over 13 years with an outstanding record of one win, three poles, 19 top fives, and 61 top tens, 35 percent of the time. His best points finish was seventh in 1957, the only season he gave the championship a serious shot. Johnny never backed down from a challenge and danger never was a factor.

Of the toughest places on Earth to start a big-time racing career, Johnny Allen and Spook Crawford picked the unknown, untested, unforgiving mile and a half, high-banked, dirt oval at Lehi, Arkansas. Less than a month after Johnny turned 21, they towed to the Memphis-Arkansas Speedway for the 300-miler on October 9, 1955.

"That was a first exposure to see what NASCAR stock cars were about," he said. "I'd run a Kaiser. This Plymouth was a four-door sedan. They kinda laughed and asked where we were going with that taxicab. [Johnny chuckles.] We were pretty ignorant when it came to knowing what we could do against Fireball, Baker, Petty, the hot dogs of the day. It was a test to see if we could come east and make a go of it. We saw the track and it was a shock. A dirt track, too, which I had never run. Big high banks. We didn't have heavy-duty things on it. It did have reinforced wheels. Airlift was runnin' a documentary filming. Ralph Liquori talked them into letting us run to get some experience. I couldn't keep up with those guys. [Johnny chuckles.] They would run off down the straightaway and leave me, then wait and we'd come back for the filming. I was runnin' hard as I could. Our engine wasn't that good. The race started and I knew what I needed to do. Be careful. Try to finish 'cause we needed to make some money. I think I qualified about 40th [actually 31st of 41]. That's deceiving because a bunch of guys weren't there because they ran somewhere and couldn't get there. The factories were in and USAC drivers also came. All the stars from both circuits were there. I out-qualified one car; a local that had a Chrysler from the dealership. [In Gene Rose's only race, he started 32nd and finished 19th. Told he outran 24 racers for 17th, Johnny deflected praise.] Well, I can't take credit for that. I pretty much outlasted them staying out of trouble. The track was horrible. It was suicide, really. A lot of cars fell out from overheating, dirt in the radiator, the ruts broke suspensions. I tried to dodge the holes. I ran as hard as I could without breaking anything; to keep from getting run over.

"Tiny [Lund] broke a suspension, right front spindle come off, it dug in, and he flipped end over end. Tiny was big, 280 pounds. Back then the doors had to open and close. They had the hinges so we strapped 'em or chained 'em. When the car flipped, it hit on the nose, Tiny's seatbelt broke, and he hit with such force against the door he broke the hinges. Liquori saw the car flippin' 'cause he was right behind. He said it looked like the car spit him out. The car came down, spit Tiny out, and bounced on. He tried to miss him and it was either hit the car or Tiny. He said, 'I was thinkin', 'Well, he's dead anyway. It ain't gonna matter' and he ran over him. Tiny had a tire mark across his helmet, so Ralph [had] hit his helmet. He was probably turnin' and had some weight off the helmet. But he ran over Tiny's head. [Tiny was sponsored by Rupert Safety Belts.] He had an old cotton safety belt out of an aircraft, you know, surplus. Cotton will rot and Tiny being so heavy, took a lot to hold him. The doctor said that if he hadn't been such a big man, it would have killed him. He had so much fat and muscle it absorbed a lot of it.

"Anyway, we were encouraged. We got a $100 for that film, a $100 for being the first Plymouth to finish; of course, we were the only Plymouth, and $95 for finishing 17th. Speedy Thompson won. Kiekhaefer tried to change from Chrysler and Ford wouldn't give him any help. So he bought a Ford, built his own, put Speedy in it, and won. That gave us encouragement. I didn't just ride around. I always try to get all I can out of what I got. You try to use your head. When you run on your own money, you're runnin' on a shoestring. We thought of what we learned. We needed the bigger engine, some heavy spindles, lots of things we could see the other guys had."

Johnny had outrun Jim Reed, Fonty Flock, Curtis Turner, Joe Weatherly, Gwen Staley, Chuck Stevenson, Johnny Mantz, Joe Eubanks, Tiny Lund and Norm Nelson. The decision was made to go for it.

"We went back to Corpus Christi. 'We can do this.' Spook said, 'I'll take six-months' leave of absence, gather up the stuff we need, and you stay here.' I wasn't married and worked on the racecar and he did at night. I sold my car. Had my musterin' out money and my car money, then stayin' with him, we didn't have any overhead. We put all the money together we could and bought an old '48 DeSoto nine-passenger sedan. [Johnny chuckles.] That was our tow car. Took the two back seats out, just had the front bench seat. Took an old army bunk and made a bunk across the back for him and his wife to sleep in. Underneath, that's where we put our spare parts plus some in the racecar. Me and the dog, a little screw-tailed Boston bull, slept up front. His wife was part Indian and a pretty good cook. We had a charcoal stove and a bunch of groceries. We went gypsy campin' ... and racin'."

The gypsy racers hit the road in 1956 to give big-time stock car racing a shot.

"Headed to Daytona in February. We were going to run the circuit for at least six months or until we went broke. The next race was a highway and a beach. That's a shocker! I'm 21 and anxious to race anything anywhere. We stayed in the car and camped out. It was in a park. We qualified on The Beach. The flyin' mile. That was a new experience. I didn't do very good. Tim Flock was on the pole in a Mercury Outboard Chrysler [at

135.747]. I think I was about 121. During the race, the sand got real thick goin' into the first turn and I got in a real soft area. It broke the steering tie rod end. The front wheels spread out and I was stuck in the middle of the north turn. Cars comin' by both ways and I'm tryin' to get out and can't. They didn't stop the race. They keep goin' unless the track's blocked. I got the seat belt loose and everytime I tried to crawl out, here come some cars. [Johnny laughs.] I finally got across the track. We didn't make any money at all."

Johnny started 67th of 76, finishing 42nd, a fine improvement, and out-distanced Panch, Thompson, Smith, Welborn, Eubanks, Owens, Roberts, Turner, Bobby Myers, Weatherly, and Mundy.

"The next race was in Hollywood, Florida, quarter-mile asphalt. We'll do well 'cause it was like Corpus Christi. We camped, ate, and slept there. Went out and practiced a couple of days and thought we was getting around good. We bought one Firestone for the right front, then found some used Goodyear Double Eagles. We thought we were in tall cotton. We're getting around fast and all the short track aces show: Rex White, Bob Welborn, Jim Reed. We're goin' to run Saturday night and they show Saturday afternoon. If you ran a track that was considered short track, you got points for short track. Jim Reed was short track champion. Hollywood was short track.

"We went to Fayetteville, North Carolina. It was a week or two before the race. We went to the Plymouth dealership to see if he wanted to sponsor the car. He said he wouldn't give us money, but he'd give us a place we could pull the car inside and work. We worked at the Plymouth dealership on commission. As fast as he [Spook] was and with me helping, we could make some money in three or four days and take off to race. We rented a trailer from Ralph Liquori. That's how we survived."

On June 10, 1956, they returned to the scene of their Grand National debut, Lehi, Arkansas, and improved upon the previous outing with a 13th. The event was marred by the deaths of Clint McHugh in time trials and Cotton Priddy in the race.

"You didn't know he got killed during the race. You're racin'. We knew the guy got killed qualifying. It concerns ya, but only until they drop the flag. You just accept that, especially then. You know the old saying, 'There's old race drivers and bold ones, but no old bold ones.' I survived. I've missed several good opportunities at Atlanta and Darlington. We were learning and trying to upgrade the car and get smarter learning the tracks. We were happy to finish and keep the car together."

Johnny and Spook get a new Plymouth from the factory.

"We upgraded to a '56 and the first race was Asheville-Weaverville. Had to buy it, but they give us a deal and financed it. I paid with on the job training from my GI Bill of Rights. We ended up financing an old rundown house and old wooden barn shop out back. We were in high cotton."

Records show that on July 1, 1956, at Asheville-Weaverville Speedway, Johnny Allen started 27th and finished 12th. On August 12, 1956, a dozen brave racers arrived in Oklahoma City for a 100 miler on a half mile of dust.

"It was a horsetrack in horrible shape. So dusty you couldn't see. Fireball was leadin' and the only place you could see was the front straightaway because of the lights hanging over. You had to look out the left window and figure where the turn was and turn. It finally got so bad, Lee [Petty] pulled in screaming at the flagman, 'Stop this race!' He grabbed the red flag out of his hand and stood on the edge of the track and threw the flag. 'Somebody's gonna get killed. This is ridiculous! We ain't runnin'!' Man, we had a riot. The people in the stands were furious. They wouldn't let us out of the racetrack."

Johnny was seventh and outran Baker and Thompson's Kiekhaefer Chryslers. Johnny's Darlington debut was the Southern 500, September 3, 1956, starting 45th of 70 and finishing 25th. He was just ahead of eventual champion Buck Baker's Kiekhaefer Chrysler.

"We really ran, but had to change tires several times. We were running a new tire for Goodyear and it was coming apart. Almost the whole field had Firestones and Goodyear furnished us tires. We couldn't afford to turn that down."

Johnny never shied from a speedway and raced the toughest, finishing well most every time. On September 23, 1956, he confronted Langhorne, Pennsylvania, one of the deadliest speedways anywhere. Johnny started 19th of 44 and finished ninth in an outstanding field.

"Langhorne is a track that everytime I went there, it scared me. The track is oiled dirt, mostly a D. The front straightaway is straight for a little bit. Not enough that you really get straight. You gotta get your speed up to get around. You get the car goin' fast enough that you get the back end hangin' way out where you're turnin' to the right and stayin' wide open on the gas. It's got ruts. It's an oiled dirt and gets tacky and you get a good grip. It's easy to get too much grip and when it does, it snaps the front end around, you hit a rut, and you'll go end over end. When you start gettin' up your speed, your adrenalin really gets to flowin'. You can't go fast enough once you get goin'. But to me, getting up to speed, you had to talk yourself through that. Felt like Darlington going into the third turn."

Johnny and Spook received the attention of Plymouth engineers. For 1957, they got a deal on a new Fury with one minor inconvenience.

"We were the only Plymouth tryin' to make all the races. They had a representative look things over. They saw we were determined and came out with the 1957 Fury. They wouldn't give us a car, but sold us a Plymouth. They ran it through the assembly line with no undercoating or nothin'. It was a barebones car. They put in their high-performance engine, Chrysler rear end, so you had the heavier suspension, and that's the way we got the car. It was a complete car, it just wasn't ready.

"We were so broke; I had to hitchhike up there. I took the bus part way and hitchhiked part way. This was Detroit in the winter. There was no heater, no floormats, nothin'. They gave us extra axles, extra gears. Ronnie Householder was in charge and sent me on my way. It was a miserable trip. There was no insulation. I had four pairs of socks on, two pair of pants. I had gloves and an ice scraper. I had to scrape ice on the inside so I could see 'cause it would frost up. We got it back, put roll bars in, and got ready to race."

Johnny and Spook were extremely competitive in 1957, running 42 of 53 races. They tallied four top fives, 17 top tens, a pole, and seventh in the standings. July and August on the Northern Tour saw them score well.

"We were on the road, working all the time. We went north to Old Bridge, Watkins Glen, finished fifth, and had to run the track backwards because the cars were set up to go left and you couldn't change the fuel pick up. You'd keep runnin' out of gas. The big problem was no escape roads. For really tough turns that were downhill, well, you're goin' the wrong way. The escape road is the other way. It made it a really fun, exciting race." Johnny laughs.

With a pole at Coastal Speedway in Myrtle Beach, they had arrived, but finished last.

"The fan blade came off. That engine wasn't used to turning that kind of RPMs. That's when I got aggravated tryin' to finish and make money, not able to go for the win. I was

Johnny Allen hustles Plymouth 64 through turn four towards a 13th place finish on October 20, 1957, at North Wilkesboro in the Wilkes 160 (Greg Fielden).

gettin' enough experience and felt like we could run better if we put a low gear in. I was in charge of workin' on the chassis and changing gears. Spook took care of the engine. I slipped a couple of notches of gear lower, then we started havin' engine problems."

Johnny shared the front row there with Fireball Roberts.

"It made me feel good. I was determined to beat him into the first turn. He beat me through the first and second, but I hung right on him till the fan came apart. I'd lapped Petty before we went out."

September 2, 1957, was the date of the tragic Southern 500 that claimed the life of Bobby Myers in a grinding crash and ended the career of Fonty Flock. Johnny made it past Flock's stalled Pontiac before Myers and Goldsmith piled in. Johnny raced to 12th.

"That was a good finish in a big race with what we had. We were strictly independent. Now they did give us a car for a dollar. Yeah, I went by him [Flock]. I saw him sittin' up there by the wall. The wreck happened behind me. The general thought was the car was black and the track was shadowed a little bit. He [Myers] was racin' with Paul Goldsmith."

Ten days later, they returned to Langhorne. In a field of 48, Johnny started 22nd charging to third, an outstanding achievement.

"Real good run for us. Whitey Norman ran second. That was a good payday."

The records reflect Gwen Staley won and Johnny copped $1,700. Changes loomed in 1958 with 22 starts, two top fives, six top tens, and a parting of the ways.

"Spook and I broke up the middle of '58. I took the '57 Plymouth, which we converted to a '58. I went to Atlanta and worked for Jack Smith. Jack was tryin' to win a championship and had two cars; a '58 Pontiac and '57 Chevrolet and needed help. Don Bailey was chief mechanic."

In 1959, Johnny ran five events, pioneering in the first Daytona 500.

"That was awesome. You come through the tunnel, look out there, and there was nothin'. No buildings or fences, just big open fields, a lake, and turns. You look down the racetrack and way off you see the bank. You turn around and the third and fourth turns are goin' straight up like a wall."

Johnny had inspection woes with his aging mount.

"That was a '57 Chevrolet Roy Tyner owned. We weren't allowed on the track because we couldn't get through inspection. They cut too much off the cylinder heads and didn't hold enough CCs. At the last minute, Norris Friel, chief inspector, said, 'I'll tell you what. Put two head gaskets under it to make up for the extra and we'll let you run,' which more than made up. That hurt us on power. At least we could race."

There was no practice; Johnny learned what he could from watching. And there was no qualifying. Johnny's first time on the track was starting the 500 dead last in 59th.

"One thing about startin' back there, I wasn't in the middle of the pack and didn't know what to expect. I could feel my way through. There were no cautions. Don Bailey was the chief mechanic. Had some guys that helped at the shop. Nobody was getting paid. Daytona was always good to me."

The record shows that Johnny drove a two-year-old Chevrolet having never been on the track to a remarkable 11th, only eight laps behind with no cautions for helpers. Incredible! He explains the few Grand National starts in 1959.

"I started thinkin' about Indianapolis. Don and I decided we would build a '57 Chevrolet out of Paul McDuffie's shop in Atlanta. I got rid of my Plymouth and got a little money. We got an old body and built a '57 Chevrolet. We were gonna go USAC in '59.

"We were gonna leave right after the Firecracker and run our first in Milwaukee, a 250-lap USAC race that had a big purse. McDuffie built a '59 Chevrolet for Fireball to run in the Firecracker [250]. Roberts switched to Smokey and the Pontiac. That left the car open and [Paul] says, 'You want to run it?' 'Sure.' I finished third and that was a good payday."

The record shows that on July 4, 1959, ever-modest Johnny started 11th, finishing third a lap behind Roberts and Weatherly with Jack Smith on his heels. In the first two major races at Daytona International Speedway, Johnny notched an 11th and third.

At Daytona, "those cars sat eight, ten inches off the ground. You had a lot of air goin' underneath. If you got a good draft down the backstretch, when you got to the turn, you couldn't 'cause the front would be so light. You had to ease out of the throttle a little bit. The car would settle enough that you could get some feel in the wheel. When you were in a pack, it would turn plumb sideways goin' down the straightaway sometimes. You had to know when to steer and when not to. Wrong time and you're gone. Usually if you leave it alone, the car will come back 'cause the wind will straighten itself out. The different body styles made a difference. A '57 Chevrolet was well-balanced. It handled real good on short tracks. The other cars were better on the big tracks."

Then he bid adieu to NASCAR.

"Went to NASCAR headquarters and told 'em what I was gonna do 'cause back then

Top: In his miraculous run from last to 11th in the inaugural Daytona 500, Johnny trails Dick Foley (66) and Joe Eubanks (82) en route (Don Smyle). *Bottom:* Up and over. While running third, Johnny's convertible leaps the rail in turns three and four in the 1960 Rebel 300 (Greg Fielden).

The incredibly mangled remains of number 69, which reads the same inverted. The entire rear of the car is bent double under the wheels (Greg Fielden).

you couldn't run both NASCAR and USAC. Pat Purcell was a big boss and said, 'You just finished third. You're crazy to leave. You have a real good career goin' here.' 'I know, but Don and I made a commitment. That's what I'm gonna do.' 'You know when you come back, it's gonna cost ya.' 'We'll have to cross that bridge when we get there.'

"We ran USAC in November [1959] and spent Christmas with our families. They had a race in Las Vegas. A mile dirt horsetrack. It was terrible. No guardrails and we ended up tearin' up the car. A guy broke a spindle and I nailed him. Tore the right side off. Don says, 'I'll take the car to Atlanta and we'll regroup.' But he got with Bill Cheeseburg and Roger McCluskey. They said, 'We're gonna build a '60 Chevrolet for USAC. You can help and we'll pay you this winter.' The guy that owned the car and Braun Plywood Company says, 'I want to run Daytona.' McCluskey and Cheeseburg couldn't 'cause that was NASCAR. Don said, 'We'll get Johnny. He runs good at Daytona. We ran third the last race.' That's how I ended up back in NASCAR. Had to pay a fine, but the car owner took care of that. This guy was a big money man."

Speedweeks 1960 were very kind to Johnny and his new 69 team. They took sixth in their qualifier and a rock-solid fifth in the 500, one lap back in a whopping 68-car field. Excellent results right out of the box.

"You know when you're runnin' good in the lead pack hangin' in there with the big dogs feelin' good. We'd open a hole together and try not to make any mistakes." Johnny is

Johnny's Chevy took out the corner of the scoring stand and tumbled down the hill to rest on an access road (Don Smyle).

so modest it often seems difficult for him accept how really outstanding he was. After a seventh at Martinsville, the third top seven in a row to start 1960, they chopped the top off Chevy 69 for Darlington and the Rebel 300 on May 14. What followed was the first of a trilogy of crashes.

"We started sixth and the race rained out short of halfway. They impounded the cars and came back the following week. Fireball was quoted, 'I'm the only driver in history to lead a race for a week.' [Johnny chuckles.] We restarted and were runnin' real good up front. The track eats up tires and after all the rain, there wasn't any rubber on it. I'm runnin third and there's already been guys stop for tires. [Firestone's] John Locks went down to Don and says, 'Get him in. The guys you lapped are comin' in on cords. He's gotta be outta rubber.' I'd been slidin' around pretty bad. Should have had enough sense to know I was out of rubber. Don walked out there, then you walked out on the track, and put the board up to come in. That was on the front straightaway and I was in the middle of three and four when the tire blew. He heard the tire blow and said, 'Good, there's a caution. Man, we needed it.' He didn't realize it was us!

"The right rear blew and the car started comin' around. I tried to get it against the guardrail, but it kept comin'. I said in my mind, 'I can spin it and keep my focus after it spins around, get it under control, and get stopped in my pits. When I locked it down to try to control the spin, the right front blew and the car shot up the racetrack, hit the guardrail, and jumped on top of it. It was in the air that quick and I was lookin' at that big board with the signal lights on it comin' right in the windshield. I wanted to get down in the seat, but you can't. You got a shoulder harness on. Just hangin' on and closed my eyes and put my head down as low as I could and hoped when the windshield come through maybe my helmet would deflect it without tearing my head off. I hit it and took the bottom of that backboard out. There was a big chunk missing, but it just caught the bottom of it with the top of the windshield. Then it caught the fence and hit one time, a bunch of sand came up in my face, and then *BANG*, a real hard hit, and stopped.

"I'm thinkin', 'I can't be stopped. That's too quick. It's gonna hit again.' I'm hangin' on waitin' and waitin' and nothin's happenin'. I finally opened my eyes and looked down and I'm hangin' upside down. I looked around and think, 'Man, there's a lot of sand in here' 'cause a lot got in my face. I put my hand down and pushed back, unhooked the seat belt, dropped down on my hands and knees, crawlin' out from under the car. I looked up and saw that stand and man I tell ya, I guess I almost had a heart attack. I just got sick. I thought I was gonna see pieces of people. I thought I'd went through the stands 'cause the stands was all collapsed and twisted and there was stuff scattered around. Man it was the worst feelin' I ever had in my life. I was lookin' around and don't see anybody. I look up in the stands and there's a big commotion, but nobody seemed to be nursin' anybody. People were real nervous about scorin' there. They said, 'You don't have to worry. We got double guardrail. The car can't get in.' I got started back where it was still a single rail. By that time people showed up to get me. All it did was bruise the bottom of my foot."

The car didn't fare as well.

"It broke the frame in half in front of the firewall on both sides and hit the back right behind the rear housing. The gas tank was sittin' over my head 'cause it was a convertible. That was my first experience. The other caught fire in '62. Our car owner quit. That was Braun Plywood and the owner was a multi-millionaire, but was bankrupting his business. You know, one of those convenient bankruptcies."

At the inaugural World 600 on June 19, 1960, in Charlotte, Johnny raced a new Chevrolet 69. He came up about 591 miles short.

"We got a chassis, body, and Plantation Club was our sponsor, a nightclub. Tommy Starr was the owner. I was fast qualifier the third day. Started 17th and comin' up the outside, got to Cotton, and we were in the top five lappin' a car [Johnny Wolford] in six laps. Do you believe that? The leaders went by him and we were just behind. He got excited and pulled down, hit the apron, and lost it. The car shot back right in front of us and I was behind Cotton. Cotton turned down to miss him and I went up to the guardrail and stayed in the gas. I'll get through before he gets there. Well Cotton hit him and shot him up there faster. Pinned me between him and guardrail. Crashed me *and* Cotton. Later, I relieved

Johnny gets sandwiched between Cotton Owens' Pontiac (6) and Johnny Wolford's Ford (88) on lap five of the first World 600 in Charlotte (Don Smyle).

Johnny Beauchamp and finished second. I ran 150, 200 miles. I hadn't been on the track since I wrecked. I was shocked. It was full of holes and loose asphalt. It was like runnin' through a mine field. We had armor plate under the oilpan, big heavy screen in front, a rock deflector on the hood. It was a time."

Johnny returned to the Southern 500 on September 5, 1960, and had a dismal race, including the loss of his friend Paul McDuffie. Johnny is reluctant to discuss it.

"I wrecked in practice. Had to run a qualifying race and wrecked. Gene White had a Chevrolet, so Gene gave me the front end off his. I put it on and lost the engine. Joe Lee Johnson was drivin' Paul's car. I drove by and saw the mess. Yeah, that's somethin' that really, really bothers you when you know it's bad. You don't know what's goin' on because they don't tell ya. You had no radios. Paul was a good friend of ours."

The season closed with a bang on October 30, 1960, at the inaugural Atlanta 500.

"We had engine trouble the race before [the first National 400 at Charlotte] and didn't have another. Don got a block from Pistone. We got enough parts to put the engine together and got it in. We got to the track Wednesday, got inspected, fired it up, was sittin' there runnin', and couldn't get any oil up to the valves. Revvin' it up and all the sudden the engine tightened up and quit. Hadn't even been on the track! Don't have another engine. We checked and nobody had a spare. Rex White said, 'I've got one in Spartanburg. It ran 400

Johnny Allen poses prior to a dismal and tragic 1960 Southern 500 (Don Smyle).

miles and was runnin' good when I pulled it. I wouldn't bet two cents it's gonna run another 500 miles.' [Rex was sixth at Charlotte and soon to be 1960 Grand National Champion.] These were stock engines and you don't look for that kind of mileage. 'You're welcome to it.' Rex sends his pick up. One of his guys and I went. Drove to Spartanburg, got the engine, brought it back, pulled the head off. That was that night. Got it ready first thing Saturday morning the day before the race. We had to run the consolation and that give us our startin' position. We was leadin' and the hood tried to come up."

Johnny started 37th and finished second a lap behind winner Bobby Johns.

"I beat Jim Paschal in a Petty Plymouth by about two foot. That was a big payday 'cause we were really hurtin'. I was at least a month behind in rent. I owed furniture payments. New wife. That was the biggest payoff we'd had, $7,500. I only got 25 percent, but that was all right. We got in the race, ended up second, and lapped Rex. [Johnny chuckles. Rex was fifth, three laps behind Johnny.] He wouldn't take any money. I said, 'Hey, we just finished second. You saved our lives. Let me pay you.' He said, 'No, I don't want nothin'. I just want my engine back. Have it out tomorrow about noon, if you will, and we'll head back to Spartanburg.' He wouldn't take nothin'."

Speedweeks meant success for Johnny and 1961 was no different: a 47th place start and eighth in the 500.

"Jarrett and I had team cars. Pistone had a Pontiac. Same car owners, B.G. and Lynne Holloway. His family was Grace National Bank and Grace Steamship Lines, Panagra Airlines. Her money was Texas oil. Tryin' to get money was terrible. They got tons of money, but cash, they ain't got nothin'."

At Darlington for the Rebel 300, Johnny had a ringside seat for a historic battle. Fred Lorenzen got his first major victory feinting past Curtis Turner with a lap to go. Johnny was third.

"I could see it goin' on. I kept hopin'."

Johnny detailed driving turn three at Darlington back then.

"Quickest way around was just scratching the paint. Straight at the guardrail and turn back left, hanging your foot in it slidin' up the track. Something you have to talk yourself into doing. I remember old Bobby Myers says, 'Third turn at Darlington is just like eatin'. When you get that food up to your mouth, your mouth automatically opens. Down there your foot automatically comes up.' You didn't want to hit the guardrail, but you had to be right on it. When you go down the backstretch, the turn's sharp. It looks like a 90 degree turn comin' toward it. The banking was one car width wide from the guardrail down, maybe a hair more. The rest was asphalt, kinda flat. It looked like you were going to drive straight through the guardrail. You had to get your timin' and get your mark where you hit it just right and back off so the car will turn. Then it would start slidin' up the hill towards the fence and you get back in the throttle wide open. It was hard to do 'cause you're slidin' toward that guardrail. It's comin' at ya at 120 miles an hour and you want to hit the brake. You don't want to hit the gas. You need to overcome that side motion with forward bite to pull you through. It's tricky to learn. If you're side by side comin' down the straightaway and you're outside, you've got the groove. If he's inside, you know he's not going to stick 'cause it's too flat. If he comes in there the same speed as you, he's gonna come up and knock you into the guardrail. You have to know at what point you're gonna out brave him. You're a fool if you go in there and see that guy's not going to back off. You're crazy to stay with him. If he wanted to he couldn't stay down. He's gonna carry you into the rail. So you back off, hit your brakes, get the car under control, and wait for him to slide up, hit and bounce off 'cause he's goin' to. He can't go in that low and make it. When he bounces off, you time it where you get through before he spins and knocks you out. It was a turn where it separated the men from the boys as hot as it was and no power steering. That's where a lot of guys got beat toward the end of the race. They always started with bear grease on it. A sealer. Almost every driver would tell you that was their favorite track because it was such a challenge to whip. Pearson was the champ. He had it figured out."

Johnny lost the Holloways as they cast their lot with Jarrett for his championship drive. Ned made Johnny an offer.

"They closed Pistone, then our team. 'Ned's leadin' in points and tryin' to win a championship, so we're goin' to support him.' We had to give our car and stuff to Ned. That was right before Bristol. Ned had a second car runnin' on short tracks. Being the nice guy he is says, 'Do you have a ride for Bristol?' 'No.' 'If you'll send somebody to my shop and get it prepared, you can drive.' On July 29, 1961, I drove it and the rear end burned up. Kenny Myler came over and said, 'I think Jack's gonna need relief. You wanna drive?' I said, 'Oh yeah.'"

Johnny relieved his old pal Jack Smith in the first Grand National at Bristol, the Volunteer 500, and won. He took over while Jack was winning and never trailed, leading laps 292 through 500; perfect substitution.

"I was in when the checkered flag came down. He was leading when I took over. It had a crack in the exhaust. The boot from the floor shift was loose or wasn't there and heat was comin' back cooking his foot. The sway bar broke and they kept tryin' to slow me down. They tried, but I had several laps lead."

Johnny led the final 208 laps unchallenged in searing July heat. Roberts trailed by two laps, Jarrett was third five back, Petty fourth seven behind, and Buddy Baker eight back in fifth. Johnny Allen won that race. He was recognized on March 24, 2006, as the first racer taking the checkered flag at Bristol in a prestigious ceremony worthy of the great pioneer he is.

"They had a celebration of the first Bristol race and Bruton Smith had a new building and museum called the Bruton Smith Building. Jack's wife and daughter brought the trophies from the race. NASCAR give a trophy and the speedway give a trophy. They loaned them to the museum. They invited me to come and give me a plaque honoring me. Instead of saying "The Winner," it says, 'The first person to receive the checkered flag.'"

Johnny's 1962 Grand National season had the highest of highs and lowest of lows.

"I started at Daytona to drive a Pontiac for Red Vogt. Couldn't get through inspection because we didn't have the right carburetor. Jim Reed got sick and asked me to drive [Chevy 7]. It had a Corvette steering box. It was great for short tracks, but on a two and a half mile track that thing was darty. The cars were high off the ground and you had to really chase them. That steering put you on edge. By the time I got used to it, we'd already lost a good bit of time."

The record shows that Johnny finished a respectable 16th of 48 on February 18. Junior Johnson quit Holly Farms' Pontiac team of Fred Lovette and Crawford Clements before the 600. Johnny stepped in.

"He [Clements] and Junior had a fallin' out. The car was white and had a black vee. All they did was change the number from 27 to 46."

The Myers Brothers 200 on June 16, 1962, at Bowman-Gray Stadium in Winston-Salem counted the same as Daytona. The field of 19 included White, Petty, Weatherly, Scott, Pardue, Smith, Jarrett, Crider, Spencer, Paschal, and Buck Baker, any one of which could win. Johnny raced Fred Lovette's 58.

"That was a '61 Pontiac Junior had been runnin' the year before. Rex was on the pole and I was outside. Rex won the last three or four at that track. We ran side by side. Rex led a while, then I led. I was in the lead at the end and Rex was right on me. Two abreast is really crowded at Bowman-Gray. Rex was right on my bumper tryin' to get by. Comin' through three and four we come up on a lapped car. I dropped down. I knew Rex couldn't run the outside with that car there. '*I got him!* No way he can beat me to the finish line.' Out of the corner of my eye he's comin' on the inside. He had two wheels on the grass and was comin'! The finish line is almost down to the first turn. You back off about two car lengths before you get there. He was up to my door and gainin'. If I'da backed off to make the corner, he would have won. Inside, he could beat on me. Well, I've wrecked a lot faster. [Johnny chuckles.] I didn't lift until I got across the line and Rex was right beside me. Morris Metcalf [chief scorer] saw how close we were and went down to the line. Otherwise, they'd have probably called it a dead heat. Ended up winning, hittin' the fence, tearing the right side off. Had to walk to Victory Lane. I wasn't goin' to lose. He leaned on me and I don't know what he did, but he didn't wreck. Rex was a tough driver, a great guy. I had a good car, too."

The 1962 Firecracker 250 had four 25-mile qualifying races. Johnny won one. In the Firecracker, Johnny lost the transmission and met television.

"I beat Junior and Banjo in '62 Pontiacs. Pontiacs had been having trouble with transmissions. They would lock up. I'd been runnin' third [in the Firecracker]; Jack Smith was leadin' me and Bobby Johns. Halfway through three and four, the transmission locked up. That was exciting! Locked up, got sideways, had my hands full. Got it gathered up into pit road, and stopped. TV came over, 'What happened, what happened?' 'I dunno. I may have blown the engine.' Crawford came over, 'Tell 'em the transmission failed!' 'You know I believe that's what happened.' All you know is you don't know what happened. You get stopped and somebody sticks a microphone in your face."

In that race Johnny was 27th of 33. He was on the pole August 5, 1962, at Nashville leading the first 46 laps until he blew a right front tire and got into the wall.

"Tore the right front up, bent the frame and firewall. Had to load it on two wreckers. You take it home, get the torches, cut half the firewall and the right front corner out. Got another frame and welded it in. Took it to the frame shop, got it lined up. Put the car back together and went to Darlington."

September 3, 1962, was Labor Day Monday in Darlington with packed grandstands and a jammed infield under a blazing Pee Dee sun. Forty-four cars were on the ready with Johnny poised in ninth aboard the newly renovated Holly Farms Pontiac 46.

Sliding for his life while running third, Johnny's Pontiac skids through turn two in the 1962 Southern 500 heading for a fiery stop (Don Smyle).

"They took so many cars each day and had two or three days of qualifying. The first day, Crawford put stiffer springs under it and the car was too stiff. We changed springs and set quick time the second day. We were third fastest in the field. The car really raced good. Third or fourth, I think, when I crashed.

"We fueled up and went back out running third, fourth, fifth, somewhere behind Panch tryin' to pass. LeeRoy Yarbrough blew an engine in one and two. I went into the corner and he [Panch] went up. He saw the oil. I didn't. I figured he'd slipped so I dove underneath him, hit the oil, and went straight up the racetrack into the guardrail. Flipped up on its side, slid along the guardrail, hooked the guardrail, flipped over on the top, and slid down the racetrack. They had a vent coming out of the gas tank and it came up behind the back glass. Slidin' upside down the gas was comin' out. Hot sparks from the roof ignited the fuel. I didn't know about all that goin' on. It was really fast. You're up on the rail, then you're over on your side, and you're on the track. Your mind is goin' fast. You know what's goin' on. Well, I'm on the track, I'm on the side, and I'm hangin' onto the steering wheel trying to make sure my shoulder don't get out the window and grind off. I'm holdin' my arm up hangin' on 'cause there ain't nothin' I can do with the steering wheel *but* hold on. You do what you can to protect yourself. You have a shoulder harness. I'm slidin' along and I can hear cars goin' by. You can actually feel them, like Greyhound buses passing. Your

Combed, cool, and collected after the fiery crash, Johnny prepares to tell ABC's Chris Economacki and the *Wide World of Sports* what happened (Don Smyle).

mind is super sensitive. Going down the track on my top I can hear the grindin'. I know I'm still on the racetrack. I know I'm not outside. I had my eyes closed, I guess, 'cause I don't remember seeing anything. You race back to the yellow. Nobody's slowed down. I'm expecting somebody to drive into the side of me any second. You know that wouldn't be good. You're upside down and don't have the frame to protect you. When I came to a stop, all of the sudden it burst into flames inside. The car turned as it was slidin'. It was slidin' backwards, so the flood of fuel was runnin' inside with the back glass out. It exploded inside and I started thinking, *'I gotta get outta here!'* There's a chance I might get run over. I gotta chance it. *I can't stay in here.*

"I'd been upside down before so I knew the procedure. It's easy to get hung up in the steering wheel, especially if you panic. The first thing you do is push your hand against the top. You have to push as much of the weight off your body as you can. With the other hand you turn the seatbelt loose and drop down on your knees on the steering wheel. You picture what's going to happen with your body. You don't just grab the seatbelt. You got room to move the way it was. I reached over, grabbed the roll bar, and catapulted myself out the passenger window. The open space was to the passenger side. My feet and knees were diggin' in and I was fast crawlin'. I thought I was on fire, but I'm not sure I was. It was hot in there. I got out thinkin' I was facin' the infield. I didn't know the car turned around and was facing out. In my mind, I could come out the window and run away from the car to the left. Well the car was turned around. I came out of the window runnin' toward the racetrack and around the backside which was burnin'. I argued that I didn't do that, but saw the film. That's why I thought I was on fire. The further I run from the car, the hotter I got like I was on fire. If I was burnin', it never showed on the fire suit."

Cartwheeling and spewing parts, Johnny sails through space toward a violent landing, broken bones, and hospital visits.

Johnny was uninjured in one of the most famous crashes in NASCAR history. It was seen nationally on *ABC's Wide World of Sports*. He escaped only scratching his watch crystal. It was the second crash of the trilogy.

"I did that gettin' out. I waved up to the grandstand on the backstretch. Holly Farms had suites there. My mother, dad, and sister and her then-boyfriend were out from California. My wife was there. Scared them to death. I waved, but nah, I didn't have any burns on me."

Johnny finished the season with a ninth at North Wilkesboro in the repaired Holly Farms 46 Darlington wreck. "It was burnt bad, but back then, burned out cars were good because they were lighter. You always fixed 'em back if there was any way. You had to really tear one up to not fix it. Holly Farms closed and Crawford went back to Spartanburg. That's when I came to Greenville [South Carolina]."

For 1963, Ratus Walters provided Johnny with a baby blue 1963 Fastback Ford Galaxie 66.

"It was a Holman-Moody Ford. You'd keep it up and they'd give you some parts. Ratus owned the car that Larry Frank won the [Southern] 500 in the year before. A dealership out of Richmond, Virginia, sponsored the car, Commonwealth Ford. They gave me a demo convertible. I ran the car until I destroyed it in Atlanta. It was a '63 until I got through with it."

On June 2, 1963, Johnny experienced an extremely hard crash.

"I ran the 600 and the car didn't handle. I wasn't runnin' as fast as Panch, Stacy, Lorenzen, and those guys. Comin' down the front straightaway, Petty dropped off in the dirt in the tri-oval. You'd kind of cut that corner. I saw rocks shoot out and said, 'I hope I don't hit one.' About that time, the right front blew and shot me straight into the wall. Back then your windshield was glass. Pieces of windshield grazed the starter. It hit so hard it knocked all the wind out of me. I slid along, stopped, and nobody hit me. I stayed against the wall past the finish line. They got the cars slowed and I was sittin' there tryin' to get my breath. They were tryin' to pull my helmet off. '*Leave me alone!*' They were tryin' to jerk me out and I was tryin' to get my breath. I hit so hard, the shoulder harness forced up against my ribcage, took the hide off both shoulders, my hips from the seatbelt. That concrete's *hard*. Those cars were stiff, too. They weren't meant to collapse. They helped me out across from Stacy's pits.

"I recovered after a while. This was the first race Stacy was back after that crash with Joe Lee in Atlanta and broke his pelvis. It was doubtful he could go distance. [Ralph] Moody come over and said, 'You think you can run?' 'Hell yeah! I'm all right.' It hadn't set in I was hurt. Stacy broke the studs off and lost time. He gets out and I get in and finished [sixth, five laps behind]. That was an eye-opener. Both '63 Fords, both Holman-Moody. It [29] was like ridin' in a Cadillac. My car [66] would beat you to death, hangin' on for dear life. That thing [29] would just cruise. I couldn't believe how deep I could drive it. How good it rode the bumps. They put softer springs and that's what I wanted."

Johnny had a demolished Ford and the Dixie 400 at Atlanta in four weeks.

"Ratus took the car to Maryland. He jacks it out and straightens the frame. His dad owned a big restaurant in D.C., Café Burgundy. A fancy restaurant where congressmen went.

"He brings it down and it will not drive. Terrible, just terrible. Practice and qualifying rained out. That put us right up against the Fourth of July race. We had to go straight to Daytona, four days to get ready. He had to bring his crew out of Maryland. 'Look Ratus, I'll tell you what. When you come back, come back with your truck and trailer. Don't bring your crew. Start the race; get the points, the car's terrible. We'll look like idiots.' He said, 'No, we need to run.' During the week I said, 'Ratus, I don't want to race the car. Load it up and take it to Daytona. We'll have time to get a new engine, get the frame checked, find out what's wrong, get it fixed, be fresh, and have a good car.' He said, 'No, we'll race.' Bad decision. It closed down the show."

June 30, 1963. Atlanta International Raceway is the scene of the third crash of the trilogy. This was perhaps the worst of all, if that's possible.

"All I did was wear out the right front. It blew, shot up the racetrack, broke through the top of the double guardrail, stood up on the radiator tearin' up the front end, knocked the engine out and forty feet of posts, and I'm ready to go sailin'. Hanging on and all of the sudden *CHOO* the car takes off. Everything gets nice and quiet and you know you haven't stopped *that* quick. You start thinkin', 'Man, it's gonna hurt when it hits.' I didn't know I'd left the track. I knew I was airborne. I didn't know which way. It hit a couple of times and bounced around. I'm hangin' on to the steering wheel tryin' to stay part of the car so you won't get beat up too bad. The guardrail ripped the front bumper off, threw the battery out on the racetrack. Fireball ran over the bumper and knocked the driveshaft out of his car. The battery hit Jack Smith's car, splashed inside, and acid got on him. The engine come out and ended up on the road. It shoved the steering column clear back into the roof. It caught me in the face. I had an open face helmet and broke my nose, tore it up. Stove my hand up. My hand hurt worse than anything. When the engine came out, the clutch pedal come down on top of my foot and broke some bones. Ended up outside the racetrack in the dirt on its wheels. Blood was running down. I was really dazed. 'I better get out before it catches fire.' I was thinkin' about Darlington. I got out the window and about passed out. I crawled away and waited. They had to get me back inside the track to the care center. It was a few minutes before I had enough strength to walk up there.

"I ended up walking back up the bank and back down on the track. They were holding me for support to get up [the hill]. You don't really hurt bad 'til later. I was sore still [from Charlotte]. They took me to the center and wiped me up a little bit. They wanted me to go to the hospital to get checked 'cause they didn't have a way there. 'I don't want to go to the hospital. I'm OK.' My foot was hurtin'. I thought I sprained it. You expected it to be hurtin' after you do that. My face was covered with blood, my nose was broken, and my hand was hurtin'. It worked, no bones sticking out anywhere. They said, 'We need to take you to the hospital.' I said, 'No, I'll tell you what. Isn't there a hospital closer?' 'Yeah, there's one in Griffin.' 'All right.' This friend, Don Hutelin, drove me to Griffin. They sewed up my nose. They made some x-rays of my foot and nose and said, 'It's broke, the top of your foot *and* nose.' I had to have it set and nobody there could. I had Don drive me to Atlanta. I guess I was thinking about Charlotte. I wanted to get a ride in somebody's car. They might even be leading. There's a lot of relievin'; Charlotte 600, Jack at Bristol, Stacy earlier. I was hurt, but walked away. It messed up some ligaments between your thumb and first finger. I guess I was holding tight against it with my arms getting ready for the impact when it hit the guardrail. It pushed the steering wheel back and that took longer to heal than anything. There was nothing broken. Stove up. I still have little problems ever now and then."

Records show that Johnny made 44 laps earning 32nd, Fireball got 31st, and Smith soldiered on in spite of his acid bath until he lost oil pressure for 24th. The 1964 season, his tenth on the tour, was one of the deadliest in auto racing history. Johnny ran only four Grand Nationals. The season opened for him in Roy Osborne's '63 Ford 92 at Augusta International Raceway, a three-mile road course hosting only one Grand National ever on November 17, 1963. It included a diverse field of 36 with Fireball winning the final race of his career and Dave McDonald second in his best stock car finish. Johnny started 23rd and blew for 20th.

"Fireball won it, a 400-mile race. Our lap speeds were not that fast. You were racing 75 miles per hour. Well, 400 miles at 75 miles and hour? That's an all day affair."

A sobering sign of the times: Of the top seven finishers, Roberts, McDonald, Wade, Weatherly, Jarrett, Pardue, and Thomas, only Jarrett was living when the following season opened at Riverside on January 17, 1965.

Johnny was eye-witness to a landmark event on December 1, 1963, in Jacksonville, Florida.

"Jacksonville was very rough. We were runnin' hot. Look at the rundown and see why cars dropped out. [Mostly axles and differentials; Johnny chuckles.] They flagged Buck Baker the winner and Wendell Scott hollered, 'Buck didn't win that race, I won that race!' 'Ain't no way in hell no nigger won that race!' Wendell said, 'I lapped you when you was in the pits!' Buck said, 'I made that up!' 'Yeah, but you didn't beat me!' Buck did have a long pit stop. They went back and forth and Wendell didn't get too upset. He knew he won and wanted it. I didn't have a clue. It was confusing with so many cautions, guys comin' in, fixin' stuff, goin' back out. When you're racing, you don't know where anybody is unless you're runnin' strong and everything stays calm. Guys come in and back out and been lapped three or four times. You don't know if they're ahead or behind. The only communication is a pit board. At night on a dirt track? It's really hard to get information. You just run your butt off."

The records show that of 22 cars, ten finished. Johnny started 19th and was ninth for the 61st and final top ten of his spectacular career. In 1965, Johnny went to Daytona to drive Red Vogt's Plymouth in spite of the Chrysler boycott.

"That was actually Bill France's car. France had a press conference and said, 'There *will be* Chrysler products in the race.' France made a deal with Red about two weeks before the race. Red calls me. 'You got a ride?' 'No.' 'You wanna drive a Plymouth?' 'It ain't gonna run.' He said, 'Mine will!' [Johnny chuckles.] 'I believe in ya, Red! How ya gonna get any sponsor?' 'Don't worry. I'll get it.' So I went down to help. Brand new Plymouth off the showroom. Made a racecar out of it. Worked day and night. Got a special cam. Ended up getting Householder to send some stuff. Slowest car I ever run. I tried to quit, but Red said, 'No!' Tried to blow it up, but couldn't. Not enough power."

Johnny started 20th in the qualifier finishing 15th. In the 500, he started 28th finishing 23rd, 19 laps behind in a race going 133 of 200 laps because of rain. Johnny Allen summed it all up.

"I did it backwards. Most people start on short tracks and work their way up. I started out on top. Those seven races I ran in Corpus Christi was my basic training. But it was good and I have no regrets. When that's your ambition, you want to get better, work your way up, and get runnin' up front. You're not satisfied with junk. It's hard to do, hanging

Fierce competitors and fast friends in the 1960s, Rex White (left) and Johnny Allen are still great friends in the fall of 2009.

out begging for an uncompetitive car just so you can be there. I saw a lot of guys do that, just hangin' on to race. I started runnin' short tracks. I won the Greenville-Pickens Championship in 1971."

Somebody said they'd rather be lucky than good. Johnny Allen was blessed with extra helpings of both. Luck certainly played a role in the outcome of his three crashes. It is unfortunate that perhaps he is best known to the public for those spectacular crashes. It was not unusual after Johnny fell out of a race to find him relieving. Over 35 percent of the time, Johnny was in the top ten in 173 starts. He raced on tracks of incredible, deadly toughness like Lehi, Langhorne, Lakewood, the Beach, Watkins Glen, and Darlington. Terrific and historic feats — such as third at Langhorne, last (59th) to 11th in the first Daytona 500 with no practice, relieving for second in the first World 600, second in the first Atlanta 500, third in the '61 Rebel 300 behind Lorenzen and Turner, preserving Jack Smith's win in Bristol's first race, and his last career top ten when Wendell won — are some of Johnny's memorable races. He did it without one single spotter, HANS device, soft wall, pit road speed limit, radio, or any of the things that have sucked the fearlessness out of the sport. He has boundless modesty, and above all, Johnny Allen is a winner. And would be even if he hadn't beat Rex to the checkers at Bowman Gray Stadium.

2

Tommy Irwin

Tough Tommy

Thomas W. Irwin was born on April 27, 1928, in Columbia Furnace, Va. Presently residing in Winchester, Va., his deep baritone makes him sound as if he could run the wheels off a stock car today. Starting in the big time in 1958 with five races, Tommy came out of the gate with three straight top tens in his first three starts. In 1959, Tommy attacked the Grand National circuit with outstanding results and 14th in final standings, somehow failing to win Rookie of the Year. He landed a top-flight independent Ford seat in 1963 and should have been on his way to fame and riches. But a devastating practice crash put the brakes on a stock car career that was just coming to full song. Along with being the first man to drive to the bottom of Lake Lloyd at Daytona, he has other claims to notoriety.

Thanks to a generous offer from a competitor, Tommy Irwin moved his family and racing operation from Virginia to Inman, South Carolina.

"Got tired of towing back and forth when I started NASCAR and we moved. I forget which race it was after and Lee Petty come up and said, 'There ain't no use draggin' that thing all the way up to Virginia and back. Bring it over to the house and leave it and you can come on down and work on it. I got plenty of room and you won't have so far to pull it.' I said, 'That sounds like a winner to me.' So I took it to Lee's and left it. I'd come back about Thursday and would work on it. See, we were runnin' three times a week. This was in '58. Now I am a fan of Lee Petty and will always be, and Richard, too, 'cause I got to know them real well leavin' my car up there. Lee give me a lot of help and he's one of my favorite people."

The last Grand National race at Atlanta's storied one-mile dirt Lakewood Speedway took place on June 14, 1959. In Tommy's only race there, he started 39th, next to last, and charged to ninth at the finish.

"I never run there but one time. I bent the push rods qualifying. We pulled 'em out and straightened them and I was wore out, worked out, used up. I went out to practice and I knew that old track was gonna dig up loose dirt. After you've seen enough dirt tracks, you know what they're gonna do. I said, 'It's gonna be like a plowed field.' I geared too low for the track while it was smooth in practice and was over-winding and bending the push rods. So I straightened 'em and went out there like an idiot and bent 'em again. So finally I got about half of 'em straight and I was so tired, I told that boy that was with me, 'I'll tell you what. If you want to run this race, you straighten the rest of them push rods and put 'em in that thing 'cause I am quittin'. I got in the car, hooked up my seat belts, put my helmet on, and sat there with my arms crossed. [Tommy chuckles.] I let him know that I was ready to go if he straightened them push rods. [Tommy laughs heartily.] So he did and I fired her up and was runnin' real good with the front cars and busted the right front tire. That track got so tore up you wouldn't believe me. The right front tire went flat and I slowed down to keep from tearin' up everything with that flat. In the meantime, I broke the cells in the battery and when the alternator quit charging, it cut off. The wrecker pushed me in and that was the end of that."

Tommy finished a respectable ninth, eight laps behind first-time winner Richard Petty, or so it seemed. He was an eyewitness to a famous controversial finish.

"Now I'll tell ya what happened there. Lee Petty had been runnin' an Oldsmobile. Lee had gone to Detroit not too long before that and got another deal and built a new Plymouth and that was the first race back with Plymouth. Richard won the race in the old '57 Oldsmobile. Lee run second in the Plymouth. But he took Richard behind the building there and you shoulda heard 'em. [Tommy laughs.] 'Richard, when that goes into Detroit that I won the first race out in this Plymouth, there's no limit to what we can get. If you win in that Oldsmobile, it ain't gonna do us a bit a good.' So Richard finally come out red in the face, mad, and told the scorers, 'Y'all scored wrong. Daddy won that race. I run second.' [Tommy chuckles.] And the guys just shook their heads. What are you gonna do when the winner

In the sweepstakes Nashville 300 on August 9, 1959, Tommy started tenth of 30 hardtops and ragtops, finishing fifth in T-Bird 36 (Tommy Irwin).

says the guy that run second wins it? You can't say, 'You gotta take it.' Well that's what happened because Lee didn't actually protest it. He made Richard go out there and tell 'em. Actually, Richard Petty won 201 races and Lee won one less."

Tommy was so good in his 99 career starts, it is amazing he never found his way to Victory Lane. He vividly remembers the ones that got away, as four days after Lakewood on June 18, 1959.

"Oh Lord, there were times I had the thing in my pocket. Columbia, man I'd rather not even, I get so mad when I think about that. Morris Metcalf was the head scorer. I wound up second. Now here's what happened. I was runnin' about fifth or sixth and the people in front of me had a wreck. Lee Petty was involved in it. He was in the pits four laps cutting sheet metal off to get back on the track. Morris Metcalf loved Lee Petty dearly. Lee was four laps down. All of them in front of me got involved in this wreck and here I was leadin' on the yellow flag. They stopped the race with the red flag. They come up there and told me that the clock accidentally got unplugged, so we're going to have to start the race over. In other words, we'd run about 14 or 16 laps or something like that. I knew right away what had happened when they said the clock had got unplugged. I knew who accidentally unplugged it. They told me, 'You can get gas if you want to.' I said, 'Can I get gas and pull back up here?' I mean my ears were burning I was so hot. They said, 'No, but you can fill up with gas and pull in the rear.' You see then, if you run 200 laps you'd run out of gas if you didn't put some in. I said, 'Naw, that's all right, I'll just stay here.' I made up my mind and I was mad and I was goin'.

"When they restarted, I lapped everybody but Petty and was on his back bumper. And the durn thing, all of the sudden I came up the front stretch and bounced off the grandstand and I said, 'What in the world!' Went down into one and didn't have a bit of brake pedal. I went down the backstretch pumping it so I'd have some. Well, I had a full pedal. 'Bout two laps it was full pedal. The next time I went into a corner and hit it, it went to the floor again. I almost hit the fence. So here I was tryin' to figure out how to get around that track afraid to use my brake. Lee come around and passed me. Now he's four laps down, but he passes me. Well I run the whole race without stopping for gas. I don't know how I done it, but found out later the carburetor had a little piston with a metering rod on it. This dust and dirt had stuck them down where that metering rod had the jets plugged up. I was runnin' extremely lean. Why I didn't burn the engine up I don't know. Anyhow, I wound up second.

"I took it back to this guy's shop the next morning and pulled the front wheels off. Before the race, I had sent the boys with me up town to get the brake linings. Unknown to me, this guy riveted the lining on the shoes with aluminum rivets. You wouldn't normally check the new rivets and they were set so deep in the pad. In the race, the aluminum rivets got hot and melted and the lining come off the shoes and wound up in there and that's what locked the wheel up and jerked me into the grandstand. Anybody knows the difference between brass and aluminum and you would never use aluminum rivets in an application like that on a racecar. After it got ground up, sometimes it would be between the drum and the shoe and sometimes it wouldn't. It just depended on where the lining was whether I had brakes or not.

"When the race was over, they hollered over the P.A. system, 'Park it out on the track.' Not to bring it in the pits. See, they were going to check my fuel cell. Well, I sure was hopin' they'd come down there 'cause I wanted to talk to them so bad I couldn't stand it. [Tommy laughs.] I went to a payphone to call NASCAR, but it was night and I didn't get no results at all. I found out later that the criteria of the race is controlled by the head scorer. I said, 'Thank you very much.' I knew that was a dead horse. But that's what happened. I won that race by three laps."

Buck Baker was third. Why did he not protest Lee Petty's win? "I'll tell the reason he wasn't raisin' hell 'cause on the last lap he blowed the engine. [Tommy laughs.] So that's the reason. Petty would have probably wound up way back. Weatherly was in the wreck, too. I actually run 214 or 15 laps on a tank of gas. But finally they just said over the P.A. system, 'Irwin, you can pull on in now.' They didn't want to come down there and check my fuel cell. Everybody knew what the deal was."

It is ironic that Tommy had such a helping hand extended to him by Lee Petty in 1958 because in 1959, an inexplicable Rookie of the Year award involved his son Richard. Tommy's Thunderbird 36 scorched the Grand National circuit in 25 of 44 events with ten top fives and 16 top tens. By comparison, Tommy Irwin clearly outran the winner of Rookie of the Year honors, Richard Petty, who ran 21 of 44 races with six top fives and nine top tens. Irwin won one pole to none for Petty. Irwin was out front for 174 laps that season and Petty led seven. In the final standings, Tommy was 14th and Richard 15th. Tommy won about $1,000 more in prize money. One must wonder how the 1959 Rookie of the Year was determined. Tommy Irwin is well aware of the discrepancy. However, Richard did finish fourth to Tommy's fifth in the brutal, oven-like conditions at Labor Day's Southern 500.

"I'll tell you something else that I still haven't gotten over at Darlington in the Southern 500. He got out sometime around the middle of the race. I think it was Marvin Panch that got in that car. Listen to this ... he got Rookie of the Race and I didn't get nothing. Bob Burdick finished second, but had Joe Weatherly relief driving for him. Jim Reed, the winner, Bobby Johns who was third, and me in fifth were the only ones in the top five that went all the way. I run the whole thing, burnt up, blistered up, that old Thunderbird was so hot inside, it baked a hole in my right leg clear to the bone.

"I was walking around after the race slushing. I thought I was in sweat, but it was blood down in my boot. Somebody said, 'You got something red on your pants there.' I pulled my pants leg up and there was a hole about the size of a silver dollar clear in and you could see the bone. That's what kind of shape you were in at Darlington. I'll tell you what, it was so hot that day, 140 degrees in the car. We put thermometers in 'em. I didn't think a man could live in 140 degrees. But you don't know it, you see. Your hands are blistered. You couldn't wear gloves. If you did, you got laughed at. So you wear blisters on your hands, bust them, and you bleed a little bit. Then the wheel gets sticky and you've got a good hold on it. Them blisters ... when you have to change gears on a caution or somethin', that gearshift lever is so hot, it feels like it's a burnin' coal of fire. Darlington will just eat you up mentally and physically. My wife used to always say, 'Are you havin' fun?'"

Tommy Irwin went to Daytona for Speedweeks in February of 1960 having gained a lot of experience and ready to go fast.

"Have you ever been on a real sure-nuff roller coaster? And for what, two rides, it's as exciting as heck. After that, there ain't nothin' to it. The first five to ten laps around Daytona is really thrilling. It's fun! Man, you're really into it. After that, it's just like drivin' down an interstate. It's just as easy as falling off a log. You can just lay your arm on the door if your car is handling right and just let 'er eat. You don't ever have to think about lettin' up. And they talk about Junior Johnson discoverin' the draft and all that. Well good god, everybody there knew about the draft. You know what I mean? After it happens one time, you realize what's goin' on. When you first go out there you understand the draft. When you can run up behind a car, pull out, and go blowin' by him, and you look in the mirror and here he comes like you're parked and he goes ridin' right by you. It don't take no engineer to figure out what's goin' on. [Tommy laughs heartily.] Now let me tell you about goin' in that lake, then I'll tell you about somethin' else."

It was February 12, 1960, in Daytona 500 qualifying race number 1 when Tommy Irwin went underwater exploring in Lake Lloyd in a Thunderbird.

"I was behind a group of cars that had the whole track blocked and I'd keep getting sucked up to 'em, but there was no room to pass. I figured I had to get by them to qualify and get whole lot better startin' spot. Nobody was runnin' that top groove right up next to the wall because all the loose gravel and rubber and everything up there. So I kept lookin' up there and that groove was wide open all the way around the track. I'd suck up behind this bunch and there was no place to go and I said, 'I wonder how that would be up against that wall.' So comin' down through the tri-oval, I backed off of 'em and pulled up against that wall in that top groove and said, 'If I lose it, I'll just slide up against the wall. It won't hurt nothin'.' At Darlington you run against the wall half the time anyhow. [Tommy chuckles.] I checked that groove out and I could hold her flat out all the way through there and said, 'Now that's where I'll go by 'em.'

"So I got me a runnin' start, pulled up against that wall, and come sailin' by the whole bunch of 'em. Comin' off a two, just almost off two, somebody slid up and caught me on the left rear corner of the bumper and turned me sideways. When he did, somebody hit me right in the door and it went out in that sand at a controlled slide. I turned the wheel, pumped the brakes, pumped the gas, nothing would change the angle that thing was settin' and slidin' at. It never slowed down at all and there were gullies where rain had run through that sand, cut gullies over a foot deep, and I said, 'This'll flip her.' I'd get all ready to flip, and it would ... *SHEW* ... right over the top of the gully and you couldn't even tell it was there. It went all the way to the water and hit the water so hard, it knocked the grill back against the radiator. And went out there, oh golly, it was 18 feet deep and the water was right under the window. Well, I thought I was on the ground so I unhooked my harness. When I did, the nose went straight down and I went down under the dash. And then it went down, down, down, down, and I felt it bump and set down. Here it is fillin' up with water. I went up then and bumped my head against the top and got some air. When they talk about it on *SPEED*, Tom Pistone said my

After one of the most harrowing rides in racing history, the 36 is pulled from Daytona's Lake Lloyd in the fading light of February 12, 1960 (Greg Fielden).

window regulator handle come off and I was down there huntin' the handle. But that's not the truth. The truth is I had that window where you could just pull it up and down. You didn't have to wind it. I could pull it up and pull it down, but I got hit in the door and bent up that linkage. So the window, I couldn't pull it down. I finally got it down far enough to get my fingers in there and said, 'Well, I'll go up and get me some more air, then I'll pull the window down.' The first time I went up, there was a lot of air 'cause it was glassed in all the way around and it was slowly fillin' up. When I went up there was only about two inches of air. My head hit the top and I didn't get there. So I had to turn my face up and jam it right up against the top. I said, 'Man, this is all I'm gonna get.' I got my lungs full of air and come down and when I got my fingers in there, and trust me when I tell ya, that window was comin' down! [Tommy laughs.] I brought that sucker down and I weighed 125 pounds then from workin' myself to death and half-way eatin.' 'Course I was tough enough that it didn't bother me none 'cause all I did was work, work, work and drive, drive, drive.

"Anyway, I pulled that window down to where my helmet would go out and when my helmet would go through, I knew I could. So I got out of there, but I didn't know how far up I had to go and was just bustin' for air. Finally, just swimmin' up just as fast as I could, of course with all them clothes on, and I had a pair of boots with a zipper up the inside. Dress boots that are not very tall, they ain't like engineer boots or nothin'. With helmet and clothes and boots and all you can't swim too fast. But I finally popped up outta there and, man, I laid back. I haven't been in any water lately, but at that time, I couldn't sink. I don't know why, but I could lay in a swimmin' pool and just float. I just laid back on my back and took me some breaths and floated around there and said, 'From now on, it's gonna take a whole lot to worry me.' Man after getting outta something like that, if I'da panicked for just a few seconds, I'da died right there. *Eighteen feet!* There was no bank, no fence, no nothin'! It was just sand. Buck Baker liked to lost his mind. He said, 'If I'da got out of the car I'da drowned 'cause I can't swim a lick!' The rescue squad was back there and they had to run to get me and I said, 'If I can hold out a little while, they'll be in here to help me.' I was lookin' for somebody *in* there. When I finally floated around and swam over to the bank, one of 'em reached in to give me a hand and I splashed water on him and he backed up. I should have grabbed his hand and fell back in there with him in that old cold water. [Tommy chuckles.] Oh, it was cold that day. The wind was a blowin' like crazy. Oh man, but I'm gonna tell ya the *bad* part of the story."

Tommy was 37th and last. The "something else" he mentioned earlier was the effect racing had on his wife.

"They got me in this old ambulance with those slanting back doors. They take me around and they're gonna check me out in the little check out center. Anytime anything happens you gotta go to the check out center. We're goin' through between Holman-Moody's building and the impound area and there's a fence there. They stopped at the gate. I looked out the window of the ambulance and there my wife stands and she's 5'6" and Cotton Owens' wife was tryin' to hold her and she's five feet. Just as I looked out the window I saw my wife's knees start to buckle. It had been rainin' and it was muddy and that place where them cars and trucks had been runnin' in and out was just horrible. I grabbed that back door and hopped out, the door fell back shut, and I caught her just as she was goin' down. I took her in Holman-Moody's building and set her on a bench. She was just sittin' there glassy-eyed looking straight ahead. I talked to her. I smacked her cheek. I got a damp rag and washed her face. I talked to her and it took me 20 minutes before she ever come to. She just set there ... *out!* I don't know where she was, but she wasn't nowhere around there. She said at the time that she knew I was in that car in that lake. That was what was in her mind. She didn't even know I was out. She didn't know I was there. All she knew was I was in that car in that lake and drownded.

"After about 20 minutes, I got her to talk to me. Finally, one of them guys in the Holman-Moody building got me a dry shirt and a dry pair of pants and a towel and I went around the corner and put on some dry clothes. Took the towel and dried my hair and everything and got to feelin' a little bit better. 'Course I was worried to death about her. I didn't know if she was ever goin' to come out of it or not. After about 20 minutes you get scared! There's the reason she never could get pregnant. We would leave one race and she would start worrying about the next one. That was the way it was. When I quit racin', we had a couple of kids *bam bam*.

"I still never had been to the hospital and the officials had been lookin' for me all over the place. Well we were getting ready to leave when they caught up to me and insisted I go get checked out. That wreck and all had happened hours before. We just drove away."

Myrtle Beach slipped away from Tommy on July 23, 1960, and he remembers it well.

"I went to Myrtle Beach and was out there leadin' that sucker all night long and with four laps to go, I blowed the right front tire and went through the fence in the number one corner. The wrecker there was from the Ford dealer and I was the only Ford [T-Bird 36] goin' good. When I went through that fence and went down ... when you were a kid, did you ever pull them things out of the ground that looked like a spear and throw 'em? Well, that's where I went. Down through a whole field of them and got stopped. It was sorta loose dirt. I got stopped, cut the switch off, and heard this hummin' sound. You know how a radiator cap will hum when a car is hot? That's the way it sounded. I looked at the temperature gauge and it was sittin' on a 180. 'What in the world is goin' on?' About that time a guy popped up in front of that driver's window and scared me to death. 'I got here just as quick as I could.' Here was that wrecker driver with the cable over his shoulder and that hummin' was that ratchet on his wrecker. He was comin' to get me! [Tommy laughs heartily.] They said he pulled right out amongst them racecars with that wrecker and went across the track and up to the fence. They were slidin' everywhere tryin' not to hit that wrecker. NASCAR run him off and told him never to come back again. [Tommy's still laughing.] He was comin' to get that Ford!

"Left front let go on me. Man I had it made 'cause Lee had been runnin' second until about ten laps to go and Buck come up. I was watchin' 'em in the mirror, and they got in a fight back there and finally Buck won out and got in front of Lee. I was sittin' there watchin', holdin' my distance with nobody comin'. That's what I'm talkin' about. Four laps and I'da had it."

According to the records, Tommy DNF'd for eighth, four laps back, due to "Tire." He added a bit of trivia about his car number and the near wins.

"That Thunderbird I run so good in was number 36 and number 36 has never won a Grand National or Cup race. I wish I could get in touch with Tommy Baldwin and tell him to change the number on that car. A lot of good drivers have had that number and they never won. I used to think it was me, but it might have been the number."

Tommy Baldwin at the time of this writing in 2010 has a Toyota team, car number

36. In the last race of the 1960 season on October 30, Tommy Irwin switched to Tom Daniels' '60 Chevrolet 2 for the inaugural Atlanta 500.

"We went to Atlanta with that sucker. That had a 348 in it and we couldn't get her to go for nothin'. So me and that Daniels boy changed cams and everything and finally put an old long-legged cam in it. It was time to qualify so I went out and qualified 27th. When that race started I lost three or four positions and said, 'Golly, we're in terrible shape.' About that time I felt that seat pushing on my back and that thing started to go. I could hold that thing flat out all the way around that track. Bobby Johns was driving Cotton Owens' Pontiac and I led two laps before the first pit stop from 27th. I passed Bobby and he passed me back and I passed him back over the finish line and then we pitted. Come out of the pits, I got out in fourth or fifth place 'cause my pit crew was a little bit slower than the other guys. When we restarted, I lost about three positions and said, 'That's all right, I'll be back.'

"And sure 'nuff, that thing laid me back in the seat and here I come on up into second and runnin' Cotton's Pontiac down. All of the sudden goin' up the backstretch, she just died. We thought it was the fuel pump, so the boys took it behind the wall and put a fuel pump on it. Went back out and just rode around 'cause we was already a bunch of laps

A disappointing 1961 Daytona 500 on February 26 netted Tommy a blown engine after 67 laps in Tom Daniels' Chevy for 45th place of 58.

Still in the T-Bird some in 1961, Tommy races Ned Jarrett (11), Junior Johnson (27), and Glen Wood (21) to ninth at Bowman Gray Stadium on April 3 (Greg Fielden).

down and ever once in a while, just to see if I could, I'd hold her flat out all the way around. NASCAR sent me $50 for leadin' two laps. That was $25 a lap for leading. Got a check from NASCAR. If I'da had the money then I got now, which I ain't rich now, I'da kept that check. I'da never cashed that sucker. [Tommy laughs.] It said right on there 'For leading two laps at Atlanta.'"

For the record, Tommy finished 18th, 34 laps behind winner Bobby Johns. On November 20, 1960, defeat was snatched from the jaws of victory yet again. At Jacksonville, Florida, as Tommy started third in Daniels' Chevrolet 2, led 166 laps, and finished second after losing the lead with 18 laps to go. "We thought it had run out of gas, but it did stop on the backstretch. Well that's the reason I got a lap down. Somebody throwed a little gas in it over there and I got her goin' again and finished second to Lee Petty. Come to find out later, they found a rag in the fuel cell. Somehow it got in the can when they fueled it somewhere along the way. That's what happened at Jacksonville when the car wasn't out of gas. There ain't no doubt in my mind that we could have won Atlanta in that thing."

In other words, there's no telling for how many races that rag had been in the gas tank occasionally clogging up the fuel flow. Tommy ran one World 600 and that was in 1961 in a factory Pontiac 18 for a cross-town car owner.

"I drove Bud Moore's car at Charlotte one time and the right rear tire kept blowin'. We qualified four laps at a time and the first lap it didn't want to run. The second, third, and fourth laps I run fast enough to set on the pole. But the first lap killed the four-lap average. Bud asked me what happened on that first lap and maybe we had it hot or something. It kinda vapor locked. It didn't want to run and at the end of the first lap she started picking up and going strong. Then the next three laps it went real good. But it wouldn't have mattered where I started 'cause I couldn't run it hard. I blew two tires just in practice. Joe Weatherly was driving the other car and they claimed they were both set up the same. By golly it would blow them right rear tires just as fast as you could put 'em on if you run 'em hard. All you could do was just kind of ride with it. It was good and fast, but if I run hard, it blew the right rear. With I don't know how many laps to go, the drive shaft come out at the front and swung around under the right rear tire, lifted me up and set me crossways. I was headed right down pit road and let her go. I stopped in the pits and before I could get anybody's attention, they had it jacked up, four tires on it, full of gas, and beatin' on the trunk lid for me to go. I finally got Bud's eye and pointed underneath. He jumped over the wall and looked under and just waved his hands at the guys. The drive shaft was completely gone. I wasn't in contention to win."

For the record, those four shaky qualifying laps earned Tommy seventh in the starting grid of 55 and he wound up 20th despite losing the drive shaft with 39 laps to go. Tommy ran a red 1962 Chevrolet 27 during the 1962 Grand National season in a car he built himself.

"With Monroe Shook I wasn't runnin' outta my pocket. But up till then I was runnin' outta my pocket and I done all the work. You know what I'm sayin'? Buildin' the cars, workin' on the cars, buildin' the engines, clear up until '63. I built that car ['62 Chevy 27] at Monroe Shooks' and Monroe had a heart attack. He had to quit financing any racing. So it set for a while. Then there was a concrete outfit in Arlington or Alexandria named Burton and Robinson. Well they bought that car for me and I took it back to Inman, South Carolina, where I'd been for a while before I come to Keysville [Virginia]. That guy that keeps these records on NASCAR [www.racing-reference.info], I don't know how he come up with that Melvin Bradley. Melvin Bradley had something to do with Holly Farms and Junior [Johnson] run 27. So he just picks up on this 27 and puts this guy as owner. See, I built the car out of a regular passenger car at Monroe Shooks' in Keysville. Emanuel Zervakis originally built the '61 Chevrolet for Shook Transfer. Then I went up there working and driving for Monroe and built the '62 and took it to Daytona as 85. But see, when Emanuel run 85, that was Monroe Shooks' number as a car owner. After this concrete company bought it, well several times I added it up and eight and five were 13. I don't like 13 and I don't like green. When I started racing, you couldn't run a green car and you couldn't put 13 on it. That was a no-no! Well see all that's gone by the wayside 'cause of sponsors whose color is green like that battery. Interstate backs Joe Gibbs there on [Kyle] Busch. Well they can't have nothing but green on their cars because their batteries are green. And Smokey Yunick put 13 on a Chevrolet. That was the first 13 I ever remember showing up; Smokey's 13 at Daytona. But that little old car [his '62 Chevy] would run. I had good luck with that car."

"I took that to Daytona. I was runnin' around with that thing and ever once in a while it would go 'bup' just like that. You could just feel a little jerk like. Well I got to wonderin' what it was. I went in, done some checkin', went back out again and I was holding her on the floor all the way around and said, 'Wonder if it could be in the ignition switch?' I was fiddlin' with the switch and cut it off. Well it didn't change the sound or nothing so I cut it back on. 'That thing didn't cut off. I'll bet that switch is bad.' I reached over and cut the switch off and that Chevrolet never changed a sound. I run ten laps with the switch off! I said, 'What's goin' on?' I'd let off the gas and it'd die. I cut the switch back on, still had it in gear, the engine started runnin'. I went on and run about two laps on the floor, cut the switch off, it cut off. So I cut the switch back on, run ten, cut the switch off and it never changed the sound. I ran another ten laps with the switch on.

"So I went in and started hunting Vince Piggins, the Chevrolet engineer that was down there. I found him and said, 'What is a goin' on with this thing? I can hold it on the floor, run ten laps, cut the switch off, it doesn't even change sounds. He said, 'Now I'm gonna tell ya what the deal is. The flame front is so slow in that 409 that you've got a fire burnin' in them cylinders all the time. That is the flame movin' from the sparkplug all the way across the cylinder. When you cut the switch off, it don't matter. There's fire in there. When the gas comes in, it lights.' [Tommy laughs out loud.] That's the gospel. He said it was

Since 8 + 5 = unlucky 13, Tommy changed Shooks' Chevy to 27, but here at Myrtle Beach on July 21, 1962, started second and finished 18th of 19 (Jack Walker).

Outside his Inman, South Carolina, garage, the beautiful Cunningham-Stewart Fastback Ford 44 was poised to ride Tommy to wins and stardom in 1963 (Tommy Irwin).

nothin' in the world but the flame front was so slow, we was losin' horsepower. If we could ever burn all that fuel, we could have another 100 horsepower. He said, 'When you tear them engines down and wipe the piston off, what does it look like?' I said, 'I gotcha.' Half of that piston, when you wipe it off with a rag, was just as clean as it was when you put it in there. Half of it had carbon on it and the other half wipes clean. That flame is burning in there all the time. It's more or less just dieseling. It didn't slow down none. It kept right on runnin' just like it did when the switch was on. He said once it gets like that, the sparkplug wouldn't even have to be firin'. It's just runnin' off itself."

Records reflect that in 1962 in Chevy 27, Tommy ran 19 races with two top fives and nine top tens. In 1963, Tommy Irwin had the rides of his life with a trio of new number 44 Fastback Galaxies backed not so much by Ford, but by the deep pockets of Briggs Cunningham III and Stewart McKinney, a wealthy Connecticut politician. They were also Tommy's last Grand National seats.

"I had a shop in Inman and built three of them. One of them was an old Fred Lorenzen car that I took the body off of and put a body on of that chestnut color. Anothern was a complete new Ford that Ford give me that was a school bus yellow. There was a guy that run that color for Holman and Moody [Nelson Stacy]. Well all of them had no interior other than just a bucket seat and a 427 dual four engine on it. But you couldn't run the dual four in NASCAR. Of course, we didn't run the engines stock anyhow. We took 'em out, reworked them, and put a single four-barrel intake on 'em. Then they gave me a ton stake-truck to drive. I went to Holman-Moody and they loaded me up a frame, sheet metal, and all that stuff. I took it back down to the shop and built the car out of pieces. So I actually had three of them built. I only had one guy helping me that was being paid. Everybody else just jumped in. Free help. Had a volunteer pit crew; some of them from Inman

Tommy Irwin finally had a good Daytona qualifying race on February 22, 1963, starting 18th and finishing 8th, then earning a fine tenth in the 500 (Tommy Irwin).

and some from Fairfield Firestone. Briggsy and them brought 'em down. I guess those from Fairfield Firestone you could consider paid people. But anybody I had from Inman, none of them were paid."

Tommy had a sponsor and impressive benefactors for 1963.

"It was Fairfield Firestone, Briggs Cunningham, and a future senator, Stewart McKinney. He got to be a senator from Connecticut. [Research found that Stewart McKinney married the daughter of Briggs Cunningham and Lucie Bedford, who was the granddaughter of the co-founder of Standard Oil. McKinney died in 1987.] Briggsy Junior [Briggs Cunningham, III] was at the shop one day in Inman. Now here's the Cunninghams, worth about a billion dollars or more. He sits down on a battery and eats the back out of his pants and hasn't even got another pair of pants with him. We go up to the house, he goes in a room and takes his pants off, hands 'em out, and my wife sews up where the battery acid eat holes in his pants. He puts his pants back on and goes to the races like that. He don't care. He was partners with Stewart McKinney. They had a Firestone store. They done tires and light mechanic work, upholstery work, in Fairfield, Connecticut. They were partners in this thing; Briggsy Junior and Stewart McKinney. See, Stewart was married to Briggsy's sister. That's how they were connected and later Stewart was elected to the U.S. Senate."

Tommy Irwin was part of the Ford domination of the 1963 Daytona 500.

"What happened at Daytona, I was runnin' up there towards the front good and one of the lug studs on the right front popped off when we went to change tires. My pit man run to the box and got one and had it in there and was pulling it in with the impact wrench. The NASCAR official thought it was taking too long and come and checked it. 'I got her fixed. It's all right.' He [the official] made us pull behind the wall, take the wheel off, and let them inspect it. Then they OK'd it and we put it back on and that's what put me tenth place. But I was runnin' good that day."

On March 2, 1963, in a late Saturday morning practice session for a 100-mile Grand National race at the Piedmont Interstate Fairgrounds in Spartanburg, before my very eyes and no more than 20 feet away, Tommy Irwin crashed his gorgeous chestnut-colored Ford 44. In my (the author's) life as a keen observer of auto racing and having later seen drivers die, Tommy's wreck that day still ranks as one of the very worst accidents I have ever seen. My friends and I were sure Irwin had been killed.

"What caused the wreck in Spartanburg, it was a brand new short track dirt car. That chestnut with those white letters made a pretty car. Anyhow, we went out there and was practicing and they throwed the red flag. They stopped to let people into the infield. Well, I come on in the pit. We worked on it some more and I went on out and was practicing real hard. I was comin' up behind about three cars and they throwed the red flag. Well when they did, these three cars in front of me went down on the brakes pretty hard. I had been working hard and was kinda tired and just laid my arms on the steering wheel resting. Had to put down on the brakes pretty hard. When I did, the left front brake grabbed and that spun the steering wheel under my arms. Naturally, the first thing you do is grab the wheel and start bringing it back around. You know it crossed up. As I'm bringing it back around, bringing it back straight, it nosed into the opening into the infield bank. There's an opening there of a three foot bank and when it nosed into that bank, the back come up over the front and it just done end-over-ends. I don't know how many times it rolled 'cause I don't remember nothing.

The twisted remains of Tommy's Ford in the Spartanburg pits on March 2, 1963, after the crash that basically ended his Grand National career.

Here's what happened: I had a stock Ford bucket seat and they're hinged, you know, on them two-doors. The bottom I had it plated and bolted to the roll cage and I had the back plated and bolted to the roll cage where it went across up behind me. Where the seat goes together, it slides on a pin on each side with a washer and a cotter pin. This hard jolt sheared them cotter pins and the back of the seat jumped off those pins and opened up and that loosened all my belts. I would go down in that hole and fly back out. It knocked my eye out on my cheek. It was hanging on my cheek just a swingin' and beat me up ungodly. I had bruises for six months. It bruised my back, my arms, my head got out because there was red dirt all over my helmet. I don't know why it didn't kill me. I had one little cut on my hand. OK, I remember smellin' dust real strong. That's all I remember during the whole thing. Some guy comes up through the infield and my wife's coming down there and he said to this other guy with him, not to my wife, she's just walking by, he says to his buddy, 'There's no use messin' with him. He's dead.' My wife heard that and she couldn't hardly make it down there then.

"They got me in the ambulance and she got in there with me and when we went up out of the track, the stretcher rolled back and bumped the back of the door and that woke me up. I talked to her goin' to the hospital and I remember my face felt funny. I reached up there and I felt my (left) eye and it felt like a hard-boiled egg laying on my cheek. They got me to the [Spartanburg General] hospital and the eye doctor looked at that eye and said, 'Forget his eye, just try to save him. The eye's gone.' Of course, they didn't even pay any attention to that thing. It was just swingin' around and I was layin' there and that was about the middle of the afternoon on Saturday. Briggsy and all came to the hospital and the doctors had to run 'em out. They was in the room, in the hall, and the doctors run 'em out of the hospital. I didn't know it, but my wife said there was a crowd there. They come from the racetrack. All the people that were with me and some that weren't. They was doing too much talkin', I guess. So the doctors run 'em out. That's when I was passin' out and comin' to.

"They wouldn't give me a shot for pain until Sunday morning 'cause they were afraid it would send me into shock. I spent all Saturday evening and Saturday night coming to for maybe 30 or 40 seconds and just pass out from pain. I remember coming to, I'll bet you, 50 times. But I wouldn't stay there long. It hurt so bad I'd pass out again. Finally about daylight Sunday morning, they gave me a shot of morphine. They gave me a pretty good one and I just laid there floatin', playin' with my eye, and talkin' to my wife and anybody that wanted to talk to me. It was just layin' there and I was just playin' with it with my dirty hands and everything. Later that day it had kinda gone back up and was settin' outside the hole, but settin' out there where I could still play with it.

"I crushed a vertebra in my back, so they took me down to x-ray me some more. I was layin' there on that x-ray table and saw a post on the x-ray table. I saw a ghost line. You've had an old television that wasn't right that had a ghost line on it? Well, I saw a ghost line of that post. Goin' back up there even in my fogged up, shot up brain, I said, 'I know you can't see double vision with one eye.' I said, 'That eye's working!' So when I got back up there, I told my wife, 'Get that eye doctor back in here' the best I could. She said, 'Now Tommy, they said that eye was gone, not to worry about it.' I said, '*Please* get the eye doctor back in here.'

"So she went to the phone and called that doctor. He come in there a couple of hours later and said, 'What seems to be goin' on?' I told him I was seein' that ghost line. Well he lit his cigarette lighter and held his hand over my good eye and said, 'Can you see that?' I said, 'Yeah,' He said, 'What does it look like?' I said, 'A light, a candle burnin' about a quarter mile away.' He put out the lighter and said, 'How far away?' I said, 'You put it out now,' and then he knew I could see out of it. He told them to keep an ice compress on it. And you know that thing sunk back in my head and when I had to get glasses, my right eye, the other eye, went first. And I still got that sucker in there! Still workin' fine. [Tommy laughs.] When they put them cold compresses on there for about eight or ten hours, it sunk right back in my head. I guess the mud went on back in there with it is all I can figure." [Tommy chuckles.]

"Over three weeks, the first week, they give me a shot of morphine every hour. That's how bad I was broke and beat up. I had a crushed vertebra in my back. I had a little cut on my hand right by my thumb about a half inch long, and everything else was bruises. My right hand had got out the door and the car rolled over on it and it looked liked you'd dipped it in black paint. My whole left arm except my hand looked like it had been sprayed with black paint. My back still had bruises six months later from getting beat around, you know. Anyhow, they give me a shot every hour on the hour for the first week. Second week, every three hours. The first part of the third week every three hours and then they backed off to whenever I wanted it. So I would get one about nine o'clock, wake up about two or three and get another, then I'd wake up the next morning and felt fine. Along about nine o'clock that night I'd get another one. Same thing three o'clock in the morning.

"After laying there over three weeks, they put a back brace on to hold my shoulders back because of that vertebrae and here I go bouncing home just feeling fine, glad to be out of that durn hospital. Food terrible, ya know. My wife was bringing me sandwiches from over at Jimmy's Restaurant. I couldn't eat that hospital food and finally got to where I couldn't eat Jimmy's any more after a couple of weeks. Anyhow, I come bouncin' home just feeling great. A bunch of us boys used to sit around and play a little ol' cheap poker. I went up there and played poker with them, went home, it got dark, and about nine o'clock I started getting a little chills. About nine-thirty, my teeth started chattering. I started freezing in the middle of the hot summertime. We had a floor furnace in the hall. I got a plastic chair over it and sit on it and turned that furnace wide open in the summer time; sittin' there chatterin' and freezing. My wife got a wool blanket and made a tent out of it and sat there and told her I was not going to live till morning. I was goin' to die right there. I knew I was goin' to die and you could hear water dripping down in that furnace off of me. I was just freezing and sweating up a storm and dying all the time. I sit there all night and about daylight, I started feeling a little better and when it got good and bright, I got up and felt fine. Went on and ate some breakfast, fooled around that morning and afternoon, and played some more poker. I come back that night and it was the same old thing again. That went on for about three nights. Then the fourth night, she piled a bunch of covers on me and I got to sleep. Then it slowly just tapered on off. The next night and the next night was better and I had a doctor's appointment in a week.

"When I went in there sittin' in the waitin' room, the receptionist said, 'He will see you in his office.' I went down there, sit down, and he came in and looked at me and started laughing. [Tommy laughs.] He said, 'How was it?' I said, 'It was seven kinds of Hell!' He said, 'I knew it would be, but there was nothing I could do for you. I could have give you something to take home with you, but you'd have bugged me for the rest of your life.' I agreed with him 100 percent. Morphine! I was on that stuff. You know they talk about people using dirty needles? I would have put it in there with a rusty nail if it had got it in there. That first night, I knew I wasn't going to live till morning. He said that's the only way you can do it. So you go through Hell for a week. It goes away then."

The demolished chestnut and white Ford 44 was repaired while Tommy healed.

Tommy Irwin in the pits recently preparing his son's late model for a race in Virginia (Tommy Irwin).

"The guys that worked for me fixed that while I was in the hospital. All kind of rumors got out the roll bar gave away and all that stuff, but it didn't. The fenders were all tore up. The top had to be straightened. It was fixed up and sold to a guy that ran short tracks up in Connecticut."

Pictures and mementos of Tommy Irwin's fine Grand National career are in short supply at his house.

"You know, it's ridiculous, no more stuff than I saved. It don't mean anything. You're just doin' it for the pleasure of it, the thrill of it. You don't think about savin' none of that. I won a boatload of trophies around here locally and you didn't get a trophy every race. They'd have special trophy races and I won a bunch of them. And that kid of mine when he was just comin' up, when he was real young got a little old adjustable wrench and over a period of time took ever one of them apart. They bolted together then. I finally gathered 'em up and put 'em in a couple apple crates and bushel baskets and when we moved in this house in 2000, I throwed 'em in the trash. [Tommy laughs.] I started to put 'em back together and I said, 'Heck, it just ain't even worth it.' So I throwed 'em away."

What Tommy Irwin cannot throw away in a bushel basket is the legacy of an independent racer holding his own with very best in stock car racing nearly every time he strapped himself into a racecar, almost all of which he built himself. He probably should have never surfaced from that frigid Daytona lake in 1960, but he did. He definitely could have been carried from Spartanburg General Hospital to the mortuary after that fairgrounds crash in 1963, but he wasn't. He never had the pleasure of driving into Victory Lane in his 99 Grand National starts, but he should have several times. And he ought to carry the honor of 1959 NASCAR Grand National Rookie of the Year because he was. Tommy Irwin is an overachiever and as tough as any racer who ever lived. Racing through his ninth decade on Earth, there is no end in sight. And his eyesight is just fine.

3

Curtis Crider

Crawfish

Curtis Wade Crider was born on October 7, 1930, in Danville, Virginia. Of Dutch-German descent, Curtis grew up on a tobacco farm near Chapel Hill, North Carolina, helped his father work on neighbors' cars at ten, and bid the town farewell before his 16th birthday to live with his uncle in Schoolfield, Virginia. Working at a service station, he became a pretty good mechanic, and at 18 joined the U.S. Air Force. While there, Curtis finished high school, traveled the world honing his mechanical skills, and attended stock car races after his discharge in the early 1950s. He saw the legendary pioneers, proceeded to join them picking up rides where he could, and moved wherever they were. That eventually led to the NASCAR Grand National circuit and 232 races from 1959 through 1965. Curtis Crider got his start just out of the service at a famous old dirt track.

"Spartanburg was one of my favorite tracks and the first track I raced on. I had just got out of the Air Force and was ridin' around and saw a bunch of people and cars. I didn't even know it was a race. I bought a ticket to watch 'em practice. This guy kept coming in skippin' and I said, 'Hey buddy! Stick your finger up in that coil, turn the motor over, and see if you got any damn spark. It's the quick way.' [Crawfish chuckles.] He tried it and said, 'No, we're not.' 'OK, get a coil and put it on real quick like.' Practice was almost over. They put a coil on and that thing cleared up. He said, 'Damn! You a race driver?' I said, 'I'm the best you've ever seen!' [Crawfish laughs.] I said that, word for word. It was the Yon Brothers out of Charleston, South Carolina. 'You wanna drive for us?' I said, 'Yeah, why not?' So I used their helmet and stuff and made out all right. We finished third. Thank goodness I got there and it was a way of life for me after that. That was my very first race and I lied myself into that one. I told them I was the best they'd ever seen, but it wasn't no lie because they hadn't seen many."

In 1955, he traveled to England with Bobby Myers, Neil Castles, and Possum Jones for the World Stock Car Racing Championship. Curtis finished second to Myers.

"Raced all over Canada, the United States, and England. The people were so nice. Most of them lived on farms. They'd talk to me, then invite me and the crew for dinner durin' the week. We had a lot fun with them on the track and off. I showed them how to make one handle, set it up, shocks and springs and stuff. I made a lot of friends like that.

In fact, one of them bought the last racecar I built, a '40 Ford number 21. He bought it from London, England. We had it all set up. I took it to Savannah, put it on a ship, and he's got it over there and goes to shows. My number 3 is in the Georgia Racing Hall of Fame. I got a '40 Ford hauler. Got the tire rack and all. It's got to be the only '40 Ford hauler. It's got ramps, a winch, and all that stuff."

Curtis explains how he got the name by which he prefers to be addressed, a fact that he made abundantly clear.

"Many years after having moved to Greensboro, North Carolina, I went back to Danville to race in my young, single days. I met a fine little girl working in a truck stop. She was working until midnight. We made a date. I would stop there after the race. We traveled light with no changes of clothes. It was agreed that I would try to stay clean. The guys on the crew would do all the tire changing and other work and I would drive. A fellow wouldn't get very dirty that way, would he? During the race, I crossed up on the backstretch and up and over I went, outside the track, and into a little old creek. Not very deep, but wet and muddy. The car wasn't damaged and I wasn't hurt, but I guess I looked pretty funny climbing out of the stream and up the bank. When I got to the pits, the guys started picking at me and one of them said I looked like a crawfish, all muddy and wet, coming out of the creek. From then on, I was *Crawfish* Crider. Many folks never knew my name was Curtis. Later while driving Grand Nationals and having to talk business with executives in Detroit, I felt it would be ridiculous to telephone and say, 'Hey, look here. This is Crawfish Crider.' I figured it would be much better to say, 'Good morning. This Curtis W. Crider.' Not only were some folks surprised to learn my given name, but others who met Crawfish for the first time would say, 'My goodness. I pictured you a heavy-set person.' Guess they figured anyone with that nickname had short legs and waddled."

One of Crawfish's best friends in racing also had an appropriate nickname that was confirmed before they hit the big-time.

"Lewis 'Possum' Jones was driving for Deese's Garage in Charleston and I was racing for the Yon Brothers down the road. Possum and I were competitors, but off the track we were close friends and ran around together. In those days, car owners more or less adopted their young drivers, took them into their homes, each with a room of their own. The drivers often ate dinner with the families. I would go down to Deese's Garage in the morning and ask for Possum. Mr. Deese or his son Sonny would say, 'He's still in the house.' I'd go in and find him still sacked out. Whether that's where he got his nickname or not, I'm not sure, but it sure did fit. That lad liked to sleep more and longer than anyone I've known. He was one heck of a good race driver. Possum always drove half barefoot, no

Curtis Wade Crider, circa 1963 (Curtis Crider).

shoe on his right foot. I never could stand the hot floorboard, but Jones always said he could have a better feeling on the accelerator wearing a sock instead of a shoe."

Not all of the moonshine came from North Georgia and North Carolina. One transporter of future Grand National fame operated in the Palmetto State.

"My brother Ike and I did our share of moonshine running from still to market. One of my most harrowing experiences came after I had picked up nine or ten cases in Greenwood [South Carolina] scheduled for an Abbeville delivery. After that, we were going to race in Aiken. The liquor was stored up front in the truck we would pull the racecar with. We piled cases of oil, gas cans, tires, and tools on top of the liquor. We looked all over Abbeville that Saturday night, but couldn't locate the customer and unload. We just had to roll on to Aiken for the race the next day. I would keep the racecar with me until it needed repairs, then go back to Charleston. At Aiken, everything worked OK until late when the racecar developed engine problems. Charleston was closer than Abbeville, so first things come first. Get the racecar repaired. Take care of the whiskey delivery later.

"We checked in at the Yon Brothers Garage and I told Cecil, 'I have some whiskey on that truck and I've got to get rid of it.' Cecil said he would make a phone call. I talked to the people, told them how much we had, and it all sounded pretty good. The buyers would come to the garage, taste the whiskey to be sure it was OK, and take it off our hands, at least out of my truck. They didn't show. It was getting late and we decided to give up and go to the motel. We unhooked the racecar and had the liquor in the truck. On the way to the motel, the police stopped us. At first, I thought someone had tipped off the police because we were cutting in on another distributor's territory. It was after sundown. We got out of the truck and walked back to the police car and the officers got out with their flashlights. They were nice, but were flashing their lights at the stuff in the truck. I showed them my driver's license and tried to stay cool. 'Where did you get these tires and wheels?' Then I got the picture. They were *not* looking for whiskey. They thought we had ripped off a tire store or were stripping cars. I explained, 'We are racing people. We race for the Yon Brothers and been working on the racecar. We're headed for the motel.' The policeman threw the beam towards the back of the truck and I could see the corner of a case of whiskey under the tires. Every time the light would aim towards the whiskey, I'd take his hand and move the light to another area. 'Those are the kinds of tires we run on asphalt.' I'd pull it to another side and say, 'Those are the tires we run on dirt.' I gave him a lesson in racing on the side of the road, whether he wanted it or not.

"I started to help Cale Yarborough with his Grand National car. I was service manager at the Ford dealership in Florence, South Carolina. I would go to the races with Cale and work on his crew. Sometimes I would be the only crew member, crew chief, or whatever. One day after a string of bad luck, Cale wanted to run some of the short tracks between the Grand National events. I had a nice little '37 Ford finished and ready to race. Cale proposed we trade even, his Grand National for my sportsman."

"There I sat with a '58 Grand National car and the Fourth of July Firecracker race coming up at Daytona. I worked on the car at the Ford place nights and weekends and was ready to leave. I spent all our savings getting the car ready. I went to the gas station where I regularly traded and asked, 'How about filling the tow car with gas, filling the racecar with gas, and then cash a check for $25 and hold the check until I get back from Daytona?' He agreed. With the cash we had from home, the $25 from the gas station, and a full load of gasoline, my wife, two children, and I took off for Daytona. We still had two or three days after arrival before checking in at the speedway, so I drove around and found a body shop. I told the owner that if he would paint my car as best he could in a hurry, I would put his name on it. He liked the idea and did a nice job.

"Then I towed the car around and stopped at a fast food place called Whataburger. I couldn't get the towcar and the racecar into his parking lot. I parked across the street, walked in, found the owner, and asked, 'Would you be interested in putting your name on the side of that racecar for the Firecracker 250?' 'Certainly. How much would it be?' I said, 'A hundred and fifty dollars for the quarter panels.' 'That sounds fine. Go ahead and do it.' I went to my Uncle Harry and Aunt Erma Hanks' house in Daytona Beach; put the car in his driveway, got a brush and some paint, and started lettering. I had never done any sign work, so it took me about all day. I would get almost through with Whataburger and it would be bigger at one end than the other. I'd have to go back and enlarge the letters. I finally got them equaled pretty good. The next day, I went to the place, parked across the street, and found the boss. The sign looked pretty good, even better from a distance. 'Yeah, that looks all right. Come into the office.' I quoted him $150 for the quarter panels, thinking both sides. He said, 'Let's see, $150 and $150, that's $300, right?' 'Yes sir. Anyway you want to figure it.' He wrote a check for $300. If he thought it was worth $300, I wasn't about to argue. Besides, I had not the slightest idea what the going rate for that kind of advertising was. This was all new to me.

Curtis' famous Whataburger Ford 83 before the 1960 Firecracker 250 at Daytona, where he went from last (37th) to 24th (Curtis Crider).

"We ran and I earned some money there, so it was not a bad experience. When I returned home, I paid my bills at the neighborhood gas station."

The record shows Crawfish started 37th; dead last, finishing 24th right behind Reb Wickersham on July 4, 1960.

"Next came the annual Northern Tour, first stop Heidelberg, Pennsylvania. When we arrived a couple of days before the race, I began to look for sponsors. An outboard motor dealer bought space on the front fenders and I left Whataburger on the quarter panels. The boat dealer was across from the motel. When Lee Petty arrived, I was out there lettering. Later at the track, Petty told the fellows, 'If you ever see Curtis sitting on a box painting his racecar, you might as well unhook because there's sure to be a race around there soon.'"

On July 10, 1960, Crawfish started tenth, finishing 15th, the last car running 64 laps behind winner Petty. Crawfish had his share of flat towing misadventures.

"In those days, we did not have trucks or trailers, just tow bars. Coming back into New York, there were seven of us towing, 14 cars in a line, running those winding roads alongside the Hudson. I was traveling light with one crew member, cousin Jerry Hanks. I was leading the parade. Two girls were signaling for a ride. They were way out in the boondocks in the mountains, soon to be dark. I stopped to pick them up. I forgot about the 12 cars behind me and when they all braked quickly, it was quite a mess. Some of them crossed up across the road. Thank goodness no car hit another. There was a farmer and his wife sitting on a porch and we scared them to death with the squealing and smoking. The girls attended a nearby college and were out hiking and worried about the approaching darkness. To make matters worse, we'd only gone about a half a mile when we reached their college. 'Lord, goodness girls, don't ever do that again! With all that commotion and you're only going that short distance, for goodness sakes!' Later Buck Baker said, 'Lookahere Curtis. I know your intentions were good, but the next time something like that happens, how about letting the last car in line pick 'em up. The first car shouldn't do it.' I couldn't argue with that.

"We were building a new racecar in the shop in Charleston while I went to Hillsborough, North Carolina, one Sunday. We left the big truck back at the shop. We were almost to Hillsborough about 30 miles below Chapel Hill when the tow bar broke loose from the pick up. All racing fans know that a runaway racecar will turn left. Moments after I realized the tow bar broke, I heard the safety chain snap. I could see in the mirror the racecar was trying to run over the pickup, but was angling to the left side of that two-lane road. Coming toward us was a DeSoto. I could see the folks, a family en route to church or a Sunday visit. I held my breath as I waited for that racecar to hit that DeSoto head on, scared to death that someone would be hurt. Fortunately, the racecar hit the DeSoto a glancing blow, mashing the fender against the front tire, crushing in the quarter panel and the chrome strips along the side. The startled driver went down the road and parked. The racecar made a left turn, knocked down a wire fence, and stopped in a cornfield. I stopped and hurried back to the DeSoto. No one was hurt, but they were frightened half to death and all shook up about as bad as I was. We pulled the fender away from the tire and talked with the man about the damage.

"He was a pretty good sport. 'How much damage do you think I did?' 'Well I really don't know.' I added, 'I don't either. I am a pretty fair mechanic, but not much on body work. How much was the car worth before I hit it?' 'Well, about $300, I reckon.' 'I'll tell you what I will do. I'll just buy the car from you and you go ahead and drive it for a week or two until I get in touch with my dad in Greensboro. I'll get him to come over to your place and pick it up. You just go ahead and drive it.' The man said, 'That's fine.' I gave him the money and he gave me some papers sufficient to consummate the deal.

"The farmer was standing outside his house and seen the whole commotion. He came over and said he would get his tractor and pull the racecar out of the cornfield. Here comes a state policeman 'What's going on?' I told him, 'Let me tell you something. This is the damndest thing you have ever seen. My racecar tore loose and hit my DeSoto.' The policeman turned to the DeSoto driver and said, 'Is that right?' 'Yes sir, both of them is his. He owns both of them.' [The cop] couldn't figure out how a South Carolina racecar could hit a North Carolina DeSoto, both headed in opposite directions, and me owning both of them. All this on Sunday morning. He shook his head. 'I'll tell you what son. You keep that racecar hooked up real good from now on.' He drove away, no problem. After the farmer towed the racecar out of the cornfield, I asked, 'How much do I owe you for the use of your tractor and the damage?' 'Son, you don't owe me a thing. I haven't had as much fun on a Sunday morning in I don't know how long.'"

One of the all time greats took time out from winning the Southern 500 to give Crawfish a driving lesson.

"Buck Baker was one super person. He was serious about racing, yet fun, nice to be around. During the 1960 Southern 500, I was doing all I could with my old car going into the corners as fast as I thought I could possibly make it. Baker and I came out of the pits one time during a caution and I was in front. The field was on the backstretch and the caution was about to end. Buck motioned me to go on. He was anxious to catch up with the tail end of the field and could not pass me during the caution. I was running wide open because the track was clear between us and the end of the pack. I dared not run faster through the corners, especially with my older car. As we came off the fourth turn, Buck planted the front bumper against my rear bumper pushing. As he carried me into the number one turn, I thought, 'Oh Lord, I'm not going to make it!' Buck backed off and that old Ford settled down in that turn and sailed through it. It was really beautiful and I couldn't believe it! Up the backstretch we went and caught the field in time for the green flag. Buck won that race, taught me something; how to drive through the turns faster and safely. I picked up two or three positions after he showed me how to get through the corners. Before that, I had been backing off early, not realizing the car's handling capability.

"Of course, Buck was not trying to be a teacher. He wanted to get around faster and I was holding him up. For us, regardless of the intent, it worked. Through the years, Buck and I had a good relationship and I was especially happy to see him honored by the National Motorsports Press Association Stock Car Hall of Fame at Darlington. Buck earned that recognition."

The record shows that Crawfish started the Southern 500 in 43rd in Ford 83 and finished 20th, running at the finish.

"In the early days at Darlington, tires were too skinny and the spindles were small. Handling in the corners was at a premium. Jack Smith's car was out of control one day in the first turn and he went over the guardrail. His was not the only car to do that. Jack once commented that every time he would go down the front straightaway after that, his right foot would automatically raise up. The most awful sound on any speedway was the big boom of a tire blowing, which sounded like a cannon. When a fellow like me was working on the car trying to get the right weight distribution, fellows like Fred Lorenzen, Nelson Stacy, Ralph Moody, or Fireball Roberts would walk by. If you looked like you were ready to scratch your head, they would jump up and down on the springs and say, 'Go a little heavier' or 'Go a little lighter.' Ralph was a former race driver before he was a car builder and was one of the best at both. When Moody would bring a car to the raceway, he would take it out first and test it. Make changes to make it handle better. Then he would tell his driver to get in. Moody knew what the car was capable of doing and it was up to the driver to practice and reach the same goal."

Darlington was tough, especially the third turn.

"It was just as fair to one as it was the other. Hell, all of us got to go through it. You just wanted to get close to it. You gauge yourself as to how fast you want to go and then right in the center make sure you don't get into the rail. Right then you can get back full throttle and come off and down the straightaway. If the other guy had a little advantage, it would be smart to let him have it because you could mess both of ya up. Maybe the next lap or two you got the advantage.

"In 1961, some of the superspeedway promoters worked on a plan to attract a variety of automobiles by offering bonuses of $1,000 for the best finish by make of car. There was one stipulation to win the award; the car must go at least half the distance of the race. I had older equipment and felt I could do better if I updated. I wanted to buy a '61 Mercury. I went to my bank and explained my need for a loan. The bankers listened, took it under consideration, and a short time later told me that being a race driver, they did not think I was gainfully employed sufficiently to borrow that kind of money to buy an automobile. I telephoned Bob Colvin, president of the Darlington Raceway. 'Curtis, why don't you come and we'll talk about it.' Colvin never told me whether he had talked to his bankers, but it was obvious he had. I went to his bank as he suggested, laid the plan on the table, what I planned to do with the money, and the potential for the bonus money. The Darlington bank lent me a third. Next I went to banks in Abbeville and Savannah getting a third from each. They were aware of what the other banks were doing, all on signature loans. I went to the Mercury dealer in Charleston and paid cash for a '61 Mercury. It had 13 miles on it when I drove it to the shop. Boy, did we hustle to get that car ready for Charlotte.

July 4, 1961, found Curtis and his new Mercury 62 looking sharp for prerace photos. In the Firecracker 250 he started 25th and finished 24th (Curtis Crider).

Vapor lock put Curtis' 1962 Mercury 62 on the hauler at Myrtle Beach on July 21. He finished 169 laps for 12th out of 19 starters (Jack Walker).

"We qualified well. There were three Mercurys which had factory support, so they were my biggest threat. I had to get ahead of those three, and of course, go more than halfway to earn the $1,000 bonus plus whatever purse I could earn. My luck was running good because those factory-supported Mercury entries went out with various ailments. Then approaching the halfway mark, *my* troubles began. Rear axle trouble and it began to smoke. I stayed on the track as long as I could, adding laps because I had to reach halfway. The condition worsened and I had to park behind the wall, then push it to the garage. I was afraid I had not reached halfway, although I knew the race leaders had. I ran to the scoring stand and after checking, sure enough, I had passed halfway and was the last Mercury running. I had the $1,000 bonus. Along with the prize money I won for qualifying and finishing that and the remaining races, I had enough to repay the three banks. I had good equipment for the rest of the 1961 season. The 1962 season was quite good for me. I finished 12th in the Grand National point standings ahead of Buck Baker [13th], Bob Welborn [15th], and Junior Johnson [20th]. I was in 52 races, had three top fives, and was in the top ten 18 times earning $9,540 in purses, plus point money and other payments."

Next he talked about his Danville friend, Wendell Scott.

"I first met Wendell when he was racing around Winston-Salem and we became good friends. We had something in common; we were both born in Danville. My folks moved away when I was a boy, but Wendell stayed. Wendell always held his own in sportsman racing and did his own work, as I did. It was the same when he moved into Grand National racing. Undoubtedly, there were some special problems being a black person in the sport. But Wendell was an independent just like a lot of us and didn't have much money just like a lot of us. Teams would help each other lending tools, tires, even engines. There are many cases when one driver would lend equipment to a competitor and then the competitor would win. If Wendell needed help, someone would help him. If I needed something and Wendell had it, he would lend it to me. At every race you would find me and others visiting Wendell in the garage and pit. We would all go to the Riverside races. It was a financial strain on independents, some more than others. In those earlier days at Riverside, a lot of people did not have haulers. It was a long, lonely trip, but we did keep in touch with each others' whereabouts to a degree."

On January 17, 1963, Wendell Scott was a winner at Riverside three days before the 500.

"Some of us left the Carolinas and Virginia earlier than Scott and heard reports that he was in Texas, then Arizona. Most of us were at the raceway, but no Scott. The word was that he was getting closer. The rule at Riverside was that all cars had to be checked in by 4 P.M. Thursday. They have rules or they would never get practice and qualification completed. With Wendell still missing, many of us were getting concerned about him while working on our cars. Stock car racing is really a family situation. Sometimes we quarreled, but otherwise we stuck together. It was Thursday noon, then half the afternoon passed and still no Wendell. Finally came the announcement, 'OK fellows. Get your tools picked up, boxed up, shut up, and get out of here. That's it for today.' As some of us were walking toward the road from the garage, here came Wendell and his racecar, barely in the nick of time. There were not even seconds to spare when he got the nose of his towcar through the gate. Then his car stalled. There were about 30 of us that reached the gate at the same time. His towcar was steaming, which was why he was late. He had to baby the thing on the highway because of an overheating problem. Thirty pairs of hands grabbed that towcar and racecar and pushed them inside the gate so Wendell would be considered as checking in under the deadline. The officials went along with it. No one wanted to see Wendell make that trip across the country for naught. Wendell did race, had a good finish, and made some money."

The record reflects that on January 20, 1963, Curtis started 36th and finished 43rd, next to last, after 26 laps. On the other hand, late-comer Wendell Scott started 33rd and completed 169 of 184 laps for 18th ahead of Lorenzen, Weatherly, Hurtubise, Pagan, Pearson, Paschal, Parnelli, Goldsmith, Sutton, Petty, and Crawfish. Wendell was a winner all the way around that weekend.

"Officials decided to hold an impromptu popularity contest, each driver voting for his favorite, and they passed out paper ballots. We were instructed to write any driver's name, our own if we wanted. I was leaning against Richard Petty's racecar talking to Lee. I had the ballot in my hand. Lee asked. 'Who did you vote for?' 'I voted for Tiny Lund.' 'Why don't you vote for Richard?' I liked Richard. Tiny's name had just come to mind when they handed me the ballot. I thought a minute and said, 'OK, I'll vote for Richard.' They were both deserving. I changed the ballot and turned it in. When the officials counted the ballots, they discovered they had a tie. They also noted they were short one ballot. Checking around they learned that Wendell was the one. He was busy working on his racecar. They sent a messenger to Wendell with a ballot and he scribbled the name of Richard Petty. It was announced that the tie had been between Richard and Curtis Crider. Wendell's vote gave the title and the trophy to Richard. I had no regrets. I was proud that the fellows thought enough of me to give me that many votes. I feel honored to have run second to Richard anytime. Jarrett won the race, Richard was second, and I was third, behind Petty again."

The record shows that on April 4, 1963, Jarrett nipped Petty for the Augusta 66-mile win, a race cut short 88 laps because of dust. Crawfish was third, two laps behind after starting 15th and last. Wendell was tenth. The road became especially rough for Curtis later in the 1963 season, and it came to a head at Atlanta International Raceway.

"I ordered a brand new Mercury which came with a 427 engine. During the blueprinting and rebuilding of the engine, I discovered the valves and heads were a bit smaller than normal. There was a four-barrel intake, and everything seemed OK, but the head assembled at the factory had valves that were slightly smaller. Not much, but still a difference. I was familiar with NASCAR rules that you can't bore the cylinders too much and you can't have items larger than normal. I wasn't worried about smaller valves. The next race was [Birmingham, Alabama] and there wasn't time to go to Charlotte and pick up another set

On July 18, 1963, a stern-looking Curtis lined up 16th for the Mountaineer 300 in Huntington, West Virginia. He finished a solid eighth between Nelson Stacy and Marvin Panch (Curtis Crider).

of heads. There didn't seem to be enough difference to cause a problem. Later I could contact the factory, find out what the problem was, and get it fixed. We raced with no problems and headed to Atlanta.

"My wife was in the hospital in Charleston, so I left the boys in Atlanta and drove straight to the hospital. When I returned, I found the car in the inspection area and the engine had not been put back together. It was covered up. The boys explained that they had pulled the engine down for inspection and the officials said the valves were too small. NASCAR confiscated the heads. I went to the trailer where Norris Friel, the head inspector, had his office. 'Norris, what in the world has happened?' 'The valves are too small and you had the wrong heads on the engine.' 'My God, Norris! I'm not cheating or anything. You know that. They're not too big. I don't understand that.' Norris said, 'It works the other way, too. You run smaller valves, you get better gas mileage. There is only one set of valves that you should run. I have no choice.' I had to agree. Here I was with a new racecar and no cylinder heads. My wife was in the hospital and I needed money. I needed to run that race and earn some money.

"Something happened that hadn't occurred before or since. I broke down. I climbed into the seat of my truck facing the infield. I had just given out from running back and forth to Charleston to visit my wife in the hospital, getting the new car ready, going to race, and back to Atlanta. I needed to work, to earn money for the hospital bills, and to pay my crew. I sat there in the truck and cried like a baby until I got it out of my system. Buck Baker spoke about adversity: 'You may give out, but you don't give up.'

"Then I got out of the truck, calmed down, and drove to Atlanta to the Mercury dealer. I asked if they had the heads and valves I needed. They did and recognized my name as one of the regular Mercury drivers. I got the parts. I asked if I could use their machine shop to work on the heads and they let me. I knew I didn't have to worry about the CCs because the 427s were usually right on the money meeting NASCAR specifications. The problem was getting the right valves and the engine back together. We used the machine shop, put the heads together, loaded them in the pickup, and headed for the raceway. I had the heads and valves inspected, they passed, and I said, 'Now let's go racing!'

"Later during practice, a man from the Mercury dealership came up while we were on pit road. He handed me a bill for the cylinder heads and valves. Up against the pit wall a few feet away was Fran Hernandez, Mercury Division's racing man from Detroit. I said to the dealership man, 'C'mon up here. There is someone I want you to meet.' I introduced the two of them and told the man from Atlanta, 'This is the man you want to talk to right here. I ordered a new car from the factory with the right kind of engine. It was delivered with the wrong cylinder heads and wrong valves. Norris Friel has your heads, Mr. Hernandez, and I have mine in the racecar. You two get together and see what y'all can do about this thing.' I walked away. I had not had a chance to let the Mercury people know about their error. I was going to take care of that after Atlanta. I never heard a word about it from anyone, not even Hernandez. My car was in good shape. I guess the factory paid the dealer. I know that Norris had my so-called illegal cylinder heads and sent them to some place and put them on display as they do with other 'cheating' equipment.

"The car was about ready. Those troubles were behind me and the crew when a NASCAR official came by and said they were taking up a collection for somebody who really needed it. No names were mentioned. We had so much expense, car and hospital,

Labor Day 1963 and Curtis' car sits for public inspection after 332 Darlington laps and a fine 16th place Southern 500 finish (Jack Walker).

that I was pretty low in that department. 'Well, I don't have much on me, but I'll give you what I can.' 'That will be fine Curtis. That's all we ask.' I counted the money, figured how much I would need to feed the crew that Saturday night and for Sunday breakfast, and said, 'I'll give you half of what I have.' I figured that was fair. The man thanked me and went through the garage area collecting from everybody. Sunday morning, raceday at the drivers' meeting, one of the NASCAR men said he had an announcement to make. They presented the collection they had taken for Mary Frances and me because of our hospital expense. After all the trouble with the cylinder heads, the Mercury dealer, my sobbing in the truck, this was so unbelievable, so touching, so emotional ... it really got to me. They had a list of guys who donated: Cotton Owens, the Wood Brothers, the Bakers, Ray Fox and crew, Bobby Johns and Papa Johns and crew, so many of them, all down the line, the car owners, officials, and some of the sportswriters. My name was on the list, too. A man never forgets and it makes one realize how auto racing is really a family, especially stock car racing. They may fuss and argue and do battle on the racetrack, but when someone needs help, they are there even without being asked."

Records reflect that Curtis ran the new Mercury at Birmingham for a solid sixth before the emotional Dixie 400 at Atlanta. On June 30th at Atlanta, Curtis was running 19th at the finish in a field of 36.

"We were back the following spring for the Atlanta 500 and had two cars. Frank Graham of Charleston was my other driver. Everything seemed set. We had qualified, the cars seemed right. It was better than 1963. Then it rained and the race was postponed. A.I.R. seemed to be jinxed back then with more rainouts or rain delays than any other track. The crews went home. The racecars were impounded. Come race day, Frank and I were there, our racecars on pit row, and one of our crewmen was there, Warren Prout from Charleston. Something happened to the rest of the crew en route. He felt awfully small standing in that huge pit with two racecars, while up and down the wall were five of six men for every car. 'Well all you can do is hope that the guys come through that tunnel. If they don't, try and get some help from some team whose car has dropped out. Just do the best you can. When the green drops, Frank and I have to do our thing out on the track.' Warren told me later he was sorely tempted to take off, but he did stick around, borrow some willing hands, and both Frank and I finished the race with fairly decent pit stops."

Life was lighter touring with a Buddy in 1964.

"It was time again for the Northern Tour, Bridgehampton, New York. Buddy Baker was to drive my second car. My crew had gone on with the equipment and the two racecars. Buddy and I were driving up in Buddy's automobile. While going through Virginia, we decided to stop in Washington and look up Ratus Walters at his Café Burgundy. Ratus owned the '62 Ford in which Larry Frank won the 1962 Southern 500. After visiting his restaurant, Ratus invited us in the country to see his place. In the garage was his '62 Ford racecar without an engine. Everything else was intact, radiator and all. Ratus said he was so busy, he didn't have time to race anymore and had sold everything except the racecar. We made a deal and bought the car. Together we fashioned a tow bar in his well-equipped shop and hooked it behind Buddy's car. We figured we would tow the car until I could buy another truck or car to pull it. We would get an engine someplace.

"Sag Harbor was way out east near the tip of Long Island. The promoters made arrangements for us to stay at a resort which had been converted from an old house built by a whaling ship captain and I do mean old. Buddy and I drove up and looked at this big, beautiful old place. Immediately I saw a drawback and pointed it out. This was a big, three-story house built entirely of wood surrounded by huge trees and overhanging branches. 'My God, Buddy. They put us all in this place. What's going to happen if the place catches on fire during the night?' The main hallway was converted into a lobby. As we were early, I suggested Buddy and I go upstairs quickly and pick out a room. We opened many doors and looked over the rooms until we found the one that suited us, a big old tree outside the window with big strong limbs really close. If something did happen, we could scramble out the window and down the tree to safety. Traveling around had taught us to be cautious."

This race could have been launched with "Gentleman, pretend to start your engines."

"Buddy and I qualified our cars OK. Ratus' car was still hooked to Baker's automobile. As the cars were fueled and pushed to the main straightway, Baker and I noticed that all the cars were gone from the pits and there was still one place left in the starting field. The promoter had advertised a certain number of cars and was one short. Spectators notice things like that. Buddy looked at me and smiled and I looked at him and grinned. We both had the same bright idea at the same time. 'Why not?' One of our crewmen got a spare helmet from the truck. We had lowered the front end to level it out for towing. Since there was no engine, with the radiator in place and hood fastened, there was no indication there was no engine in it. We pushed the car onto the track and lined up at the tail end ready to go. I went back to the tow trucks and asked one of the drivers if he would mind pushing our car for a start as we were having a trouble getting it fired. 'Not at all, that's what we're here for.' With one of our pit crew guys in the driver's seat, I told him, 'When you go past

Curtis Crider was sharp at Daytona Speedweeks in 1964 with a crisp-looking '63 Mercury 62. In the 500, he was the last man running, finishing 21st of 46 (Curtis Crider).

the flag stand and grandstand and scoring stand as the wrecker is pushing you, flip the switch and appear to do anything to start the engine. They won't start the race until that wrecker is off the track. Let him push a full lap, then coast in behind the pit wall, throw your helmet down in disgust when you get out, get mad, cry a little, kick the tires, whatever.' Sure enough, the wrecker driver pushed him a lap, my man dove behind the wall, and went through all the motions of a disgusted driver. Buddy and I hadn't cheated anybody. The promoter advertised a full field and he got 'em. By the time we got to the next race at Islip, New York, the word moved fast and we took a lot of kidding. Another riverboat gamble and it worked."

The Bridgehampton race was next.

"Marvin Panch and I got our cars tangled up in one of the S curves of that road course and let me tell you we were doing figure eights side by side at high speed through an area of little scrub trees and shale dirt that covered the infield. We did not have windows and the dust and stones and branches were flying into the cars. We were spinning in a cloud of dust, but every once in a while I could see Marvin face to face and next I would be looking at the back end of his car. We ended our wild rides side by side, close enough that I could have reached out and touched his car. My engine choked down and I couldn't get restarted.

I could see Marvin's car had its right front fender jammed against the tire. His engine was running, so I climbed out, pulled the fender off his tire, and checked the other three wheels. Everything looked OK so I signaled Marvin to get going and he was off. There my car sat with a stalled engine, well off the backstretch, so they were not stopping the race. In fact, I don't even think they missed me.

"There were two security guards at a gate nearby, so I called them. 'Hey, how about letting some spectators out here and give me a push to start my car.' 'No, we can't do that. But if we can get you down inside that gate, they can push you all they want.' 'OK, let's try it.' The two men pitched in. We pushed the car back and, fortunately, it was downhill and close to the gate. The car was rolling; they opened the gate, and in the car went. I climbed in, buckled up, and I'll bet there were 300 spectators wanting to push. Of course, there wasn't room for 300, but enough pushed and the engine fired. I turned the car around and out the gate I went onto the racecourse. Every time I drove down that backstretch there was a mob cheering and clapping and waving. They had a piece of that racecar and I had my own cheering section. Marvin and I both finished the race in top ten positions, even after all that mess."

The records reflect that Buddy drove for Crawfish once in his career on July 12, 1964, at Bridgehampton with no record of the old Walters Ford entered. Baker finished 20th with engine trouble in 01 and Crawfish had a fine fifth in 02, two laps behind fourth-placer Panch and ahead of Ned Jarrett. Crawfish was eight laps behind winner Billy Wade.

"In Islip, I went to the Mercury dealership where there was a wrecked station wagon, a new one that had been rear-ended. I bought the engine and we installed it in Walter's '62 Ford. Now Buddy and I had three cars. During the race on that little quarter-mile [actually .2 mile] asphalt track, a car in front of me lost the rear end cooler hose, sprayed the track, and covered my windshield with grease. It put out the lights. I couldn't see a thing. A driver never wants to lock up the brakes going through an oil slick because sliding tires will speed up the car and be out of control. I knew there was a wall out there. It seemed like I slid 40 miles and found the wall. It cleaned out the front end and I managed to roll around into the infield. When they restarted the race, the rear end was pointed toward the second turn. I was sitting on the hood with my back against the windshield. Lee Petty and some others were leaning against the front watching the race. A couple of cars got crossed up in that turn and one was spinning through the infield headed right for my battered car. I didn't see it coming. When Petty and the others started running south, I knew something was coming from the north. All I could do was flatten myself on the hood and hope for the best. That car hit hard and rolled the rear deck lid right over the top. I never saw such a mess for a car parked quietly in the infield. Fortunately, I escaped."

The record reflects that a pair of Charleston drivers, Pete Boland in Mercury 01 and Frank Tanner in Ford 66, finished 22nd and 21st respectively at Islip on July 16, 1964. Buddy Baker shows 20th in Ray Fox's Dodge 3. It appears Boland was traveling with fellow Charlestonian Crider, and Tanner could have been a Crider mechanic in the Ford 66, which matches the make and number of the old Ratus Walters' Southern 500-winner purchased by Buddy and Crawfish with the new station wagon engine. Crawfish remembered the way it was before 1964.

"I remember the exhilaration of the beginning of my racing career. You are sitting in the racecar with the best equipment you can come up with. Hopes are high as the cars roll around on the pace laps. Then we get the green and the butterflies are gone. We are racing!

The excitement, the accelerating, easing into the corner you can feel the tires biting. The car is working good and *you* feel good. By the time the race ends, whatever was going to happen had happened. You have done well or not. You accept it and work toward getting ready for the next race, another green flag, another moment of excitement."

For Curtis "Crawfish" Crider, the fun died as his friends did.

"When I was running Grand National, I began to get strange feelings thinking about good friends who had died in races, en route to races, or in tire testing. 'What am I doing out here to start with?' I would climb in a racecar and it wasn't fun anymore, not the way it used to be. There was the great Fireball Roberts. We used to buddy around a bit after practice, going bowling, getting something to eat. That terrible day at Charlotte, there were two cars burning. As I went by I could see one driver out of the car and I just knew the other driver was still in the car. I couldn't tell who it was. The flames were terrible because there was 42 gallons of fuel flowing on the track from the two cars. That was before we had fuel cells. I felt really queasy. Later, I learned that Roberts had been in the racecar and taken to the hospital where he died of burns [39 days later].

"Other friends I lost were Little Joe Weatherly, Jimmy Pardue, Larry Thomas, and Billy Wade. The last time I saw Billy was at Spartanburg after we tangled and I demolished my car. Wade was out of the race, too, but he was driving for the factory-backed Mercury team and would have another car for the next race. I was independent and it wouldn't be easy putting together another competitive racecar. Billy said, 'Curtis, I am so sorry. I'll do something for you as soon as I can.' Billy Wade died tire testing. I have the memory of a good friend. With so much sadness happening in 1964 and some business deals working, I drove only a couple of races in 1965. I decided it was time to cut back to some short track racing or even retire. When you lose the fun part of anything, you are just not going to do it as well. It is time to think about making some changes."

A series of events in the winter between the '64 and '65 seasons were the last straws for Crawfish's Grand National career.

"My moving away from major league racing in 1965 was in part because of the friends who passed on. There was another factor. The 1964 season had been very good to me. I had run 59 of 61 races, finished among the top five seven times and 30 times in the top ten. I was sixth in the standings for the championship. It was the best year of my career as an independent, and [I] had acquired the lowboy trailer for hauling two racecars, a Mercury and a Ford. The fun was going out for me, but life does go on. There are negotiations with sponsors, car owners, car owner backers, and sanctioning associations. Sometimes the drivers, crews, and car owners are caught in the middle during a contest of power between corporate leaders and the racers have no voice or control.

"There was an offer of a good backer for 1965. The catch was that I had to switch to Chrysler products and run a Dodge. The deal was I would be given two Dodges, engines, and equipment. With that in mind, I began to sell off the equipment I had been running in '64. Stick Elliott took the truck-tractor and lowboy trailer. One of the racecars went to Tennessee and the other to Georgia. As long as I was going to be racing Chrysler products, all the spare parts went with the racecars. Beyond our control, there was a debate between NASCAR and the racing divisions of Ford and Chrysler. Chrysler had the hemi, so Ford come with a new engine of its own. NASCAR could see themselves in the middle of a Detroit war and the danger of the word 'stock' in stock car racing would have little meaning.

There was no way everyone could be happy no matter what the rules. Chrysler showed their unhappiness and pulled out. That left King Richard high and dry and the decision hit me like a ton of bricks. I decided there was no way I was going to start over. I had sold all my equipment. Building back up would have been too tough. I spent time around Monks Corner [South Carolina] trying to figure which way to turn, became involved in co-promoting racetracks, and doing a lot of flagging around the area. It was a new field and I enjoyed the change."

In 1965, the Grand National road came to an end for Crawfish Crider. In his three starts, Crawfish had one of his best career finishes in his two-year-old Mercury at Richmond on March 7 with a fourth. He followed that with an eighth in Sam Fogle's Ford at Hillsborough seven days later, and closed out a 232-race career at Martinsville on April 25, finishing 17th in David Warren's Ford 53, a week before Jimmy Helms took it over for the next two seasons. Crawfish summed up a big time career.

"There is a tendency to compare the super-high salaries of major league athletes — auto racing, baseball, football, and basketball — with the dollars earned by the comparable athletes in the 1940s and '50s and to declare that those in the latter group were born too soon. As an auto racer in that earlier era, I have no regrets. I do not feel deprived. In our day as today, there were haves and have nots; factory teams and independents. I do not feel you can measure the success of a career or the quality of life strictly in terms of dollars. The cost of living was so much lower then for the needs of life. Expensive technical equipment had not been invented. We stayed at the mom and pop tourist cabins alongside two-lane highways named U.S. 1 and U.S. 40. Loretta Lynn once said, 'We didn't know we were poor.' The road had many detours and potholes, but I raced on the World's Most Famous Beach and on the Daytona International Speedway. My goal was to do the very best I could with the equipment available to me, to try to be the best in my

Curtis Crawfish Crider stands with one of his restored sportsman rides at a recent car show, looking like he could climb in and run with them today (Curtis Crider).

bracket. It was all good, believe me. We had a finishing record that was out of this world. We finished sixth in points in 1964.

"Those of us who were independents did not begrudge Fireball Roberts, Curtis Turner, Little Joe Weatherly, and Bob Welborn, who had factory rides. I can assure you I enjoyed the hell out of what I was doing. Both groups, the haves and have nots, got along well. One case in point was the 1964 World 600. The factory teams used engines for practice and qualifying, then switched to race day engines. The deal was that [a Mercury team driver] would qualify his car, then give his engine for my qualifying and it would be mine to keep. The two crews worked feverishly to install his engine in my car, then I qualified. Two cars qualified the same afternoon with the same engine, then I drove the race with that engine. There are many people to whom I owe thanks for assistance, support, and most important, for their friendship through the years. God bless. Tell every damn body I said, 'Howdy!'

Curtis Wade "Crawfish" Crider finished in the top ten in Grand National competition nearly a third of the time. He is one of the breed that actually hauled moonshine at great personal risk. The high-water mark was his outstanding sixth place finish in the 1964 standings. In that deadliest of seasons, he earned top tens in 30 of 59 starts and top fives seven times. In two of the toughest races ever run, Crawfish was 11th in both; the World 600 when he watched his friend Fireball Roberts receive fatal burns and the Southern 500 where pal Buck Baker won his final race. Crawfish retired from the big time only to continue his assault on the short tracks, becoming Florida Dirt Track Champion 1970 through 1972. He won 52 Late Model features, 21 in a row in 1973, and was the 1974 Volusia County Speedway Champion. It was a long haul from Curtis W. Crider slithering up that muddy red creek bank in Danville earning the nickname Crawfish to becoming a modified sportsman legend and one of the greatest big-time independent stock car drivers ever. Entering his eighties, Crawfish is still crawlin' and still haulin'.

4

Elmo Henderson
The Lone Pioneer

Charles Elmo Henderson was born on October 14, 1932, in Cherokee County, South Carolina, and lives in Spartanburg, as he has since his racing days. The U.S. Navy veteran takes a long walk every morning, rain or shine, hot or not too cold, and is a gold mine of information about the independent NASCAR Grand National racer of the late fifties and early sixties. He was a dominant personality in sportsman racing in the 1950s through the Piedmont Carolinas along with other racing stars-to-be. "Leadfoot Elmo Henderson," as the *Spartanburg Herald-Journal* called him back then, won scores of races and the captured the Greenville-Pickens Speedway Track Championship in 1958, the year before fellow Spartans David Pearson in '59 and Floyd Powell in '60 through '62. In 1959, he launched his scattered 21-race Grand National career spanning parts of five seasons in which he took four top tens and one top five. Elmo's 1960 Grand National efforts found him running well in signature and inaugural events remembered for their toughness. While he only once piloted a first-class Grand National ride, he was in the top ten nearly 20 percent of the time. Elmo ran with best and often beat them. His Grand National start was on June 26, 1959.

"Jack Purser paid Joe Eubanks $100 to let me drive his '58 Ford at the Charlotte Fairgrounds. That's my first Grand National race. The car was originally Eddie Pagan's from California that hit the guardrail when it was new. [This well-documented devastating crash was in the 1958 Southern 500.] There's a picture of it just plowin' that guardrail up. They fixed it up. I don't know how much work they had to do to fix it, but that's the car."

The record shows that Elmo started 12th, overheated after 160 laps, and finished 22nd of 35. The second start was Labor Day 1959 in the Southern 500 where *Thunder in Carolina* was being filmed.

"Joe Eubanks was gonna drive the '58 Pontiac 'cause that's the one Cotton had. The movie people took the deck lid off, put a tripod in, and this dumb cameraman stands in the back of that Pontiac. He's standin' up in the back of a racecar and it's runnin' on the apron. I'm gonna tell ya them cameramen's crazy. [They used a car out of the showroom for the racer driven by character Les York.] That's a stock automobile. It wasn't even a racecar. It was a stock Oldsmobile painted up. He'd come out of the pits, run down in front of the camera, and they'd jack it up. The camera would shoot it just like a regular pit stop.

But Joe's making money [driving the camera car]. He didn't care nothin' about runnin' the race no way. He called me and said, 'Elmo, if you want to, take my car, the '58 Ford down there.' Why I jumped all over it. Well, I got Joe Tate. He'd helped me on my sportsman cars around here."

Elmo's car owner arranged lodging accommodations.

"Watson [W.H. Watson, the Pontiac's owner] calls down there. He tells me these people are friends of his. Told us where to go, the address, you can stay with them. Now he ain't put up no money either for rent. They wasn't gonna put no money on that car. Anyway, we go down there and find that place. I told them who I was, that W.H. Watson had told me that y'all would put me and Joe up. They didn't seem like they was too enthused about it. They put us in a little old guest house and it didn't have no bathroom in it. No shower. 'You'll have to come in the house to use the bathroom.' I didn't like that at all. Didn't have no money either. Didn't have no choice.

"Then at the racetrack, we got it through inspection. I got out on the racetrack, you could run two laps. It started missin'. I had nearly everybody at Darlington, Ray Fox, work on the carburetor and we done everything. You pull the distributor out of a '58 Ford engine, the shaft goes down and turns the oil pump. It's supposed to have a little O-ring. I didn't know it at the time. Well everytime we'd pull the distributor out to get somebody to check it, that rod would fall and you could hear it hit the bottom of the oil pan. We must have pulled the oil pan six or seven times on that thing and they finally run us out from under the garage and made us get out in the dirt. And them sand fleas and it was a hundred degrees if it was any temperature at all. Joe finally got mad and headed back to Spartanburg and left me there by myself. I give up on it and made one lap to get startin' money and parked. That's it. That's the end of the '58 Ford."

According to the record, Elmo actually made 16 laps before retiring officially with engine trouble and finished 48th of 50. He opened 1960 in the ex–Cotton Owens 1958 Pontiac 70 owned by W.H. Watson.

"Jack Purser, he's the guy that built my first racecar and he run the Esso station. W.H. owned two trucks and he leased them out to haul merchandise ... a truckin' company. How I got this car is how crazy I was to even fool with a Grand National car. Cotton got that car. That was a factory car from Nichels. Nichels and Goldsmith was in the deal with Pontiac. Cotton had done wore this car out. Watson goes up there and drives the car down to the service station, run the car up and down the road two or three times, and I didn't even know nothin' about that. So the next day, I was there and Jack said, 'We got the car back and you always said you wanted to race a Grand National.' Oh man, I was in hog heaven. 'Man yeah!' "'OK, take it down to your house and we'll go through it.' We got Louis Clements before we figured out who was going to work on the car. Louie did some head work on the Pontiac engine. We didn't have no brand new engine. Homer Bearden had a garage right behind Purser's service station, 1481 Asheville Highway. Tinsley's Junk Yard was right across from it. I had drove for Homer, a '34 Ford coach, red 22. He had a '34 Chevrolet with a Wayne head, a six-cylinder. Most of your six-cylinders had the exhaust, carburetor, and intake on the same side of the head. Wayne is the guy's name that invented this head; had the exhaust on one side and the intakes on the other. And run? It sounded like a bunch of hornets in a fruit jar when you were turnin' RPMs."

On to Daytona for the 500.

Elmo Henderson close up and ready for his first crack at Daytona in February 1960 (Elmo Henderson).

"At that time, you had to be in Daytona for a whole week. So they took up money to buy David [Pearson] Jack Smith's old '59 Chevrolet. So me and him had raced together for four or five years. We decided to go together in case one of us had any trouble. That was a pretty long haul. The night before, Homer had a trailer he towed that '34 Ford on. You're talking about something that didn't weigh but about 2,600 pounds. That Pontiac was heavy. It had black iron pipes for roll bars and it must have weighed 5,000 pounds. Anyway, we decided we'd check it out on the trailer. We'd worked on it and had it ready. It was about ten o'clock and Asheville Highway in Spartanburg was two lanes. We pulled it up on the trailer. Jack's pickup, an F-100, was pullin' that big old trailer with that car. There was a dip right out here right across from P.J.'s Bar and Grill. I went up to the circle, turned around, and come back. Everything was all right. I hit that dip and that Pontiac was so heavy, it picked the rear end of that pickup off the ground. I was this way, that way, and it took me all the way to the top of the hill to get that thing without wreckin'. I said, 'I ain't pullin' that trailer nowhere with this thing.' We back it off and got a regular old tow bar that car dealers use and put it on there. David had a bigger trailer. I guess we met down at Rogers' or somewhere [Rogers' Esso on North Church Street was Pearson's sponsor]. We took off. David could run faster than I could. I could get runnin' fast, but couldn't stop. It just wanted to push that pickup straight ahead.

4. Elmo Henderson

The tank-like '58 Pontiac was solid in its qualifying race, finishing 12th of 40 a lap behind. In the 500, Elmo crashed on lap 31 for 59th out of 68 (Elmo Henderson).

"We got to Daytona about three o'clock in the mornin'. There was a service station on South Atlantic that had an awning on it. We pulled in there. David had a pickup with one of them little aluminum camper tops on it and he could lock it up. I was by myself and Gerald Pruitt was with David. I said, 'We'll camp out here and get some rest.' Gerald got in the back of David's camper. David come up there and jerked the damn door open on my truck and said, 'Git over! Git over! Git over!' I says, 'What the hell's a matter with you?' He said, 'I ain't sleepin' in that truck by myself.' So help me, that's the God's truth. I had to get up, lean agin the window and he leaned agin the window on the other side. That's how we slept. There's the front seat of his truck with nobody in it. We got a motel the next day."

Elmo's 1958 Pontiac 70 was a heavy.

"That old Pontiac was long and big and the Chevrolet was lighter. It was made out of heavy material. Cotton always built a safe racecar. He put every brace and everything. There's another thing that added to the weight. He didn't want to get nobody hurt and didn't want to hurt himself neither when he was drivin' it. I wish I still had that car. I'd restore it and put it in a museum. We sold that car to a guy that run over at Greenville-Pickens and he put a '59 Pontiac body on it."

Elmo describes his first look at the Daytona International Speedway.

"When I went through that tunnel, I looked and said. 'My God!' I had my doubts about that track and I don't think there was a soul that went down there that didn't. I think he's lyin' if he didn't ... till you get on it. It scared me to death until I got on it. When I went around the first time in one and two, I was on the apron. I hadn't picked up no speed. So I had to go down the backstretch. Now that bank looks terrible when you're runnin' slow. It looks like you're runnin' straight into it. Once you get up speed, you don't notice it that much. I got up to a hundred miles and hour and it felt good. I wasn't runnin' fast enough for it to be weaving around, you know. There wasn't nobody out there with me, I don't think, and if there was, it was only two or three cars and wasn't very close to me. So I got my confidence built up a little bit and I says, 'Well, here it goes this time.' I put all it'd do down the backstretch and got me a good run. I just wanted to see if I could hold it wide open. You wanna lift that thing when you're coming up on them corners. But they'd done told me you could hold it wide open. 'Well, we'll find out in a minute.' I was more cautious. I didn't try to race nobody. If I couldn't just drive by him, I'd run what I could. 'I gotta get in the 500.'"

And what about sleeping with Pearson?

"Once we got there, we went our own ways. We might see each other and throw our hand up, but you don't have time. I wasn't too proud of him to start with right then."

W.H. Watson, the car owner, "didn't come down until the next week and Jack [Purser] had to run the service station. They give me some spendin' money to get a motel and I'm by myself in all this. I think he give me $300 for the week. That was supposed to cover the room and everything. I did what I had to do myself. Dewey Owens, Snicker Woods, Jack Purser, Homer Bearden, and somebody else all come down for the hundred mile [qualifying] race, I think. They didn't come till then. Gettin' the car through inspection I did all by myself. There wasn't nobody else to do it, so somebody gotta do it. Cotton didn't come over and help me. Louie Clements, he come and I pulled the heads off. You had to pull the heads off back then for inspection so they could check your bore and stroke. I had a set of gaskets and Louie was runnin' with Rex [White]. They was havin' trouble with their car and there were two days I didn't get nothin' done 'cause he didn't have time for me and I can understand that. He was rentin' a building from Jack [Purser in Spartanburg] and Jack, I think, was gonna give him a month's free rent to help me get through the inspection. The people was comin' down on the weekend for the race. Of course, you don't need a crew in a hundred mile race. If you have trouble in it, you're out anyway. You don't have to put gas in it but one time. You really don't have a pit stop."

On February 12, 1960, Elmo Henderson virtually by himself with all the pressure in the world on his shoulders ran a worn out, two-year-old 1958 Pontiac in the second qualifying race for the Daytona 500. Elmo started 27th of 40 cars and finished 12th, one lap behind in the 40-lap race. Only eight cars were on the lead lap and Elmo was right behind Banjo Matthews at the wire. After this extraordinary feat under harsh conditions, Elmo found himself solidly in the Second Annual Daytona 500 in 24th position in a field of 68. It is nothing short of miraculous, as Elmo humbly acknowledged.

"That's what I got thinking about the other night layin' in bed. I must have been completely out of my mind to even get in a Grand National car without any factory backing. I did somethin' that not many could do. They mighta coulda done it, but they didn't have to do it. I *had* to do it. I called my wife Betty. She wasn't down there then, but she stood beside me my whole racing time. I don't recommend it anymore. It was hard on her and we had a kid. I guess Kim was about eight or nine years old going to school. I wouldn't do it over. My wife made the livin'; I'll be honest with you. I'd make some money every once in a while. I worked until I could bring some money home [racing]. She stood by me the whole time. I'll tell you what. I loved it so much. I know how stupid I was."

On February 14, 1960, Elmo's first Daytona 500 was a crashfest.

"We didn't have radios and in that pack, they give us free gas, Pure Oil. I could run 43 laps on a tank of gas before we run out. Everything was set. The crew was happy; we had one set of tires, and a set to back it up. Had the air wrench set up. Your adrenalin is runnin' so high, you're high. You can't explain it until you've done it.

"I wore a T-shirt and a pair of white pants. I had a pair of black, three-quarter length boots, helmet, and goggles. No shoulder harness, lap belt only. Crazy? Tell me about it. Everything was fine. Wasn't in no big hurry. Just runnin' a good race right then 'cause the cars were bunched up pretty good. Wasn't takin' no chances. We knew it was going to be a long race. We were using our heads. We *thought* we was. I think part of this was as much my fault as anybody's. This guy I could gain on. Then I'd back up. Then he started losin' some oil and it was gettin' on my windshield. He was driving a Dodge from Georgia somewhere. I knew when I started down the backstretch, it was long shot, and I was gonna go by.

"Well I held it down and as we started to come off of two, I was done right to his door [on the inside]. That's the shortest way around. That's why I think I learned a little bit about the wind. I was runnin' that close to him, I guess [Elmo puts his palms about a foot apart], but that's no big deal racin'. There's certain places you can't do that or you'll get into them. I found that out in the corner right then. Now if I had been runnin' perfectly straight, I coulda run that close. [He puts his palms almost together.] It wouldn't make no difference. It would have probably been smoother. But anyway, I don't know whether it turned around ... it hit him. Just all at once, I was in it. Part of that could have been from the oil that he was losin', or it could have been the wind suckin' me into him. But I never did loop it. Now he looped on around. I corrected it and by the time I corrected it, I was sideways on the grass. And it went all the way to number three down that long backstretch. And two or three people, spectators said, 'You slid the furtherest of anybody I ever seen.'

"That's when the windshield come out. That wind just sucked it right out. And it packed mud around my helmet, face, and goggles. Packed it up in the roll bars. It sucks grass, you wouldn't believe what it will do. Once I got it stopped, then I just pulled it down into low gear come on to the pits and told Jack, 'Get me a shop rag.' I thought I could just put it around my face. Another education I got. They gave me rag and I took off and man, it wasn't long before I got down on the apron. Them cars go by and that sand down there on that track, it was tearing my head up. It was liftin' my helmet choking me to death. You know, air goin' under. That was the end of my day. We went to try to find one [a windshield] and if we'd have found a Pontiac settin' in the infield, we'd have took it out and settled with the man later. I think we got $700 ... $750. You didn't make any money 'cause you'd done spent $300 or more. All that driving, gas, and more. I think it was a good indication. It learnt me a lot about going to another race like the Southern 500. That's what I wanted to do. I wanted to be a racecar driver. I wanted to be a Grand National driver."

The record indicates that Elmo slid in 59th of 68 after 31 laps. He raced Grand Nationals at Daytona five times, more than anywhere else.

"I liked Daytona. It's easy to drive. You don't realize you're runnin' that fast. What you've got to do is figure out that when you're runnin' up on a car, you know you're gonna be there quick. Once you allow for that, it just comes natural. You learn by experience. You get too close and it'll suck you right into them. I've done that down there, too. That's nothing new. In fact, it drifted more back then. You didn't have the spoiler on it and it was more bulky. I talked to Junior Johnson down there when he won in a '59 Chevy, Ray Fox's car. Junior told me he was followin' Smokey's car, Bobby Johns' '59 Pontiac, and that was the first time he knew exactly what was happenin' to the car. The wind was catchin' it. He was behind them and Bobby was racin' with someone, I forget who it was, and Junior was runnin' third. He said he seen the whole back of Bobby's car come off the ground. [Bobby Johns' back window was sucked out with two laps to go and he spun, costing him the 500.] He said that's when he knew that you had to be careful and start payin' attention to the wind. Concentrate on that and pay more attention on what to do with the steerin' wheel and accelerator. Junior taught me a bunch."

Elmo next moved on to Martinsville.

"They had used axles that Cotton had pulled out and everythin' went up to Martinsville. But I knew that was gonna be a dead end to start with. And I wouldn't have known how to fix the car anyway. I go up there and practiced a good bit and I'd get in the throttle and that thing would push straight into the wall. Never been on the racetrack before. In fact, another thing, you gotta back out of it at the flagman's stand. You even do today. I think I was carrying it in too deep and when I'd jump in the throttle ... well I wouldn't just say 'jump in,' but just as fast as you can take it down without bustin' the rear wheels loose ... it would push when I turned and I said, 'This ain't gonna work. I'm gonna blow a damn tire and tear the car all to pieces.' But I didn't have to worry. In a couple of more laps, the rear axle broke. Now we had a trailer that time. We borrowed one of them tractor trailers that Pierce Tractors had over there [in Spartanburg]. They set high off the ground, but they won't sway with ya like them little old light trailers."

The record reflects that Elmo actually time-trialed 26th of 37 and finished 31st, dropping out after 130 laps with a broken axle. He got some factory help for the 100-miler at Greenville on April 23, 1960.

"I wanted to run Greenville 'cause I'd won the championship there in the sportsman car. So Ray Nichels was over the Pontiac Division at that time. I had met Ray downtown [Spartanburg] at a party at the Village Supper Club. I didn't have a short track gear. I think we needed about a 586 or somethin' like that. All the gears I got are speedway gears. The factory didn't make many gears. You had to use a ten inch or twelve inch ring and pinion; used a different model rear end housin'. That '58 had a smaller housin', so we put a different housin' under there. Nichels sent me a gear to Cotton and told me to check with Cotton. Well Cotton called me and told me it was up there. So we got it in time to go to Greenville."

Elmo hit the Greenville-Pickens clay with something to prove.

"I went out and made a couple of laps and man that thing felt good. I qualified that car sixth. I beat Junior Johnson. He qualified eighth. [He also out-qualified Buck Baker, Rex White, Bob Welborn, Joe Weatherly, Jimmy Pardue, and nine others.] That was one of the happiest days. To beat Junior Johnson on a dirt track? Listen, I just got lucky or he got all screwed up. I knew how to get around it."

But trouble found the old Pontiac during the race.

"We run probably three-quarters of the race and I smelt it. We didn't have a rear end cooler. All at once she just went *RRRRAAAW!* That was it. Just sheared the pinion gear and all the teeth off of it. Burnt it up. If it didn't have no other problems, we'd have had a good finish."

For the record, Elmo was 11th, completing 120 laps and beat Johnson, Weatherly, Turner, and Buck Baker. On June 19, 1960, Elmo and his race-weary '58 Pontiac 70 went to the opening of the Charlotte Motor Speedway for the World 600. The 400 grueling laps around the mile and a half unfinished facility featured a 60-car field and everybody was a rookie that day. Making the race was an ordeal.

"We didn't get to qualify the first day. They was having trouble. The track kept comin' apart. They'd put more asphalt and it would come apart again. Well, in fact, we wasn't ready for it either. So what NASCAR done, ya know these belts that tractors had with a pulley on it? We had to put mud flaps on the racecars. NASCAR went and got [those belts] and sawed the pieces and give everybody two mud flaps. We had to make the brackets ourselves, borrow a drill; it was the damndest mess you have ever seen in your life. Lee Petty carried his cars home and made a steel mesh wire in front of the windshield. We went and got another windshield and put a double windshield one on top of the other one. It don't fit too good, but we had braces drilled with straps. So we finally did get to qualify. David [Pearson] qualified first and there was one or two cars beat him that day. David qualified before they tore the asphalt up again. I had to wait late. They put it [more asphalt] down and told me, 'Ride the top lane right against the guardrail. Don't get in that asphalt.' Hmm, this ought to be fun. Anyway, I done it and I didn't hit the guardrail. I didn't have to make but one trip around there. And I qualified right behind David. It made me maddern hell. I wanted to beat him. [Pearson timed in 19th and Elmo was 22nd, both excellent in a 60-car field.] He [Pearson] run them all. His daddy mortgaged the house to keep him runnin'. My daddy didn't have no money."

Of course, it paid off for Pearson, as he won 1960 Rookie of the Year.

Elmo has equally vivid recollections of the Inaugural World 600.

"What happened to me, I come off four and turned the wheel and the wheels wouldn't turn. I headed it for the infield between the pit road and the track. What it done, it broke the tie rod end right off of the sleeve where you adjust it. I got out of the car, waited for the wrecker to come get it, and figured that was the end of it. Papa Johns said [Shorty Johns, Bobby's father, is mimicked in Elmo's quick, deep, gruff voice.] '*What-a-matter?*' 'Tie rod broke.' '*Go-get-it! Go-get-that-damn-thing-and-bring-it-here.*' Well, one of my boys went over there and jerked it off and brought it over. That's another stupid thing you shouldn't do. Papa welded that thing back. '*Put-that-on!*' We put it on ... finished the race.

You do what you had to do. Everbody would help everbody. I got to know Papa. Bobby Johns come here [to Spartanburg] and Papa would be with him. They'd sleep in the back of that van they had. I got to know him and me and Bobby got to be real good friends. That Bobby was something. We finished."

The record states that Elmo, with time lost during Papa's tie rod repair, completed 212 of 400 laps for 32nd place, last of the 18 cars running when Joe Lee Johnson took the checkered flag in Paul McDuffie's 1960 Chevrolet. Once again, Elmo Henderson endured an incredible tale of hardship and persevered. It got worse for him in 1960, but not the way you would think for a veteran and proven short-track racer and champion. "Jack and them decided to run two of the worst short-track races in the business, Columbia Speedway and Martinsville. Columbia was dirt, but it's sandy and packed and it'll eat a set of tires up. And us with no money, we had no business doin' it. Anyway, I'd been runnin' my sportsman car down there doin' good. Won some races there. So we go to Columbia and unhook the car and go out there. I'm familiar with that track and get used to the heavier car, you know, than them '37 Fords and stuff. Felt pretty good and I knew I was gonna have to take care of the brakes. You had to slow down pretty good to get in them corners because it was so sandy. You get in too deep and you just go right over the bank. Anyway, I got out there and run me two or three laps doin' pretty good. So I decided to put the hammer down and see if I could cut me a good lap. I come off two and snapped the axle practicing. Now here we are.

"We flat towed it down there ... no trailer. Well, Rex [White] had a trailer. See, you didn't have a floatin' axle back then. If you start pullin' up the road, the wheels will come off. You ain't gonna have no wheels. So we hooked Rex's trailer to Jack's truck and I left. I didn't even stay for the race. I was so mad and disgusted. So I get up close to Jonesville and run out of gas. No interstate. I was tired and give out. I said, 'Well, they'll be along after while.' I was out in the middle of nowhere. They was workin' on the road down there or somethin' where you usually go through Union and we had to come out there close to Whitmire. Everybody that was comin' from Columbia had to come that way so I wasn't worried about it. I just laid down in the front seat and went to sleep. Well, Rex and them come by and seen me sittin' on the side of the road, but they didn't get out and look down in it. 'Well he ain't there; he must have got a ride on home.' He [Rex] had to tow his car back on the road 'cause I had his trailer. Once again helpin' each other. When I woke up, I walked up to a man's house and he was a farmer and had some gas in a five gallon can. He put me some gas in it and I paid him, cranked the truck up, and brought it on home. That was that little trip to Columbia."

The apex of Elmo Henderson's Grand National career was on September 5, 1960, in the 11th Annual Southern 500. This was a typically blazing-hot Labor Day at the height of the storied race's history and had it all: a star-studded field of 48, an enormous crowd of 80,000, an international radio audience, a frantic race-long, lead-changing battle, grinding crashes, an incredible finish, a scoring dispute for the win, and most sadly, three fatalities. Spartanburg's Elmo Henderson started 26th and should have been somewhere in the top ten at the conclusion. Elmo had to overcome a little dust up in practice.

"I don't know if anybody is puttin' any money in the car. Homer didn't have any room up there at his place. He needed room for his customers' cars. My building was 18 by 22 or somethin' like that and that's where we worked on the car. So ... we go to Darlington. I

Into turn four, Elmo soldiered on with seven cylinders ahead of Pearson, finishing an outstanding 12th place on a grueling, deadly Darlington day. Pearson fell out for 27th.

done been to Darlington before in a '58 Ford of Joe Eubanks.' Marvin Porter was driving that Oldsmobile that some old men bought. Pops Racing team, you might of heard of it. Well they bought that car that Lee Petty won Daytona with [in 1959]. Marvin was drivin' it at Darlington. We was out there practicin' and Marvin had spun out up in one and two. He's settin' up there crossways in the racetrack. Well, I just bent the old Pontiac and got it on the apron and here he comes backwards *wide open*. He caught me right behind the right rear wheel and sent me round and round. I was so mad I didn't go talk to him. Messed up a set of brand new tires and Goodyear come over there and looked at 'em and said, 'Take them off and bring the wheels down there and I'll put you a new set of tires on.' I couldn't have run these and I didn't have any money to buy anymore.

"The 500. "We coulda really done good. We started the race. The car run good. I was tickled to death. I had my regular crew and just went with it. They didn't make no money either. They'd just do it. I was runnin' real good and all at once it started missin'. I figured a plug wire come off 'cause it was runnin' perfect then all at once it started skippin'. I stuck my hand up and told 'em I'd be in the next lap. They gonna put gas in it anyway. So I come in and pointed to the hood and Jack stuck his head in the window. I left it runnin' and said, 'I think a plug wire's off.' They checked and it wasn't no plug wire. Couldn't see nothin', ya know? Jack says, 'Run the damn thing till it blows.' But it wouldn't run fast enough to blow. I run that thing all day. We run the whole race and finished 12th. If that thing had been on all eight cylinders, there ain't no tellin' what. But another thing happened.

"The wreck starts happening comin' outta two and they're [the Paul McDuffie crew] about not quite half way down the backstretch and we're pitting right above 'em [closer to turn two]. When McDuffie and them got killed, I come off of two, I seen Bobby [Johns] upside down. The wreck had done happened and that was his car [Joe Lee Johnson's] going down pit road. He had done made his pit stop. McDuffie had the jack. He's goin' back over that wall. Bobby's upside down and the bumper of Bobby's car catches Paul McDuffie between the wall and the back bumper of Bobby's car and cut him in two. Paul McDuffie had the jack and Joe Lee was leaving his pits. They told him to go. Johns catches him. He's slidin' on his top. I didn't see this, but they said Fireball was leadin' the race at that time. They said Fireball stopped and it really shook him real bad. He seen him. He was dead. They were real close. Somebody told me Fireball said, 'I'll win this race for Paul.' I don't know if it would have helped if he [Johns] had hit Joe Lee's car or not, but it cut one of them guys right in two. I didn't pay no attention to 'em and they was out in the race track. I just looked at Bobby and then I gotta watch where I'm goin'. I didn't figure Bobby was hurt. The car wasn't pushed in or nothin' and he was still buckled in. Bobby was still in the car, but it's upside down. Time we come back around, they didn't red flag it. I was thinkin' they might ought to red flag it. We kept going, ya know, real slow.

"Once they got the mess cleaned up, we started to race. I'm still on seven cylinders. So, we figure, I forget how many laps to go, the last 200 miles or so, they motion me to come in. Gonna put two tires on. Well, we had an air bottle and had a gauge for the air wrench; so much pressure. The handle where you set the pressure, we had it drilled and wired so you couldn't turn it off and had the same amount of pressure for the air wrench. 'Cause them tanks is under about 2,500 pounds and you don't run but about 90 pounds, somethin' like that, for the air wrench. It blowed the hose off of the gauge. Now this is how crazy my crew was. They wasn't no outside wall. The wall was back here between the fans. But you're out on the track. There wasn't no wall between you and the racecars. They changed two outside tires with a lug wrench and sent me on my way. I didn't know [three people had been killed]. But they did. They knew it and that's when I said they [were] crazier than I was. That was the job and you gotta do it."

Henderson's unsung crewmen, fully aware of the carnage that had taken place only feet away, changed right side tires on Elmo's 70 with a manual lug wrench, unprotected from stockcars speeding by furiously behind them. Incredible!

It was a truly amazing finish for the car and to the 1960 Southern 500. In a car two years old that was worn out at the beginning of the season, Elmo Henderson finished 12th on seven cylinders in the biggest race of the year.

"You know why it was on seven cylinders? Rocker arm stud. They was pressed. Used to press 'em. Now they make that stud with a screw and you tap it in there. You screw it in. Well it's forced in there and it slipped up enough to let the rocker arm jump off the pushrod. So that valve ain't workin' and that was the problem. I wanted to blow it up."

Seven cylinders, 26 laps behind and all, Elmo still finished ahead of the others running at the finish, like Clem Proctor, Shorty Rollins, L.D. Austin, Herman Beam, Curtis Crider, and G.C. Spencer.

"Turns three and four you *had* to hit the guardrail. It would sound like you tore the whole side off and all you'd see were little scratches. It ain't no good feelin'. I never did like it. I had to run fast. You had to run right against that rail and you cannot run side-by-side and run fast. Durin' the race you'll see 'em like that, but they're both slowin' down. If they was wide open, you're both goin' into that guardrail. You'd scrape it. But you'd just go up there and you just turn it. You don't hit it when you first go in there. You throttle back in there and she'll just go up there and *RRAAAARRAAARRRAAAH!* You just hold it steady and ease it back down. You hope you don't every time. You usually get to where you can keep from doin' it. You don't want to be a lane down and do it. You gotta be right up there against it. I never did like that 'cause it makes you think you just tore your racecar all to pieces. It makes the durndest racket you've ever heard. You can't even hear the engine for the racket it makes. *RRAAAARRAAARRRAAAH!"*

Elmo ran four times in 1961. He was hired by a Californian named Charlie Chapman.

"These guys from California only run one race a year and they picked me to drive their car. Bill Stroppe built it in California. He was a big wheel with Ford. He built it for 'em. They were some of the best guys you ever wanted to meet. They had enough money. They owned a wrecker service in California. I think we finished 20th or something. It just was draggin'. They changed cams and everything. It just wouldn't go. I don't know what it was. It drove good. It just wasn't fast enough. Them people, they sent me fancy shirts and stuff after they got back home. They made you happy to drive. They were just as happy because I didn't scratch the car or nothing. They didn't care if we'd have won it. I didn't outrun anybody, I out lasted 'em. That's all they wanted to do. He was a sportsman and all he wanted to do was be a part of that race at Daytona. That's all he wanted to do."

For the record, Elmo drove a 1960 Ford 41 for Charlie Chapman from 57th out of 58 to 23rd only 16 laps behind, out running top-line cars and drivers like Flock, Matthews, Allison, Joe Lee Johnson, Frank, Buddy Baker, Stacy, Junior Johnson, Paschal, Johns, and Turner. Next was Atlanta and the surprise ride. If you're a racer, always take your helmet.

"Here's my trip to Atlanta. I wasn't runnin' full time Grand National. Me and Jack Purser, we decided we'd go to Atlanta to see the race. So I take my helmet just in case I pick up a ride. I go in there and Jimmy Thompson had blown a tire and hit the wall the day before. [That was in the modified sportsman race on Saturday. He still had to run the Grand National on Sunday.] Jimmy was all bruised up. He'd run in the modified race and we knew each other at Daytona and I asked him, 'Who the hell got holt of you?' He said, 'That damn car hit the wall. Elmo, did you bring your helmet?' I said, 'Yeah.' He said, 'Listen. I don't think I can make this race.' I said, 'All right.' He said, 'We'll split the money. I'll get out and you can have it.' So I went and got my helmet. These guys [the owners] were from Indiana, I think. One of them old, big T-Birds. It wasn't no first place car, but it ran pretty good. We finished the race. Anyway, I got a few bucks. The guys must liked the way I was drivin' 'cause I'd never met the people before. Before we left, I thanked them and everything. I told them, 'I live in Spartanburg. If you guys ever come down this way, come by and see me.' I give 'em my address and everything. Well, one of them said to me, 'You got a place we can leave this racecar instead of draggin' it all the way back to Indiana?' 'Yeah, you can leave it at my house. There ain't nobody gonna bother it cause I had an old racecar sittin' out there anyway.'

On June 2, 1961, Elmo started 12th in a 21-car race at the Piedmont Interstate Fairgrounds in Spartanburg and the number 55 T-Bird's owners did not know it.

They left the car there and they had this race comin' up at The Fairgrounds. Joe Littlejohn [the promoter] said he needed me. I said that I ain't got nothing over here, but these guys' car from Indiana. I said, 'It's got an Atlanta gear in it. I ain't got no gears and nothin'.' 'Come on. I'll take care of ya.' Like *heck* he did! I went over there and I couldn't run with them boys. I was pullin' a mile and a half gear under that thing and I needed a half mile. I was runnin' and tryin' it in second gear and that was too much. Turnin' too many RPMs I'd blow the engine. All was well until I was goin' down the backstretch and popped a tie rod and it hit that little old guardrail and I went over the bank. And that big old oak tree down there? It laid up right agin that tree. And it was dark down in there. I got out of the car and crawled up the bank and here all them front-runners were comin' down the backstretch. I run back down in the hole!"

Once again, Elmo got a factory boost for the 100-miler in Greenville on June 8, 1961.

"Junior [Johnson] was drivin' for Holly Farms and they had a couple or three cars. At the time, Crawford Clements was chief mechanic on Junior's cars. Well, Pete and Tom Blackwell [Greenville-Pickens Speedway promoters] got together with Crawford and he talked to the people up there [at Holly Farms] and worked out a deal to bring another car [for me]. The day before race day, I caught the flu. I was sick, mister, I was sick. Somebody drove me to Greenville. Got over there, got over to the car, and I told Crawford, 'I'm sick. I got the flu.' They had done advertised. I had to go through with it. I don't care if I would have died. I got in the car. Got the belts adjusted and all and I went out and qualified. I didn't do too good. I'm not sure, but I think I qualified about 14th or 15th and I was expecting more out of myself in that car. Of course, I was sick and couldn't concentrate. When you got the flu, you're sick."

Records show Elmo qualified 11th in a field of 26. Junior and Elmo drove 1960 Holly Farms Pontiacs that night, numbers 27 and 7 respectively.

"They had the track real muddy. They watered it more after everybody qualified. Richard was starting up close to the front. Junior started up front. The race started and in a couple of laps, Junior coasts in the pits. I was right up in the middle of all the mud slinging and I was getting my windshield really screwed up. We run about thirty laps and the caution come out. That tickled me and everbody else that was in that mess. We all made a beeline for the pits to get the windshields cleaned. I told Crawford, 'Put Junior in the car.' 'Nope, this is your deal.' They filled my car up with gas, cleaned the windshield, and Crawford told me, 'You can go all the way.' So I never thought anymore about it. I'd say about fifteen or twenty laps later, I run out of gas. Coasted into the pits, put gas in it ... the engine was dead. It wouldn't crank. Pushed it up pit road, back quick, and the race is goin' on. It started, so I went out there. I'd got to feelin' better. Adrenaline, I guess, and then I was mad. I was mad because Crawford told me I could go all the way and I'd run out of gas or they didn't get it full. It shouldn't have been no problem 'cause we hadn't run but about thirty laps. I drove my butt off and wound up in sixth. Some cars had fell out, some of the good cars, but I finished the race and got sixth out of it. I was the happiest person in the world to get to drive Junior Johnson's car, but when you're that sick, you don't care if you live, die, or what."

For the record, the five finishing in front of Elmo were Jack Smith, Ned Jarrett, Emanuel Zervakis, Joe Weatherly, and Jim Paschal. Notables behind him were Richard and Maurice Petty, White, Pearson, Welborn, Buck Baker, and Elmo's teammate Junior Johnson. Elmo recalled the 1961 National 400 and another one-shot deal in a black '61 Ford 82 racing out of Spartanburg.

"That was Budgy Dunbar's car. I think Marvin [Porter] drove it at The Beach. I didn't drive it but one time and I don't think he drove it but one time. But Budgy, all he done was pull cars and sell them. He didn't have no money to be messin' with that. It was one of them [Fords] that its back come straight down [the roofline]. They won't run on a racetrack. That's why they come out with this Fastback Ford on account of the aerodynamics. Well anyway, I didn't have a ride at Charlotte. I was runnin' a little old garage down there on 221 and Budgy come down there and said, 'How 'bout drivin' my car.' I said, 'All right.' So we went to Charlotte. I don't even know where we qualified, but it wasn't good. [Elmo was a decent 23rd out of 43.] During the race the water pump broke, it run hot, and that was the end of it. I don't know where we finished, but it was way back. [Elmo finished 27th. That race involved a grinding crash that Fireball Roberts said was the worst of his career, until the one that cost him his life.] As I come out of four I seen Fireball settin' with his nose up agin the concrete wall. All I did was bend it hard, I didn't spin or nothin', went under him and kept going. The caution come out and when I come back by, Fireball was settin' in the infield on the ground holding his head and Smokey was with him. It shook him up 'cause that was a bad lick. He was hurt, I know. That thing [the T-bone by Bill Morgan] drove the [passenger] door to the center of the car. I could see that just as plain as day."

After omitting 1962 and 1963 from his Grand National career, Elmo Henderson cast his lot with one Paul Clayton, a Spartanburg businessman and drag strip owner in 1964. Clayton had a two-year-old ex–Jack Smith Pontiac 70 and they set out for Speedweeks in Daytona.

"This guy here in Spartanburg [Paul Clayton] bought one of Jack Smith's old Pontiacs. So Bud Moore's younger brother Don was the mechanic on it. This thing started off bad. He [Clayton] knew I had driven Daytona and everything and said, 'How about drivin' my car.' I didn't have a ride, so I said, 'Yeah.' Here's three of us, Don, Paul, and me. We get to Jacksonville on the old road where you go across the bridge and go all around before you get to the toll road. Right there the truck quit pullin' in that curve before you start across the bridge. There was a lake or river or somethin' off to the side. That was only two lanes there back then. We were settin' in the middle of the road on our side. I didn't know it, but he [Clayton] already knew this had happened before. [Elmo gave a detailed explanation of the small part of the intricate axle and gear assembly that broke.] We jacked the back of the truck up and told Paul to go back up the road about a hundred yards and get them people over in that other lane. So we're up under the durn truck workin' on it in the highway with a trailer hooked to it with a racecar on it. All at once I heard this damn truck, an 18-wheeler slidin' the wheels ... *ERRRRRRRRRRRRRRRRRH!* Paul had jumped out of the road and down the bank near that river or lake or everwhat was there. And that truck was in our lane and he locked the brakes down to keep from runnin' over us. I cussed him out [Clayton, not the truck driver]. He got it stopped and got on around us. He locked the trailer down so he could steer the tractor to miss us. I wasn't too happy. We didn't fix it [but it was drivable] and so help me God, it happened again once we got to Daytona."

After the ordeal on the road, Team Clayton finally arrived at their destination.

"We get to the racetrack and get the car through inspection and all. Go out on the racetrack and fouled a plug out … started skippin'. I come in the pits; Don pulled the plugs out, and found one that was oilin' up. Must have had a broke oil ring or somethin'. We thought it was just bad plugs, so we put a new set of plugs in it. We go back and in two laps, same thing. Now Don's got a brand new engine settin' on the truck. He done rebuilt it. I said, 'Don might as well go put the other engine in. Ain't no need foolin' with this. It's internal, foulin' the plugs and pumpin' oil into the cylinder.' Paul wouldn't let us change engines. On top of this now, I had done went to Firestone, they was friends of mine. You know I got a big deal with Gene White when I quit racin' and went to the race parts business. I told Gene, 'This guy ain't got much money. Anything you can do me for four tires?' At that time you put tubes in them. 'I can let ya have four tires, you give 'em back to me, and I'll turn 'em in as an experiment, ya know, or somethin'. You know how that works. So it wasn't gonna cost Paul nothin'. So I done him that favor. People I know, usin' my friendship. Then, after he wouldn't let me do that [engine change], all he wanted was that $750 for starting the race. He didn't want to tear his racecar up.

"That was one of my nightmares, that trip. I was so mad I wouldn't even speak to him. Me and Don was sleepin' together in a rented little old cabin. Cheapest thing he [Clayton] could find. I knew what he'd done. They paid the driver at that time. So I made my one lap. [NASCAR records indicate Elmo made four, remarkably for 39th in a 46 car field.] I pulled in the pits. I told Don to pull the wheels off and take 'em down there to Gene White and give him his tires back. Then Clayton tried to steal the four band new tubes! Man, I cussed him for everything. 'You take them damn tubes back down there and give them to Gene.' Or I took 'em. I don't remember, I was so mad. I met some friends out there and I

This is the Paul Clayton '62 Pontiac 70—that Elmo unhappily raced at Daytona Speedweeks in 1964—being flat-towed at Darlington (Jack Walker).

4. Elmo Henderson

Spartanburg stock car legends and neighbors seen together in June 2009 are Bud Moore (left) and former "roommates" David Pearson and Elmo Henderson.

was fumin'. They was in the infield. 'How 'bout takin' me back to Spartanburg. Y'all goin' home tonight?' They said, 'Yes.' I said, 'Good. I gotta go over here and get the money, then I gotta go to our cabin and get my clothes and wait on Paul.' They said. 'That's all right. We'll just go over there with you.'

"We stopped at the liquor store and got a fifth of liquor. I don't usually drink hard stuff. I like my beer. We was settin' over there drinkin'. Poor Paul come runnin' in the house. He thought I'd done gone with all the money. Wasn't but $750. 'There lays your money. I took my thirty percent and I'll see you later.' We hit the road and I come back to Spartanburg. I wouldn't drive back with him. And I found out later, that truck, they had to fix it again and I think that broke Don from racing. I ain't spoke to him [Clayton] since."

Elmo confirmed that Paul Clayton has since passed away.

Elmo Henderson was part of an elite Ford Motor Company Team in 1965 that went to the tip of South America and drove a fleet of Mercury Comets north to Alaska. Elmo was a top-notch race driver and did something about then that many, many racers never could do knowing clearly that they should. Elmo hung up his goggles at 33 years old and used his friendships, expertise, and business sense to move into the racing parts business and live comfortably with his wife to this day.

"I was taking money and puttin' it in the parts business. I was gettin' past the age when anybody wants to hire you as a young driver. I had gotten my goals and I didn't want to be a has-been, ya know, like some others, and just ride around. If I couldn't race, I'd just hang it up. So I did hang it up. My wife had been through enough without making any money. I had a house. I had a chance to make some money. I had come to the conclusion that I wasn't gonna get any backing at that time at my age. Rex White and I started it [the racing parts business]. I had seen that I could make a livin' doin' it myself. I'd talked to Betty. I said, 'Honey, keep me up for a year, we'll be in business.' She said, 'OK.'"

Elmo Henderson walked away from driving racecars. He wasn't a good driver, though. He was a great racer. He was a track champion, a top contender, and always a threat to win any sportsman race he entered in the 1950s and early '60s. But this is about his Grand National career. He took on the best racers on the biggest stages NASCAR had and managed some fantastic runs. His remarkable 1960 season often traveling alone and preparing an exhausted two-year old Pontiac by himself makes him a true pioneer of auto racing, the likes of which will never be seen again. He made great friendships at all levels of stockcar racing and left when he could still run with anybody. He stays in shape, looks 20 years younger than he is, and as Cotton Owens said, 'If you want to find Elmo, he's out there walking up Asheville Highway every morning.' It's true, if it's not too cold. And of course, he's all alone.

5

Reb Wickersham
The Flying Rebel

Charles "Reb" Wickersham was born on January 11, 1934, in Longboat Key, Florida, and currently lives in Newberg, Oregon. Reb raced as an independent from his first start in a 1960 Daytona 500 qualifying race until a grinding crash in the 1965 Southern 500 ended it. He sprung onto the NASCAR scene debuting a new, gleaming-white, 1960 Oldsmobile 33 sporting Confederate flags and sponsorship from the Flying Rebel Racing Team, which he drove in 16 races through the first race of 1963. He captured four top-tens in his 41 starts, three of which were 10th places. Reb's best career finish, an eighth, came in the 1965 Firecracker 400 at Daytona. His best year was 1964 when he ran 14 races with one top-ten and a career-best 33rd in Grand National points. Colorful describes the career of the Great Northwest's most prominent confederate.

Reb Wickersham started stock car racing after attending the inaugural Daytona 500 in 1959 with his boss, an Oldsmobile dealer in Sarasota, Florida. They had just witnessed what they thought was Iowa's Johnny Beauchamp in a Thunderbird edge North Carolinian Lee Petty's Oldsmobile for the win.

"I was walking down the stands with my boss, Ed Cooke, and whole bunch of people and said, 'You know it's bad enough to get beat by a damn Yankee, but to have a Ford beat you, too … that's really bad.' Everybody started laughing and I said, 'I'm gonna come down here next year and take that Oldsmobile around there.' And my boss said, 'You not gonna be driving here, Reb. That's for the big boys.' One of the guys said, 'I bet you don't show up' and I took him up on it.

"So the boss sold me a brand new Oldsmobile at cost and we built that thing in the garage area of the dealership, Ed Cooke Motor Company, not knowing what the hell how to build a car. Like I said, it was done on a dare that I wouldn't be there the following year. I was with six rookies working on my pit crew. None of us knew a darn thing about building up a Grand National car. I got the car in the summer [of 1959], a brand new all-white 1960 Oldsmobile Super 88 hardtop. I had some mechanics there at the shop, Parker Tunis, Bob Woods, and Jimmy Pironi, and we all took the NASCAR specs and started building that car. We did everything you could do to it according to specifications. Of course, by the time we got there [Daytona], the specifications we used were a year late. We had to do a lot of new things once we got to the track. We got it to specifications and went out there and qualified.

An aching back rode with Reb in the Oldsmobile at Daytona Speedweeks in 1960 in preparation for the 500 (Reb Wickersham).

"We were assigned the number 33 early and my sign painter was great and put it on the top and both sides of the car in Dayglo orange. I came up with the Flying Rebel Racing Team because I used to do a lot of backyard boat racing and my boat was *The Flying Rebel*. I formed a corporation, my brother was vice president, a friend of mine was treasurer, and I was president of it. We called it the Flying Rebel Racing Team. I used it for a couple of years. They called me everything when I first started racing; Johnny Reb, Johnny Yuma, Reb, I got all kinds of names. You know my name is Charles and it was joked about, 'How you gonna get your whole name on the car?' Well, that's when I said, 'Let's just be Reb then instead of Rebel.' I shortened it down to Reb and that's what I've been for 45 years or better.

"I had no experience other than running a little sportsman car a few times on a quarter-mile asphalt track. I've always loved speed and I just went out there and drove the thing. After a while it felt normal out there and was no big deal. I loved speed. We qualified real well [eighth] for the first hundred miler. In those days, we thought 137 miles and hour was flying."

The record shows that Reb finished 25th in the qualifier and lined up 49th of 68 for the Second Annual Daytona 500, a race he was dared to run. Before the start, he got an offer from a veteran driver.

"This guy used to be an inspector, Bill Gazaway, and he and his brother built this '60 Olds and Tiny Lund was driving it and didn't qualify. The day before the race, they came to me and said, 'We want to use your car because Tiny needs a ride. He's trying to get in the points.' I said, 'I've gone too far and done too much to let anybody drive my car.' They were going to start 50 cars, but the reason they let the other cars in [68 total] was because of a couple of drivers, Tiny was one of them, and another well-known driver."

In a crash filled race, Reb recalled one horrendous accident.

"Talking about my first Daytona 500, there was a lot of action happening that day. I'll never forget coming off number two turn, I forget the boy's name [Tommy Herbert] from Miami driving a Thunderbird and that sucker hit the outside wall and he started rolling and that thing fell apart. I remember looking out my windshield and there the engine was up in the air and I thought it was going to come right down on my car. That engine was up there above me as I went under that sucker. He didn't die, but he sure got plenty beat up."

Reb did better in the 500 than he originally thought.

"Being the first time at a big track associated with NASCAR, if anything came along free, I'd take it. That was the beginning of Autolite that year and they came to me and said, 'Can we give you Autolite plugs and stuff? We'll set your car up, do all your tuning, everything for you. We'll just set you up.' I said, 'Free? OK, fine, go ahead and do it.' So we went to Autolite 'cause everybody else was running Champions. Only about six or seven cars signed up with Autolite and I was the first Autolite car to finish. It was really funny 'cause two weeks after I got home, I got a check in the mail for $4,000. I had already gotten something from NASCAR, then a week later I got another $500 [from Autolite]. Anytime anybody came and offered me anything, I'd take it. I didn't really care. I took Goodyear tires and they were called 'Maypops.' I was one of those guys taking freebies."

Living accomodations were easy for Reb around Daytona.

"I was very fortunate at Daytona. My sister lived there and she had a hotel. She gave us two rooms right on the beach and that's what got me through Daytona. As much money as I made, I had to split it up among my crew. When I got done, there wasn't a lot left. With the Autolite money, I was able to hide enough to make it on down the road. I didn't carry a big crew to Charlotte. I only carried two guys with me. I never run anything else but Autolite. Honest and truly, when I went to Daytona for the first time, that's all we planned on running was one race. Of course, it got in my blood. We were just getting our feet wet. It was a lot different in those days. I didn't have no support. My little small corporation I was runnin' with, we were runnin' on low fuel most of the time. But thank God for the free give-aways I got."

The record states that in Reb's first major race, the Daytona 500, he finished 33rd, 25 laps behind winner Junior Johnson, and pocketed a purse of $700. Reb the Rookie finished ahead of pole-sitter Cotton Owens, Weatherly, Panch, Lund, Langley, Parnelli Jones, Red Farmer, Roberts, Bob Burdick, Speedy Thompson, and Joe Lee Johnson. Reb also finished on the same lap with and right behind the famous Herman "The Turtle" Beam. He pioneered in his rookie year by starting the inaugual races at the Charlotte Motor Speedway [World 600] and the Atlanta International Raceway [Dixie 300]. He recalled that first World 600 on June 19, 1960.

"That was a bad day. They sent me a telegram. I have it today in my scrapbook. It says, 'The race has been delayed.' They tried to get that race off on Memorial Day, but the pavement was green. We came in and started out practicing and the asphalt started peeling. Man, it was just peeling off in hunks. They were out there trying to patch the darn thing and we all went down to different places. We all got pipe and put chicken wire up in front of the cars to keep the asphalt out of the grill and radiator and things like that. Looked like a bunch of chicken coups running around out there. We had everything that day. It was a very slow 600 miles. Joe Lee Johnson won it. It was a fun race. I think it took six hours. It seemed like we were out there forever and ever."

For the record, Reb's next start after Daytona was this brutal first 600-miler which he completed while many of the great drivers and teams of the day did not. Reb started 50th of 60 and perservered for 26th, running at the finish, which is terrific under deplorable conditions. In just his third career start, Reb outran none other than Jim Reed, Jarrett, Pistone, Zervakis, Roberts, Turner, Lorenzen, Weatherly, Joe Eubanks, Owens, Allen, both Pettys, Bob Welborn, and Junior Johnson. Reb Wickersham was far too good to beat those winners by only luck. Reb recalled his rookie test at Darlington at the 1960 Southern 500.

"If you go back, way back, when I took my drivers test in the '60 Oldsmobile, Fireball and Junior took me out for my rookie test. I got out there and I thought I'd been driving pretty well. I thought, 'I'm getting along here pretty good.' The speeds weren't that hot in

Reb sits in the convertible version of the Oldsmobile. Note the stock instrument panel with the addition of gauges, dash-mounted tachometer, and mirror (Reb Wickersham).

Two racers with great nicknames, Possum Jones (2) and Reb Wickersham (33) battle in the 1960 Firecracker 250. Possum was 36th and Reb took 23rd of 37 (Reb Wickersham).

those days and Fireball would get beside me on the straightaway and try to crowd me a little bit. And Junior would catch me over here and put pressure on me to see what I'd do. So I'd come around and go back to the garage area. I'd come out and Fireball walked around and looked at the right side of my car. He says, 'I thought you were driving out there?' I said, 'I was.' 'No you're not. You haven't got a Darlington Stripe on that car yet.'

"Darlington scared me. Daytona didn't scare me. You come down the backstretch and go into three, if you were side-by-side, somebody had to get off of it. It was a very scary moment going down there knowing you're beside 'em. They gotta let off or you gotta back off. It was a scary track. Of course, turns one and two weren't too bad, but three and four just scared the hell out of me. Especially that backstretch. Every time I come off turn two and started down that backstretch I'd wonder, 'Man, am I gonna get through that sucker or am I gonna get my ass busted?' I went around and put it on the rail. When you run hard, you had to hit that number three rail. When you went into that turn, if you were holding power, you'd slide up just enough to rub that side of your car, then you could kind of ease her off coming through the middle of the turn and into four. But I went out there and got it and Fireball said, 'OK, you're in.'"

During the 500, Reb flirted with disaster.

"I was right behind Bobby Johns and Roy Tyner when they got together. I came around off number two. I saw, I think, Roy Tyner's car upside down in the middle of the track [actually Johns' car]. I didn't right off hand see where Bobby was, but I saw this person laying out in the middle of the track. Well my pit was right by Joe Lee Johnson's crew. I came in and went right past his pit and there was all this commotion going on. They flagged me by and I pulled in and I asked my pit crew guy named Billy, I said, 'Billy!' I thought it was Bobby laying out and I says, 'Bobby OK?' He said,

'Don't worry about it. Get outta here!' He wouldn't hardly let me stop. He got me out of there. Later, I found out, after I got my axle broke, what had really happened. Three people had been killed and Joe Lee Johnson's crew had been beat up pretty bad. That was a sad day, it really was."

Joe Lee Johnson's chief mechanic, Paul McDuffie, a winner with Fireball Roberts in this race in 1958 and the first World 600 with Joe Lee Johnson earlier in June, was killed along with Johnson crewman Charles Sweatlund and NASCAR official Joe Taylor. Three others were badly injured when Bobby Johns' Cotton Owens Pontiac locked bumpers with Roy Tyner's Oldsmobile and crashed into the unprotected pit area, creating a deadly shower of concrete shrapnel. Reb had had an ironic encounter on that very race morning.

"That morning, my former wife and my pit crew and some of their wives were eating in a restaurant in Florence, I think it was. I was sitting there and Paul McDuffie was sitting across from me. He got up and walked over and said, 'Hey Reb, this is your first race here. Take it easy or you can get killed out there.' I'll never forget that. I'll remember that the day I die. I was telling Rex White that. He said, 'Be careful or you can get killed out there and *he* got killed.' Of course, that's when they started putting up pit walls at Darlington. Everybody was just out there in the middle of the racetrack in those days. It was dangerous. Darlington always has been a dangerous track. I wanted to be there because it was a challenge, but I just never really had a good time there."

According to the records, Reb lined up 38th of 48, broke an axle on lap 163, and crashed for 32nd. He ran the first National 400 in Charlotte on October 16, 1960. David Pearson ran six more races than Reb after Darlington.

"In 1960, I was up for Rookie of the Year. He beat me out of it. After Darlington, I don't think I did another race, maybe one more. He got in it and he just kept going. Norris Friel told me, 'Reb, you got a good chance to get Rookie of the Year.' I didn't even think I was in on the thing and he said, 'You're up there, buddy.' The next thing I knew, David got it."

Then there was the day Reb loaned Olds 33 to a fellow competitor.

"A guy named Bob Barron lived about 15 miles from me. He was a transplanted Yankee with a little radiator shop in Bradenton, Florida. He had an old Dodge and was actually finishing worse than I was. He was always back there with Herman [Beam] somewhere. He was trying his best to drive all the races. He was putting them things together with glue and rubber bands and everything to keep going. He said, 'Can I drive your car down at so-and-so?' 'Yeah, Bob, but you can't trailer it.' He said, 'I'm going to tow it with a tow bar.' I said, 'Don't tear my car up, will you please!' [Later on] I come back to North Wilkesboro and Jimmy [Pardue] says, 'I think Bob's got something to tell you.' I said, 'What?' He [Barron] said, 'The hitch broke loose and the car went out into a tomato field.' That car had tomato seeds all over that sucker. The front bumper was knocked up under it where he went over this ditch and hit this fence post out through this tomato field somewhere in North Carolina. He said the farmer come out and said, 'If you hadn't been a race driver, I'd be making you pay for this.' The car was so full of tomatoes. It was in the grill and the radiator. It was tomatoes everywhere! Seeds were all over the hood of my car. I'll never forget that. He was so scared to tell me. But Pardue told me before he got back to town with it. I just said, 'Hey Bob, you're going to have to help me find a bumper for it. We went out and found another bumper and kept on truckin'. That was a good old car. It was just a homemade racecar. Had fun with it and drove it wherever I could when I could."

Reb was a participating eyewitness to one of the most infamous events in NASCAR history in his last start of 1961 on August 13.

"I was up at Asheville-Weaverville when they had that riot. I'll never forget that as long as I live. Jimmy Pardue and his wife and my former wife and her kids, she was pregnant with her daughter at the time. The wives stayed there in Asheville at the motel and Jimmy and I went out to the track with our cars. Well the track fell apart. The promoter knew the track was coming apart. There was holes in the track and it was beating the hell out of the cars. He left town before the race ended and they called the race at 251 laps [actually 258]. We all came in and were over in the garage area. But there was only one way to get out of that track. That was right next to the grandstands. There was an opening in the guardrail and you'd drive through there.

"We come on in and the fans started getting a little grumpy. They were yelling that they wanted the race finished and all this crap, you know. We were minding our own business and some of us started to get ready to go. This guy had gone across the driveway with a big pickup truck. It was sittin' across the road there so we couldn't get through that gate. There was these guys standing up there in the back of the bed and they were all drunk on shine screamin' and yellin'. The people were kind of milling up behind us. The state troopers said that they couldn't come on the property unless we broke through the thing. They were sitting outside, we're inside. I was loaded up ready to go and they really started getting nasty. I'll never forget that. Old Pop [Giant Eugene Eargle, Bud Moore's right hand man] walked up. This one guy had a two by four in his hand. Pop grabbed that damn two by four and laid 'em down like bowling pins. He grabbed that two by four out of that guy's hand and he just kinda wop wop wop and wopped 'em down. They started comin' across the rail after that. Those suckers come through and started comin' across the track and I grabbed a ball peen hammer. I didn't know what else to do. I knew I was going to fight with something. I grabbed this ball peen hammer and I run out there and Richard Petty got hit right in the face with a watermelon. Somebody hit him with a damn watermelon. I ran up and this guy was comin' and I pulled my hammer back and pulled my hand forward and somebody jerked the hammer out of my hand. I crawled back under that crowd and back to my truck and my damn crew chief, he's locked himself in the pickup truck. I couldn't even get in my own truck.

Top: On April 16, 1961, at North Wilkesboro, North Carolina, Reb drove to his first career top ten in the Gwyn Staley 400. Reb and the repainted Olds still look racy (Reb Wickersham). *Bottom:* Bristol's Southeastern 500 on July 29 was Reb's only 1962 start for a 39th. Others racing are George Green (1), Bill Morton (64), and Ray Hendrick (35).

"They broke through enough that the cops started comin' and gettin' 'em after they broke through that gate there. But old Pop, I'll never forget that. The other bunch was comin' from the other direction. There was another guy, he always used to carry, we called them 'frog stickers,' knives, ya know. He got somebody in the ass with one of those. He stuck that sucker up his ass. Damn good mechanic. I forgot who he worked for. But anyway, I know he stabbed this guy. There was a lot of blood flowin' around after a while, but it was a weird day.

"I'll never forget it. People yellin'. It kind of scared me to be trapped. You got drivers and a few mechanics and thousands of people out there. You got 'em all wound up and they're all against ya. It was scary and I don't want to see it again no matter what. I thought they were our friends, but I guess they weren't friends *or* fans. They thought they got cheated out of half of a race. They were drinkin'. You could tell they were all drunk. That was an exciting one. I had more excitement with my Oldsmobile than I did with most anything else."

The old Oldsmobile's final run, now number 67, was on November 11, 1962, and was rather special.

"The final race for the Oldsmobile was in November of '62 at Golden Gate Speedway in Tampa. About 25 Grand National cars came in there on a third-mile track and it was kinda crowded. We went out and qualified and had trouble. It was reversed order. They put me on the inside pole and Herman Beam on the outside. There were some cars behind me that were about the same speed and the big boys were in the back. I figured when I went into that first turn if I started to slide, I'd have Herman to bump up against. When the race started, Herman just pulled over and almost parked and I was out there by myself. I was able to get it around the turn without anything happening. That was the final Grand National race for the Oldsmobile. That was the first time I started on the pole."

The record shows Reb was the last car running in 18th ahead of Jarrett, Roberts, Spencer, and Dieringer, and Larry Thomas. Reb's Wilkes County, North Carolina, days living with Jimmy Pardue had to involve moonshine at some point.

The famous Miss Pure Firebird Linda Vaughn and Reb pose trackside in the early 1960s (Reb Wickersham).

"That was an interesting thing in my life. Ted Lowe, who worked on Jimmy Pardue's car was from North Wilkesboro and he had served time for runnin' shine. Ted was a nice guy. He died not too many years after that. So I asked him, 'Ted, do you know where I can get a jug of shine?' 'Yeah, I can set you up with some. Let's take the truck.' We went out in the woods way out there in the middle of nowhere and I blinked my lights. Some lights blinked back at me. I went down there and told the guy I wanted a half gallon. That's five bucks. He says, 'Well, why don't you just take six half gallons and maybe you can make some money.' I took the six or whatever it was and he put them in the bottom of an oil can crate. I took 'em home and I kept one. You could mix them, 180 proof, half and half and get drunk on it. Just a shot of it and mix a whole bunch of water with it and you had the same thing you would if you bought at a store. I sold the rest of it for, I think, about a hundred bucks. So I paid for my expenses there and back. That was the Moonshine Capital of the World."

Reb recounts when he and pal Jimmy Pardue bought a pair of year-old Ray Nichels Pontiac team cars for 1963.

"I went up to Highland, Indiana, and bought Len Sutton's old car and Jimmy Pardue bought the one A.J. Foyt had driven. It was 18 below zero and Billy Gill and I had never seen it that cold. We had a fifth of whiskey in the back of the car and went out there the next day and it was frozen. I said, 'We better get the hell out of here!' Some boys down at the shop [Nichels'] said, 'Why don't you guys come over to our house tonight and we'll get together,' and we said, 'Fine.' They told us how to get there. So we were driving the streets in his car and all of the sudden the street lights and everything just disappeared and we kept going. I said, 'What do you think about this country, Billy?' He said. 'I don't know.' We drove on about a quarter mile and guess were we was? We were on Lake Michigan! We stopped and I said, 'There's ice under us.' So we turned around and went back. That lake was solid as a rock out there. We'd have driven all the way across the damn thing to Michigan or somewhere 'cause we were on our way. I've been to Alaska and lived in Colorado and never seen anything like that."

Reb went north to race in 1963 with some other NASCAR invaders.

"The Yankee 300, that was a USAC race on the road couse at Indianapolis Raceway Park, and we went up there. Jack Smith, Fireball, four of us went to drive the USAC course. Ray Nichels' whole crew was there and they worked on my car and got me set up for it. I finished seventh and A.J. Foyt won. I felt pretty good against all those big USAC cars, all those big names back in those days. Foyt, Rutherford, Sachs, all of them run that day. I felt pretty good about that. I finished seventh and made a few dollars. You see, they pay different in USAC. They pay according to the amount of the gate receipts. You get a certain amount of that. So I got a pretty good hunk of money out of that thing. I was surprised. I was signed up to run Milwaukee, but something happened. We went back to Florida. We were lucky to have Ray Nichels there. He took good care of us and they were a good bunch of guys and he was a good man himself."

The ex–Nichels/Sutton 1962 Pontiac carried 67 and Reb's Sport Shop as a sponsor. In the 1963 Daytona 500 qualifier, Reb started ninth and finished 21st. The 500 was worse, as he started 40th and finished 46th, just ahead of Ralph Earnhardt, Pearson, and Crider. "We blew right off the bat going down the backstretch and somebody brought me home," he recalled.

Reb had a decent streak after that with a 17th at Atlanta, 11th at Bristol, and then another bad day at Darlington in the Rebel 300 with a troublesome competitor. It was for hardtops for the first time and had a screwy format of twin 150-milers with a Lemans-style start for the first race where the drivers dashed across the track to their cars, climbed in, fired them up, and raced away. They lined up for the second race as they finished the first and averaged out the finishes of both "Little Rebs" to determine a winner.

"I finished one of those and in the second, Tiny Lund, I think, was in those days probably one of the dirtiest drivers of the bunch. He caught me coming off the fourth turn right down the straightaway. There used to be a little dip right there as you come off number four going down the straightaway. He was riding my bumper and hit me as I went over that bump. Of course when he did, it knocked me sideways and I went into the wall. I steered into the wall and the car climbed up and actually was up about as high as the chain-

The Rebel 300 (actually two Little Reb 150s) found Reb the Racer gridded 25th on May 11, 1963. He was crashed out by Tiny Lund for a dismal 23rd of 31 (Reb Wickersham).

The ex–Ray Nichels/Len Sutton Pontiac frames a very proud Reb during his 14-race 1963 season (Reb Wickersham).

link fence. I fell back down on the track and pushed it back into the wall so I wouldn't go out in front of the cars. They put the caution flag out and I was crawling out and had my foot and my leg out looking for an opportunity to get out and run across the track. I heard the race announcer say, 'Fireball doesn't see him!' Gosh, I saw him coming down the track running alongside that wall. I got back in and wrapped my legs and arms around that roll bar waiting for him to hit me. He had not seen the caution or anything and he just veered out, really, I mean, the wind shook me so hard when he went by. After the race, he said, 'Reb, I never saw you until the last second.' If he had hit me, it would have been all over with 'cause he was coming full bore and I was just sitting there in that track. A race fan came over after the race and said, 'You're the first white man to ever scare the livin' hell out of me. I thought you were comin' in the stands with me.' I just never really had a great love for Tiny. I always thought he was kind of a dirty driver. I mean I know he's gone, passed away, I know he got killed, but that's just my feelings."

The Reb nabbed his first top ten at Birmingham.

"I finished tenth and ran out of gas with three laps to go. I was running about fifth and knew I was getting low on fuel. My pit crew said, 'Keep going ... *Go!* Don't come in.' I ran out of gas and finished tenth. I would have been up there that day."

Reb strung together some top twenty runs consecutively at Atlanta [18th], Bristol

[18th], Asheville-Weaverville [12th], Huntington [15th], Martinsville [17th], North Wilkesboro [15th] and a ride in Buck Baker's Pontiac at Charlotte, which blew for 26th.

"A lot of stuff you don't get credit for. In those days you had a pickup and a trailer and we threw all our junk in the back of the truck and went racing."

He picked up a last minute ride on July 4, 1964, at Daytona.

"At the [Firecracker] 400, I had my Pontiac over there. We had blown an engine and I didn't have a car for the race. Bobby had a number two '64 white Pontiac that belonged to his dad. Didn't have anything on it, but number two. Shorty [Bobby's dad] was a hotheaded little Greek. He was following me in the pits. Bobby had jumped over to the Ford. They had a factory team there. [Bobby Johns replaced Fireball Roberts at Holman-Moody after Fireball's injury in 1964.] Anyway, I was in the pits and Shorty says to me, 'Hey Reb, you wanna drive my car?' I said, 'Yeah.' Bobby had already qualified it or something, I don't know. I think I was 19th. Never had been in the car. I just went out on pit road, jumped in, and cranked that sucker up and we went off down the track. Comin' down I looked off the turn and I saw old Johnny Bruner, Jr., who was the flagman in those days. I saw him up there, the flag in his his hand, and he was holding it up there and he hadn't let the green out yet and we were all showering down on it, you know, in third gear. Cranking it down! We were probably running 135 down through there. A.J. Foyt's right on my bumper starting right behind me [Reb started 17th, Foyt 19th].

"He drops that flag. Haulin' ass now and I get just past the starter's stand, jam that sucker down in gear, and all of the sudden that sucker jumped sideways on me. I only had one choice ... to hang on to it! I kept it that way. Everybody went by and I dropped down and drove around the apron all the way back to pit road. Of course, A.J. came out in the papers the next day and said, 'Man, that boy did a hell of a job. If he'd had let that sucker go, he'd have taken out the whole back of the racetrack.' Anyway, I was talking to Buddy Baker when I was there at Darlington [in September 2008], and he said, 'You remember turning that sucker sideways on the start?' I said, 'Yeah.' He said, 'You don't remember what Papa Johns called ya? He called ya everything but a white man.'

"I drove around just short of the area behind the pit wall. I got out and left. I could have come back in and probably got the tires changed and kept on goin', but I just pulled it back in because I didn't know what was wrong. I dropped down. I hit the damn thing and I locked it in. I don't know what gear it was. The car just jumped sideways and I turned the wheels and rode it down. It was a new car. It was the car Bobby had been driving until he made the driver switch. That was it. You know Shorty got killed. They robbed him and beat the old man down. Yeah, that was terrible. [Reb refers to the Miami riots in 1980.] He was a good old man. He was hard-nosed, but he was a good man. Bobby's a good man. I always liked Bobby."

In 1965, Reb Wickersham secured without a doubt the best ride he ever had.

"I was driving for Ray Underwood of Cartersville, Georgia. My mechanic was a young fellow who had worked in the engine department at Holman-Moody named Bruce Bacon. He came out of there and built that engine, a 427 side oiler. There were seven '65 Fords running. They were factory cars. I had the only outside car of the '65 Fords. A kid had bought it somewhere outside of Cartersville and got behind in his payments. He tried to burn it when they tried to reposses it. They saved most of it. Underwood owned a wrecking yard, picked it up and brought it in there, and built the racecar."

Car 03 debuted in the second qualifying race for the 1965 Daytona 500 and the red Galaxie started 20th and finished tenth. In the 500, he started 20th and came in 26th in a race stopped by rain. The Dixie 500 in Atlanta on June 13 was an especially good run for Reb.

"We went up there and outrun I don't know how many of the factory Fords. I came back to my garage and in the meantime there were 16 wheels and tires. I pulled in there and asked Bruce Bacon, 'What is this?' He says, 'Ralph Moody come over here and said you'd outrun some of his cars, Holman-Moody cars, and he wanted to give this to ya 'cause they figured you'd be runnin' up there with 'em on Sunday and if you needed anything to please let him know because you were runnin' on their team now.' In the race, ten laps to go I blew the engine and I wound up 12th. It had been a rainy day and the racetrack sits down in a bowl. The fumes got down in there and when I got out of my car, I couldn't hardly walk. I staggered toward the field hospital and fell over and Buddy Baker took me on down there. Len Sutton and several other people were in there. They kept us a while, but it was a good race. I was runnin' fifth, I think, when I went out."

The summer brought some respectable starts and finishes and then Reb returned to his favorite track, Daytona, for the Firecracker 400 with his best car ever.

In his best career finish, Reb took eighth in the 1965 Firecracker 400 at Daytona on July 4. His Ford 03 moves through the garage area afterward.

Skeen's demolished Ford 23 rests after another hit by a skidding Bert Robbins as Reb's smoking wreck sits nearby pouring fluid from both ends.

"We blew an engine qualifying for that race and I didn't have anything but a short block with me. I went to Holman-Moody and they had a whole trailer full of engines 'cause they had their factory Fords out there. We went over to see John Holman, a man I didn't care much about. Ralph Moody was a hell of a nice guy. Holman was just hard to get along with. He wanted to screw ya every way he could. So I went to him and said, 'Can we buy an engine?' Engines were going for about five grand in those days. He said, 'No, I'm not selling any. I don't have any to sell.' I went back to Norris Friel, technical inspector for NASCAR. He and I were pretty good friends. He's the one I first saw when I signed my first papers in 1960 in the Oldsmobile. He was always for the little man. He was always trying to get the factory guys for doin' some screwin' around. I went to him and said, 'Norris, I need to get an engine.' He said, 'Did you go to Holman-Moody?' I said 'Yeah.' Norris said, 'What did he say?' I said, 'John Holman said I couldn't have one.' Norris said, 'Let's go!' We walked over there and he told Holman, 'Sell him an engine or get your damn cars off the track.' So Holman made a grumbling sound and pointed back in the back and we went and picked one out. It wasn't as strong as the one we had in there, but it ran and we just stayed in the race till we finished and that was it."

It was to be Reb's best career finish, an eighth, nine laps behind winner A.J. Foyt. After a blown engine left him 15th at Bristol, Reb Wickersham hauled 03 to Darlington for that Labor Day classic, the Southern 500, for what would be his 41st and final Grand National event. Reluctantly, he remembered.

"September the fifth, 1965 [actually the 6th]. I always tell people I enjoyed racing, but that is one of the things that always hung with me. I can tell you, right now, I'll be honest with you, I don't remember the day at all. I remember waking up 13 hours later. I gotta thank God that he took that out of my mind because I think if I could see it happening, or seen what was going on, it would have been really, really bad. I do know that Neil Castles came up to my car, my crewmember said. He hadn't qualified. He was driving one of Buck Baker's old cars and he come up and told me he'd be in the pit. Of course it was a hot day like it was in Darlington and he said he'd be there in case I had to get out. But I don't remember anything. I woke up that morning [the day after the race]. I was still wearing my old dirty coveralls. They had sewed my jaw up where I had busted my jaw where the steering wheel got me and I had spleen injuries. I always thought it was the third [lap], but it was the second. [The crash was on the third lap in the third turn, so he completed two laps.] I saw the video and I tried to think what I did and what I tried to do. What I think I tried to do was he [Buren Skeen] dropped down, you know, that track used to be one lane. There was a big infield on that end and if you ever dropped down, especially with a lot of speed on your car, there wasn't much you could do with it. It was like driving off the side of the road. You get the tire caught in the edge of the road or something. Well that's what he did from what I understand. He dropped down and lost it and spun around and came back up tail first into traffic. Evidently the old theory was, you know, 'When you see it, aim at it, and it won't be there when you get there.' Evidently, I tried to drop down and they said he must have started putting the brakes, the binders, on or something and slowed it down and I hit him. *T-boned him.* You had to stay above in that third turn. I mean that's one thing I learned.

"Well, I woke up in the hospital in Florence. My scorer was with me then. She was in the scorers' stand and, I was told this later, when she didn't hear me comin' around, she jumped out and ran down the front straightaway with these cars comin' around. They had cautioned it and she got down to the car evidently and my pit crew had got there first. They took me out of my car. My car started to burn, smoking, and they put me in the ambulance. They thought they saw Buren moving in his car and they knew I was out. My car had a little flame and they were throwing the dust on my car. Evidently, my crewman jumped into the ambulance with me and my scorer came up and the guy said, 'No. We can only carry one.' A deputy sheriff picked her up and carried her to the hospital. But I woke up in the hospital. I know I was out about 12 or 14 hours. I had a broken jaw. I had a ruptured spleen, and my harness really busted up my shoulder. They figured it probably impacted at over 180 mile and hour, he coming back and me goin'. I hit him right in the door. I woke up and they were standing to my right by the end of my

With his arms stretched above his helmeted head and an apparent jaw injury, Reb Wickersham is lifted from his battered Underwood Ford.

bed, a man and a woman, and they kept saying, 'Reb, it wasn't your fault.' I didn't even know what they were talking about. I said. 'OK,' or something like that and they left, you know. They said something like, 'Buren's hurt, but he's still alive.' They told me, 'You were in a bad wreck. Buren's in a room across from you.' I went home two days later and I got a phone call that he had died. I was on my ranch and that kind of messed up my life for a while.

"While I was recuperating from my accident at Darlington, I was on NASCAR compensation or workers' comp or whatever. They were paying me $75 a week, which was big money in those days. I came home and a friend of mine was a big inboard hydroplane racer. He says, 'Why don't you get into boat racing?' I said, 'I don't know. I don't like those hydroplanes.' They got those big California skiboats with the big motors in the back of them and it sounded like fun. I finally got on the phone and found a boat out in Bellflower, California. We drove out there, picked that sucker up, and brought it to Florida. It had a Bill Stroppe engine it, a big Merc in that sucker, and I took it back and put straight pipes on it. Went to a race down in Palm Beach and was runnin'about 125, 130. The boat was only 17 foot long and weighed about 1,200 pounds with that big engine in the back of it. I was runnin' this race on the intracoastal waterway and was just kickin' ass, nobody staying

Driver's side view of Reb's racer. In his final official Grand National start, Reb won $505 for 43rd while Buren Skeen's family got $510.

near me. Somebody took a picture of me goin' under the bridge and my boat was out of the water about three feet. That picture hit the damn papers on the west coast of Florida and the next thing I knew, NASCAR called and says, 'We're cuttin' off your money right now 'cause you're not hurt.' That was the last of my workers' comp."

After many years passed, Reb reached out to the family of Buren Skeen.

"I tried about ten or 12 years ago to make contact with Belinda, that's his wife. I didn't know her or the boys at the time. I did know Buren 'cause he was a rookie that year at Darlington. I knew him before. I had raced somewhere else with him prior to that. About 12 years ago, there was a guy in their area named Frank Smith. He had contacted me years before about buying my coveralls, whatever I had to sell. He had opened a little museum up there in Archdale [North Carolina]. We talked and talked and carried on and finally one time I asked him, 'Do you know Belinda Skeen?' He said, 'Yeah, I know her.' I said, 'Would you mind asking her if I could call her? I'd like to talk to her.' I mean I was kind of spooky about it. He called me back and says, 'She says, "Why does he want to call me?" or something like that. So I figured it in a negative way and just kind of dropped it."

Reb eventually got the phone number of the Skeens and wondered one night if he should dial it.

"I finally did and got the younger boy, Chris, he was only two at the time [of the accident]. He answered the phone and I said, 'this is Reb Wickersham.' Boy, it hit me pretty hard. I said, 'I been wanting to call you folks for a long time and I kinda felt like your Mom didn't want to talk to me.' He said, 'No, don't you ever think that way because we've thought about you at family reunions. We always wondered how Reb Wickersham was doing.' Then a half hour later, Eric, the older boy, called me and said, 'Just talked to my brother and we're just so glad we finally made contact with you. We didn't know how to get a hold of you.' We talked a minute. It was just before Christmas. Since then, Eric and his daughter and I went out together and had a great time. It has really healed me a lot because I hurt.

"I was talking to Johnny Allen when I was sitting down there in the President's Suite at the track [during the historic festival at Darlington on Labor Day weekend 2008]. We were looking up at the third turn and I said, 'That's where it happened. Johnny, I haven't ever gotten over it.' 'Reb, it's just racing,' he said. 'Johnny, it's just racing, but you've never been in an accident like that one. It never leaves you.' 'Well, I guess you're right,' he said. It's a lot better. She [Belinda Skeen] told me many times, 'If Buren had his way to go, he wouldn't want to go any other way.' At least you go out and leave this world the way you enjoyed doing it. You don't want to go out there and die, but if you go, you're probably doing what you love. Not having your wife knock you in the head. His son Eric told me when we were up in Charlotte when we went out to dinner that he has the door. He said, 'I have my Dad's helmet. I knew your car was red because there is red paint on his helmet.' He was four years old at the time. We talk now and she [Belinda] will ask me about how my family's doing. I'll tell her if somebody in my family's sick or what's going on. When I had my knee replaced last time, she called me and said she was praying for me. I'd call her and she'd say, 'Boy Reb, I'm laughing. You made me laugh and I feel so much better.' I'll call her up, we'll start talking. She'll say, 'I like hearing from you.' She worked hard and sent both those boys to the University of North Carolina. They both graduated and she worked two jobs to put them boys through school. I've talked about the wreck and I told her, 'I have a few pictures on my wall. You wouldn't mind sending me a few pictures of

Buren, would ya? Of one of his cars or something? I just want to put it on my wall for a memorial thing.'

"I saw his son this past September [2008] and when I walked out in the lobby of the hotel, I saw him standing there. He looked just like his dad. I could just see him [Buren] after all those years. You know I've put it behind me and I'm sorry it had to happen, but it happened and that's it. That's life."

Ford number 03, the ever-present flirt with death, and a shot at Rookie of the Year— Reb recalled.

"The car was junked out. The engine was taken out of what was left of it. I heard somebody bought that car, stripped the thing, and sold the frame and the body. Some of the drive gears was taken out of it. Somebody said somebody tried to fix it up and drive it, but never could get the frame straight. It was a hard stop. I had another pretty good one up at North Wilkesboro, I think it was in the Pontiac. I blew the right front and that sucker shot up that wall like a durn bullet. Kinda scared me up there a little bit. I was really lucky. You know you always think about it when you get in the car, especially on the big tracks. You always think, 'Is this my day?' I thought about it a lot ... a lot of times. You knew something could happen. You'd sit there on pit road and they'd say, 'Gentlemen, start your engines!' and it was all over with. It was gone. I've always done a lot of things and jumped in feet first. I just had the urge. It turned me on so much to see those cars runnin' at Daytona, the speed they were runnin', which wasn't that fast, but it was fast for that day. A 135 to a 145 ... that was flyin'. I was 25 when I got into it. Guys now runnin' at 17, 18 years old. But the only persons younger that me was Buddy Baker, Richard Petty, and that was it. I was the next one and they were a lot younger than I was.

"A lot of guys are gone. Darel Dieringer was a good

Reb went to the water after his Grand National career ended as seen here piloting "Rebel a Go Go." He was named the 1966 Florida Boat Racer of the Year (Reb Wickersham).

friend of mine. Bobby Johns I still like. Bobby Johns is a good guy, period. Bobby Johns and I got along great. We were both Floridians. A little side story on that one ... back in '66, I was racin' boats and the governor of Florida at that time, Haydon Burns, a Democrat, was at the Hialeah Racetrack. I got invited as the top boat racer in Florida and Bobby Johns got invited as the best auto racer in Florida. We met down there and they had this big dinner for us and I had only been driving boats a few months. We had a great time."

Reb remembered some missed opportunities.

"I went back in '66 and I don't even get credit. I can't tell you who it was. I drove a couple of, kinda did a little bit of a free-lance. I'd go around the track and get a ride or something. I didn't get credit for nothing. Norris Friel was still an inspector and he had come over to my part of Florida a couple of times and called me up. We'd gone out for lunch or breakfast or whatever it was. I don't know if he was lonely or what, but he'd come over. He came to Bradenton one time and called my house and my former wife said, 'Reb's not here.' Then I came home and she said, 'Norris Friel called and he's at a Holiday Inn over on the other side.' He'd come over a lot of times and sit around and sometimes we'd be talking, talking, talking and I'd get a little bored. But he came over and I didn't see him again until I went up to Atlanta. I was going to try to find a ride. He says, 'Where were you?' I says, ' Norris I was doing something, I don't know.' He says, 'Man, I came over for

At Darlington's Historic Racing Festival in September 2009, Reb and the author sport Flying Rebel Racing Team hats, two of only four in existence.

one reason. There was a lady in Valdosta, Georgia [Betty Lilly] related to the Coca-Cola people. She called me up and asked me do I have a driver?' He said, 'I got three people. You were number one, Bobby [Allison] was number two, and Joe Caspolich from Jackson [Mississippi]. You three were on the list and you were number one, Reb.' He said, 'Guess what? Bobby's in that car.' I said, 'Well, that's my luck, a day late and a dollar short.' Bobby Allison got the ride and today my wife says, 'You know what? It coulda been you. You're better off that you didn't get that ride.' I was kinda glad I didn't get the car. I was already having problems and I didn't need no more."

A phone call and a final chance to climb throught the window of a Grand National go unanswered.

"I came back into racing and I had an offer, I don't remember who called me up, and said, 'Hey, you wanna drive?' I said, 'No, I'm runnin' my ranch and driving boats right now. Let me call you back.' I never made that call back. I miss it. I miss it more than anything in the world. You don't know how much I miss it. I kick myself in the butt for not getting back in there and going full force again. It was the greatest time of my life."

Reb could not close without thanking those independent mechanics, crewmen, and others who helped him throughout his career.

"I've mentioned some of them and left out quite a few. Unfortunately, some are not with us anymore, but deserve some recognition for helping me in whatever success I've had in my life. They are Pat Morrison, Parker Tunis, Jim Peroni, Odell Hood, Billy Gill, Bruce Bacon, Bill Young, Buddy Adams, Bob Anders, Frank Wickersham, Butch Wickersham, and my wife, Gail. Without them, I would not have made it."

Reb Wickersham, and do not call him Charles, was credited for 41 Grand National races with probably a dozen more undocumented starts. As is evidenced here, he accounted for himself very well. He boasted and bet at the first Daytona 500 he'd be in the next one. He won the bet and went one better: he finished well. His career coincides with the dawn of the superspeedway age, which he attacked in a homemade car with zero speedway experience. And not just any car, but a big, white, brand new, off the showroom floor 1960 Oldsmobile gaudily sporting dayglo orange 33s and the Confederate battle flag of the Flying Rebel Racing Team. A disasterous Southern 500 in 1965 snuffed out the best year and ride Reb ever had. So he took his lust for speed to the water and made a name for himself there, too, standing out from the rest, as always. Charles Wickersham was a rebel. Reb Wickersham still is.

6

Paul Lewis

Gentleman Teacher

Paul Lewis was born on September 28, 1932, in Surry County, Mount Airy, North Carolina, Andy Griffith's hometown. Paul served during the Korean Conflict as an instructor and was discharged in 1953. He honed his driving skills ferrying soldiers on leave back and forth between New York, Pittsburgh, Philadelphia, D.C., and their camps in his Cadillac sedan. He moved to Johnson City, Tennessee, in 1955 and is still there. Paul started racing modifieds in 1956 and went Grand National racing in 1960. After his racing days ended, Paul began to mentor young men on the short tracks of east Tennessee, producing winners and champions.

His well-worn first Grand National ride, 1958 Chevrolet Impala 32, is on exhibition tours today and is a story in itself.

"It looked terrible. It was a rust bucket. The first car I ever drove in NASCAR in North Wilkesboro in 1960, spring race, and we were poor, dirt poor. We went with dirt track tires on asphalt. I spun that sucker four, five, six times. I think the last two I was sittin' between three and four laughing. Some guys came over later and said, 'We know you were havin' trouble, but what were you laughin' about?' I realized how bad I must be out there in that thing. That car weighed 4,450 pounds on dirt track tires on asphalt. You couldn't hold it in a ten-acre field. [Paul laughs.] That was my first race and learned from that."

The record shows on March 27, 1960, Paul started 20th and finished 12th in the Gwyn Staley 160. There's more seat time to come in the '58 Chevy.

"Brownie King built a '60 [Chevrolet number 1]. He went to Daytona with a hurried up racecar. He didn't finish well in the race. He'd borrowed money to build that car. He had to pay it off and got worried. Jess Potter asked me to drive this '58 Chevrolet in 1960. Other people drove it; George Green and several others. I continued to drive the '58, you know, learning curve. Jesse didn't have much experience and we learned together. I bought that car from Brownie. We had to rebuild the front end, get the car where it would handle. We did pretty good for a couple of country boys. We ran a '60 on super speedways and the '58 on dirt. We ran a lot of dirt."

The record shows in the 1960 Daytona 500, Brownie King drove Potter's 1960 Chevrolet to 30th, earning $200 while George Green torched the '58 Chevy 32 for 55th. This is followed by an unexpected helping hand.

6. Paul Lewis

Paul's original ride, Jesse Potter's restored 1958 Chevrolet Impala. This car took Paul to his first seven Grand National starts, including a sixth in the last at Weaverville (Paul Lewis).

"We had to tow the thing, no trailers, no haulers. The last track we ran was Saturday night in Wilson, N.C. Jesse had to come back to work, so on Sunday I went to Bowman-Gray [in Winston-Salem] myself. That's when they run grand touring cars against the Grand Nationals inside the stadium. It had chains and concrete pillars sticking up. I broke a right front ball joint and tore the whole right front out. I worked and worked and had it pretty close and it was late. Everybody had left. They turned off the lights. I turned the towcar around and the headlights on so I could see. One man saw what was happening and helped me. I'll never forget it and I tell the story every time I get a chance to give him credit ... Lee Petty. Lee pulled his truck over and helped. We had to get that thing where we could get a tow bar on it. I had most of it done, but had to finish tightening stuff. I had to beat that thing to get the bumper on so we could get a tow bar on it."

The record shows that on April 18, 1960, Paul drove the '58 Chevy 32 to 11th, retiring with spindle trouble.

"Late at night, I'm comin' back from Bowman Gray on country paved roads. On a curve there was swamp on both sides and I started into that curve. That sucker got away from me and tried to jackknife. I hit the gravel, but maintained control. I threw gravel all down in a frog pond. [Paul laughs loudly and claps.] A couple of guys were down there frog huntin'. 'What the hell's goin' on up there?' I say, 'Guys, it's just me. I almost wrecked my racecar. You just go on doin' what you were doin'. They said, 'OK, thank yi.' [Paul laughs heartily.] Fortunately, the towcar was heavy enough to maintain control. It was as heavy as the racecar. It weighed 4,800 pounds and the racecar weighed 4,450."

He recalled one more ... for the road.

"I was goin' to Hickory pullin' the old '58 down Jonas' Ridge Mountain with a tow bar. I ran out of brakes and started gearing down. I got the tow vehicle in second and burned the transmission up. All I had was second. I had very little brakes. I'm wiping out ditches with that racecar. [Paul bursts into laughter.] This lady was sittin' in that back seat and we'd go into a curve and she'd let out a squeal [Paul is laughing, trying to finish the story] all the way down that mountain. When I got down to 64, all I had was second gear all the way to the racetrack. Somebody brought the [race] car home, but I had to drive that sucker home in second gear."

Paul described promoters back in the '60s.

"Some promoters in those days were unfair. There are multi-millionaires now that treated us unfairly. We needed financial help. If you blew or crashed, you had to make at least a couple of hundred bucks to get home. They would promise us deal [appearance] money and after the race, they would come up with an excuse not to pay us the money. Who was the backbone? *We* were the backbone. If you crashed and needed money, Larry [Carrier] would help you. I've had him ask how things were. He wanted to make sure all of us were ready to race. I knew if I had trouble, he'd come through. I never did ask him for a deal. But at other tracks, I would have to. Almost all of us had to work the tracks to get some appearance deal 'cause the purses weren't worth a flip."

Paul was in the inaugural World 600 on June 19, 1960, and had problems like most everybody with the disintegrating speedway. He started 34th finishing 58th.

"I fell out, broke a ball joint. Up in three and four there were two great big places torn out. There was just enough room between those two places where if you could hook your left front on the lower side of one, your right front wheel would miss the big hole. It would stay just enough on that asphalt where it wouldn't tear the ball joint up. But you would get forced into that big one every now and then by lapped cars. After a while it broke a ball joint. Before I fell out, Joe Lee Johnson, the eventual winner, was seven laps down. I was runnin' second and Jack Smith was leadin' when I broke a ball joint. I kept watching him [Jack] hittin' that thing and thought, 'He's going to tear the right front corner out of the Pontiac.' The story is he [Joe Lee] won, but at the time I fell out, he was back in eighth. I think he was so far down when Smith fell out they had to wait and let him catch up before counting the laps again. I was running second and on a pit stop, I remember Jess and I looking and Johnson was a lot of laps down. Of course, if I hadn't broken a ball joint, I would have won it. But so would a lot of people."

Paul found out later that he didn't get credit for any laps that day.

"There was a wreck on the front straightaway and I got into it and cut a left front tire on the debris. I spun, but when I got under control, I was still back far enough I could cut across to my pits. They said before the race, 'No cuttin' across the infield.' I put a tire on and got back in the race. Now this happened early and I ran the rest of the race and was already disqualified. I didn't cut across to gain anything. I tried to tell them, 'Hey, I had a flat tire. I would have to gone all the way around spreadin' debris and tearin' my car all to pieces. All I had to do was get over to the pits. I didn't gain anything and they still disqualified me. Didn't get any money. I used up my tires and gas and didn't think I'd done anything wrong. When it was over, I told them why I did it, but it didn't go anywhere."

The record reflects that positions 55 through 60 were Richard Petty, Lee Petty, Bob Welborn, Paul Lewis, Junior Johnson, and Lennie Page respectively. Each got credit for zero laps and zero money won. NASCAR let them continue to risk their lives in one of the most crash-filled events in history, the longest stock car race ever, without compensation.

Paul's fiery crash at Nashville on August 7, 1960, was quite spectacular to everybody ... but Paul.

"I came off the second turn, blew a right rear, spun around, ripped the gas tank open slidin' along the guardrail. That's what caused the fire. That was sort of an insignificant thing as far as crashes. It's just something you did quite often. Just another wreck. Flame out. Burned it. You have so many different kinds of wrecks. [Paul laughs at its insignificance.] I went to Greenville with a brand new '61 Chevrolet. It was a dirt track and I went practicing and it slipped out of high gear. You use deceleration instead of the brake. When it got a bite, it went straight into the inside bank. I rolled eight times. It landed on its wheels on fire. I got out with my own fire extinguisher and put the fire out. My two front teeth are porcelain. I broke my teeth on the steering wheel. [Paul chuckles.] We had just built that car. We only ran it on paved tracks and super speedways. Promoters paid us better for newer cars ... evidently they paid us pretty good or I wouldn't have taken that brand new car there on dirt. It was a loss."

At Darlington for Southern 500 in 1960, Paul confronted Chevrolet about the availability of racing parts necessary to compete. He went to bat for all independents.

"The engines weren't worth a flip. You could put the clearances in and they would not stay together. I had been raisin' cane with Norris Friel of NASCAR. I made up my mind, when I get to Darlington, something's going to give. Norris had been listening. He knew everybody had been gripin' about it. So I got there and the same old problem. All we're gettin' is drag racing, street stock stuff. I said, 'Norris, I've talked to an attorney and if we're not going to have parts numbers we need to race with, what the factory guys are runnin', there's gonna be problems. If I can stop this race, I'll do it, get an injunction.' I left and heard Norris over the loud speakers, 'All you independent guys and the people from Chevro-

A fiery crash on August 7, 1960, in Nashville did not stop Paul from continuing on to a tenacious 16th place finish in the rain-shortened race.

On August 14, 1960, Paul took tenth in the Western North Carolina 500 at Weaverville. Note the two plates bolted on to keep the driver's door closed (Paul Lewis).

let, up in my office.' So we all met up in the stands where the scorers stood on the inside of the pits after the regular scoring stand was knocked down by Johnny Allen in the previous race. Norris said, 'Tell these people [two Chevrolet engineers] what you told me.' I said, 'This is supposed to be *stock* car racin'. You're not runnin' stock engines. Now I can understand doin' this trick stuff inside with the clearances. But your rods, your pistons, valves, valve springs, the stuff you're runnin', we can't get it. We're blowin' engines right and left.' All of the guys have been talking to me about this, the independents. We either get access to the parts your people have been runnin' or Mr. Friel can tell you what I'm going to do.'

'This man's talking about doin' legal things' [Friel said,] and that got their attention. [The engineers said], 'We'll take care of the situation.' I said, 'Norris, they're buyin' time. They're not going to do anything. They were supposed to get us paperwork to get the right parts numbers, not the ones they had there to hand out. They brought parts around later for us to look at and I said, 'We're dummies, but not that dumb. I have been racin' Chevrolets for years. These parts are the same parts I run in my '60 El Camino that I went drag racin' with.' The engineers said, 'Well it is the good parts.' I said, 'It is not! These parts are not any better than what I've got now. It won't live.' 'Can you and your crew chief come out in the infield?'

We went there and they opened the trunk and got a set of heads and headers out. It was parts probably not as good as what I had. They were going to give me these parts and Jesse wanted to take them. 'Noooo way. They're tryin' to bribe us. We're not going take their junk. Go over to one of those factory cars and get a set of heads and headers and I'll shut my mouth.' 'We can't do that. Those cars don't belong to us.' I said, 'Come on. You people been spendin' money on racin' for years. Racin' wouldn't be what it is today if the factories didn't get involved.' I wouldn't take it. I went back to Norris and I gave them a length of time to come up with parts. They kept writin' me and sendin' me part numbers. Fortunately, I had people in both the Chevrolet and Ford place that could recognize the parts weren't very good. We were able to buy some better parts than we had, but we never did get the real super trick parts."

On August 13, 1961, Paul was an active participant in the abbreviated Western Carolina 500 at Asheville-Weaverville Speedway where angry fans all but caused a riot. "When we started, the asphalt broke up and got bad. The windshield got broken early on and the glass got down inside my uniform and in the back of the seat. I was sitting up tryin' to drive like this. [Paul leans forward.] I couldn't see with all the dirt and debris. I couldn't drive because it cut up my back. They red flagged us because of the track conditions. They [the fans] didn't want their money back, they wanted to see the race. A bunch of drunks got a pickup and backed it in the pit entrance and eight or ten were in the back. We were all gathered around and couldn't get out. I looked down in turn one and saw one of those old army six-bys with the tandem axle; a crane ... a wrecker. I said, 'I'll move that truck if you guys go and stand on the runnin' board. If the keys are in it, I'll move that truck.' I went and got that sucker cranked, got it turned around, and drove toward pit road. [Paul chuckles.] The two men on the runnin' board weren't paying attention and these guys ran up and jerked the key out. Richard [Petty] and I were standin' side by side. Richard's pretty tall, maybe six or seven inches taller. They were throwin' bottles and everything and a bottle hit Richard in the top of the head. BONK! Richard dropped down and I saw him walkin' through there

Paul Lewis had a brand new 1961 Jess Potter Chevrolet to campaign for 21 of 52 races that season. He finished 28th in the Grand National standings (Paul Lewis).

in a squatted position. He said, 'It's too rough up here for me.' Well Pop Eargle went and got a loggin' chain. That chain was ten or twelve feet long and he had it run through his hand and wrapped around his right arm. He said, 'I'll move 'em.' Buddy, he came up with that log chain [Paul laughs.] and began swinging it. They scattered like somebody had thrown a snake in there. I think he hit two or three of them. I didn't do it, but they shoved the truck down pit road with no driver in it after those guys fell out of the bed. A guy was runnin' to get in and get it stopped. [Paul laughs.] That was the end of that."

For the record, Paul finished 20th, one spot ahead of Reb Wickersham. The 1961 Southern 500 on September 4, 1961, found Paul following a crash trying to happen.

"Poor ol' Tiny. Norris made the statement, 'Give Tiny an anvil at eight o' clock in the morning and he'll have it tore up by five.' [Paul chuckles.] Bless his heart. Run a 500-lap race and I'll guarantee you somewhere down the line he'd get his and your sheet metal mixed

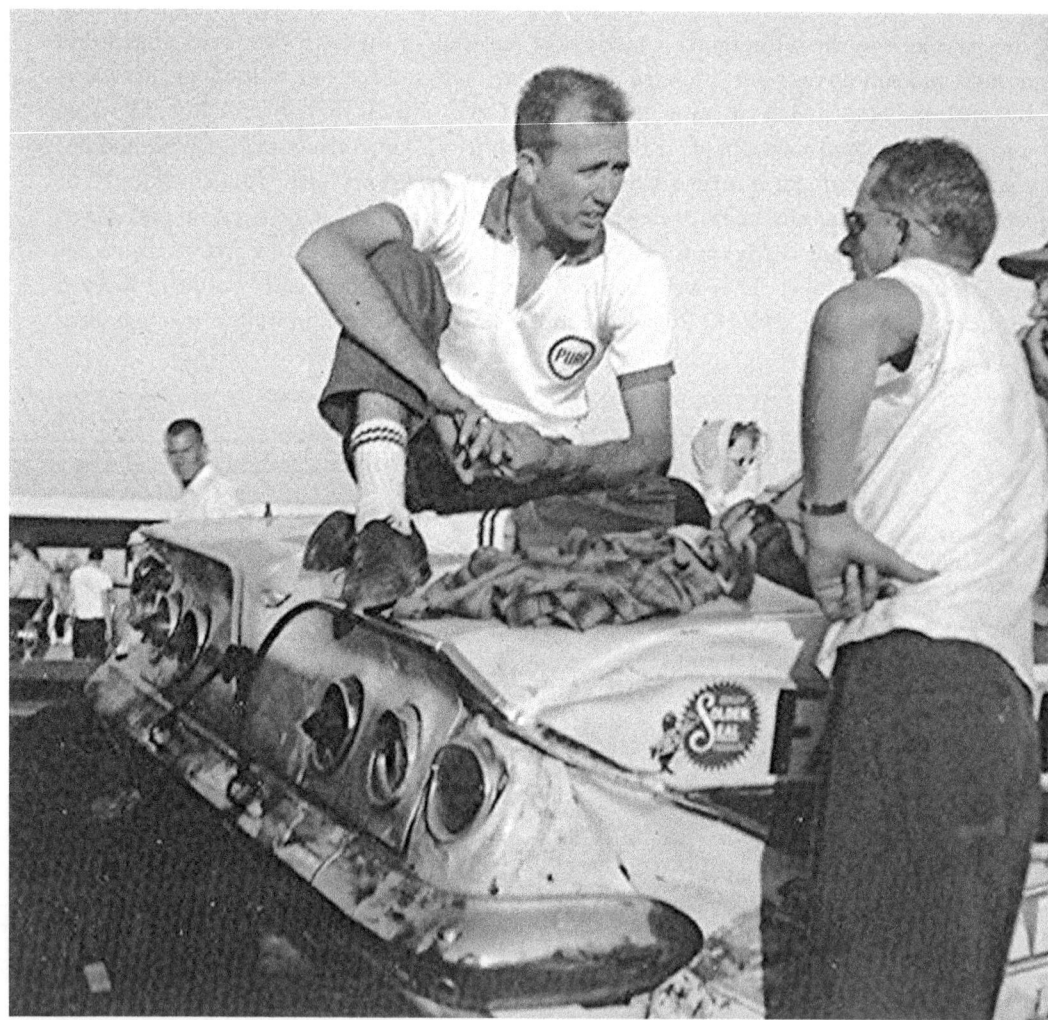

Paul holds court on the rear deck of his '61 Chevy, which shows signs of wear and tear. Note the taillights still mostly in place (Paul Lewis).

up. He kept bouncing off the fourth turn rail and I knew sooner or later he was going to come off too hard and cause a spill. I'm runnin' too close behind him and the guys behind are runnin' all over me. They can't see what's goin' on like I can. So I kept pushin' 'em back and pointin' at Tiny. [Paul looks back making hand gestures.] After four or five laps, he came off that corner and clipped the guardrail and when he came down, I backed off a little to see if I had a chance to get by. He came down and his right rear corner had already come around and caught the right side of my car, spun me, and I got it perfectly backwards. I slid all the way to the finish line. Bob Colvin [president of the Darlington Raceway] named me 'Spinner' after that because I had the longest slide backwards at Darlington. [Paul laughs.]

"When I got stopped, it was in the middle of the straightaway. I'm sittin' there gettin' ready to pull out and Marvin Porter from California came through full bore. When he saw me, he locked it down [CLAP], the car spun around [CLAP], and it struck me [CLAP]. I was holdin' the streerin' wheel so tight it pulled the column out of the dash. I had that steering wheel in my lap. I looked at him and realized he was unconscious and jumped out of my car right fast because I was all right. I got him out and Marvin Porter was a big man and I couldn't handle him. [Paul chuckles.] I got him by the nape of the neck and dragged him across the track to the pit road. I didn't think about it, but that had to be funny. [Paul laughs.] He was knocked completely out.

"Anyway, that's how I got my nickname. We were at a press conference at Bristol. People standin' around and I walked through the door and Bob Colvin said, 'Hey Spinner!' How ya doin'?' He proceeded to tell people why. He was a super guy. Bob Colvin and Larry Carrier are the two best promoters I ever dealt with and they looked out for the small people. Bob Colvin and Larry Carrier were just super good to the independent guys."

The record shows in the 1961 Southern 500, Paul, Marvin, and Woodie Wilson crashed together for 33rd, 32nd, and 34th respectively. Tiny motored on for nearly 300 more laps before finally crashing out near the end for a decent 15th place finish.

The attempt to unionize the drivers in 1961 provided an opportunity for his peers to see exactly what Paul Lewis was all about.

"That organization thing, Herman Beam and I were the only ones that wouldn't go along with it. We went to Weaverville, pulled up to the gate, and were goin' to sign in. A guy had a form he wanted me to sign attesting that I never was a member of any organized labor, blah, blah, blah, and the whole nine yards. I looked and said, 'I don't need to sign that.' He said, 'You do.' 'No, I won't

On October, 14, 1962, in the National 400, Paul ran the Osborne Brothers "dragster" to the front chasing Junior Johnson when it blew for 35th (Greg Fielden).

sign it. I don't have anything to do with that. I don't have to sign.' He said, 'Well you can't get through that gate.' I said, 'Fine with me, but you call Bruner [chief steward Johnny Bruner], Bill France, or somebody that knows what's happenin'. I do not have to sign that. The car belongs to me. If he don't want me to run, fine! I'll just take my car and go home.' He said, 'They said you're gonna have to sign.' I wouldn't do it. So I was getting in my car and he must have called Bruner or somebody. He came runnin' out there 'Hey, wait a minute.' I'm in my car ready to pull out. He said, 'Come here and sign this pit pass.' He was very arrogant. All those people were arrogant back then. These people had to be smart back then. Had a little authority, you know. I wasn't going to sign because I hadn't been a party to it. I didn't approve because I didn't want to be a part of a national organization of labor. I told them at the Nashville meeting that I would gladly be part of a local. We do it ourselves. But I don't want to be part of a national organization. It would have probably made us a little more money for a while, but eventually they would have taken us over entirely. I didn't believe in it."

At Charlotte for the 1962 National 400, Paul was in Lewis Osborne's Chevrolet Old 97, a dragster.

"They called me to drive. He had a drag racing engine in that thing. Man that thing was strong. They said, 'Now we want to get recognized. This won't live very long, but take it to the front if you can.' He told me what kind of engine it had in it. When he told me about the parts, I *knew* it was strong. When they dropped the green flag, I went towards the front and ran, but I knew that engine was going to come apart. Junior Johnson was leading that tank driver from Cincinnati, Nelson Stacy. I worked my way through the field and got by Stacy and Junior was in front. Stacy was behind me. He couldn't do anything with Old 97. He was runnin' pretty close, though. I felt that engine rattle in the straightaway and knew it was gonna come apart. I did like this to Stacy [Paul points he was going low]. Sure enough, it came apart and I held it down. Stacy should have went to the outside. He didn't. He came to the inside. Well, when the car got sideways, it caught him. It came around and he went up against the guardrail. If he had went the way I pointed, he would have cleared it. I was headed to the front. It was strong. I started somewhere back in the thirties and around thirty or forty laps I was up there chasing Junior Johnson down ... with a drag racing engine. I could set a car up and get by 'em quick. With a car that fast, it was hard to work your way around those cars. Once I got to the faster cars, I was able to get around them pretty good. It was strong."

The record reflects that Paul started 25th and finished 35th, completing 142 laps. At the 1965 Atlanta 500, Paul partnered with the legendary Herman Beam. The back-story must be told first. (Note: Anytime Herman Beam is quoted, read it in a slow drawl.)

"Ford Motor Company gave Herman two cars for Cale [Yarborough]. They were '63s. He and Cale changed the sheet metal on them. I think they ran all of '63. Herman messed up at the 500 at Darlington [in 1964]. Cale would have won, but Herman, being the conservative that he was, never had any extra parts. Prerace, he took the wheel bearings out instead of putting new ones in, which all the factory cars did. They put everything new in before each race. He didn't want to jeopardize his deal so he took the wheel bearings out, cleaned them, spec'd them to make sure they were good, and put them back in. Normally, independents do that. That's what *he* did. Cale was runnin' real good. He come in the pits with a burned out wheel bearing and Herman took it apart. Two factory men saw the wheel bearing and said, 'Herman, were those new wheel bearings?' Herman says, 'Well ... no. I took 'em all apart all the way around and cleaned 'em real good and they all looked real good and I packed 'em and put 'em back in.' The factory people just walked away and he lost his deal with Ford. You can't really blame him. He didn't have any idea he could go to Holman-Moody and get anything he wanted. He had never been able to do that so he didn't think about getting new wheel bearings. He was just doin' like he always had."

The records show Herman and Cale ran 14 races together in 1963 and 19 in 1964. Paul bought one of Herman's 1964 Fords for the 1965 Mopar-less season.

"I bought one of the cars. I hired Herman to be crew chief, to keep the car ready. Bless his heart, you had to really push him to get him to do things. We ran real good in that car. I sat on the pole at Harris. The first short track I'd raced it. They [Cale and Herman] never sat on the pole and didn't finish a lot. Herman was real good. That's the reason I wanted him. I mean a perfectionist, an absolute perfectionist. He was slow as seven-year itch, but that's just the way he was.

"After qualifying, we got ready to put the car on the racetrack, it started missing. Could not find that miss. They kept hollerin' to bring the car out because I was on the pole. G.C. Spencer was outside. Finally, it ran pretty good and stopped misfiring. I thought, 'Maybe I fouled a plug.' I put the car on the line and on the parade laps it didn't misfire until they dropped that green and [CLAP] I'm gone! Dick Hutcherson qualified third, G.C.'s on the outside pole. Hutch rooted G.C. out and was second. I pulled out eight or ten car lengths and the thing started misfiring. So Hutch caught me and hit my bumper because my car wouldn't pull out of the corner it was misfiring so bad. When it would take hold, I'd pull away. We ran forty or fifty laps and finally the car got so bad I thought, 'I'm going to have to pull it in.' At least we could find the misfire and finish. We never did find the misfire. After the race, Hutch said, 'I want to know what in the hell you were tryin' to prove.' 'What do you mean?' 'Tryin' to make an ass out of me?' I said, 'Man, I had a bad misfire in that thing. The reason you was catchin' me is it had a misfire. If it hadn't, you would have never seen me. I'd have run away and left you, man. It would pick up and I'd run good and it would start misfiring again. That's why you were catchin' me. I wasn't doin' anything intentionally. Believe you me, I wish that thing hadn't been misfiring because I would have blown your doors off! You wouldn't have seen the rear of my car.' He was in a factory-backed Ford from Holman-Moody."

Paul ran into the same problem with Ford he had years earlier with Chevrolet and confronted top man Jacques Passino. Paul phoned Dearborn.

"'Mr. Passino, this is Paul Lewis.' 'Yeah Paul, I know you.' 'You may or may not be aware, but this engine stuff that we're tryin' to run, my past history with Chevrolet I couldn't get good parts. Now I'm in a Ford and I still have the same problem.' He said, 'You're not supposed to have a problem. You're supposed to be able to go to your local dealer and order those.' 'No sir, cannot do it. They don't have part numbers.' So we talked about things, the independents, NASCAR rules, so on and so forth. He said, 'Can you be at Holman-Moody in the morning?' 'I sure can.' 'You be at Holman-Moody in the morning.'

"So I go to Holman-Moody and back up to the loading ramp. Some smart guy says, 'What do you want?' 'Mr. Holman or Mr. Moody ... either one here?' 'Well, I don't know. What do you want?' 'You just go back there and ask if Mr. Passino has talked to them.' So he took off. Ralph Moody came out and says, 'What's goin' on out here?' I said, 'Did you

Paul pits during Charlotte's National 400 on October 17, 1965. He notched a fine ninth place finish near the end of his busiest season (Paul Lewis).

talk to Mr. Passino?' 'I didn't talk to anybody.' I said, 'You better talk to Mr. Holman. Mr. Passino is going to call you people. I'm over here picking up a short block. He said for me to be here and I could buy one.' 'What I got was before they blueprinted it.' I said, 'That's all right, I can blueprint it. I can put all the clearances in.' Boy he went back in and was gone a long time. Evidently he must have called Passino. Mr. Moody came out and said, 'What's this about you and Passino?' I said, 'I was wantin' to buy an engine. The local Ford dealers can't get this stuff that you guys are runnin'. I'm tired of blowin' engines and want to buy what you guys are runnin'. Passino told me to be over here this mornin' and I could buy a short block.' He said, 'You got any money?' I said, 'How much?' He said, 'Four hundred dollars.' He told that guy to get that forklift, get one of those crate engines, and put it in my truck. I paid him and left. Four hundred dollars for a short block 427 was dirt cheap, but you had to do all the machine work.

"I butted heads with Ford. I didn't butt heads with Chrysler, but I give them a hard time. And Chevrolet, I really raked them over the coals. I'm the guy that's the spokesman for the independents. I will play by their rules as long as they are fair for everybody. But don't make your rules favor some and everybody else have different rules. I'll play the game as long as I get a fair chance, but don't jerk me around."

Subbing for Cale Yarborough at a local showing of the 1965 Hollywood racing classic *Redline 7000*, Paul peers from the cockpit of the competitor's racecar (Paul Lewis).

Wendell Scott was Paul's good friend.

"Wendell Scott, bless his heart. He would make a pit stop with only a lug wrench, floor jack, and his son. I said, 'Jesse, let's change his tires for him.' And we did. 'Now Wendell, when we have a caution, let me come in first and as soon as I get out, you come in. We're going to change your tires for you.' So we had the air wrenches and we started changing his tires. He started writin' columns in the Danville, Virginia, paper. I had an uncle there and he used to tell me how Wendell used to talk about me in the newspaper. I believe in being fair with everybody. Treat everybody equal. If the Lord blesses you with something and you can do for other people, then I think you should do it. Spread it around."

Always the teacher, Paul helped The Turtle find some speed.

"We were at Daytona. It was tough at times for him to make the field. 'Herman, you're not going to make the field.' There were some cars at the end runnin' faster than him. He'd say, 'What am I runnin'?' I'd give him his time and say, 'You're going to have to pick it up.' He'd go back out and come in. 'Herman, you're just not runnin'. I can hear it. You're lettin' off on the front straightaway way too early. You need to drive on down into the corner.' He said, 'Well ... it's like this ... I get down at the end of that straightaway and I tell myself, "Don't lift here," and that heel stays down, but that foot just comes up automatically.' [Paul laughs.] 'You have to run farther down in there.' Finally, he began running a little faster.

When he would come in, I'd give him a false time. I was still showin' him runnin' a little slow, but he was pickin' it up. I got him running fast enough by givin' him slower times. He qualified and made the field because he was runnin' fast enough on those last few laps of practice. I never did tell him about givin' him slow times."

After a 1966 summertime string of Maryville [third], Weaverville [third], and Bristol [fourth and second], Paul returned to Maryville on July 28 for the second time in six weeks.

"Started dead last because the boys jacked the car up to get the asphalt tires off and put the dirt tires on and knocked the fitting off the rear end housing cooler. Spent the whole time gettin' it back on. Had no practice, no qualifying, started dead last, ran them down, and won. I kept workin' my way through the field and got with the faster cars. Those guys were beatin' and bangin' all over the place like they do on dirt and they finally beat themselves to death. Once I got the lead, I ran off and left them. I made the car win at Marysville because I made it handle and stayed out of trouble.

"The way I won was unique. If I had qualified in the top five and won the race, it probably wouldn't have been so outstanding. But starting dead last with no time trial, no practice ... I guessed at the chassis. It was a torsion bar car. I had never run a torsion bar car on dirt. That car was a whole new deal to me. Richard [Petty] said to me one time, 'What did you do to that old car? I never could get that car to handle.' He had tore it to pieces and never could get it handling. His racing outfit was settin' over there with all this extra stuff and my old truck sittin' over here. Dodge truck, stake bed with a couple of extra wheels and transmission. I said, 'Well Richard [CLAP], it's like this.... I got two sets of

July 28, 1966, in the Smoky Mountain 250 in Maryville, Tennessee, Paul attacked from the back, beat the best, and became a first-time Grand National winner (Paul Lewis).

torsion bars from you and two sets of rear springs and one or two extra shocks. One of those setups I use on super speedways and one on short tracks.' I really didn't have much choice. [Paul chuckles.] He wanted to know what *I* was runnin'. What *I'm* runnin' is what *you* sold me. That's all I've got. I *had* to make it work. He turned, scratched his head, and walked off.

"We had to be super good at chassis setup because we didn't have much. These guys with factory-backed cars had trailers full of parts. They'd try all kinds of springs and shocks, combinations of gear ratios, and the whole nine yards. I pulled a real tall gear at Marysville. Richard asked me what kind of gear I pulled. He couldn't believe I pulled a gear that tall. In essence, what happens, you have a super horse-powered engine and if you're runnin' dirt, and if you're not getting a hold of the dirt, you're not getting anywhere. I had a tall gear and no horsepower. After that track dried, I was hookin' up. Of course I knew how to run that track, too. I was getting a bite and those factory cars were spinnin' all over. They'd come off the corner spinnin' and I'd just drop down, get a bite, and go on. When I got in the top ten, I got to lookin'. I said, 'Man! Hey! Fifth, fourth, third, second.' I gotta ease off a little bit and not push the car real hard. Once I got the lead, I didn't want to run any harder than I had to. We were good with what we had. I know this sounds like bragging, but there was a lot of good racecar drivers that were independents. Had they had factory rides, their names would be on top of the sport today."

The independents lacked only the deep pockets of the factories, not the intelligence and know how.

"We drove a racecar by the seat of our pants. I mean guys that knew how to tell people what to do to the car. You didn't have chassis people and shock people that drivers have now. We told the people what to do to the car. Change this, change that; it's doin' this, it's doin' that, and we'd tell them what to do. Back then, we knew what we were doin' and could set up a racecar. We were settin' a car up the way we wanted it to feel and knew what it would take to get that done. I always ran good at Martinsville. It was flat, but I had a lot of flat track experience. I'd run that old '58 on dirt and go to some other tracks and they'd give me a hard time. They'd say, 'You been runnin' outlaw again, ain't ya?' I'd say, 'Yeah I have.' The dirt was all over my car. [Paul laughs.] Bill Gazaway used to really give us a hard time when we run outlaw."

Paul Lewis partnered with legendary Herman Beam, a competent driver on the track and a genius in the garage.

"Herman was brilliant! He was a chemist. We were at Daytona. My car wasn't runnin' real good and the engine wasn't turnin' like I thought it should. I had a lower gear in it than he liked. I came into the garage and he said, 'How many RPMs you turnin'?' I said, 'That old hemi's turnin' sixty-one, sixty-two hundred.' Man, he almost came unglued. He didn't want it to turn that kind of RPMs. He'd been turnin' his engines fifty-five hundred. I wanted to turn about seventy, seventy-one, seventy-two to get up in the horsepower. He got his pencil out. He took a tape and measured the diameter of the tire, took the RPMs of the engine, took the gear ratio in the rear end, and said, 'Well, you're runnin' about 213 down that back straightaway.' [Paul slaps the table.] Brilliant! Absolutely brilliant! [Paul laughs.] Man, that's unbelievable!"

"I'd go to the garage at night and he'd be working. He wouldn't work during the day. He was a night person. We'd be workin' at ten or eleven o'clock. The helpers needed to go

Paul and the legendary Herman Beam pore over an engine block with the care and precision that was the hallmark of their work and cars together (Greg Fielden).

to work the next day. Well, he didn't have to because I'm payin' him a weekly salary. While building an engine, he'd have a block of glass and a main bearing cap with some sandpaper workin' on the clearances. Then he'd get his calipers out and he'd measure. We didn't have anybody to do that kind of machine work. He'd sit there and hand-fit that blamed engine on a cinder block with a piece of glass on it and sandpaper. And, by George, they lived! I turned a lot more RPMs than he and Cale ever thought about. Herman wouldn't lie. I'd say, 'Herman, what kind of clearance do we have on that rod cap or side clearances or piston clearances or main caps?' and he'd tell me. If it wasn't enough, I'd tell him that we needed another thousandth or half thousandth. Went to Daytona with that Plymouth and blew. Brand new fresh engine. The engine hadn't been runnin' good. I figured out when the car got hot, it would start boggin' down. It wouldn't turn enough RPMs. I knew those rings on the pistons were swellin' against the cylinder walls. I asked him, 'What kind of clearance were you runnin'? 'Uh, 'bout one and a half.' I knew it needed to be two and a half. He didn't put the clearances in it I told him in the pistons to walls clearance that was needed and that's why it seized up.

"He didn't like low gear ratios and we were at Richmond when it was dirt. The car

Instrumental from the start with Larry Carrier in the creation of the Bristol International Speedway, Paul poses there from his potent 1965 Plymouth 1 (Paul Lewis).

run pretty good, but wasn't turnin' enough RPMs. We had way too high a ratio and I said, 'No wonder it's not fast. Put that 588 in there and this car will come alive.' He didn't want to put that low a gear in because it would turn too many RPMs. 'Herman, you work for me. I pay your salary. It's my car. If we blow the engine, it's my fault for puttin' the gear. I ran in the top five about the whole race and came up to lap Curtis Turner. For some reason or another, Turner had it in for me. I never did figure out what. They gave him the move over flag for a couple of laps and he wouldn't. Runnin' on the inside of me and Pearson, we couldn't run real hard because he's down on the inside. Finally, he muscles his way between Pearson and me. Pearson's getting away from Petty and me and those on back are on our bumpers. [Paul chuckles.] I took him down to the first turn with my foot on the brake still acceleratin'. I took him too far and backed off my brake and by that time he'd gone too far. That's the last time I saw him." [Paul laughs.]

The record shows this 100-miler on September 11, 1966, was won by Pearson five laps ahead of Buck Baker with Paul third, and Turner fourth, eight laps back. The Lewis-Turner rematch was at Martinsville two races later on September 26, 1966.

"I don't know what his problem was, but he ran me up over the curb in three and four. I was tryin' to get underneath him and he came down and I got in the grass and spun. I didn't lose anything 'cause they threw the caution. He went in the pits. I didn't go around the racetrack, I went in the pits to check the car and change the left front. I go back out, but it had done a little more damage to him. He came startin' out of the pit and the wall was right there. I was coming off the fourth turn, the rest of the cars were ahead of me, and he started easin' out. I pulled down out of the fast groove and headed straight for his door. I meant to run halfway through him! He put that thing in reverse and backed it up. [Paul laughs loudly.] That's the way we settled our problems back then."

The record shows that Paul finished sixth, ten laps behind winner Fred Lorenzen. Curtis dropped out for 31st. What followed could be called the Chicken Dinner Peace Talks.

"We were at Wilkesboro and Junior Johnson and Holly Farms always fed us on Saturday. I was standin' in line and his [Turner's] crew was around. One of his crew said, 'We wouldn't have to do so much work if certain people would quit beatin' and bangin' on our cars.' I said, 'I'll tell you what you do. You tell that stupid driver of yours to respect other people on the racetrack. Quit runnin' over me, I'll quit runnin' over him.' They started laughing. They knew I was right. They had to do extra work because I was beatin' and bangin' on their car. I was tryin' to get to him before he got to me. As far as mad, I can't remember havin' any problems with anybody. I try to get along. If my car wasn't runnin' good, I'd stay out of people's way. If my car was runnin' good, I expect them to return the favor. I didn't intentionally run over people and beat and bang. I didn't want to tear my car up [Paul laughs]. I wasn't some smart aleck that thought I knew it all. I just rolled with the flow, so to speak."

Not only a top-notch racer, Paul knew a thing or two about what it took to make a race car go, sometimes with a little sleight of hand.

"Householder, the top man at Chrysler, and Bill France were buttin' heads right and left. NASCAR waited until late in the year to announce the new cubic inch displacements on super speedways for the next year [1966]. Chrysler got caught with no 405 engines. I got caught, too. They announced it so late; Chrysler couldn't get the production set up. Householder got a machine shop in California to build the crank units to destroke the 426 engines. You could run a 426 on the short tracks, but you couldn't run on the super speedways. Had to be 405. Well, I keep thinking about it and races are comin' up. 'I'd like to have a 405 and I can't build one out of what I've got. I don't have the money and the facilities.' I kept thinking and remembered the kind of cubic inch testers NASCAR used. You take the plug out, spin the engine; it goes up to a certain amount of pressure. I remembered the brand and it was made in Sioux City, Iowa. So I said, 'Herman, I want to run Atlanta and I think I've figured out how to do it. I'm going to order this tester. What we're going to do is use brass shims and shim the valves on the valve seat all the way around so when the engine cranks up to full compression, it'll bleed just enough by the valves that it'll crank up 405.' Herman said, 'Oh no, that won't work. And that's a lot of work.' 'Well Herman, do you want to race or not? We're out of racin' except on short tracks.' I convinced him, so I ordered a cubic inch tester. The night before we went to Atlanta, we started real early. We shimmed the valves on a 426 hemi. It took all night long gettin' the right thickness of the shims. The valves come down and the shims get creased it on the valve seat and the shims would stay there as long as there isn't any ignition with the plugs out. I took it to Atlanta, pulled into the garage, and go through inspection. The inspector came up with his cubic inch tester, stuck that thing down in that hole, 'Cranked her over ... 405. 'OK, you can go.' There was a guy leanin' up against the gate goin' into the garage area. We got the engine ready. I fired it up. It blew those shims out of the exhaust pipe. They hit the guy's leg over there. He has no idea what happened. [Paul laughs hard.] He looked down and brushed them off. He probably thought I broke something in the engine."

Next was Shims Part II.

"Householder came up to me one day. My truck was sittin' next to the Pettys. He stepped between the trucks and said, 'I'm going to tell you a story, I hope you'll tell me one.' 'Mr. Householder, whatever.' We had been cordial. So he proceeded to tell me what he had done and how he had not got all his engine assemblies. He figured that the guy [contractor in California] had sold extra engines assemblies and I ended up with one. I said, 'Mr. Householder, I couldn't afford one. There's no way I could afford one of those assemblies.' I told him that I destroked mine. He kept questioning me, 'What did you do?' 'I destroked it.' 'How'd you do that?' 'You destroke one by short rods and the throws on your crankshaft. Biggest thing is your rods.' 'Where'd you get the parts?' 'Well, you know there's a lot of good crank people in Charlotte.' He said, 'Yeah, there's some real good machinists over there.' I said, 'I had to get the crank turned for that 405 stroke and they made the rods.' He said, 'That's real good. I'm glad you're makin' the race.' He walked off.

"He came back a later and said, 'I'm havin' a little trouble with your story. I got to thinkin' about that crank situation. I don't believe you did what you did. I don't think those people in Charlotte could have done that, not takin' anything away from them. I don't think you told me exactly what you did.' I said, 'Mr. Householder, that's a 426.' [Paul claps and laughs.] 'You got that 426 through inspection?' 'Sure did,' and told him how. He absolutely could not believe what I did. I had that much desire to race that day. He said, 'That's just absolutely amazing!' From that time on when Householder came around, he'd go, 'How ya doin' Paul? How's everything with you today?' I gained his respect. I outsmarted NASCAR. I got more of a charge out of out-smartin' them than I did getting the car in the race. It's not cheating. It's engineering. It's ingenuity. As an independent, if you run halfway decent, you had to bend the rules."

The record shows that on March 27, 1966, Paul's "modified" Plymouth started 36th and finished 17th in the Atlanta 500. Then he took a shot in Petty Plymouth 42 for the 1966 American 500 at Rockingham.

"Blew an engine. Matter of fact in the next lap or two, he [Richard] blew. That was my time with the Pettys. It was a recognition thing and I knew Chrysler was lookin' at me

Paul got a chance in a second Petty Plymouth on October 30, 1966, in Rockingham's American 500. He started 15th and had engine trouble for 29th (Paul Lewis).

after a win and runnin' a Plymouth. That may have had somethin' to do with the Pettys puttin' me in their car. But it turned out really bad. The problem was they pitted waaaay down at the end and I could not see the pits. When they wave a caution flag, Richard goes in first, then I go. They only had one crew. I had to wait until they got him out. Maurice [Petty] was tryin' to hold the board and I couldn't see anything. I knew about where it was, but didn't want to go in the next lap until I knew. I think he [Richard] got mad because Maurice slipped and fell down. But, I went in and made my pit stop the next lap. That could have had something to do with them not stayin' with me. I hope it didn't. That car was there to finish. His car was to run out front and win. If he fell out, everything went back on it [42]. He wouldn't get in the car [42] unless their other driver needed him. He couldn't have driven my car because I had to revamp the seat. Richard was tall and I was short."

For 1967, Paul moved to the handsome, swift, and winless A.J. King Dodge 1. After an eighth in the qualifier and 46th in the Daytona 500 due to a hub failure on the second lap, the King team met at Bristol where Paul was master.

"We came from Daytona. Hadn't run the car and they came to Bristol with the same bars, shocks, and setup we ran at Daytona. That car was terrible. I couldn't make the crew chief understand you can't run the same setup at Bristol you run at Daytona. He thought he knew it all. Qualified pretty good, in the top ten [actually 11th]. I ran 30 or 40 laps and had to get out. I've never had relief because I've never smoked, drank, caroused, or partied. I was always in pretty good physical shape. They put Sam McQuagg in. He went out and

In eight of Paul's 14 starts in 1967, he hustled A.J. King's beautiful blue Dodge Chargers, finishing in the top ten half the time (Paul Lewis).

run five or six laps and spun two or three times, and had to get out because he couldn't drive it. They got Bobby Isaac. Bobby ran four or five laps and couldn't drive it. He pulled that sucker in. I got back in and finished decent because a lot of cars fell out. Isaac paid me a compliment and I'll never forget it and don't hesitate to tell people. We were in the shower room and he looked at me and said, 'I'm going to tell you something. You gotta be some kind of a hell of a race driver.' I said, 'Well, gee, Bobby. Yeah man, whatever.' He said, 'That was absolutely the ill-handlingest, sorriest racecar I have ever set down in. Anybody that could drive that damn thing has got to be super human!'"

The record reflects that Paul lost the engine and finished 16th in the Southeastern 500 on March 19.

"The car was always beautiful and we went to Darlington and didn't have any lettering on the side of it. He put gold leaf lettering on it. I said, 'A.J., what are you doin' with that gold leaf on the quarter panel?' I already had a few marks on it. He said, 'I wanted it to look pretty for Activated Angels. That was the name of his cannin' company. I said, 'A.J., you don't want to do that. That won't stay on there. When I get to runnin', that'll all be gone.' He said, 'Don't get so close to the guardrail.' [Paul laughs.] I go back out practicing and I'm really gettin' the car handlin'. I set the car up like we all do and get that Darlington

Stripe. I came back in and had scraped all that gold leaf off the right side. He said, 'Oh my God! What happened to my gold leaf?' 'I told you not to put that on there. I told you what was gonna happen.' He said, 'Well you shouldn't have got up against it.' I said, 'I didn't come here to stroke. I came to race. If you're going to run fast at Darlington, you're going to get the Darlington Stripe.' I walked off."

The records show that on May 13, 1967, Paul had an outstanding sixth after starting 13th in the Rebel 400.

"The fast groove is when you go in to turn three, you know you're probably going to hit it every now and then. You try to get in the groove without hittin' the guardrail, but you don't have complete control because the cars were so heavy and the aerodynamics were terrible. The big block engined cars would run real fast down the back straightaway. The groove in turns three and four was right up to where you could feel and clip the guardrail. The more you pushed, the faster you got, you'd hit it a little bit more. If you went in too low, you would slide up and have to back off or really get into the guardrail. But if you hit it just right, you could pull it down just a little and let the car drift back up and it would stay in the groove. Tippin' the guardrail would set the car just right to really wade into it. It was a thrill! When you clipped it, you were just barely touching the accelerator because you wanted instant bite. When you touch the guardrail, you want that right rear wheel pullin' a little. You have your foot on the brake so you could tap it if you needed it. You clip the guardrail, hit the accelerator, and get that side bite. You were pickin' up the banking. It was like a dance. It was rhythm. You had to do the same thing every time and do it right. It was a thrill. I've raked from the door all the way back. If you back off you're really going to get into the guardrail. Don't let it scare you. You know you're runnin' good if you clip it."

Passing added a new dimension to negotiating Darlington's third turn.

"It's like a chess game. You planned your strategy from the beginning of the straightaways to the end of the straightaways. If you had somebody set up comin' off two, you run side by side. If you were underneath him, he knew you couldn't stay down. He was going to have to back off and let you go or you were going to have to back off and let him go. It depended on how brave you were. If you had your nose out a little, most of the time you could force him to ease off and let you go on in. If he didn't, it would crash us both. If somebody had me set up and got underneath me, I would ease off. I would wait to see if he would ease off first. Whichever one had his nose out front would be the one goin' in. You knew the ones not to race with. The ones you give plenty of room. Most of our passing at Darlington was in one and two. You had to be brave. You had to know your abilities and what you're doin' and stay on that accelerator. That was one place you really had to use your accelerator to maintain control. If you're havin' a rhythm problem, it was somethin' you had to work out for yourself. When a car gets out of shape, there is a certain amount of driving skill you have to apply as to whether you think you can drive out of it or go ahead and spin and try to save it." [Paul laughs.]

Paul Lewis took over the famous J.D. Bracken Chevelle 2 when Bobby Allison got the Holman-Moody factory Ford for the 1967 Grand National finale. After four races in 1968 — including a top five at Montgomery and a 13th in the rain-shortened World 600 — Paul Lewis' Grand National career was done. He raced some local sportsman events and later taught others on the short tracks of Tennessee. Along with his protégé, 2000 championship-winning driver Jeff Gilder, Paul formed RacersReunion.com, a successful and fascinating website devoted to the preservation of auto racing history. Throughout his career, Paul Lewis proved himself not only as a top-notch driver and mechanic, but that rarest of racer, a winning independent. He fought for the rights of the independent against NASCAR and all three manufacturers at one time or another. He shrewdly manipulated the rules to compete, pulled a much larger driver from his car to safety, and went fender to fender with legends. He could dish it out as well as take it. Paul was in shape then and near the end of his eighth decade looks like he could climb in the window of a stock car and do it all over again. Paul Lewis is a winning racer, a crafty mechanic, and a respected spokesman. But this gentleman would rather teach.

At Occoneechee Speedway's September 2009 historic festival in Hillsborough, North Carolina, Paul was fit and ready to buckle up and take on all comers (Paul Lewis).

7

Gene Hobby

The Racing Marine

Charles Eugene Hobby was born on October 17, 1937, in Apex, North Carolina, and still lives there. Gene, as he is known, was very athletic, playing football and other sports at Apex High School before attending East Carolina University from 1956 to 1958. He turned twenty-one in boot camp with the U.S. Marines Corps at Parris Island, South Carolina, where he again played football and won the championship. Gene was later stationed at Camp Lejeune, North Carolina, with the same troops that landed in Lebanon earlier that summer in Operation Blue Bat, which had prompted him to join the Marines. He was trained as a sniper in Hawaii due to his expertise as a high-scoring marksman and became a member of the Viet Cong [VC] Hunting Club, serving in the Vietnam War. Gene was honorably discharged in the summer of 1961. He mustered out of the Marines in time to drive his 1957 Ford Fairlane to Daytona for the 1961 Firecracker 250 on the Fourth of July.

"I got there a few days before the race and checked in at the Lynhurst Hotel. I had always heard about Smokey's Best Damn Garage in Town, so I went by and saw the Pontiacs he was preparing; a '61 for Fireball and a '60 for Panch. Also doing work on their cars were Curtis Crider and his '61 Mercury, Tiny Lund with Lyle Stelter's '61 Pontiac, and Roy Tyner and his '61 Ford. I hung out with these guys a couple of days. On race day I helped with Tiny's pit crew."

Curtis "Crawfish" Crider is a legendary racer from North Charleston, South Carolina, with vast experience winning hundreds of sportsman races in the Carolinas, Georgia, and Florida. Curtis opened his home to Gene and a life-long friendship was born.

"Curtis, his wife Mary Frances, and their two kids had an extra bedroom built next to the garage. I stayed with them about ten days after the Daytona and Atlanta races and helped Curtis on his racecar. They had to run Columbia on Thursdays. Curtis, his family, and I left Wednesday for Columbia towing the '60 Ford with their family car. We went by Tiny and Betty's fish camp outside of Monks Corner at Lake Moultree and had a very nice time. When we got to the outskirts of Columbia, the towcar ran out of gas. Curtis told me to get in the racecar, crank it up, and push the towcar. So we did, right through downtown to a truck stop when we got pulled over by the police. Curtis put his mouth and brain in gear, as he was a great talker and bull artist. He told the cops what happened and his kids were screamin' and dyin' for somethin' to eat. The only choice we had was to keep goin'. Before long, we were all out there laughin' and jokin' and they let us go. But it was a waste of time because a bad storm set in and the race was rained out."

Gene planned to start racing on his own, but his heart got in the way.

"I talked to Curtis about buying his '60 Ford racecar. I could make arrangements when I got home. I told him I'd see him at the Myrtle Beach race in about two weeks. My dad was a longtime produce trucker out of Pompano Beach, Florida. I found out when I got home that he was in bad financial shape and was about to lose his home and his rig. Crops had frozen a couple of times in Florida that winter and he hardly did any haulin'. So I gave him the funds I'd been savin' and would have to put off racin' for another year or two. It was a very disappointin' time.

Gene Hobby ready to race in 1964 (Gene Hobby).

"I started racin' in the spring of 1964 from the burnin' desire I'd had for years. I started to buy Herman Beam's car, but I couldn't get the Ford place up there, I was workin' in Henderson [North Carolina], to get off of it, you know? I didn't have a sponsor. My first racecar was a 1962 Dodge with a 413 cubic inch engine purchased from Larry Thomas from Trinity, North Carolina, for $1,500. Larry had three cars, all of them '62 Dodges, and he had run this one on all the short tracks. I stayed up there on weekends for about a month and worked on the car before I brought it home. I ate many a meal with him, his wife, his mother, and dad. I learned a lot about the car by spendin' time at his home and shop. He had a factory up there, boy. Anything you wanted in the Dodge. He had some hook-up with the Dodge factory somewhere 'cause he had everything a Dodge could possibly have. He wasn't needin' anything. He had a four-bay garage. They were country people, farm people, the nicest people you'd ever want to be around. Wade Thornburg was his chief mechanic and Darrell Bryant was there quite a bit."

Gene Hobby joined the Grand National tour.

"The first part of the 1964 season, I towed my 1957 Fairlane 500 with a tow bar and no trailer. Later that year, I purchased a 1962 Ford pickup and still used the tow bar. In order to have safety lights on the car when towin', I connected coated electric wire to the taillight wires of the towing vehicle and used safety pins to make the connections. I ran the wires down both sides of the racecar to the lights in the rear glass, and PRESTO ... I had safety taillights! In order to tow the racecar with a tow bar, you took both rear axles out so the rear gear, drive shaft, and transmission would not be affected with wear and tear. You used regular street tires and wheels on the front. In order for the engine to run cooler, we snapped every other fin off the water pump propeller to slow the water flow. Just a few little tricks I used now and then. Sometimes I'd tow to my parents' house before a race and need to go to the garage to work on it. Ron Ritter, the police chief in Apex, used to escort me to Prince's Auto Service with the blue lights on and I'd be behind him on the streets in 99. When I finished, I'd call Ron and he'd escort me back to my parents' house.

"I found out pretty quick that independents had to work a lot harder than the other drivers just to get through inspections. The big factory teams had crews to do all the work and we didn't. Usually, the first thing you would get from an inspector was a long list of things to do to the car. We would lose a lot of seat time, as far as practice was concerned, just making the car acceptable. The dirt tracks were not as bad about inspections as the paved ones and that is what I was running, the short paved and dirt tracks."

He explained some Gene Hobby racing R and D.

"I had a nice back yard for my research and development program. I did most of the general mechanics on the chassis, front end, rear end, tires, etc. I always found a good engine and carburetor person for tuning. Friends were a very important part of an independent's ability to go racing. I'd like to thank M.E. Whitmore and his dealership, Cotton Owens, Buddy Arrington, Roy Tyner and crew, Ollie Yates, Sr., Earl Sears, Ronald Hinesley, Barney Humphries, Bob King, Marvin Adcock, John Bennett, and Joe Holder.

"Before the races, I would check my race schedule and start phonin' promoters for the tracks ahead. They all wanted a full field of cars and some would agree to put you up in motels, but most would always pay you $200 to $300 'deal money' over what the purse paid. Some would hinge on it when you got to the pay-off window after the race. Buck and Buddy Baker were my friends. The promoter at one track owed Buck for the year before saying he would 'send the check,' which was a common cliché. Buck asked Buddy and me how much 'deal money' he promised us. When we got to the promoter, it was a very long story ... made short! Buck grabbed him up by the shirt collar and got close and personal with him. Buck got all of our deal money and his back pay."

Wendell Scott's crewman came to the rescue at Martinsville.

"Sometime durin' the race, I got tangled up with some other cars and continued on not knowin' anything was wrong. Even as I was getting passed by Fireball Roberts, he was pointing at the front of my car as he went by. Then NASCAR black flagged me and I had to come into the pits. When I did, I climbed out, looked at the front end, and to my surprise the front bumper was bent out on one end like a batterin' ram. Since I had accidentally pulled into Wendell Scott's pit, his son Frank just reached down with both hands and ripped and twisted that bumper off. He threw it aside, I jumped back in, and off I went. I'll never forget Frank Scott for doin' that."

The record reflects that on April 26, 1964, in the Virginia 500, Gene started 29th finishing 19th, the last man running. Fireball was fifth in his third from final start.

"Marvin Panch was one of the good guys, down to earth just like Richard [Petty]. We

April 12, 1964, at Hillsborough, North Carolina, Roy Tyner (9) slides off course as Gene, in his third big time start, chases Larry Thomas (36) down the backstretch (Gene Hobby).

Gene's Dodge (99) is at full right lock as he slides past John Anderson (20) with Ned Jarrett (11), Richard Petty (43), Fireball Roberts (22), and Wendell Scott (34) passing at Martinsville on April 26, 1964 (Gene Hobby).

were runnin' at South Boston in '64 and at the end of the race, Richard was in front and Marvin was behind. They came by me on the front stretch and as Marvin come off four, he clipped the right taillight, which was all plated up. It took the plate and the chrome. I didn't think anything about it with three or four laps to go and he went on. After the race, I was in the pits gettin' my car ready to tow back home and Marvin came up and said, 'Hey Gene. I'm really sorry I bumped your right rear back there. I was really after Richard and I wanted this race. I was tryin' my best to get him and I'm really sorry that happened.' I had no idea. He did. He looked me up and apologized."

The record shows that on May 17, 1964, Petty won and Panch was second at South Boston while Gene soldiered home in 11th. Getting to the races before the completion of the interstate highway system was arduous and preparing the racecar on the fly was worse.

"A lot of times we towed all night and all the next day. I left North Carolina on Friday night for the Southern Tour, which took in Nashville, Chattanooga, Birmingham, Valdosta, and the infamous Spartanburg race on June 26, 1964. I-40 was being cut through the mountains to Nashville with lots of detours. We got to Nashville at 4:30 P.M. on Saturday for the race on Sunday. We stayed at the same motel as Roy Tyner and his mechanic. We planned pit strategy and combined our two mechanics and tools. While towing from race to race, the people at truck stops would flock around the racecar and ask questions. One was always, 'Do you take pills before the race?' 'No!' But secretly, I did take a couple of bennies during towing at night to stay awake. I could see how you could get addicted to them because they would make you think you could whip King Kong! It was a $50 fine per pill if caught. I got them from my Dad, a produce hauler with Horace DeWitt, L.G.'s brother, out of Pompano Beach."

L.G. DeWitt was the famed car-owner of 1973 Winston Cup Champion Benny Parsons.

"We worked on our racers at truck stops and motel parkin' lots. I helped and witnessed a driver pull the engine out of his racecar using 4 x 4 lumber as a hoist support over the engine. We stripped the bed down in the motel room and placed a piece of plywood on top and set the engine on the plywood. He washed the engine parts in hot soapy water in the bathtub and rinsed them in a bucket of gasoline and put the engine back together and ran the race the next night.

"I got my first bump draft from Buck Baker in Nashville. He bumped me and how I saved it I don't know. He came up to me after the race not exactly to apologize, but to more or less let me know that he had to hit me because I was holdin' him up. Buck was always there to win and had to do what he had to do. If he hadn't liked me, he wouldn't have mentioned it. I understood completely.

"After most dirt track races, we had to magnaflux front end parts for cracks. The day of the race at Chattanooga, Joe Lee Johnson invited us to use his garage for repairs. I did not have the right rear gear to run the track. He gave me a rear gear out of a burned Plymouth wagon. I figured the ratio from the transmission and rear gear and ran in second the whole race. We did that on tracks of ⅜ths of a mile and less. From time to time, the Pettys brought me parts to the track. Lee was in charge at that time. All I had to do was call. I once towed to Manassas alone, which was about six hours, one way, and towed back home the same night in time to work my day job. In getting to the track, I stopped at a truck stop nearby and picked up a mechanic. I let him use my friend's NASCAR license that I borrowed before I left home. At a few towns where we raced, I picked up a one-deal sponsor for about $200 to $400 to put his name on the rear quarter panel. Once we bought an oil cloth and cut a rectangle out of it, duct taped it to the car, and put the sponsor's name on it."

Prior to the Chattanooga race on June 19, 1964, Gene found that it was possible to get his whole foot, boot and all, in his mouth.

"I had been tryin' to get with the promoter, but I never could get him to get a deal. We got to Chattanooga Monday night about ten o'clock and stopped at a big service station right there on Main Street. It was all lit up and everything and [Gene chuckles], had a phone booth right there on the corner. My wife's with me and I pulled my car in and we was towin' on the pickup truck. I went in and asked the station guy, 'Listen, we just got into town late and would it be all right if we parked out here in your parkin' lot and stay the night 'cause there's a lot of lights out there?' He said, 'Oh yeah. Sure.' We were gonna sleep in the pickup and eat hot dogs and drink a beer. I said, 'Look. I'm gonna try to get up with this promoter before it gets too late.' So I went over to the phone booth. Right there in all these big bright lights, my car sittin' there number 99 hooked to my truck, and got him on the phone. 'I'm on my way from Nashville to Chattanooga and I've got to do some work on my car before I can run your race Wednesday night. I've been tryin' to get with you to get some deal money. I'm really in need of some parts and all. After we got through talking he said, 'Yeah, we made a deal, ya know.' I think it was a couple or $300. I'd already told him I was between Nashville and Chattanooga and had my car in the shop and had to get it out and tow it on the next day. [Gene laughs.] He said, 'Oh by the way, that your car number 99?' I said, 'Yes sir.' He said, 'Wasn't that your car settin' up there at the service station in the middle of town a while ago?' [Gene really laughs hard.] He knew I was puttin' him on. I got caught red-handed tryin' to get a deal. I told him all this damn sob story about my car in the shop. I said, 'Godamighty! You done caught me shore nuff! I do need some change.' He said, 'You're not the only one. I hear this story every week. I know what's comin' from you guys. I need some cars so come on up here.' Larry Thomas came up to me after the race and said, 'Where'd you finish?' 'Tenth.' 'Damn. I can't believe that. In my car, too.'

The record shows that Gene finished tenth of 19 in the Confederate 300 at Boyd Speedway in Chattanooga. Larry Thomas from whom Gene bought the 99 crashed out for 14th. The tour continued to Valdosta, Georgia.

"The next night during the Valdosta 100-miler about halfway, my accelerator spring broke. I kept switchin' the engine off and on to get into the pits. Cale Yarborough had mechanical problems and was out. When I got into the pits, Cale was standin' with wrenches in hands. Two guys raised the hood and Cale dove in and put double accelerator springs on it. Cale, Buddy, several others, my wife, and I got a midnight snack at the local truck stop and then sat around the pool at the Holiday Inn until 4:30 A.M. If only I had a recorder then."

The records show that Gene took 18th at Valdosta as Buck won his 45th and next to last Grand National race. Next, he had a fine run in the best race this writer ever saw.

"The infamous Spartanburg 200-lapper, June 26, 1964, was the last race of the Southern Tour. I had a white car, but it looked like a rainbow after the race. I think I collected paint from every car there. It was a very intense 200 laps. Most all drivers had a one-gallon Thermos jug strapped to the floorboard behind the driver with a rubber tube running up over his shoulder to sip on. I have known a few to have something other than ice water in the jug and that was called 'spirits.' Before the race, I was going to different cars talking to the drivers and around a couple of cars I kept smellin' something like spirits. I was secretly asked if I wanted a 'draw from the straw' meanin' the jug behind the seat. I declined, being that I never had and never did.

"The field was set with 21 cars. Pearson on the pole, Richard on the outside, Billy Wade was third, and Ned was fourth. Pearson had mechanical trouble about halfway. I passed J.T. Putney and Buddy Baker got in behind J.T. A few laps later, I came off two, headed down the backstretch, and glanced in my mirror and saw Buddy and J.T. tangle. Both cars rolled and were out of the race. I was later involved in a crash and knocked my right front fender in on the tire. I pitted and continued. Ned and Billy were putting on a show, knocking and banging and a little bump drafting, to say the least. Ned took the lead near the end and both of them tangled and rolled a couple of times. During the long caution, Billy was stomping back to the pits, wiping his face, and spitting, looking really upset. I thought for sure the race would have to be stopped to watch a serious confrontation. I just knew there was going to be a four round bout between Ned and Billy. But it continued. I finished eighth, Petty won, and LeeRoy Yarbrough was second. That ended our five-race Southern Tour. I was lucky in that I left home two weeks earlier with $150 in my pocket and returned with $2,000 after all expenses."

Gene remembers his good friend Jimmy Pardue.

"One of the most intense guys in racing that I knew was Jimmy Pardue when he was behind the wheel. Just a down to earth guy, country-talkin', real slow drawl, talk to ya anytime ya stop by him to ask a question ... just a good guy. In '64 we were up at Bowman-Gray in August and Jimmy was behind me and we run a couple of laps together. There was about 25 cars on that quarter-mile flat track and he stayed behind me and all of the sudden goin' down the backstretch he bumps me. Bump draft. [Gene chuckles.] I looked in the mirror and his windshield had fell in his lap. [Gene laughs hard.] I said, 'Lord have mercy!' He had to come in and I didn't have to stop. Later on I think he fell out with mechanical trouble or something. I'm tellin' ya, when he grabbed a hold of that steerin' wheel, he won't joke or carry on with anybody. He was focused right out that windshield. He had his left hand white-knuckled at eleven o'clock, his right hand white-knuckled at two o'clock, and his chin just about on top of the steerin' wheel. I mean he was *intense*. He came by after the race and apologized because the bump actually backfired on him. We had a good laugh about it. That was really tragic 'cause we lost a good guy [later when he was killed] and he would have really gone somewhere. I think he had four sons."

The record shows on August 22, 1964, Gene was running at the finish in 14th of 24. Jimmy Pardue was 16th dropping out due to linkage trouble. That day, Jimmy Pardue had exactly one month to live.

The top drivers of the early to mid 1960s gave Gene inspiration.

"Some of the hotdogs of that time were Ned and Richard, Marvin, Buddy and Buck, Cale, Jimmy Pardue, Darel Dieringer, ole Pistone, Tiny, LeeRoy, Cotton, and David ... all those guys. They didn't think a thing about stopping and talking to ya a few minutes. A few would even go around and have a beer with ya. They were really down to earth and it gave us a little bit of pep to talk to them. That happened quite a bit throughout those three or four years there. It was just great.

"At the end of the '64 season, I was gonna run the fall race at Martinsville. About a week before, I had already sent my entry form in and Tommy Porter from Savannah called me. He and Bubba Into and another guy came up there to Henderson and we talked. He said, 'I want to buy this car and try to get it ready for the race the first of November in Augusta.' He give me a down payment and I told Tommy that I had already committed to run Martinsville. He said, 'Well just bring it back in one piece.' I said, 'Well....' [Gene laughs hard.] I better protect this money and put it under my pillow.'

"I went on to Martinsville and about halfway through the race, Doug Cooper in a '64 Ford was comin' down the front stretch. I was right behind and he spun out in one and two. He was exactly taking up the whole track. The nose of his car was against the inside where the little berm was and the tail end was sticking right straight up the track. I don't know how I got between him and the wall. He was settin' there lookin' right straight at me and all I could see was the whites of his eyes. I would have hit him right in the door 'cause Bobby Johns was behind me and when I saw what happened, I just jerked it to the right. Somehow soon as I did that and got right behind him [between Cooper and the wall], Johns crammed me in the rear and I know my car left the ground. I must have been airborne a couple of seconds there. It put a whiplash in my neck, boy, I'm tellin' ya right now. All I could see was the wall comin' towards me. I said. 'I'm gonna knock this wall down.' I never touched it, but for the right rear quarter panel. How I missed it I'll never know. Bobby Johns tore the whole front end off his Holman Moody Ford. I never stopped. That was a *good* bump draft. I didn't even know what kind of damage I had back there or nothin'. Only thing I know was that I had a little vibration. 'Must be somethin' hangin' off the car.'

"I came in, made fuel stops, never checked back there. After the race, that bumper and deck lid was knocked in a foot and a half. [Gene bursts out laughing.] I couldn't believe that! I never stopped. Sure didn't. Doug Cooper came up to me after the race and asked, 'How in the hell did you miss me? You even took Bobby Johns with you so he wouldn't cream me.' I said to myself, 'Oh hell! I'm gonna have to tell Tommy Porter now.'"

The records show that on September 27, 1964, Gene finished 21st of 41, while Cooper and Johns crashed out for 29th and 30th respectively. Gene wound up 44th in his first season in the Grand National point standings.

"I got back home that night and said, 'I gotta call Tommy right now.' I call and said, 'Well Tommy, you wanna come get what's left of it?' [Gene laughs hard.] I didn't tell him what happened, ya know. He came up there the next week and got that car and towed it back. I went down to Augusta, I believe it was the last race of the season and they had that car immaculate. It was painted metallic blue just like it come out of the showroom. They were out there qualifyin' and askin' me about gears and stuff and it had a 413 in it. They had rebuilt the engine. 'We got a 583 [gear] in this.' I said, 'Tommy, that's gonna be a little strong for the track down here.' It's a half a mile, high-banked, asphalt track. I mean you could boogie down there. About a 567 was as strong as you want to run. They had a 583 in there and shore 'nuff, he might have got halfway through the race, but the engine went out. I think it popped a valve or something."

The record shows that on November 1, 1964, Bubba Into started 29th and finished 22nd in a 1962 Plymouth 91. Likely this is really Gene's '62 Dodge 99. Gene got new wheels for 1965.

"For the '65 season, I purchased a '64 Dodge from Buddy Arrington which was a previous Cotton Owens car. I also had somewhat of a sponsor, M.E. Whitmore, Inc., of Henderson. I could use one whole bay in his large Buick-Dodge dealership. I also obtained a one-ton, stake bed, '65 Dodge tow truck and racecar trailer. I still had to take care of all phases of the operation alone. The first race on my 1964 number 99 Dodge was at Spar-

To start the 1965 season, Gene was armed with a spotless Dodge stake bed truck, trailer, and a shiny ex–Arrington '64 Dodge 99 (Gene Hobby).

Ready for war, Gene poses with the 1964 Dodge 99 that would take him to Grand National fame (Gene Hobby).

tanburg in February. At most all the tracks, drivers that were running for the Grand National Championship would ask other drivers to start their cars for the points. Shortly after the race started, they would pull in and the regular driver would take over. In fact, Darel Dieringer asked me if I would let him start my car for points because he had finished second two weeks earlier at the Daytona 500 in Bud Moore's Mercury behind Fred Lorenzen. I told him he could. Soon after that, he told me that Doug Cooper had brought a second car to the race and needed a driver, but he wound up in Sam Fogle's '63 Ford 31. I finished fourth there on Saturday afternoon. The next day, we went to Weaverville, where I was 13th, and the next weekend we went to the Richmond 250 and I took sixth."

The fourth-place finish at Spartanburg on February 27, 1965, was the highest finish of Gene Hobby's Grand National career. Gene was off to a terrific start in 1965, and then came The Big One.

"The very next Sunday, March 14, 1965, I went to Hillsborough, a .9 mile dirt track. I started 17th and while they played the national anthem, I thought that I should tighten the shoulder harness as tight as possible. This was the first year they were mandatory due to Joe Weatherly's death the year before. By the 35th lap, I was in seventh place per my scorer. Junior Johnson came around me and I stayed with him for several laps and in doin' so, I brushed the fourth turn bank twice with my right rear quarter panel. Shortly after I came off four the next time still right behind Junior, I got it straight and when I got back into it, the right front went down and jerked to the right. I went end-over-end once and rolled four or five times, windin' up past the flag stand right side up with the front end up the bank and into the wire fence. All I could see was people hangin' on the fence lookin' inside the car with no windshield and no back glass. The first thing I did was to cut the ignition off. Looked back toward the fourth turn and saw Neil Castles, J.T., Lil Bud Moore, and several more turn into the inside lane to miss my car. I did not attempt to unbuckle and get out until all were under caution. When it went end-over-end, it hit on the top of the drivers' side, upside down, and I thought to myself, 'Blankety blank ... I better grab the steerin' wheel with both hands and hold on' while at the same time spitting out a mouth full of Orange County clay! It seemed as if I was in a 55-gallon drum rollin' down a very rough terrain. My crew thought I was unconscious because I did not get out right away. I told them I wasn't about to get out until all the traffic got by me.

"Several guys came runnin' to the car and helped me out as I was unbucklin' and we looked all around the car for damage. Then I said, 'Well, it's been a hard day's night, someone call the wrecker.' The only place I could tell I was hurt was my left shoulder, a bruise from the harness. Also, a bruise on my left pelvis and one finger on my right hand was cut from the windshield glass. The inside top of the car was painted white and it left blue zigzag marks and a dent from my blue helmet, directly over the driver's seat. For a fact, the shoulder harness saved the day. It kept me from free-flyin' through the pines. After all was said and done, I went to my regular job the next day."

Gene Hobby's record shows without a doubt he was

On March 14, 1965, at Hillsborough, the shiny came off Dodge 99 as Gene rolled and flipped down the stretch within feet of the crowded stands (Gene Hobby).

A famous headline of the event from *Southern Motorsports Journal* read, "What was a hobby is no longer a hobby for Hobby." (Gene Hobby).

Gene hauled the remains of his car home. With the help of his many friends, he had it back on the track in 42 days at Martinsville (Gene Hobby).

a fine driver, but his Hillsborough flips are probably what he is remembered for the most. He was a flipping number 99 fifteen years before Carl Edwards was born. After the crash, Gene Hobby had a decision to make.

"I was then in a dilemma of whether to build the car back, or not. About two days later, my mechanic and the dealership, unknowing to me, ordered about $1,500 worth of parts and all my friends were ready to help me build it back. I purchased a '64 Dodge body from Jack Kochman's Hell Drivers Show and put it nose-to-nose in the dealership garage. Nothing fit except the body. The whole underside of the car was modified. We were rushin' to get the new car built for the Martinsville 500 several weeks away."

Cotton Owens came through with a key part to get 99 back on track.

"He played a good part in gettin' stuff for me. When I wrecked, that right spindle really messed up. That spindle was as big as your forearm. It was made to fit inside a reinforced hub and I called him. 'Cotton, I really need some help. I gotta get this car ready and I don't know where in the world to get a spindle, but I know you can do it.' He had to machine it, ya see. He's got a machine shop and all. He said, 'You send it to me.' I packed it up and sent it to him on the bus and a week later got it back. It was perfect. I just hooked it right up. I remember payin' that bill, $200. [Gene laughs.] Yes sir. My sponsor, M.E.

Whitmore, paid for it. But I paid him every month for some things. Cotton was real good about doin' stuff like that. A super guy and a friend to all. On Friday before qualifyin' on Saturday, my friend, race driver Jimmy Helms, phoned to see if I'd be ready or not. We worked until four Saturday mornin' and got to Martinsville in time to qualify. We only had a primer coat of paint on the car and my number. The owner of the dealership, Mickey Whitmore, slept in one of the cars he had in his showroom until we left there at four that mornin'. He was a very good sport in all aspects.

"When I pulled into the track with my slick new year-old Dodge and all the accessories, I stopped in the pits. Cale, Buddy Baker, Dieringer, Wendell, and several more surrounded me, ribbing me about factory help and eyein' the new racin' rig. I pointed to my hip pocket and said, 'It's all comin' out of Hip National. That's my story and I'm stickin' to it.' Before qualifyin', everyone was checkin' over last minute details of their set up. I had my right front wheel off the car and Herb Nab, who was Junior Johnson's crew chief, came by talkin' to me about Junior's car not handlin' like it should in the corners. I told him I was runnin' a 3/8-inch spacer on the right front wheel, which was illegal, and that he could borrow it and bring it back after Junior qualified. He put it under his shirt and walked back to his pits. Junior got the pole and that is fact. Herb returned the spacer under his shirt. Unfortunately, I had handlin' problems during the race and had to pull out early."

The record reflects that on April 25, 1965, Gene started 31st and finished 27th of 36, only 41 days after his Hillsborough wipe out. However, Junior crashed for 22nd after winning the pole courtesy of Gene's ⅜-inch spacer. Gene was an undercover racer for a while.

"As I planned to start racin' Grand National in 1964, I was employed with a finance company and racin' was not allowed. My name was Charles Eugene Hobby and I went by Charles. So as a front, I decided to start usin' Gene to cloak my identity and this worked very well. The company's home office was in Ohio and the manager, Ron, kept in touch with me weekly and visited once a month. He knew me as Chuck, a third name for me. I was runnin' all short paved and dirt tracks and the results appeared in newspapers, car magazines, radio coverage, etc. After I had my spectacular wreck at Hillsborough, I got a call from Mr. Ron and he asked, 'Chuck, do you race stock cars?' I said, 'I had intended to talk with you about that.' He came to town later, we had coffee, and he told me I could not be doing this. I told him that I had a lot of people on our books that were big race fans and also *my* fans. I asked him if he played golf and he said 'Certainly.' I said, 'Well, I drive racecars, what's the difference?' He went back to Ohio and phoned the next week and said I had to quit racin', or else. I resigned and went fulltime racin'."

At Bristol, Gene and the other independents made a show of strength.

"During Saturday's practice, we had a bit of a protest that started when our cars were lined up to go onto the track. The inspector was slidin' a four-inch tall hoe under the cars to determine the height of the chassis. If the top edge of the hoe hit the chassis, it was too low, and we had to correct it. They caught me and I pulled to the pits. Next in line was Buck Baker and the same thing happened to him, but the inspector was about to wave him onto the track. Wendell, his crew, and several more independents were standing by and saw the incident. Wendell said, 'If you let Buck on the track and don't let Hobby on for the same thing, none of us are going to run!' There were a few minutes of commotion to say the least because we threatened to get Norris Friel involved, which was the head technical inspector. We all stuck by it and the inspector made Buck come in and adjust the height on his car."

Another incident that illustrates the cooperation between independents occurred after the race.

"Tom Pistone crashed out and damaged his '64 Ford so bad that after leavin' the track, he was stuck at the motel unable to tow number 59 home. He was flat towin' the car and it was too messed up. He asked Bob Derrington if he could borrow his trailer to get back to Charlotte, but Bob refused. I offered to let Tom use my trailer and I would flat tow mine. But Tom and his boys kept workin' on it and would test it by towin' it around the motel, out onto the highway, and back through the parkin' lot. This went on for several laps. He almost went around that motel as many times as he did at the track. When they finally got it adjusted enough to hit the road, we all left for home."

Gene recalled that not all the accidents took place on the track.

"After runnin' Langley [Field] on a Friday night then tryin' to make Bowman Gray Saturday night, and Hickory on Sunday, a lot took place. I spent the night near Langley and hit the road about 5 A.M. Saturday to go by the shop in time to get to Bowman Gray. At approximately 7 A.M., I entered a small town just south of the Virginia-Carolina line. The highway was a four lane strip with no median. I saw a school activity bus parked on the left side of the highway. On the right side was a large group of high school students at a sandwich shop and one black guy was standin' at the edge of the highway waitin' to cross over back to the bus. It was good and light and I slowed my tow truck and trailer down to 35 miles per hour. The guy had a drink in his left hand and a hot dog in the other. As I got closer, he took off runnin' across the highway to the bus directly in front of me. I swerved hard left and he ran into the right front fender, runnin' board, and west coast mirror. A bright red substance spattered all over my windshield and I yelled 'I've killed him!'

"I stopped around the middle of the center line of the highway, jumped out, and went around to the right side of my truck where he was lying on the pavement moanin'. Everyone came runnin' and surrounded us and someone even grabbed the keys out of the ignition. They started takin' notes, names, etc. The red substance that spattered my windshield was found to be a cherry smash drink, thank God! The police and rescue squad arrived, put him on a stretcher, and drove to the hospital. I was interrogated by the police for several hours. How long was I on the road? Did I fall asleep? On and on. I even took the officers and all the rest of students out to the scene and showed them the smashed hot dog with a perfect imprint of my tire tread over it just to the right of the center line of the highway. They finally ruled it 'unavoidable.' I could not leave the police station until the guy was brought back from the hospital, which was around noon. He was on crutches with his foot and leg in a cast, his head was bandaged up, and he had torn shirt and jeans. They found both of his shoes in the ditch. Holy moly! A close call and what a nightmare! I missed the Bowman Gray show Saturday night, but made the Hickory race on Sunday. I was afraid to go to the mailbox for a long time after that thinkin' I'd get a letter from some lawyer, but never did. Whew, at least not yet!"

The record indicates that Gene finished 17th with fuel pump problems at Langley Field in Hampton, Virginia, on May 14, 1965; missed Bowman Gray on the 15th; and took 23rd at Hickory on May 16, again with fuel pump trouble.

"I would like to mention a little conversation with a one of a kind and quite the character and friend, Wendell Scott. After a race at Myrtle Beach in 1965, we were in the payoff line in the promoter's office and several of us were talkin' about our qualifyin' time. The dirt track was so that if you ran off between turns one and two, you could drive outside the track through a cornfield outside the backstretch and get back on. Wendell commented, 'Did you see Tiny leave the track between one and two, run through the cornfield, and get back on the track? All you could see was the top of his car and the corn stalks gettin' mowed down. Do you know he still had a better qualifying time than I did?' We all laughed. Wendell was quite the character, a good friend to all, and always funnin' around like that. He is really missed."

For the record, Tiny started third and finished third on the night of June 24, 1965, at Myrtle Beach. Wendell started 15th and finished 16th; Gene started 16th, came in 11th, and a young rookie named Buren Skeen started seventh and crashed out for 12th.

On July 25, 1965, Gene went to Bristol and felt the strong arms of NASCAR.

"Went back there and this is goin' back to how the independents had to work. We worked on our cars and they give us a list a mile long. Piddly stuff, see? And we needed seat time. One of the head inspectors, Bill Gazaway, had a list of about ten or fifteen things and one of 'em was my roll bars. He didn't like the way the roll bars were welded in. I said, 'Listen, I paid a guy an astronomical fee, a professional welder, to put these roll bars in there. They come in there and I been runnin' the car all season.' He was just pickin' on it, evidently. I thought he was picking on me. Before, Ron's Ford would always be open that weekend all night for guys to work on their cars over there. The time before, I went over there and worked on my car because I couldn't get it handling and took a half inch out of the A-frame and got it perfect. I was determined I wasn't goin' to do it this time. I got in an argument with this guy and listen, if it hadn't been for Buddy Baker and Cale Yarborough, I'd probably still be locked up in Bristol! I was fit to be tied.

"My car was on the infield there and he said, 'Gene, all you gotta do is take it over there to Ron's Ford, he's gonna be open tonight.' I said, 'I'm not takin' it anywhere. I'm gonna pull it outside the gate and leave it. I know Larry [promoter Carrier] needs the cars up here.' I got so upset that Buddy had to restrain me and Cale was over there tryin' to keep Gazaway straight. [Gene has anger in his voice as he continues.] Gazaway was about six foot two and I was about five eleven, ya know. I don't know what would have happened, but I'm tellin' ya I was after him because he kept getting kind of smart with me. I said, 'I ain't gonna do it! I'm fed up with it! There's two or three more independents the same way and we're fed up with it.' Curtis Crider had already pulled out. Several months before that he started another racin' program around Charleston called the NUCAR Series. He was pissed at NASCAR, also. I parked my damn car outside the gate. Larry Carrier came out there talkin' to me and said, 'Gene, listen. We'll give you some help. Whatever you need to do.' I said, 'Larry, I'm fed up with it. I'm not the only one. I ain't takin' no more of it!' I pulled my car outside the gate and parked it over at the motel. He didn't like the welds. That's what really ripped me off. All I could see was VC. Man, all I could see was VC. I gotta take my blood pressure." Gene laughs, but is still angry 44 years later.

Gene Hobby decided to tackle the Granddaddy of Them All, the Southern 500, a race he had only dreamed of running.

"I entered the Labor Day Southern 500 in 1965 arrivin' at the back gate check-in durin' the afternoon on Friday before the race on Monday. Elmo Langley, Wayne Smith, and Buren Skeen were parked there also. Buren was a short track ace, especially at Bowman Gray Stadium. We were all shootin' the breeze and the Winston-Salem race came up, which had been about ten days before. Buren had raced in it while testin' the Grand National circuit. I had talked to him before and after the race, in which he ran seventh. He was very satisfied with his finish. We were talkin' about him enterin' the Southern 500 and it would be his next race. He was very excited about it. The next few days, gettin' through inspections, practicin', and qualifyin' was pretty busy. All the drivers and mechanics ate lunch at the infield cafeteria each day. There was a lot of camaraderie among us. Durin' the practice just before qualifyin', I blew a right front between three and four and did right much damage to the front end and could not get it repaired in time to make the race. Independents didn't have a back up car back then. Buren qualified about half way back in the field of 40–44 cars."

Buren Skeen had run seven times previously with very promising results. He scored four top ten starts and three top ten finishes. In two starts at Bowman Gray near his hometown of Denton, Skeen notched fifth and seventh place finishes. A day or so before Gene's practice crash, he had another bout going through inspection. Gene and a couple of others failed and had to take corrective action.

"They checked the fuel capacity of our gas tanks and me, Wayne Smith, Bob Derrington, and several others had 23-gallon tanks instead of the required 22. NASCAR told us a place in Florence to take the tanks to at a welding shop. There they vatted them out and cut a rectangular hole in the tank, welded inside a gallon gas can like you'd use to fill up your lawnmower, and sent us on our way. I stood there and watched them. That's exactly what they did to bring our gas tanks down to 22 gallons."

The Southern 500 was run on September 6, 1965, with 44 cars. Buren time-trialed his Reid Shaw 1964 Ford 23 a solid 21st behind J.T. Putney and G.C. Spencer, beside H.B. Bailey, and just ahead of Reb Wickersham and Buddy Arrington. All except Skeen were experienced independents.

"About the second lap, Buren lost control in the turn and was T-boned in the driver's door by Reb Wickersham. It was completely unavoidable. Buren's driver's seat was knocked to the center of the car and the steerin' wheel was stickin' out through the busted windshield. It took about a half hour to extract Buren from the car and he was unconscious. Reb was pretty shaken and very concerned about Buren. They took both to the hospital. Reb was released overnight, but Buren passed away about a week later. This incident was very tragic and emotional for many of us."

Gene almost sold his racer in late 1965 and, as it turned out, was glad he didn't.

"I had my car parked for the fall race up there [at Charlotte] and some guy called two or three times and wanted to buy my car. It was for Harold Kite. They wound up buyin' this other car from somebody else [Ken Spikes] and that's when Kite got killed. I'da really felt bad, naturally, if he had been in a car that I had and got killed in it. That was terrible."

The last race for 99 was the Capital City 300 on September 18, 1965, at Richmond. Gene started dead last in 37th and dispatched 24 competitors for a very respectable 13th place. The penultimate race for Gene in the Grand Nationals occurred at Dog Track on May 29, 1966.

"The last race we ran at Moyock was in 1966. We ran there and about halfway, my water pump messed up and started overheatin'. I pulled into the infield. I got out of the car and inspected everything and said, 'Well I gotta wait till everybody gets out anyway.' I got up on the hood and set there. All of the sudden Richard had ignition problems. He came in, parked his car, and they put it on the hauler. He came walkin' through and saw me sittin' there. He stopped and talked to me for a couple of minutes and got up on my hood on the other side and set there to the end of the race. We sat there and talked and carried on, just he and I, on the hood of my car."

The record shows that Gene drove a 1964 Dodge 58 instead of 99 and dropped out for 23rd after overheating. Pole-sitter Richard Petty had ignition problems and settled for 18th. He was an "outlaw" before his career ended.

"From time to time during our Grand National racin' careers, we would run outlaw tracks meanin' other than NASCAR. We would tape or paint over our name and number, etc., and enter the races. They had a hotshot quarter-mile dirt track at Rockingham and one Saturday night I took my car down there and ran fourth. I had to be in Richmond the next day for the NASCAR race. I stopped at a service station on the way home, washed all the mud off my car, cleaned it up, got two hours' sleep, and towed to Richmond."

Gene Hobby's finale came at Richmond in the Capital City 300 on September 11, 1966. "This guy was in the process of buyin' my car and was a good mechanic. We were racin' on the Northern Tour in '65 and were together again that summer. He got registered and the car was now 58. His name was Joe Holder from Franklinton, north of Raleigh, and I was runnin' it for him. He run it a couple of races. I had run an outlaw race on a quarter-mile dirt track at Rockingham on Saturday night and ran fourth. One of J.D. McDuffie's guys towed me up there and I had messed up a gear, my half-mile gear, and was runnin' another gear or something. Anyway, I blew a tire and kept runnin'. They finally flagged me off. I came in and decided to park it because I didn't have the right gear. I had a deal with Paul Sawyer, the promoter up there. I always started callin' two weeks ahead of time. That's one of the first things you learned. You call these promoters and they'd help you out."

The record shows that in his final Grand National start, Gene Hobby started 28th and finished there, being flagged off after seven laps.

"When I got hooked up with Joe Holder, we were gonna run North Wilkesboro and the car was up in Franklinton. Me, my wife, and another friend were gonna drive up to North Wilkesboro and run the car. [Gene laughs.] We got up there about nine o'clock and the car was sittin' outside the gate on the trailer. Enoch Staley, the promoter, whistled for me to come over and told me to open the hood. I did, we looked at the engine, and he was kind of amused at what Joe had done. I wasn't! Then Joe came up and I said, 'Joe, whatsa goin' on?' He said, 'They didn't like the carburetor I had on there.' He had two two-barrel carburetors on there instead of one four-barrel. They wouldn't let us run. I said, 'Well damn, Joe. Didn't you read the rule book?' He said, 'We're legal. It's four barrels.' [Gene laughs hard.] It was real hoot."

Other opportunities arose for Gene and he left the Grand Nationals behind in 1966.

"I had a chance to go drivin' late model sportsman cars for a couple of different people and that's what I started doing. Had more time to spend at home with Gina and Christy. The guy that was buyin' the car decided to give it up. So, I took the car back. He didn't want any of his money back. I actually sold it a time and a half. [Gene laughs hard.] In fact, Buddy [Baker], LeeRoy, and J.T. started the car. Things were getting too expensive. I had a fuel cell ordered from Akron, Ohio. Thought I had a sponsor goin', ya know. The

In August 2009, Gene Hobby was honored with a weekend at Occoneechee Speedway and is joined by his daughters Christy (left) and Gina (Gene Hobby).

sponsor fell through and the fuel cell was like five or six hundred bucks. I called and cancelled it. I'm gonna get out of it. I got enough to do around here besides mess with this. It was gonna cost an arm and a leg to do all the extra safety stuff without a sponsor. I sold it the same day I was gonna take it to Hillsborough. A guy called me from Shelbyville, Tennessee, and wanted it. He and a buddy came and bought that car the time they ran that fall race at Hillsborough. I ran local stuff in North and South Carolina runnin' late model sportsman from '67 to '82, then NASCAR Dash cars for a few of years from '83 to '86."

Gene Hobby is the picture of good health. At 71, he goes to work every day starting off with a dose of honey in his coffee. With Gene, just about everything goes better with honey. I can attest to trudging around the pits at the Darlington Historic Festival in 2008 with the mercury well over 100 degrees. At 56 years old, not only was I having trouble masking my difficulty keeping up with Mr. Hobby 15 years my senior, but I was secretly hoping he knew CPR. Gene and the bees know something. Aside from honey, Gene Hobby is inspired by his faith, family, friends, and the man and his music, Elvis Presley. He is especially fond of The King's recording "If I Can Dream." In 35 Grand National starts, Gene had a career best fourth in Spartanburg in 1965. He was the 99 that made flips famous more than three decades before today's 99 flipper Carl Edwards. The Hillsborough Historic Speedway Group honored Gene for three days in August 2009 at their annual festival. Thanks to his honey, Gene Hobby has a sweet life and keeps busy as a bee.

8

Jimmy Helms

The Dreamer

Jimmy Helms was born on August 7, 1935, in Monroe, North Carolina. He graduated from West Mecklenburg High School in Charlotte, joined the U.S. Navy, and served eight years including reserve time. It was there Jimmy began racing micro-midgets and dragsters. In 1958, he started running modifieds while working at Folger Buick as a mechanic. Then in 1964, Jimmy went bigtime with the NASCAR Grand National Division when he raced for a legend.

"Neil Castles came to me one day. I was working at Lacy's Alignment doing front end and frame work 'You wanna drive a racecar?' I said, 'I'm thinkin' I do.' 'Well, come out to Buck Baker's shop.' I talked to Buck and he told me what the deal was. Buck Baker, he's my hero. I had run with Roy Tyner and Neil and some of the other guys at the Robinwood Speedway in Gastonia. Neil knew my background in racing and he and I were good friends, had been for a long time. I went with him and worked in the pits. We worked for Speedy Thompson at Daytona two years. Got my first ride with Baker and stayed there a little over a year."

Neil drove Baker's 1962 Chrysler 86 while Jimmy saddled up 88. Jimmy ran 18 races that season for Buck starting in Atlanta on April 5, 1964.

"Never had run asphalt. I talked to Buck. I always called him 'Boss.' 'Boss, you're gonna have to give me a little education here.' He said, 'You go out there and find where people have been practicing and that normally is the groove. You just mash the gas and turn left.' [Jimmy laughs.] I do my best to stay off the wall. Most of the time Buck wouldn't let you run the whole race 'cause he was saving the car for the next one. Startin' money, that's what Buck wanted. We're not spendin' a lot to repair the cars. We're not tearin' them up and beatin' them all to pieces. He kindly held us down and by doin' that, I learned a lot. I really wanted to race. I wanted to go wide open, but it was his car. I believe in some cases I could have held my own with about anybody. He was doublin' up usin' us in the pits as well. I enjoyed it. It was my first real thrill in the big time."

Driving his sixth race, Jimmy got his first top ten at Savannah on May 1, 1964.

"You stay out there and stay out of trouble, you can usually end up there."

The record shows that was one of the few times Jimmy did not start and park, completing 152 of 200 laps. It was his first time in Grand Nationals running at the finish. In the 1964 Rebel 300 at Darlington, Jimmy's teacher was the best.

Jimmy Helms poses at the wheel of one of Buck Baker's Chryslers in 1964. It appears to be the one normally driven by teammate Neil Castles (Jimmy Helms).

"'Boss, how do you get around *this* track?' Buck said, 'Ya see that white line down there in three and four?' 'Yes sir.' 'You put the left front wheel on it and don't let it come off.' [Jimmy laughs.] That's what I tried to do and Daytona the same way. You see where the faster cars are runnin' and set the groove up. Then you run accordingly.' Beautiful. Just like sittin' back in a rockin' chair on a Sunday afternoon. We were racin' hard, but back then we was only runnin' 135, 150 miles an hour. It was a thrill! We'd go down to the corner and if your car is set up good, you'd go through it, you'd pull out the other side, and it's real smooth."

In nine starts from Darlington in May to Darlington on Labor Day, Jimmy ran Buck's Chryslers a remarkable 18 laps in competition. Imagine Jimmy's frustration at being bridled, parking his perfectly good racer every single time. The most laps he completed was in the World 600 when he ran four and retired 86 on the same lap Neil parked 88, for 39th and 38th respectively. Just three circuits after Jimmy and Neil won a combined $1,275, Ned Jarrett, Junior Johnson, and Fireball Roberts tangled in one of racing's most tragic scenes.

"I pulled into the pits and looked across the track and could see smoke risin'. I said, 'Lord, somethin' done happened over there bad.' A few minutes later we found out. Fireball and Ned Jarrett, I believe it was Junior, got into it and Fireball burned pretty bad. Brought him to the hospital at the infield. He was in a mess. Just barely [saw him]. You don't like to look at stuff like that, but he died in the hospital" on July 2, 1964.

On May 30 at Greenville Pickens Speedway, Jimmy parked Buck's 86 for last after two laps and witnessed an interesting event. "Let me tell a story about Wendell Scott. I loved that old boy to death. Wendell was something else. I was in the pits. Wendell came slidin' in, got out, walked around the car, and kicked [the tires] nonchalantly. Got over to the concession stand, got a hotdog and a drink, woofed that hotdog down, drank the drink, tossed the bottle, got back in his car, buckled up, put his helmet on, and left a rooster tail of dirt as high as the grandstand gettin' out like he was leadin' the race. [Jimmy laughs long and hard.] He just made a pit stop. He finished the race. I died laughing. I'd heard it, but I'd never seen it."

Wendell Scott bought Buck Baker's 1960 Chevrolet to join the Grand National ranks.

"Buck told me about Wendell buyin' his first car. 'Old Wendell came and paid me for my car. It was settin' there in the stall. Wendell said, 'Mr. Buck, you gonna help me load this thing?' Buck said, 'I leaned my butt against the workbench, took my foot and put it on the bumper, and shoved it out the door and said, 'Yep, there ya go.' [Jimmy laughs.] How true that is, I don't know. If you know Buck, you can see him doin' it."

After finishing one lap for 20th in Spartanburg on June 26, Jimmy and the caravan returned to Charlotte. In that caravan was Buddy Baker, who finished 12th after flipping. He was towing J.C. Parker's Dodge 87.

"It was about one or two in the morning before we got back toward Charlotte. You come down off Wilkinson Boulevard from 85. There's a road that cuts through and Buddy's car came loose. They lost it. We flat-towed. Got to lookin' for his car and didn't know where it was. He don't even know when he lost it! When they come loose, you don't usually feel 'em. The house they found it next to is still there. The reason they didn't find it [sooner] was because it went in behind a bunch of bushes. It was hid back there. Out there lookin' for it at two o'clock in the mornin'.

"Neil lost one one night. We came from the shop down Morrisville Drive on the way to a race. I think that was the Oldsmobile Buck had. We got over to his [Neil's] house and the car was gone. They looked a couple of hours for that car. Ford Motor Company had a plant on the corner of Morrisville and Wilkinson and they found it down an embankment sittin' between some cars. Didn't hit a thing, run down that embankment. I think we've all lost one. I've lost two."

You had to beware of freeloaders on the road, too.

"One time when I had my Ford Buddy [Baker] said, 'Why don't I ride with you?' He wasn't drivin' for Buck. He was gonna' drive for somebody up there. 'Fine. You can pay part of the gas bill.' 'I don't think so.' I said, 'What do you mean? You're gonna ride with me.' 'Yeah, but wherever the front seat goes, the back was gonna follow. I'll ride in the back.' [Jimmy laughs loudly.] We'd go up the road just like a bunch of gypsies, just havin' a big time. Goin' through Richmond it was so hot and miserable, I said, 'We can put air conditionin' in here, Buddy.' 'How you gonna put air conditionin' in this thing?' I stopped and got two or three bags of ice, put it in a little ice chest, closed the windows, stuck a hose in the vent, run it down in the ice chest, and it cooled. It got so hot goin' through Richmond, you couldn't hardly breathe. It worked."

On Labor Day, September 7, 1964, Jimmy put 88 on the outside of the 20th row and two laps later rolled in for 42nd of 44. Neil followed Jimmy to the garage 15 laps later for a combined one grand in winnings. Meanwhile, Buck battled the heat, the competition, and "The Lady in Black" (the Darlington Raceway) for his third Southern 500 victory. It was his 46th and final Grand National win. He was a happy "Boss."

"He made money all the way around. He was drivin' a Ray Fox car. After it was over we'd pack our tools up and get ready to go. Of course, we waited until the race was over, go get a little bit of change. Sometimes he'd collect it. He'd pay us. I was on salary and when we'd run a race, I'd get a little extra.

"We ran a shop at the airport. Did front end alignment and that's mainly what I was doin'. When we weren't, I was workin' on the racecars. Buck would take off and leave me and Buddy there. Buddy was driving a Dodge for someone. Buck would tell him, 'Buddy, straighten that fender out while I'm gone. If you need any help, ask Jimmy what to do.' Buddy would get over there hummin' and foolin' around with it. 'Jimmy! Come here a minute. Show me how to do that.' Everytime I'd show him, it was done. [Jimmy laughs.] Next time that happened, he said, 'Jimmy! Come here and show me how to do this.' I walked over and said, 'You pick up that hammer and that dolly and you start doin' it.' 'Well show me how.' 'You'll never learn if I set down here and do this.' [Jimmy laughs louder.] Buddy was sharp. He had me doin' his work for him. We had fun. We had a good team. We all got along good. He [Buck] was good to work for. He was real good to me."

What about driving Buck's old Chrysler?

"It had to weigh more than 4,000 pounds. [Jimmy laughs.] I drove it in Jacksonville, North Carolina, and it [the track] was full of holes and I'm tellin' you what's a fact. It just rolled in 'em. In the other cars you could see guys bouncin' up and down, but it would roll through those holes it was so heavy. It was a really good handling car. I liked those Chryslers."

On September 11 at Hickory, North Carolina, Jimmy strayed away from Buck for the first time and drove Bob Cooper's 1962 Pontiac 61. He started 26th in a 27 car field and had the green light to race.

"I don't remember why Bob didn't drive, whether he was sick or what. I didn't have a ride when I went or I wouldn't have got in. I always took [my helmet]. That's like leavin' home without your credit card. You just don't do it. Bob said, 'You wanna drive my car?' I said, 'Yeah, I've got no problem with that.' They'd had it set up pretty good, too. So, I'm out there runnin' just as hard as I can lookin' down at the oil pressure and it was scarin' me. There's very little oil pressure. I pulled in the pits and said, 'Hey! We don't have much oil pressure in this thing.' He said, 'That's where it runs. Don't worry about it. Go out there and mash it!' I did. I went out there and mashed it."

The record shows that Jimmy finished tenth right behind Wendell and just ahead of Buddy Arrington, two top independents. Jimmy knew what it was like to start and *not* park.

The best year statistically in all categories for Jimmy was 1965. He was no longer with Baker and ran 39 of 55 races, had four top tens, completed over 5,700 laps, and pocketed $12,049 finishing 18th in points. Consider that 161 drivers earned points and Jimmy outscored such notables as Johns, Lund, Arrington, McQuagg, Langley, Pistone, and Tyner. He opened it up with a unique ride in Ford 98 for his first Daytona 500.

"That was Benny Parsons' car. That was a real good car. Benny had won the ARCA race. He was hoping to get his car in the field. Same car [ARCA winner], but Norris Friel [chief technical inspector] told him that NASCAR wouldn't let him run 'cause he had never run a NASCAR race. Now figure that part. [Jimmy laughs.] Norris told him, 'Let Jimmy Helms start your car for ya and at least you'll get starting money and that'll give you enough to get home.' I started his car and ran several laps, I don't remember how many, and pulled in. I think he paid me $100, which that was good goin' home money for me. I was workin' for Baker at the time. Just happened to have it [my helmet]."

The record shows that Jimmy's first Daytona 500 started 39th and finished 38th after two laps for Benny.

"I had been down there [Daytona] in January doing brake tests with Buddy for Grey Rock. I never got into testin' except that deal. They may have paid Buck somethin' to let me come down there. I just got my normal salary. Of course, all expenses and everything. Buddy and I had a room together and a bar below us! It wasn't the highest priced place in town, I can tell ya, with Buck payin' the bill. He'd take care of ya, but he wanted to be conservative with his money."

Jimmy parted company with Buck Baker on good terms.

"I was lookin' for another ride. I had quit Buck after February and Buddy was tryin' to help me find rides and Buck, too. Buck, to my knowledge, never said an unkind word about me. In fact, he even said some kind ones. He said, 'Yeah, if you can't find somethin', come on back.' [Jimmy chuckles.] He had the cars, there's no doubt about that."

One of those cars was a 1965 Plymouth Fury 86 with a proud history. When Mopar pulled out in '65, it was the Chrysler standard bearer on super speedways. Numerous top fives and tens on dirt and asphalt were highlighted by back-to-back seconds to A.J. Foyt in the Firecracker 400 with Buddy driving and to Ned Jarrett in its next race, the Southern 500, with Buck relieved by Buddy. It was a really fine racecar and should have easily notched a victory or two.

"We built that car at the shop. It was sold to some folks in Columbia, a construction company. In '67, it came back to Charlotte and I was gonna get a ride 'cause I'd gone to work for Goodyear. That was enough of workin'; I wanted to go back to racin'. Neil said, 'Gotta a car over here. It's one we built at Baker's. You want to drive it?' 'It works for me. I'm not opposed to drivin' a Plymouth.' That was the year you could put the hemi back in them. They did. I started practicin'. When you'd mash it, I swear that car would have flown if you could have got it straight. You go to the corner, it would push so bad it would go straight to the wall. Then you gotta take both hands and pull it off. I was first [alternate]. If I coulda got in it, the car wouldn't have lasted because they didn't change the torsion bars and you couldn't get enough pressure on the right front to hold it up. Couldn't get enough spring under it."

Jimmy went on to Atlanta and a ride in 48.

"I went to Atlanta, got a ticket on the way down, and that didn't help matters any. I had to run good to pay for that ticket. What's G.C. Spencer's number? [G.C. drove a 1964 Ford 49.] It was his dirt car. G.C. wanted somebody just to start to get that extra four or five hundred dollars. Buddy told him, 'Get Jimmy, he don't have a ride.' So G.C. said, 'How 'bout startin' my car for me.' 'Sure. Am I gonna make anything?' 'Well yeah, I'm gonna pay ya.' G.C. did good by me. I went out qualifyin' and I had the second fastest time of the day. The only reason I didn't make it first was because it was rainin' so durn hard in one and two I couldn't see. I came back in and G.C. was standin' on the pit wall. He didn't wear his teeth durin' the race, which I don't blame him. You hit somethin', they're gonna fall out first. G.C. was standin' there, his hair was wet, and he was soakin' wet grinnin' from ear to ear. I stopped and he come runnin' over and said, 'God-a-mighty!' I said, 'What's wrong?' 'That car's not s'pose to run that fast. That's my damn dirt car! [Jimmy laughs.] You know what you qualified?' 'Naw, I really don't.' I couldn't see the scoreboard or hear the speakers. I was second fastest of the day and, I guess, if it hadn't of been for rain, I might have done better. I think only two of us got there the second day 'cause it started rainin'."

The record reflects that 24 cars qualified the first day and Jimmy was 26th. He was, however, the second fastest of day two. Fastest of day two was Castles in Buck's '65 Fury 86. Jimmy completed 46 laps in G.C.'s dirt 48 car for 34th and $600. On May 2, 1965, Jimmy finished an outstanding 12th in the Southeastern 500 at Bristol and began of a solid relationship with David Warren and 1963 Fastback Ford 53.

"David was a gentleman out of Statesville [North Carolina] and was actually a truck driver who loved racin'. He bought this car and I don't know who first drove it, but he went to Bristol. There again, I don't have a ride and I'm lookin'. I don't know who told me about it, but it may have been Darel Dieringer. He said, 'Hey, you wanna ride?' I said, 'Yeah.' Darel said, 'I don't want to drive this car. You might talk to the man.' I went over there and he [the man] said, 'Darel's got another ride.' I said, 'I'll be glad to drive it.' So I got in the car and no time to practice. Darel set a car up where most of us would go into a corner easy and come out hard. He'd go into the corner two or three car lengths ahead of everybody else 'cause that's the way he set it up. He'd go in there still drivin', but then when you'd come off, you'd come off easy. I didn't know how to do that and didn't have time to make changes. When I got through with that race, both of my hands had blisters from tryin' to wrestle it. My hands were actually bleedin' when I got out of the car. I didn't have my gloves. I had my helmet, though."

With his fine Bristol run, the man, David Warren, hired Jimmy. Warren's previous ten career car owner starts netted nothing better than a pair of 13th place finishes. Jimmy latched his bloody hands around a 12th the first time out in the 53. Jimmy recalls his new boss, David Warren.

"Dave was a real nice fellow. I enjoyed drivin' for him. Had a good relationship and when he could, he went with us. He was on the road drivin' a truck. He'd listen [to the radio] so he'd get his money. I had an agreement that I would give him so much right off of the top. It didn't matter what I made, I'd give him a percentage right off of the top. The rest of it was mine. I paid all the bills and kept the car up. It worked out fine. If I needed an engine, I'd go to Holman and Moody and buy one taken out of a car that had qualified. I'd buy them right out of my pocket. Never charged anything. It didn't cost David anything. Normally, I could run a block six or eight races and most of the time, you'd run till you broke it. Then you'd go buy another. I gave Holman-Moody $600 for a short block, which to me was a good price. Ford probably didn't even know we existed. Dave was a real nice guy and I always thought a lot of him."

David Warren wasn't exempt from fun at his expense.

"He was crippled. He had polio at a younger age. We went to Savannah and [Tom] Pistone was behind us in his car towin'. Me and David come out in mine and Tom told the police at the gate, 'You better check that guy. He's drunk.' They pulled David out of the truck, gonna make him walk the line. Tom 'bout got David locked up! David didn't drink a drop. [Jimmy laughs hard.] He was cripple! Couldn't walk the line. Tom got to laughin' so hard, he was tryin' to tell the police he was playin' a joke and police got mad at him. They didn't have no sense of humor at all. I forget where we were goin' after that, but I told Tom, 'Don't ever do that again.' Course I got even with Tom a time or two."

One of those times was at Charlotte.

"We'd been clownin' around and I said, 'I need to get even for what he did to David.' I got a big bunch of salt and we'd take a Thermos jug and tape it to the roll bar and run a hose up to our shoulder harness. If you wanted a drink, you'd just get a sip. Filled his full of salt. [Jimmy laughs hard.] He never did know who did it. Probably will now. [Jimmy laughs real hard.] I don't care."

There was more fun to come with Tiger Tom.

"He liked to procrastinate. I wanted to get my thing ready, then sit down. He had a nice shop and we worked day and night. I looked down and he was asleep one morning. I said, 'I got to go Tom. Darlington's comin' up and I got to get down there.' 'Ahhhh, just wait a little bit.' I said, 'No. You won't get there until tomorrow or the next day.' So I went on down into the office and was talkin' to Bob Colvin [Darlington Raceway president]. We always got a little deal money back then. Promoters looked after us pretty fair. Went in to see if I could get an extra hundred or two. 'Yeah, I'll take care of ya Jimmy. Don't worry about it, OK?' While I'm there the phone rang and he said, 'Excuse me a minute. Yeah? What do you want, Tom?' When he said that, I knew who he was talkin' to. 'I'll tell you what I'll do. I'll send you a $100 to stay home so you won't come down here and knock all my fences down.' [Jimmy laughs.] Tom came down, but he was late as usual."

The Hob Nob Restaurant was Jimmy's sponsor on Warren's 53, and hob nob there they did.

"It was a restaurant down on North Tryon Street [in Charlotte] a Greek ran, named George Poulos. He was really and truly a racefan. He loved race drivers. He'd feed us. As far as me getting any cash, I never had a sponsor that paid me anything. I just kindly got to goin' in his restaurant and eatin' there. It was a real good restaurant. We'd have some of our press parties there. One day I thrilled George real good. We was at Charlotte and I asked Petty, 'You got any plans for lunch today?' 'No.' I said, 'Let's go to George's to eat. He wants to meet you.' He'd never met George. Ya know, Richard's one of the finest people I've ever met. He said, 'OK, lets go,' just like that. So we go downtown and we're ridin' along talkin' about racin'. That was after I had my wreck out there and he'd had his little incident. I said, 'You know somethin' Richard? I don't really care anything at all about racin'.' He looked at me with this puzzled look and said, 'Why?' I said, 'I just like to ride fast.' [Jimmy laughs.] He liked to died laughin'.

"We got to the restaurant and I thought George was gonna have a conniption. He was overwhelmed with Richard comin' to eat at his place. He came and sat down with us. He was the chef, cook, bottle washer, everything. But he took time to sit with Richard and chat. I don't know how he stayed in business. He fed 'bout all of us. Elmo Langley, Buddy, myself, some of the news people, Max Muhlman, Bob Myers, a couple of great writers. It was just a great group of people."

The records show that in 1967, George Poulos competed in 23 of 49 races in his own Plymouth, usually number 57, finishing 46th in the Grand National standings with one top ten, a ninth at Savannah.

"There was a dentist office around there, Dr. Roach, and he was one of my fans. He'd get up in the truck and ride with me. [Jimmy chuckles.] I had a guy that furnished my windshields for me. He did a great job, too. I bought a windshield from him and he said, 'How 'bout putting my name on your car?' I said, 'How 'bout furnishing my windshields?' He said, 'OK.' So I did. You'd go to a race and sandblast a windshield at Daytona or Charlotte. You couldn't see out of 'em next trip around. I'd try to make one last three or four races if I could 'cause I didn't want to get into his pocket too bad. I've got my tool at home that I used to change 'em with. I can change a windshield in 15 minutes if I have to." Jimmy chuckles.

At the Rebel 300 at Darlington on May 8, 1965, Jimmy time-trialed 21st, finishing 18th in a field of 31. "Everybody was knocking door handles off. I had just got through paintin' my car and it really looked pretty. I was proud of it. Norris Friel [chief tech inspector] came over and said, 'Jimmy, you gotta take your door handle off and cover it up with a piece of aluminum on the right side.' I said, 'For what?' You know we ran with door handles. He said, 'Well they're knockin' 'em off when they hit the rail over there.' I said, 'I'm not gonna run fast enough to hit the damn wall. Don't worry about it. I'm gonna keep my car in good shape.' 'TAKE IT OFF!' 'OK!' I took it off, start to practice, and the car was runnin' real good. The first thing I did was get my Darlington Stripe. Would have knocked it off anyhow. [Jimmy chuckles.]"

Jimmy explained his technique of obtaining the Darlington Stripe.

"That was in my Ford. I didn't hit it with the Chrysler, but I did with the Ford. I learned a lot. Don't hit the rail! Of course if you do, unless you really slam it, it'll help you get through there. You know you're gonna wear your sheet metal out. Then you have to work hard Monday mornin'. You'd go up there and it would sound like a train goin' down the track, 'ch-ch-ch-ch-ch-ch.' Scared me first time I heard it. I knew what it was and said, 'Damn, there goes my Darlington Stripe.' I went back to what Buck told me the first time I was there. 'Put your wheel on that white line and keep it there.' If you go in there hard enough, you can't keep it there. That's when you get to the rail. It wasn't that far. So I'd go in there and aim, try to keep my wheel right where he told me, and it would go to driftin'. If you're runnin' fast enough, you're gonna drift into the rail. When it gets there, you're gonna hear that 'ch-ch-ch-ch-ch-ch.' Like I say, it's gonna slow you a little bit and you're gonna pull right on off of it. It could help you, course it could hinder ya, too. It could really hurt ya if you weren't careful."

The third start in the Warren 53 was on May 14, 1965, and produced Jimmy's best finish to date and ultimately of his career, a sixth at Langley Field in Hampton, Virginia. "I was better on dirt than on short asphalt. That's what I grew up on. I think it was at Hampton I got Pistone to help me set my car up a little different. Tom was pretty good at settin' up a car. It got to where I could get around without any problems."

The record reflects that in the 21-car field, Jimmy finished ahead of Spencer, Lund, Doug Yates, Junior Johnson, Tyner, Moore, Scott, and was right behind old pal Neil at the checkers. Nine days later, Jimmy scored another fine finish, improving from 38th to 13th in the 44-car field World 600. "My front bushin's came out of my A-frame. When you'd go in the corner it wouldn't matter because all your pressure was hangin' on it. But when you go down to the dogleg, you're runnin' straight then you got that little trick there, you could feel it movin'. I mean it would actually move you into another lane if you weren't careful. I went into the pits and had a fellow named Carl Stairs who run a brake shop here in town. It used to be Marvin Panch's Four Wheel Brake Service and Carl and I worked together for Marvin for a while. Carl was in my pits with a couple of other guys and I said, 'How 'bout checkin' this thing. It's comin' apart or somethin'. He said, 'The A-frame bushin's are completely gone.' I said, 'Too late now to try to put one in.' He said, 'Well it's not goin' anywhere. Go ahead.' 'Yeah, we ain't runnin' but about 130, 135, but go ahead.' 'I don't care. It ain't my car. Go on.' [Jimmy laughs.] He made a pretty good evaluation. Carl was an excellent mechanic."

Jimmy Helms' Hob Nob pit crew was never permanent. "Dave [Warren] could do some work when he was there. He would do what he could. He could handle it. He was stout. But most of the time I [would] pick up some of my friends. They'd go to the track and help out. Just like when I started, you'd go and do what you can. Bob Derrington had a brother named Junior and mechanicked for me a lot. He couldn't get along with Bob at all. But Junior was a good mechanic when you could keep him there. Most of the time he was with me when I was with David's car. Carl Stairs helped along with a few others. Once in a while you'd come in and have a flat and get it changed and probably wouldn't go through the second set. Ross Huggins was the Goodyear man and would give me one set, but everything else I had to buy. So I'm gonna keep that set as long as I can. That's something I had very little trouble with. Once in a while on the asphalt I'd have to change one or two. I'd have probably run faster if I hadda changed 'em. You gotta do what ya gotta do to survive. David wanted you to run."

The summer of '65 sizzled as the tour hit Myrtle Beach on June 24 and a rough ninth for the Hob Nob Team.

"I worked my way up on those marbles down there. Man, it was like skatin' on ice. That's the night Derrington come down and run all over me. I mean he just tore the door skin all to pieces. After the race I said, 'Damn Bob! You didn't have to hit me that hard did ya?' 'I didn't mean it.' I said, 'OK. That's all right. There's other races. No harm.'"

The record shows Bob Derrington was seventh that night and Jimmy had a little feud brewing. Three nights later the circuit rolled into Valdosta, Georgia, for a 100-miler on dirt. Jimmy qualified tenth and finished last.

"We got to Valdosta and said, 'I gotta new engine [to install later]. I'm just gonna go ahead and run the fool out of this engine tonight.' We qualified that afternoon and was practicin'. Pistone was out there and I got to runnin' around with Tom [Pistone]. We run several laps and I'm right on his bumper. 'This old car's runnin' pretty good.' We were runnin' bumper to bumper all the way around and I said, 'Damn! This thing's movin'!' 'Bout that time ... *KAPOOF!* There I go to the bottom of the track, oil everywhere, blew the engine. I didn't make the race. I been settin' out there when they wouldn't start and somebody would push you off. They'd be playin' "The Star Spangled Banner" and I'd be settin' there with my engine idlin'. That was in one of Baker's Chryslers. [Jimmy laughs.] They hadn't said, 'Gentleman, start you engines' yet, but I was already runnin'. I had to go."

Jimmy was credited for last because he made the field before he blew and was forced to miss the race. Daytona on the Fourth of July is where Jimmy started 32nd, finishing a decent 24th and had an off-track encounter with Derrington.

"My door was still wrinkled up pretty bad. I mean Bob did a number on my door. The first thing I did was I get my car in the garage. As a matter of fact, I pitted next to A.J.

[Foyt, the race winner] that year. I got under the shed this time. They always put us old boys out in the back that didn't have the big money. But this time I got in the shed and by God I stayed there. Jimmy laughs. I went over to the Ford place after I got settled in and ordered a door skin. I was gonna go back, put my door skin on, and I'd look good. They said it would be in in a day or so. Well I go back over to the Ford place and they said, 'Oh yeah, your door skin came in. Somebody picked it up for you.' I said, 'I didn't send anybody over here for it.' They said, 'Yeah, a guy named Bob Derrington.' [Jimmy laughs hard.] Bob had his beat all to hell, too. I said, 'Son of a bitch!' Anyhow, I go back and start beatin' and bangin' and framin' on my door. It was beat so bad, you couldn't make it look like anything. At Daytona, they want your car to look new. So I get me a gallon of Bondo and started spreadin' it all over. It looked ratty 'cause I was sick. It was about two inches thick. One of the inspectors come by and said, 'Can't let ya go out there with that car lookin' like that.' I said, 'Why?' He said, 'It don't look new.' I said, 'Man, them people in the stands can't see that.' I went to Chief Inspector Norris, my buddy. 'Hey Boss, let me ask you a question. Derrington took my door skin and I done spent money on a gallon of Bondo and used it all up. I'm runnin' out of money. Look at my door.' He came over and looked and said, 'Well see if you can smooth it out just a little bit better and go ahead and paint it.' 'OK.' I tried a little bit more and said, 'OK, here we go.' Painted it with a spray can. Put my number back on there and away we went. I asked him [Derrington] about my door. 'Well, I needed a door skin myself and they had one in stock.' I said, 'Yeah Bob. That was my door skin that you beat off my car the other night.'" Jimmy laughs.

They rolled into Darlington on September 6 for one of the most torturous Southern 500s ever: the Wickersham-Skeen fatal crash early, Cale Yarborough launching over the first turn rail, numerous other spins and crashes, and Ned Jarrett holding on for dear life in an ailing car to beat Buck's Plymouth 86 by 14 laps. Through the carnage and heat, Jimmy persevered from 37th to a splendid 12th for arguably the finest race of his big-time career. Jimmy supplemented his purse with a little movie work.

"I made part of the in-car video of that. They edited it out apparently. You know after we slowed down, I pointed the camera at Buren's car to see if they wanted to see that part. They edited it out of there. They never showed it. I don't know why. I may have missed the button and didn't get that particular shot. I tried as I came back around on the caution lap to get it again. I aimed the car. The camera wouldn't move. They taped the camera to the roll bar and I had a button I mashed if I wanted to turn it on. I think I got an extra $100 or so for shootin' that film. It may have been somethin' Norris told them, 'Go get Jimmy to do it.' Norris Friel was my friend. A lot of people didn't like Norris and he was a cantankerous old gentleman. I thought the world of him. We got along great. Before the video got out, I called the guy I had done it for. I said, 'Could I get a copy of that film I made for you?' He said, 'Yeah. I'll send you one.' I said, 'I don't mind payin'. How much do you want?' He wanted about a $1,000. I said, 'Whoa. Wait a minute. There seems to be something wrong with this picture. I don't believe I want one that bad.' Short period of time I got somethin' in the mail about videos and things of racin'. I said, 'Hey, I believe that's the one I made.' I got it.

"After that it was a sad day. You could tell he wasn't with us anymore. He asphyxiated. The story we got was it pushed all his intestines up into his throat. [Similar to Billy Wade.] Billy hit the wall at Daytona and it left the imprint of the car on the wall and you could

Riding with Jimmy as he shot film footage on September 6, 1965, at the Southern 500. Here he passes the wreckage of Buren Skeen's fatal crash (Screen shot).

see the outline of the colors that Bud [Moore] had. I think his body stretched so far that there was a dent in the glove box on the other side."

Buren Skeen lived one week, passing away on September 13, 1965. The record shows Lorenzen was just ahead in 11th and right behind Jimmy in 13th was Bob Derrington.

October 17, 1965, was one of those days that auto racing had to endure much too often in the 1960s and had just experienced at Darlington. The National 400 at Charlotte Motor Speedway found Jimmy starting mid-pack with a mixture of veterans, inexperienced, and perhaps even rusty drivers. Those drivers with their starting positions were Rock Harn [22nd], Sonny Hutchins [23rd], Harold Kite [24th], Frank Warren [25th], and Jimmy [27th]. Disaster struck quickly.

"That's one of the worst experiences in my life. On the last parade lap, I'd always put my feet against the floor, push back in the seat, and tighten my shoulder harnesses as tight as I could. I'd just got settled in when they dropped the green flag. I'd rather be at the front or the back. Startin' in the middle, I never did like that. I was comin' down the backstretch lookin' through the side of the glass to the corner and you could see a couple of cars get together and start to slide. If you head toward the wreck, nine outta ten times, they're gonna separate and be gone. I headed toward the wreck and as I got closer, he [Harold Kite] stopped. He stopped goin' thisaway [up the bank] and all the sudden started back down. I'm tryin' to get around him here [low] and by the time I got on the flat part of the apron down here [the very bottom], you don't see on the hill. All I could see was it [Kite's car] comin' and I said, 'Oh crap!' I had no idea what car it was. I was doin' all I could to get out of his path. That's all I was tryin' to do. When I saw him comin' this way [up the bank], I thought, 'I got plenty of room.' We were on a collision course, that's what it was. He was still up here [high] when I first started down. I had gotten down. I wasn't all the way in the grass yet. By the time we hit, I was in the grass and so was he. That's about all I remember. One of my friends was in the turn and he got across the fence to me. He was the first one there. He said I got out of the car on my own. I was tryin' to walk and didn't know what I was doin'. I told him, 'I better sit down. I don't feel very good.' I sat down and laid down.

"The next thing I remember I'm in the ambulance goin' to the hospital. I was kindly goin' in and out of the situation. Finally I got to a point where I could talk. I said, 'Um, OK. I'm good to go now.' I was feelin' pretty good, a little dizzy. But hell, I still am. [Jimmy chuckles not because it is funny, more of a tension-breaker from the terrible memory he is reliving.] I wanted to see how bad my car was and get it fixed and go. But with the front wheels sitting up in the cowlin', there wasn't much I could have done with it. Didn't realize I was cut on my chin and had lost a lot of blood. I told the doctor, 'If you can get this thing sewed up, I can get on back over to the track and finish up.' 'No. I don't think you're goin' back today.' They got me sewed up and did a pretty good job. Fortunately, it hit in a place where all my wrinkles are now, so it don't show. I have no idea what got it. I don't think it was my helmet. There was a picture from some photographer. He was makin' sequence shots. When the cars actually hit, you couldn't even see me in the car 'cause it hit so hard, it knocked me down below the window and I sit up pretty high in my car. Of course my shoulder straps kept me from leavin' the car. I never did figure out what cut me. I got in the room and kindly had my senses back a little and said, 'How's the other guy doin'?' They told me he died at the wreck. The doctor didn't want them to tell me 'cause they was afraid I'd go into shock. I wanted to know because I felt so bad our cars were torn up. I mean I wasn't hurt that bad. Evidently when I found that out, it did my day in for me."

Jimmy had met Harold Kite earlier in the week.

"That week Richard Howard [track president] liked to have us come out a week early and ride people around the track on Sunday to help promote the race. I think I borrowed a tire from Harold. I had one that had gone bad and we weren't runnin' that fast. That's the only time, I guess, that I ever talked to him. I didn't know him.

"Somebody told me later that he and his buddy were bumpin' goin' down the backstretch. I think Rock and the other one [Kite] started getting together. I'm not sure where Frank [Warren] was. It took me a good spell to get over. I felt more for his family than anybody else. I was still breathin', so ... I was lucky in that respect. Norris came by my shop and I said, 'Boss, I sure hate what happened. Do you think I should write the family a letter and apologize?' He said, 'No. That's somethin' you don't do.' I had to go on the advice of Norris because he'd been around this business longer than I had. So I never did write the family. I just hoped they never felt bad about me. Could have been me as easily as him."

The involved drivers' Grand National experience at the time of the crash was as follows: Harn — one race at Augusta in 1962 and one at Martinsville three weeks earlier; Kite — eight starts including a win in his first race ever, the 1950 season opener on Daytona Beach, but none since 1956 at Shelby; Warren — two short track starts in 1963 and 1964 each and two in 1965. Warren had just finished eighth in Southern 500; Hutchins — one race in 1955 and nine in 1965, including Charlotte and Darlington; and Jimmy Helms — 55 starts at all major speedways over two years. Jimmy was by far the most experienced driver in the crash.

A major T-bone accident had not involved a fatality in Grand National history. However, in the previous major race, the 1965 Southern 500, Reb Wickersham similarly and unavoidably crashed into Buren Skeen, who died from his injuries. Two consecutive super speedway races involved T-bone crash fatalities. It happened again in 1975 with Tiny Lund, but not again as of this writing.

Jimmy's recuperation was interesting, just like everything else he did.

"I got out of the hospital on Wednesday and had split a tooth, this eye tooth, and it was just sort of hangin' there. I went by the dentist office [Dr. Roach] and he wasn't there. At the race, Doc was leavin' and fell down the hill and broke his arm and was in the hospital himself. So I asked his nurse, 'I need to pull this tooth 'cause half of it was hangin' and the other half was loose.' She said, 'Jimmy, you can't pull that tooth.' I said, 'If you'll let me borrow the pliers, I can.' She gave me a pair of pliers and that lady had been with old Doc forever, I think. She was well up in years. A sweet woman, I mean, really nice. I thought she was gonna pass out. I got in front of the mirror and pulled the rest of it out. I couldn't go with it like that. That was on Wednesday and I went to Hillsborough on Sunday."

Any second thoughts about racing again?

"Not really. I think I wasn't quite as aggressive for a while as I was before. But you kindly get settled back in to it. I don't care what any driver tells you. They go out and have a crash and say, 'Ah, that didn't bother me.' Well, I don't believe 'em. If you got any feelings at all, you think about things like that. I think in some cases it probably slows ya down. You look back at some of the drivers that's had bad crashes over the years and look at their record later on. I think you'll see they might have slowed down a little bit. You get a bit more conservative. Look at Dale Earnhardt. Doin' real well for years and all of the sudden, he's gone. It can happen to anybody at anytime."

The following Sunday at Hillsborough, North Carolina, Jimmy drove for Henley Gray in a last place effort.

"I started Henley's car and went a couple of laps. I don't recall anybody even mentioning what happened [at Charlotte]. Look at what we were driving. A 4,000 pound automobile with factory-built chassis and if you get hit sideways, head-on, even the hoods back then would come back in your windshield if you weren't careful. We did fix 'em where they wouldn't break away. They were somethin' else back then. They were stock cars."

For the record, Jimmy Helms' best year statistically was 1965 with four top tens in 39 starts and 18th in points. Notable finishes were 12th at Bristol, 13th in the World 600, 11th at Watkins Glen, and 12th in the Southern 500. There was plenty in 1965 of which to be proud.

A second year with David Warren, 1966, held promise, but ultimately produced no top tens in 25 starts. David and Jimmy never discussed building another car. Major finishes were 25th in the Daytona 500, 22nd at Atlanta, 16th in the World 600, and 19th at Bridgehampton with a funny tale.

"I tore my transmission up before the homestretch. They got a curve that you shift down in and then you got a long stretch and you go to another corner. I think that's where Buddy saw me comin' and thought somethin' had happened [to him]. I came up behind Buddy on a straightaway and he said, 'I looked in the rear view mirror and saw you comin' up through there and I looked down at my oil pressure to see if my engine was seizin' up. I checked my foot to see if it was mashed down, see if my brakes locked up.' He said, 'Hell,

The Hickory 250 on April 3, 1966, was a dismal DNF for Jimmy's '64 David Warren Ford. Tom Pistone (59) rides the cushion, but also DNF's for 22nd.

you ain't never run that fast! [Jimmy laughs.] What's wrong with *my* car? He's passin' me!' I liked road courses. Seems like they worked real well for me."

On July 30, 1966, ill health and a chance meeting in Nashville led to a genuine thrill and lasting friendship.

"I was sick and Junior Derrington was with me goin' up through the mountains. I had Junior drivin' part of the way 'cause I didn't even have any driver's license. My insurance had lapsed and I didn't know it. I couldn't see that I drove any worse or any better with or without a license. Got up there in the early afternoon and Marty was walkin' around the track there and I said, 'There's Marty Robbins, man!' It was like the first time I met Richard Petty. 'There's Richard Petty, my hero.' I said, 'Have you got a car here today?' He said, 'Naw, I don't.' I went over to Norris and said, 'Hey Boss, do you mind if he drives my car? I ain't feelin' worth a damn anyway.' He said, 'If you don't mind, I don't.' So me and Marty hooked up and I let him drive it. He was involved in a wreck. Couldn't get away from it, but he was comin' up through there. He was a heck of a driver."

The record reflects that Marty Robbins qualified the Warren 53 Ford 17th and retired after 48 of 400 laps for 25th in the 28-car field.

"I was workin' for Goodyear and Pistone called and said, 'You gonna be there?' 'Well, yeah Tom, I'm gonna be here all day.' 'I got somebody I'm bringing down to see ya.' I said, 'Come on.' Tom brought a whole entourage with him. [Jimmy laughs.] 'I just wanted to bring Marty by here to see ya.' I said, 'You gotta be kiddin'!' These people up here in the store, I been talkin' about some of my racin' career. I told 'em about Marty Robbins. They don't believe ya, ya know. 'You don't know Marty Robbins. You're makin' these stories up.' I said, 'Marty, if you don't mind, come up here. I want these people to meet you.' He walked up there and this one woman, she was a country music fan from way back. I thought she was gonna have a fit. She could not believe it. He was really a nice a gentleman."

The David Warren partnership ended after one of the most infamous races in NASCAR history, the 1966 Dixie 400. In that event, Jimmy started 39th and finished 17th. Two of the most outrageous racecars in NASCAR history paced the field. One was the ⅞ths scale, Smokey Yunick pole-sitting Curtis Turner-driven Chevelle 13, which blew after leading 59 laps for 24th. The other was the equally illegally chopped and dropped Junior Johnson–built, Fred Lorenzen–driven 'Banana Boat,' which crashed out while leading nine laps later for 23rd.

"We changed our pay scale. I'm not sure what he thought. I was makin' too much money or what. He wanted to switch things and give me a percentage for drivin' and workin' on the car. 'OK, that'd be fine.' We needed an engine to go to Darlington. It come time to pick the engine up from Keith Dorton and David didn't have the money. I said, 'What we gonna do?' He said, 'Can you get it?' I said, 'Well no, David. We have another deal now.' I let him pick the car up and all the spare parts I accumulated. David just kindly of run out of money or I don't know what. I never did quite figure that out."

Bouncing around to end of the 1966 season, Jimmy ran his finale in a 1964 Ford number 96 owned by the Carolinas' major promoter of Saturday night grapplers, Homer O' Dell.

"I got to knowin' Homer through Swede Hansen and Rip Hawk. I used to go to Spartanburg with Swede. Swede died here a year or so ago. Swede had Alzheimer's. Bless his heart, he was a good guy. I got to knowin' quite a few of those wrestlers and after I got with Homer, I got to know more. Homer come to me and said, 'I want to race a car.' 'Homer, it takes money.' He says, 'I got money.' 'OK, let's buy one.' Homer bought that car and I didn't like it. I asked another buddy of mine, 'Would you want to drive this car for Homer?' 'Yeah.' So, he got into it. It was Sonny Lamphear. Sonny's the one that got me the sheet metal for my car [to convert 53 from a '63 to a '64 Ford]. He started drivin' and I think Homer ended up sellin' it. Homer wanted to make it a production like wrestlin' shows. [Jimmy chuckles.] He said, 'I want to get a red carpet so you can walk out to your car. We're gonna put you in a nice uniform, one of them fireproof uniforms.' 'OK Homer,

Jimmy battles fellow independents Elmo Langley (64) and Roy Tyner (9) at Martinsville in the 1966 Virginia 500 on April 24. He lost the brakes for 27th (Don Smyle).

but....' [Jimmy starts laughing and can't finish.] I wasn't gonna go for that. He was a character. He'd get to drinkin' and get a little mean. He'd had a hard time with police. I wouldn't put up with him. He was always as nice as he could be. He'd show his butt in a restaurant. He was a good guy. I liked old Homer. Last I heard, he was over in Knoxville, Tennessee."

The Homer O' Dell era was but one race on the dirt in Richmond to end 1966 for Jimmy. They started 27th and blew an engine for 14th a little past halfway, one spot ahead of Junior Johnson. O'Dell's career as an owner spanned 16 races with five drivers, ending with Jimmy, and his car never finished a single race.

The 1967 Grand National season was short and sweet for Jimmy. It started at Bristol on March 19 in his old Hob Nob Restaurant pal George Poulos' Plymouth 58. On June 24, 1967, at Greenville Pickens Speedway, Jimmy Helms crawled through the window of a big-time stock car for the 88th and last time. He went out in style wheeling Gene Black's 1966 Galaxie 75 from 12th in a field of 21 to a solid ninth. The only other car running at the finish was Mr. Hob Nob himself, George Poulos in 12th. Jimmy reflects on 1,175 days as a Grand National pilot.

"You know, it's strange when you're growin' up you see all these people and boy, you kind of worship them as heroes. I used to ride a bicycle from Hoskins out to the old Charlotte Speedway and climb up on a hill. I couldn't see the whole track, but I could see Tim Flock, Fonty Flock, Bob [Flock], Buck Baker, Ralph Earnhardt, all of 'em runnin'. My heroes. Marty Robbins, you listen to his singin', Hawkshaw [Hawkins], those people were nice. I'd like to meet them. You end up meetin' the people and find out they're just good, down to earth people like you'd like everybody else to be. I'd be goin' to Myrtle Beach with my girlfriend back then, go by Darlington and say, 'You know what I'm gonna do one of these days? I'm gonna race on that track right there.' 'Ah, you ain't gonna do that.' 'Yeah, I'm gonna race that track.' I'd go to Daytona and I'd say, 'I'm gonna race this track one of these days.' I kept on and my dream came true. And I loved it. I had a good time racin'. I've got probably a couple of regrets, but sometimes you can't help things happenin' to ya."

In 2009, Jimmy Helms spends his days selling boats and sailing supplies at West Marine on Lake Wylie near Charlotte.

Jimmy Helms' stock car story is divided into three distinct sections. The opener was with the old 1962

Chryslers where he was absolutely reigned in from actually racing, but visited nearly all of the tracks learning the ropes from an icon, The Boss Buck Baker. Then he was turned loose with the aged equipment of David Warren and did a fine job. At the very end, Jimmy took whatever he could land. You could also divide Jimmy's career into two periods; before the October 17, 1965, crash and after. No matter how his career is measured, Jimmy Helms dreamed an improbable dream, made it come true, and proved he could race, which makes him the biggest winner of all.

9

Joe Frasson

Jackhandle Joe

Joe Frasson was born on September 3, 1935, in Minneapolis, Minnesota, but made Golden Valley famous in his Winston Cup days. That colorful-sounding location is fitting for one of the most flamboyant drivers to ever frequent a speedway. Joe was a big, burly throttle stomper who put himself in position to win races on the premier stock car circuit and probably did win once. On the tour for a decade from 1969 to 1978, Joe took the green 107 times, with four top fives and 19 top tens including thirds at Darlington and College Station. His antics are legendary and he never shied away from confrontation or publicity. Being independent in USAC was just as wild as in NASCAR. Joe remembered his first major stock car race.

"My first USAC race was in New Bremen, Ohio. I bought a car from Dave Hirschfield. They weren't gonna let me run because I didn't have a USAC license. This was the last race of '67. I said, 'I'll buy a license.' 'Well, you've got to have a physical exam. We just can't do that at the track.' Some guy says, 'What did that guy say his name was?' I said, 'Joe Frasson.' 'That's that crazy son of a bitch that drives that yellow Chevrolet. Get him a license. We've got a doctor here.' 'Yeah, I'm right here.' 'Take him out behind the truck and give him a physical.' 'All right, if that's what I have to do, let's go.' Went out behind the truck and he says, 'Are ya healthy?' 'Yeah.' 'Got any heart trouble?' 'No.' 'OK, you passed.'" Joe laughs.

With a season of USAC under his belt, Joe went NASCAR.

"I run a full season of USAC, must have been '68, and A.J. talked me into going to Riverside, California. He said, 'Hell, them NASCAR boys ain't nothin'. We'll blow their doors in.' Gurney, Foyt, Andretti, these guys I raced with. Who was up front every road-course? The guys *I* raced with. That Plymouth didn't come close to fittin' NASCAR specs and we worked on that car. A guy I had never met ask me if I needed help and wound up bein' part of my crew for several years there. His name was James Gardner. We rebuilt that racecar at the racetrack, got it through inspection Saturday morning. Had one lap of practice, then it was qualifyin' time. I set fast time that Saturday. Something happened and the car dropped out of the race."

The record shows Joe started 25th in Plymouth 32 and fell out after three laps with ignition trouble for 41st.

"Bill Gazaway gave me the raspberries. 'We don't have to worry about him comin' back. We schooled him.' The next year, I bought a Dodge from Nichels Engineering. It wasn't new, it was one of Snuggy's [Don White's] cars. I took it to Riverside. When I pulled in, Bill Gazaway told his brother Joe, 'Hey look! That damn Yankee's back. You think you're ready for us this year? You're gonna rebuild this car, too.' I said, 'I'm ready for ya.' 'Joe, go inspect the Yankee's car yourself. I'm sure you can find somethin' wrong with it.' He inspected that car and I was the first one through. He said, 'Where'd ya get that?' I said, 'Nichels.' He said, 'No wonder everythin's right.'"

The record shows Joe started Plymouth 132 in 11th of 44 and was the next to the last car running at the finish in 20th. Super Tex convinced Joe to head east.

"A.J. talked me into going to Daytona. 'I don't know A.J.' 'You showed 'em here,' he says. 'You got in the top five and there was no one ahead of you except Parnelli, me, Al Unser ... USAC boys. They're no problem. Our guys won't come to Daytona. You'll do good.' So I went."

As a NASCAR rookie in 1970, Joe went to Daytona and really got schooled.

"The biggest thing I had ever seen was Milwaukee. We went through that tunnel and I says, 'Where the hell's the racetrack?' The driver said, 'Look behind you.' 'Oh my God! You don't run on *that* thing.' He said, 'Oh yeah.' I had the Nichels Dodge and we got through inspection no problem. I went out on that racetrack and did everything I knew how to do 'cause A.J. was really givin' me the raspberries. I think we were closing in on 200 miles per hour. I'm 30, 40 miles an hour off the pace. I'm liftin' in the corners, hittin' the brakes. A.J. says, 'What the hell's the matter? You got no guts?' I said, 'By God, if you can do it, I can do it.' He says, 'I'm fixin' to go out to practice. Come out with me. I'll show you how to get around. I can do it. You can do it. Don't be scared. I won't carry you in over your head.' [Joe laughs.] 'You'd probably kill me if you got the chance.' 'Nah, come on.' I've tried puttin' both feet on the gas pedal and they both come off when I go into that corner. Joe laughs heartily.

"Went out, got up to speed, went down that looooong back straightaway, we hit that third turn, and A.J. said *WHOOOM* and was gone. 'Where the hell did he go?' He slowed up and waited. Put his hand out the window givin' me the finger. We tried it again and he still pulls away from me through the corner. He slowed up and waited for me again. This time, he's tellin' me I'm number one, shootin' me a bird. That pissed me off and I says, 'If he can do it, by God I'm gonna do it or I'm gonna wreck this thing, one of the two.' He went through that corner and I'm stuck to his back bumper. We went through there and I said, 'Hmm, maybe I am a racecar driver.'"

Joe had a good run in a sad qualifier.

"I think I was runnin' third. A good friend, Jim Hurtubise, blew an engine comin' down pit road. Back then they had no speed limit on pit road. I'm comin' in for my last pit stop hot. I hit that oil from when Herk blew, spun all the way down pit road, gathered it up, went back out, finished the race. I don't remember where I finished, but I shot third in the foot."

The record shows that Joe was 13th three laps behind, one position ahead of his mentor A.J. Foyt. Tab Prince was killed on lap 18. In his first 500, Joe started 26th finishing just ahead of James Hylton in 21st. Joe recalled the Atlanta 500 on March 29, 1970.

"I showed up with a 1970 square-nosed, recessed-grill Dodge. Ronnie Householder [Chrysler racing boss] come over and says, 'We're having a meetin' of all Chrysler drivers at the Holiday Inn. I would like you to come.' 'Yeah, I'd be glad to. I'm not a factory driver.' He said, 'We know that, but we want you there. At least you're strong.' Everybody there was drivin' a winged car. I had my square-nosed Dodge with the recessed-grill, which definitely was a disadvantage. Somebody said, 'What the hell you doin' here? You ain't drivin' nothin' but junk.'

"The next day, LeeRoy Yarbrough, says, 'Joe, you got an extra pair of gloves?' Now he runs factory. 'I've lost my gloves. I ain't got enough money to buy another pair.' I got a pair and give him my gloves. 'What are you gonna wear?' I said, 'I don't like them damn things.' I outran six or eight of the factory winged cars. When I pulled into the garage area after the race, the first thing that got my attention, I was still married at that time, four of my girlfriends were standing there talkin' to my wife. 'I'm gonna get killed!' Right in the middle of where I pulled was Householder, the two Larrys [engineers from Chrysler], Ray Nichels, Paul Goldsmith, all the factory brass. I get out of the car, Householder congratulates me and turns to the head of Chrysler Racing and says, 'Why doesn't that man have a wing?' [The Head] did not like me because in 1969 I won a USAC race at Milwaukee and had a big decal on both front fenders that said, 'This car independently owned and operated with no factory assistance.' He told me to take it off or never get any factory help. I told him to go to Hell! 'You start helping me and I'll take it off.' Householder says, 'I want a wing on that car.' [The Head] says, 'I don't have any.' Ray pipes up, 'I got a shop full of them. Where's your next race?' 'Charlotte.' 'On your way home, drop the car off at Nichels Engineering. You'll have your wing.' 'OK.'"

The record shows that at the 1970 Atlanta 500, four winged Mopars were ahead and

Joe got his wing just in time for the 1970 World 600 on May 24, 1970. It paid off with an outstanding 12th place finish on a hot, crash-filled Sunday.

seven behind Joe, a considerable independent non-winged achievement. Then Joe won his wing.

"I brought the car up there, left it. 'Bout two days before I needed to be in Charlotte, I called Nichels and asked, 'Is my car ready?' 'Yep.' 'OK, I'll be there tomorrow.' So I drove to Nichels with my truck and walked in the loadin' dock area. There's my old car exactly the way it came off the racetrack in Atlanta; dirty, tire marks all over it. They hadn't touched it. I said, 'Oh my God! I gotta be in Charlotte tomorrow.' Minnie, who was Nichels' brother-in-law in charge of the engine shop, says, 'That ain't your car.' I said, 'Minnie, that's my car and I gotta be in Charlotte.' He says, 'THAT'S NOT YOUR CAR! Your car's inside.' Went inside, there's a winged car all painted, lettered, decaled, ready to go; number 18. While we're there, a couple of guys come in and want a motor. I told Minnie, 'I need a spare motor, too. Hemis. He said, 'We got a bunch of them.' They had 'em in cubicles three high. I said, 'How 'bout that one right there painted yellow and black?' The tag on it says, 'Hold for Snuggy.' Snuggy was Don White who drove the house car for Nichels [in USAC]. Minnie says, 'You don't want that motor. That's one of Snuggy's. Yes I do!' 'No you don't!' He says, 'Take *that* one down. Put that in Joe's truck.'"

While Joe loaded up his new motor, the two other guys went after Snuggy's. "Minnie says, 'I'm not supposed to sell that one. That's one of Don White's motors.' 'Yeah, we know. We want to buy it. How much does it cost?' 'Well, five hundred dollars extra. I'll let ya have it, but you get outta here before anybody knows what happened.' They peeled off the cash and fork-lifted it to that truck and was gone. Minnie come back in and I said, 'You son of a bitch! You sold them the motor and wouldn't to me.' 'I told you ya didn't want *that* motor.' He turned to another guy and said, 'OK. What other motor on the dyno didn't come up to horsepower?' The guy said, 'This one here.' Minnie says, 'Paint it yellow and put the tag back on it.' [Joe laughs heartily.] He said, 'I told you ya didn't want that motor.'"

Joe flirted with factory assistance.

"[In] 1971 we built a new car. Householder called and said, 'Go to Petty's. Send your truck there and get the jig. You need a new car.' I says, 'I ain't got the money to build a new car.' 'Don't worry about money, we're gonna have the two Larrys at your shop and show you how to build this car.' John Greene was the crew chief and he could cheat worse than me. I sent the truck to Petty's and this guy calls back and says, 'They won't give me the jig because they're buildin' a new car for Daytona and it'll be next month before we can have it.' I called Detroit and told 'em Petty won't give us the jig. 'You tell your man to stay there.' He called back 20 minutes later and says, 'The Pettys are not happy. They are loadin' the jig on our trailer.' [Joe laughs.] Ronnie made 'em take Richard's car off the jig. They knew I didn't mind cheatin' a little bit. Richard Petty ... 'Oh we don't ever cheat.' Like the Wood Brothers ... 'We don't ever cheat.'

"Anyways, we built the car and at that time, NASCAR didn't have templates. They had a stick they'd run under the car to make sure it was high enough and that was basically it. We showed up at Daytona and the top of our hood had to be three inches lower than anything there. 'Oh no! That's not gonna fly.' We had one devil of a time getting through inspection. Wednesday, the day before the qualifyin' races, it had been rainin'. Bill Gazaway says, 'Well, you finally got it through, but I don't know if we want you to bring this thing back or not. The bad news for you is if you don't get on that racetrack and turn a lap at 170, you don't start the qualifyin' race.' I told Skip [McCarthy], 'Put the car on jack stands.

Start the motor, warm the motor up, put it in gear, warm up the transmission and rear end.' He said, 'What the hell you gonna do? It's rainin'.' 'Just do as I tell ya and I'm gonna go get dressed.' Went and put my fire suit on, came back, got in the car, put my helmet on.' Skip says, 'It's rainin'!' 'I don't care. Put the car down. I've got to go turn a lap at 170.' I think we was qualifyin' at 196, 198. I went straight out of that garage, down pit road, out onto that racetrack, put the hammer down! I said, 'Damn, I hope these tires stick.' I don't know how they stuck, but I got one complete before they pulled the fire trucks across the racetrack. I spun that thing down pit road, came to a stop, brought it to the garage. I mean here comes everybody; Bill France, Joe Gazaway, Bill Gazaway, Billy France, you name it, 'bout that high off the ground and maddern a hornet. I says, 'How fast did I run?' 'One hundred and seventy one in the rain!' 'I get to start the race tomorrow.' 'That just cost you a $1,000.' 'I'll make it up Sunday.'"

Joe Frasson Racing was a two-car operation.

"I had two cars. Jackie Oliver was in my other car. I was in the first race and missed the big wreck that Friday [Hassler] got killed in. I went on that wet grass and slid almost all the way to the third turn before I stopped. Didn't hit nothin', heard it comin', and hung on. J.D. McDuffie found the same hole and come through there, blasted me. Took us both out. We missed the wreck on the track, but hit that wet grass and tore both cars all to hell. There's my new car out of the race. We still got that other race with Oliver. It was 125 miles. I'm standin' in the pits. He's runnin' third or fourth. He come down pit road for his stop, shuts the car off, and gets out. 'Where the hell *you* goin'?' [In an excellent British accent Joe says,] 'I cannot win the race. There's no need to keep running.' I hit that son of a bitch right smack in the jaw, grabbed a helmet, and jumped in the car. By the time I got in the car, got buckled up, we went a lap or two down. We loaded both cars up and come home. NASCAR was gonna fine me for fightin' in the pits. There was no fight! He pissed me off and I hit him! [Joe laughs wildly.] I had a bad reputation back then. I'm 75 years old now and still got that bad reputation. I don't understand why."

Joe Frasson won the Alamo 500 at Texas World Speedway by two laps on June 10, 1973, or so a lot of people thought.

"I won the Alamo 500. Total with all the baloney money you're supposed to get off the decals on the fenders, $15,000. Contingency money. Contingent upon havin' the decals on the fenders and contingent on whether or not that company was stable enough to send ya any money. I'd lapped the field twice, not once, twice! A lady friend in Texas got sick scorin' the car. Bobby Allison's wife Judy picked up my scorecard on the 20th lap and scored. She's done it a thousand times. Took the checkered flag, pulled into Victory Lane, and they stopped me. They had a pow wow. Gazaway come over and says, 'Back yer car outta here.' 'Why?' 'We just were told you didn't win.' 'Whatta you mean I didn't win? I got two laps on the field that I know of.' 'No, you didn't win. Richard Petty won.' I said, 'Bull shit!' I hoofed it straight to the scorin' stand. Joe Epton was the head scorer and I says, 'Hey! You people screwed up!' He said, 'Well, you had a long pit stop.' 'Yeah? They cross-threaded a lug. It was a long pit stop or I would have lapped the field *three* times!'

"The first thing that come out of Petty's mouth when they pulled him into Victory Lane, 'Boys, I didn't win this race. I know I'm two laps down.' 'No, uh, must have been a mix up in the scorin'. You won it.' They had Waltrip second. Jaws came up to the scoring stand. 'You people screwed up. Richard didn't win. I didn't finish second. I know I'm two laps down, if not three.' 'No, you're wrong. Joe finished fifth.' Judy piped up, 'You're all nuts! We got two laps on the field.' She went to bat for me. Bobby was drivin' the damn Matador and was out of the race right away. They said, 'Well, I guess Joe finished third on the same lap with the leaders.' 'NO!' 'Well, were gonna take the scorecards to Daytona and examine them.' 'I sued. They paid me 12,000 bucks for winnin', no contingency money, but gave the race to Richard. We went in the court in Daytona. They brought the entry blank over to me and the judge says, 'Mr. Frasson, is that your signature on the entry blank?' 'Yes it is.' 'Would you read the line right above your signature please?' 'All decisions by NASCAR are final and binding.' [Joe claps his hands loudly.] 'Case dismissed.'"

The record shows that Joe finished third, three laps behind "winner" Richard Petty, one behind Waltrip, with Cale Yarborough fourth on the same lap as Joe. Then there was the Great Talladega Bust Out.

"I was leadin' the race. I blew an engine, got back in the garage, and was loadin' up. We gotta go home, work, build an engine, get to the next race. I run four or five nights a week on short tracks and dirt tracks. Anyways, I'm gonna leave. Bill Gazaway says, 'No, you're not leavin'.' I said, 'The hell I ain't. I gotta go home and fix my car. Build another motor.' 'No, no, no. You ain't leavin' till the race is over. We're gonna inspect your car.' 'The motor's blown up!' 'We're still gonna inspect it.' 'I'm goin' home.' They closed and locked the gate. That didn't even slow that WT9000 Ford down. Went through that gate and took down 200 feet of chain-link fence. I was runnin' so fast they wanted to tear the motor down."

For the next race at Talladega, Joe redesigned his Dodge.

"I still have the belt buckle." Joe displays a belt buckle he was wearing shaped like Talladega International Speedway.

"I sat on the pole ten or twelve miles an hour faster than anybody. We came back to the shop [after] the race before. I noticed a car smokin' and the smoke was just boilin' behind it. I thought, 'If I can break the vacuum, that car has got to run faster because that's where the slingshot's comin'. I sat and looked at the back of that Dodge and the chrome bumpers were painted white for a reason. We narrowed up the front three inches and the back four. We painted the bumpers because it was cheaper than having them re-chromed. I got to thinking. Read that rule book about six times. The rule book said on Dodge, the inside of the back bumper must be covered. Didn't say covered with what. We all covered it with aluminum. Had it lettered Dodge with 18s on the corners. 'Skip, get a drill. Take those pop rivets out.' 'Whatcha gonna do?' 'We gonna make this car go fast at Talladega.' So we took the aluminum panel off, put a screen there, painted the screen, lettered it to say 'Dodge,' and put the 18s. You stood ten, 15 feet back, if you didn't look close, it looked like the car did before. Then we put that aluminum panel back up with Dzus fasteners.

"Skip says, 'What good's that?' You ain't gonna get no air in the trunk.' We take these lower panels where the quarter panels come down. Harry Hyde had gas tanks in his. He forgot to put the plug in one [one time] and they're gassin' the car. I said, 'Harry, gas is runnin' out of your quarter panel.' [Joe laughs.] 'If we make a couple of spring-loaded trap doors that'll drop down, that'll catch air off the back tires if they weren't very big. Maybe six inches wide and a foot long.' We took it out on the road where my shop was, a little rough. You'd hit a bump and those trap doors would just flap. You'd stop and the springs would bring them back up. 'That'll work!' I had NO idea what it was gonna do on the racetrack.

One of Joe's "modified" Dodges. Note the white painted chrome bumpers. He narrowed the car and painted the parts white rather than rechrome them (Joe Frasson).

"Went through inspection. As we're pushin' the car out, they flipped those Dzus fasteners, took that aluminum panel, laid it next to the fence, pushed the car out on the line, and I'm thinkin' Cale sat on the pole at 198 or somethin'. I went out and come through that tri-oval, got that green flag, and went into that first turn. I could feel the g-forces pullin' it. 'Holy shit!' I got a head a steam on. Two hundred and twelve miles an hour! [Joe laughs long and hard.] Two hundred and eleven something! Took the checkered flag, went around the track and nobody went out behind me. I come down pit road. They had every truck NASCAR had across pit road, across the grass, and they're all standin' out there. 'STOP!' 'What's wrong?' 'You're not goin' back in the garage. Right here. Go get a jack, jack stands. We're inspectin' your car right now. Here!' 'Not in the inspection station?' 'No, right here!' All the inspectors were there. They went through that car from one end to the other. Couldn't find nothin' wrong. Joe Gazaway told Bill [France], 'Far as we're concerned, the car is legal.' Bill said, 'That's impossible! He's twelve miles an hour faster than anything here.' He's standin' behind the car scratchin' his head and he looked ... and he looked ... and he came over and he touched it. *'Oh hell no!* That won't go!' 'Why?' 'You're supposed to have aluminum back there.' 'Read the rule book, Bill. Read me the rule book out loud, please.' I mean we got a crowd here now. 'On the '71 to '73 Dodges, the inside of the rear bumper will be covered.' 'Covered with what, Bill?' 'It'll be covered! Everybody uses aluminum.' 'That's not what the rule book says, Bill. It's covered. Is it not covered?' Oh, he went to the back of his rule book where he had six blank pages. He wrote it in that rule book right there in front of us, God be my witness. He says, 'Now it's in my rule book, 'It will be covered with aluminum.' You are [Joe slaps the desk] disqualified! You'll start in the rear.' But I got to keep the belt buckle. I started in the rear and they never found the trap doors! [Joe laughs devilishly.] Those trap doors would drop down and the air off the back wheels would go up into the trunk."

Joe laughs loudly, then related more independent skullduggery.

"In '74, I had an aluminum box made that I put my radio on right next to me clear of the shifter. It's up a little higher and I could reach my radio while drivin'. What they didn't know was that I mashed the button on the side and that aluminum box and radio would flip over and I had a small Port-A-Power jack underneath. I'd release the pressure and I had a line that ran through the frame, through the roll cage, to the right front wheel. I had a dummy shock up there that was actually a Port-A-Power ram inside of a shock. It would take four pumps and raise the car over an inch and half. When I released it, it would drop that inch and a half. They took pictures of that car sitting on pit road. They took pictures on the racetrack. In all the pictures when it was sittin', you could see the top of the front tire. When the car was on the racetrack, you couldn't see the top of the front tire, just wheel. Back then the Dodges had torsion bars. We used to take plastic marbles and stick them underneath to hold the car up. First bump you hit, the car would drop, but there's no way to raise the car back up. It didn't take long for NASCAR to figure that out. That's when I went to this set up. They tore that car apart. Never did find it. And the crazy thing, Joe Gazaway had that dummy shock in his hand. [Frasson laughs long and hard.] He said, 'You better get another shock. This is leakin'.' 'Cause when he took it off the car, the o-ring, we had it machined, that's where the oil come out where the shock mount was."

Joe sold the tricked-up Dodge.

"I sold that car to Buddy Arrington. He run that car a whole year. At the end of the year he called and cussed me out. 'Whatta ya cussin' me out for?' He says, 'Why didn't you tell me you had nitrous oxide in that car?' 'What?' He says, 'I found your nitrous oxide system.' 'No nitrous oxide in that car.' 'Well sure there is,' he says. 'When I cut the front snout off to make an engine stand, I found your copper line runnin' through there.' I says, 'Didn't you ever use that?' 'Use what?' I said, 'Did you find the shock up there leakin'?' 'Yeah. We were changin' shocks and that one was leakin' so we threw it away.' [Joe laughs heartily.] I said, 'It would raise and lower the car an inch and a half!' At Talladega, for every inch the nose goes down, you're pickin' up two miles an hour.' I'm just a dumb ol' country boy."

Racing under the radar continued.

"We went to Jackson, Michigan, when they come up with restrictor plates. We built a carburetor, Crawford [Clements] and myself. When you tightened the air cleaner, the carburetor would come up .008 and it would suck air through the bottom. When you unscrewed it, the carburetor set back down. I'm out there practicin' and Crawford says, 'Just half-lap it. We don't want to show our hand till qualifyin'.' I'm half-lappin' it. I come off the racetrack and boy, there's all NASCAR's trucks and cars across pit road again. They stop us right on pit road. 'You ain't got a restrictor plate!' 'Yes we do!' 'We need to look at it.' I looked at Crawford. He looked at me. 'Open the hood and take the air cleaner off.' This was Bill Gazaway. As Crawford was takin' the air cleaner off, one of the inspectors took a knife and stuck it under the base of the carburetor. When Crawford turned the bolt that held the air cleaner, it dropped the carburetor and the guy says, 'This thing grabbed my knife! My whole knife blade was under the carburetor.' Crawford says, 'You're crazy as hell!' He says, 'Take the air cleaner off.' So Crawford whooped it off. The inspector says, 'I'll show ya.' He went all around that carburetor and says, 'I swear, my whole knife blade was under there.' I said, 'Man, you crazy!' 'Take the carburetor off.' By this time, they got Earl Parker the Champion Spark Plug man, the Holley carburetor man, Junior Johnson, Glen Wood, we got a crowd gathered around. Crawford said [softly], 'I told you to half-lap it.' 'I *did* half-lap it.' He said, 'You're ten miles an hour faster than anything here.' [Joe laughs.] I *was* half-lappin' it.

"Took the carburetor off and Gazaway says, 'Take the base off that carburetor.' I said, 'Crawford, hold the carburetor and I'll take the screws out.' He's holdin' it and I'm takin' the screws out. When the base plate come apart, Crawford caught all the little check balls and springs in his hand and stuck it in his pocket. We handed the carburetor and base plate to the Holley man. He looks at it and says, 'That's strange.' Gazaway says, 'What?' 'There's nothin' wrong with the carburetor except half of the idle passages are soldered shut.' We had tubes in there with little check balls and springs. That thing would split open and suck

On April Fool's Day 1973 in the Atlanta 500, Joe passed Mark Donahue's sick Matador, but also fell out 20 laps later for 28th after starting seventh.

air. They couldn't find anything except the idle passages had been soldered shut. NASCAR fined me a thousand dollars and that was a lot of money in '75. Took the carburetor and made us start in the rear.

"Ten years later, Bill Gazaway asked me, 'What the hell made that car run so fast?' I said, 'I don't know. You got the carburetor.' He said, 'It's in the Darlington Museum with the rest of your cheatin' stuff!' [Huge laughter erupts from Joe.] But I'm just a dumb old country boy with no money. If I could do that stuff, what were people with the money and intelligence getting by with? They had the factory engineers workin' on cars."

Joe described an experiment in 1975.

"I think Petty and I were the last two with Chrysler 'cause NASCAR wanted Chrysler out. That was 1974 where we took the hemi heads off and put Windsor heads on so they

The pretty, ill-handling Pontiac LeMans that Joe raced one time on May 4, 1975, in Talladega's Winston 500. He fell out for 18th after a very fine run.

weren't hemis. I blew mine up in Atlanta in a ball of fire. That was the last race of '74. I told Crawford, 'We cannot win with a Chrysler.' Bill France called and says, 'Are you gonna be hard-headed and stick with Chrysler?' 'No Bill.' 'What are you gonna build?' I says, 'I don't know, probably a Chevrolet. General Motors always been good to me.' They called the year before and offered me a Chevrolet. I told them, 'I don't want a damn Chevrolet. You got two runnin', Friday Hassler and Coo Coo Marlin. Neither one of 'em can get out of their own way. I don't want one.' They gave my car to Junior [Johnson] and he put Charlie [Glotzbach] in at Charlotte and won with my damn racecar. [Joe laughs.]

"Crawford talks me into buildin' a Pontiac LeMans. The car was fast, but you couldn't hold that thing in a ten-acre field. At Daytona and Talladega, I'd brace my arms so I wouldn't wiggle the steering wheel. That thing would change a lane by itself. The trunk lid dropped off so fast that spoiler didn't do anything. NASCAR wouldn't give us a spoiler. I set fast time at Darlington in 1975 and got the pictures somewhere of the remains of the car. Took the checkered flag and that's the first time that car felt stable. I went down to the first turn and the throttle stuck. I hit the outside wall, spun, hit the inside, flipped it over into the infield. They wouldn't give me the record for Pontiac because it didn't start the race. I come out of the hospital and told Crawford, 'You gotta get that car fixed.' He said, 'There ain't no car left.'"

Joe executed the Pontiac and got a lot of publicity and a nickname.

"We fixed the car. Rebuilt it. Went to Charlotte and didn't make the race. I thought about it and thought about it. If that car went back to the shop, we're gonna be at the next race with it. I was standin' lookin' at it. It was a pretty car, red, white and blue. I unscrewed my jackhandle and Crawford says, 'Whatter ya doin'?' 'I'm gonna kill that damn Pontiac.' I started beatin' on it. I hit it three, four, five times. Here comes a crowd and the news media. 'Man, if we knew you were gonna do that ... you shoulda told us. We'da got some pictures.' I said, 'Well gather around, we'll do it again.' So a crowd gathered, I took that jackhandle, and flailed every panel on that car. I did not hit anywheres near the carburetor or air cleaner. I did not hit the windshield, top, or back glass. I can use that to make a Chevrolet.

Joe executed the LeMans after failing to qualify for the 1975 World 600. He did not hit places that would keep him from converting it to a Chevy.

"We took it home and Crawford was really upset. I said, 'So now we make a Chevrolet out of it.' I called Detroit and says, 'Hey! This is Joe.' 'Joe who?' 'Joe Frasson.' 'Whatta *you* want?' 'I decided we aren't gonna run Pontiac anymore and thought maybe you'd give me a little help goin' to Chevrolet.' He says, "Didn't Big Bill call and offer you that new Chevrolet before the season started?' 'Yeah, but I changed my mind.' He says, 'We changed our mind, too. We don't need you anymore. Good-bye.' *CLICK!* That was the start of the end for me 'cause I didn't have money and big money started pouring in.' Everytime we'd pick up a sponsor, NASCAR would step in and take him away."

The first big one got away.

"Darlington, '72, '73, I had been talking to Kodak. Three or four of the brass from Kodak showed up. Oh they were impressed. We finished third. Should have won. Kodak is happy. 'We are gonna sponsor you. *You* are our man!' When we get back to New Jersey, we will call, send you a plane ticket, you and Crawford come up. We'll have a press conference announcin' that Kodak will be on your racecar for the next two years.' Two weeks went by, hadn't heard anything. We called and 'Well, somethin' come up when the race was over that we have to look at.' When the race was over, I noticed they were talkin' to Billy France, Jimmy France, Gazaway. They took 'em to the country club, wined 'em and dined 'em, took 'em to Daytona. There went Kodak. This happened to me three times with NASCAR. They announced NASCAR Camera Days sponsored by Kodak. Nobody had to explain that to me. I'm not the only one they've done it to. If you didn't have a factory ride, if you didn't have money, NASCAR didn't have time for you. Billy France asked me several times, 'Why don't you quit? Why don't you get the hell outta here? New drivers can't come in and run against you guys. You got too much experience. We need new, young blood. Fresh blood with money.'"

The record shows that on April 16, 1972, Joe was third behind Pearson and Petty in the Rebel 400. Then, it happened again.

"Crawford and me made three trips to St. Louis. I've still got the letter in there. Budweiser was going to back us. They wanted to know how much money we needed for the season. I think we asked for somethin' like $200,000. Crawford kept tellin' me, 'We gotta have more.' I said, 'They won't give us that kind of money.' The head of Budweiser, a guy named Tom, said, 'We need demographics. We need spectator attendance, radio, and television audience.' I says, 'I don't know where to get that stuff. I'm just a dumb ol' country boy.' 'We'll get it,' he says. 'We'll make another appointment for you in two weeks. That'll give us time to get these demographics and still get you money for the year.' 'Great!' So Crawford and I drove to St. Louis for that next appointment. Sat down in this big office and I'm looking on the desk. There's a check made out to Frasson Racing Enterprises for $2,000,000. We talked for a bit and Tom says, 'Joe, I like you. We really want to sponsor you.' He picked the check up and tore it in half and tore it in half again. He said, 'I'm sorry.' His exact words. 'We will not be affiliated with an association that would stoop so low to steal one of its own member's sponsors.' '*What did I do?*' 'You didn't do anything. NASCAR did and I'm not gonna give it to you. Look what NASCAR has done for Winston. Look what NASCAR can do for you. Do not sponsor a racecar, sponsor NASCAR.' And that cost me Budweiser. The next year, NASCAR announced their Busch Series. What does that tell ya?"

Then came strike three.

On May 2, 1976, in Talladega's Winston 500, Joe's axle broke so he got a Miller and a push back to the pits for 36th in the Excuse Lounge Chevy.

"I have no love for Jarretts. The old man cost me Miller Beer for a sponsor. We blew a rear tire leadin' the damn race [a 300-mile Busch Grand National race at Charlotte]. Caution come out, we come in and got tires and came out fourth or fifth. The race was over and the crew had drank all the beer. I'm thirsty. Ned's goin' by and he had the Busch truck. I said, 'Ned, you got a cold beer in there?' 'Yes!' I was standin' next to the Busch truck drinkin' Busch beer. Ned takes my picture. Guess where that picture went? Milwaukee to Miller. I got a phone call, 'You just lost your sponsorship. You go see if Busch wants to sponsor you.'"

Joe had a friendship that did flourish with The Big Fisherman Tiny Lund. However, it started slow.

"Tiny was drivin' the 16 that belonged to Bud Moore. He was either leadin' or up front. I caught him and was tryin' to get by and he kept blockin'. Well, my motto back then and always has been 'Lead, follow, or get the hell out of my way.' I'll knock once. The second time I'm gonna knock a little harder. Third time I'm gonna put ya in the wall. And I did! [Joe chuckles.] After the race, Tiny come stormin' down pit road and everybody scattered. 'There's gonna be a hell of a fight. Tiny's mad!' He come down and I said, 'I don't think you want to mess with me big boy.' Tiny was from Iowa and I was from Minnesota. We knew each other, but weren't friends. Words got to flyin' and he was gonna kick my butt. 'You better pack a lunch, big boy 'cause I'm gonna clean this pit road up with ya.' He looked at me real funny and says, 'You gonna fight me by yourself?' 'Yes sir and I'm gonna whip ya!' Tiny said, 'I think we ought to go over here and talk about this.' He said, 'Me and you could whip everybody here.' Between Tiny and I, we could have cleaned out the whole racetrack. Back then I was 6' 3" and 260–270 and in excellent shape. Not a fat old man like I am now. We became very close friends. In fact, just before he died, we were makin' plans for me to move from Spartanburg to Cross [South Carolina]. I was gonna build a new shop. Tiny was gonna give me a piece of property and we were gonna race together."

Joe laughs. Imagine a racing team with Joe Frasson and Tiny Lund as the drivers. On the hot Alabama Sunday morning of August 17, 1975, a drama played out in the garage and pit areas.

"Race day mornin', he come over and says, 'Come on and walk with me.' I says, 'I gotta get my car through inspection.' 'No, c'mon. I'm spooked. That's the most ill-handlin' thing I ever drove.' I says, 'Did you put them steering arms and parts under the front end I gave ya?' 'No. They [A.J. King's crew] said you didn't know what you was talkin' about.' I says, 'Get outta here!' He said, '*Please!* Come walk with me and talk to me. I'm spooked.' 'Tiny, I gotta get through inspection. Get the hell away!' When they called the drivers to the cars, Tiny was startin' in the back and I was towards the front. As I walked by Tiny's car, that big arm came out and grabbed my arm. I says, 'What are you doin'?' 'Joe, be careful.' I said, 'I'm startin' up front. You're the one back here with the junk.' He wouldn't let go of my arm. He said, 'You're my friend. Be careful. *Please!*' It spooked the hell out of me."

The record shows that Tiny started King's Charger 26 from 31st while Joe had his Crawford Clements–tuned Chevrolet 18 gridded 22nd. Tiny's and Joe's future plans came to a grinding halt on the backstretch minutes into the Talladega 500 on lap six.

"They threw the green and I started fallin' back. Crawford called me on the radio and said, 'What's wrong with the car?' 'Nothin'! You wanna drive this dang thing?' 'Bout that time, Tiny come up on the outside and looked at me and I thought, 'What in the hell am I doing back here with him?' I put the hammer down and as we come off the second turn, that's where Tiny brushed the wall and the back of my car. It turned me a little, I gathered it up, and looked in the mirror. He was spinning down the back straightaway and came to a stop back end to the wall. I was really mad at myself for letting him spook me like that. [Joe pounds his fist into his palm a couple of times loudly.] I'm cussin' him out. Caution was out, of course, and we came by again and Tiny's still just sittin' there. Come by the second time and the ambulance was there and the doctor was in the car with him. The boy doin' the flaggin' on the back straightaway, I pulled up and stopped and he said, 'Joe, get outta here!' I said, 'How bad's Tiny?' 'Well, he's hurt, doc's in the car with him, but he's gonna be OK. Just get outta here!' I figured he was hurt, so I took off. The race got goin' again and I seen a helicopter land at the track hospital. I thought, 'They'll fly him outta here. At least he's alive.' [Joe pounds his fist into his palm again.] I can't remember where, but I got back up front and had a decent finish. When I came into the garage Crawford was there. I looked at him and the helicopter was still there. I said, 'Tiny's dead, ain't he?' 'Yes.' 'Why didn't ya tell me?' He says, 'Because you'd have pulled the car off the track.' I said, 'Yes I would've.' He said, 'Nothing you can do. He's gone.'"

Tiny Lund was T-boned by Pontiac Grand Am 66 of Terry Link and credited with 46th winning $620. Joe had a fine day finishing eighth, five laps behind pocketing $2,745. The unthinkable confronted Joe and a terrible day turned into a horrible night.

"We loaded up and drove to Spartanburg. I called Tiny's house and Wanda answered. I says, 'You OK?' 'Yeah, why?' I said, 'Anybody there with you?' 'Yeah, Ma's here.' Ma Lund, Tiny's mother. 'Did you hear the race today?' 'No,' she said. 'I had a bad feelin' about it. Didn't want to listen. Ma and I went to the movies. What's wrong?' I said, 'Nobody's called you?' '*No.*' I said, 'Wanda [Joe sighs deeply], Tiny's dead. He got killed at the racetrack today [Joe's voice trails into a near whisper]. I will be there in just over two hours.' I threw some clothes in the bag, jumped in my car, and I was in Monks Corner [South Carolina] in a little over two hours. [Joe laughs.] That's a three and a half four hour drive. [Joe again pounds his fist into his palm.] Nobody ever called her from NASCAR, from the hospital, *nobody!* To say the least, NASCAR's not my most favorite outfit."

In retrospect, "it wasn't so much a bad car; it was ill-handlin' because they had the wrong components. Chrysler products had bolt-on steerin' arms. Left sides had L-1, L-2, and L-3, different lengths. The right side had R-1, R-2, and R-3. At Talladega, you did not want a long steerin' arm on the right and a short one on the left. That's gonna make that left front wheel turn too hard. It's gonna make the car do tricks. They had the wrong torsion bars on the car. Whoever set the car up had no earthly idea what they were doin'. If I seen King today, I'd sure as hell let him know. I knew he [Tiny] was in Hickory [North Carolina] the night before, won [a sportsman race], and flew to Talladega. The thing that angers me is I gave him all the parts to make the front end right. The next year at Atlanta, somebody came up as I'm getting in the racecar and had a *World Book Encyclopedia*. They had me listed as the only fatality for NASCAR that year. [Joe laughs.] I said, 'No, that wasn't me. That was Tiny.'"

Joe was instrumental in the outcome of arguably the greatest finish in racing history on February 15, 1976.

"David would not admit it until a couple of years ago. 'Yeah, I wouldn't have won if I hadn't hit Joe. Goin' down that back straightaway, they slingshotted me because back then, you could really do it. David got out first, then Richard passed him goin' into three. I come up behind David to give a push by Richard. Richard shut the door. I seen that one comin' and jumped on the brakes lookin' for a place to go. I should have never touched the brakes, although I'da hit Richard if I wouldn't have. I pulled down and David came down and caught me in the side. I remember getting airborne comin' down pit road at 200! I got across the finish line before David. Richard's stuck in the grass. When David hit me, it turned him right back up on the racetrack. The whole right side was tore off my car. Right front wheel was gone. Right rear was flat. I limped all the way around. Once I stopped, they had to get a wrecker 'cause the car wouldn't move. I went to David and said, 'Dad

Sponsorless independents battle at Rockingham on March 5, 1978, in the Carolina 500. "Big Joe" finished 16th and D.K. (40) DNF'd for 26th.

gummit David. You wouldn't have won that race if I hadn't been there. I'm broke. How 'bout seein' if you can help me get my car back together.' 'Nah! If you wouldn't have been there, I would have been in good shape.' We argued about that for years and he finally admitted it in the Daytona paper that he would not have won that Daytona 500 if he hadn't hit me. He'd have really got tore up if he'd a hit the pit wall at those speeds."

The records reflect that Joe Frasson's Excuse Lounge Chevrolet finished 14th, 17 laps behind. The 1976 Southern 500 saw Joe involved in an extremely violent crash I (the author) witnessed and photographed. Skip Manning, 1976 Rookie of the Year candidate, took an innocent slide between turns one and two and very nearly bought it on the spot.

"Skip lost it and started to go up the track and I had no choice but to get under him. He kept his foot in the gas and shot right straight down in front of me. I never even got to hit the brakes. I T-boned him. I got beat up pretty bad because my shoulder harnesses broke, the two-inch belts. The only thing that kept me from goin' through the windshield was the steerin' wheel and the three braces behind the windshield. I busted the windshield and those braces stopped me and set me back in my seat. I raised total hell with Bill Simpson over it. He said, 'My seat belts don't break!' I said, 'I had these tested at U.S.C. and they broke at 2,000 pounds. They figured with my weight, 260 pounds, and the speed I was goin', it was 3,000 pounds of force against the belts. They won't hold.' 'My belts don't break!' It wasn't a week or two later that a UPS truck pulls up, drops a package off from Simpson. He sent me two sets of *three*-inch belts. That's how we ended up goin' with the three-inch belts."

On September 5, 1976, Joe rammed Skip Manning in turn two during the 1976 Southern 500. It appeared that both men were very seriously injured or worse (Steve Jeffords).

Manning's injuries were not as serious as those that killed Buren Skeen and Harold Kite in nearly identical crashes 11 years earlier. Skip missed one race and became 1976 Winston Cup Rookie of the Year. Joe was, and still is, very close friends with Dick Trickle, a fellow shorttracker from the Midwest. They had a couple of racing arrangements in the '60s and '70s.

Joe's head punched out the windshield when his belts broke upon impact. He took 34th and Manning recovered to win 1976 Rookie of the Year.

"Dick and I tried not to go the same track because only one of us is gonna win. Dick said, 'Are you going to Odessa?' 'Got to go to Odessa and piss off Rusty Wallace.' 'Well, you go there and I'll go to Rolla, Missouri.' 'All right, deal.' The promoter came to me and says, 'Why don't you come to my track in Rolla? I'll give you $3,000.' 'OK.' [Joe chuckles.] We get there and Dick comes up and says, 'What the hell are you doin' here?' I says, 'Man paid me to show up.' I sat on the pole. Dick was outside. They threw the green and we went down the back straightaway side by side. We got to the third turn, I turned, my car went straight. I hit Dick and drove him head-on into the wall. I hollered at the crew, 'What did you do to the car?' 'It's so cold, we put ten extra pounds of air in the tires.' 'Get that air out of those tires now!'

"It had to be at least ten years after that, I get call from Humpy Wheeler. 'Bring your second car for Dick Trickle.' We put a 99 on the car for him. He was at the racetrack very quiet. 'Bout end of the second day he's lookin' at me kinda funny and I said, 'Dick, what's on your mind?' He says, 'Did they really pay you 500 bucks to put me in the wall in Rolla?' [Joe laughs.] I says, 'You gotta be kiddin' me. You been stewin' about that all these years?' 'Yeah! I couldn't believe you accepted 500 bucks to put me in the wall.' I told him what the crew did. He said, 'You son of a bitch. Why did you tell me they paid you 500 bucks?' I said, 'Thought that's what you wanted to hear.'"

Joe slapped his hand on the desk and laughed loudly, then talked about Janet Guthrie.

"Humpy come over and says, 'How 'bout putting Janet in the car.' I said, 'Janet *who*?' [Joe laughs.] I still wonder if she really was a girl. [Joe laughs heartily.] Hey, she's as big as me. Back then I was still a good 6'2" or 6'3". She sat in my seat and did not have to adjust the belts. She reached up a stack of tires with liners in 'em. Grabbed one by the sides and said, 'Are these things really as heavy as they say?' She did about four or five lifts from the top of the stack over her head. Those things are 80, 85 pounds. You can quote me, 'That's one big momma.' She's a nice lady. She did all right. She did better than Jackie Oliver!"

By 1978, Joe had enough of big-time NASCAR and chose to make a living on short tracks, which he terrorized and dominated.

"I was runnin' four or five nights a week on the short tracks to make enough to keep the Cup car going. Gene Granger [Spartanburg motorsports writer] documented 450 wins. I asked him about these dirt tracks, state fairs, county fairs, 'cause I used to be king of those.' He says, 'We can't document it and prior to 1980, NASCAR has no records. What was the sportsman series became the Busch Series and is presently the Nationwide Series.'"

The Permatex 300 at Daytona on Saturday, February 17, 1979, is a landmark in Joe Frasson's post–Cup career. Interviews with Joe inevitably led to the story of this horrendous crash that Joe survived, but another didn't.

"Preacher [Marion Cox] called me and said, 'Joe, I need ya to drive my car at Daytona.' 'Nah, I gotta bad feelin'.' Everytime I'd get one of these bad feelings, something bad happened. He says, 'I fired my driver, lost my sponsor, and you're the only one who can make money in that car. This is the last race for that Mercury.' 'Ah Preacher, I love ya to death, but I really don't want to. OK, one condition; I will set the car up my way.' He says 'OK.'

"I went to his shop, set the car up, we went to Daytona, and was quick. It was the fastest thing there. Had a problem with the motor and we had to drop the oil pan. Preacher was one of the best with Ford motors. We worked until right at closin' time. We put the oil pan back up with just a couple of bolts. Came back the next mornin' and got under there to finish boltin' up the pan. 'Preacher there's somethin' wrong here.' He said, 'Why?' I said, 'The pan doesn't want to go all the way up in the back.' 'That's impossible. I *had* it all the way up with two bolts holdin' it before they run us out of the garage. Take the pan back off.' I took the pan off and there was a Holiday Inn towel inside. You tell me people don't want somebody runnin'? They knew that with me in that car we was gonna win. We have the motor runnin' in the car and have some problem with NASCAR. We had the fastest car and NASCAR says, 'You start in the rear.' We had a tire that somebody ice-picked. Changed the tire, took the towel out of the oil pan, and have to start at the rear.

"Preacher says, 'I want to back off on the gear 'cause in the draft, you'll run faster yet.' He changed that gear and was right. I would never argue with that man. In seven or eight laps, we came from 43rd to some place up near the top five. The 43 owned by the Pettys of Gaffney [South Carolina] have my dirt trackin' buddy from Kings Mountain [North Carolina], Freddie Smith, and if I hit him in the door, I kill him. So I turn Preacher's car into the wall. Hit him in the quarter panel so hard it spun him around and I came down on the hood of his car and burst into flames. I went down the back straightaway off the track. Sittin' there dead still and [Delma Cowart] hit me so hard; it drove the right rear wheel all the way to the front wheel. The yoke and the rear end come up through the shift lever. It drove the drive shaft through the transmission, through the engine, and knocked the crankshaft out. I didn't know the windshield was gone. I couldn't see 'cause my goggles melted on my face. The crazy thing is, just before the race started, I went back in the garage, took my fire suit off, put the fireproof underwear on, and put a new fire suit on. You could

Incredibly Joe was rammed by the Delma Cowart while sitting still on Daytona's backstretch on February 17, 1979. Note individual parts flying away (Joe Frasson).

The Great Escape. Goggles melted to his face, Joe scrambles from his would-be funeral pyre and dashes to safety. Great mental and physical strength saved his life (Joe Frasson).

take that fireproof underwear and just peel it off. They told me I died in the car. That's when Don Williams got killed."

Don Williams was comatose for ten years and passed away on May 21, 1989.

At a very active 74 years old, Harley-riding Joe Frasson never pulled a punch in his life and he didn't when he summed it all up.

"I very well remember when Davy Allison came to the racetrack and played with my kids. Bobby and I were standin' there one day doin' an interview and they asked, 'Davey, who's your favorite racecar driver?' We all figured he'd say, 'Dad.' He said, 'Big Joe.' Bobby said, 'What's the matter with me?' 'Oh, you're nothin' but my Dad.' [Joe laughs.] Billy France, if he said

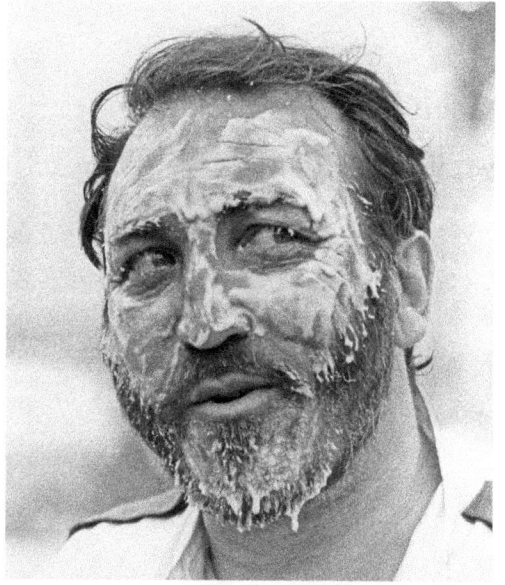

Top: A little dab'll do ya. Joe got all greased up in the medical center and came out to meet the press and the public wearing a thick coat of cream and relief. *Bottom:* In June 2009, Joe mounted one of his Harleys, his preferred means of travel. He runs a successful insurance agency in Spartanburg, South Carolina (Joe Frasson).

it once, he said it fifty times to me, 'When the hell are you old farts gonna quit so we can get some new, young blood in the sport?' He was dead set on getting rid of all the old-time people that made NASCAR what it is today. NASCAR killed them [and some touring series] so they could take the money. Billy said, 'We will make the trucks successful!' Look at the grandstand when the trucks run. We went to Bristol, the trucks went first, we went last, and had a packed house. The next year, we ran first and the trucks ran after us. Over half the grandstand got up and left before the trucks ran. You'd think that would tell NASCAR something. They want nothin' to do with us unless your name is Richard Petty or David Pearson. I don't even know how much *they* are getting along with NASCAR. I don't go where I'm not wanted."

Joe Frasson is of the mettle that made stock car racing what it is, but not necessarily what is sustaining it. He is of a different age. He is not a pioneer. He came too late for that. He is of an age when cheating leveled the track, but if a guy needed slugging, Joe slugged him. He showed up a tad before television gave it to us live weekly, but still coverage was abundant. Racing today is propped up by lucrative television contracts that fall far short of expectations. Empty seats are so plentiful that cameras shy away from long shots of the stands. Anything other than a Cup race is played out in front of a mostly empty house. Joe Frasson's ilk took a reasonably accurate example of what sat on showroom floors and put it to the test on the speedways. Folks showed up in person to watch. Sometimes Joe cheated to keep up and got robbed when he actually won. He says he won't go where he's not wanted. Speaking for thousands and thousands of racing fans that appreciate everything he's accomplished and what he represents, "It's so, Joe! We want you more than you know!"

10

Raymond Williams

Captain America

Raymond M. Williams was born on April 15, 1939, in Durham, North Carolina. He currently lives in the historic city of Hillsborough. Raymond graduated from Durham High School and attended Louisburg College. His is an amazing story of guts, incredible luck, and as great a devil-may-care attitude as ever crawled through the window of a stock car. Raymond raced in the second one he ever saw and picked the deadliest track on the circuit at which to start. Death swirled around him throughout his 93-race career covering parts of six seasons. Only in 1972 did he give the full schedule a shot running 28 of 31 races while managing five top tens and a very respectable 14th in Winston Cup Points. Anytime Raymond Williams is mentioned, the other party usually smiles and says, "Captain America." Competent, fun-loving, and looking twenty years younger than his driver's license indicates, he was the happy-go-luckiest of all independents.

As a teenager, Raymond got a degree in the pool rooms around Durham. That atmosphere exercised his wanderlust and desire for adventure and danger.

"I grew up in Durham and hung around the pool room. When the guys come home from the Second World War, they hung around the pool room until their money run out. All told stories of combat in Europe. When they formed one of the first airborne divisions at Fort Bragg, they asked for volunteers. You had to be a volunteer to be in the airborne. They volunteered because they thought they would be stationed at Fort Bragg, the nearest base. As soon as they went through training, they sent 'em straight to Europe. [Raymond laughs.] At the Battle of the Bulge, that was the airborne division out of Fort Bragg. The guys that hung around the pool room were in the Battle of the Bulge. I tried to join the military and go to Korea in 1953 when I was 14 years old. I got a guy at the pool room to say he was my daddy and sign me up to say I was 17. [Raymond chuckles.] I went to basic and was there for one week before my parents found out. They brought me home. [Raymond laughs.] My military career was about four or five days, but they cut my hair off. [He laughs again.] Elmo Langley was at Guadalcanal and was only 15.

"I got my driver's license in 1955. Everybody was street racin'. Anybody that had a fast car hired me to drive. I turned one over out in the flats in Durham. The first one I rolled, I rolled at over a hundred miles an hour across a field."

No fence could prevent Raymond from literally breaking into Grand National racing.

"In 1969, Ted Mann, athletic director for Duke University, hooked me up with Blue Ribbon Beer. I sold more beer than any other location in North Carolina from a little convenience store in Chapel Hill. I was makin' a little money. I came by Charlotte Motor Speedway the last race. That's the first time I'd seen a super speedway race. So I climbed the fence in the garage area when the race is over and went up to Elmo Langley and asked did he have a racecar to sell. He said, 'No,' but pointed me to Bill Seifert. I asked him if he had a racecar. He says, 'Yeah, but I ain't got time to mess with you. Here's my card. If you're interested, come to my shop.' His shop was in Asheville. I took his card, went home, and told my wife I was gonna take some time off. 'I'm gonna go racin'.' She said, 'I don't care what you do. Whatever.' I'd never been in the window of a racecar. Back then, I only slept about two and half, three hours a night. I worked 20 hours a day. I didn't really need sleep back then. Hell, I was 30 years old.

"I drive to Asheville and go in Seifert's shop. He had two cars, the 45 and 47. Seifert drove 45 and Cecil Gordon drove 47. Cecil was gonna form his own team the next year, so Seifert had a car. I said, 'I'll buy that car.' I had no pit crew, nothin', no trucks or anything. 'We'll work a deal where you form two teams and we'll work somethin' out.' When I bought the car from Seifert that mornin' he says, 'You ever drove a racecar?' 'Yeah.' Nobody ever asked me again if I ever drove a racecar. I asked him, 'Where we gonna run first?' The first race was in Riverside. 'We're not goin' to California. It's too far. Can't make no money. We'll go to Daytona in February.'"

In February, Raymond took off for Daytona Speedweeks 1970.

"Allen McMillan had been part owner in a car that Bunkie Blackburn drove. Allen and Bill Barker were friends of mine and they had some motorcycles. They wanted me to take the motorcycles down. We was there about two weeks before because everybody went early. We go over to Bunkie's house and Bunkie had had a bad crash and quit racin'. We were standin' in Bunkie's garage unloadin' these motorcycles and Allen says, 'Raymond's got a car. He's gonna race at Daytona.' [Bunkie] asked me where I been racin'. I said, 'I ain't never drove a racecar. I never been in the window of one.' He says, 'You gonna get killed. *You will get killed!*' [Raymond laughs.] I said, 'Well, that's the way it is.'"

Raymond and the Daytona International Speedway, or any speedway, met for the first time.

"I come in and looked at that racetrack and couldn't believe it. We go in and start unloadin' the cars. The first thing, Seifert asked me to put some shocks on the car. I put 'em on upside down. [Raymond laughs hard.] I didn't even know how to change a sparkplug. [More laughter.] I'm in the dressin' room puttin' on my uniform and Elmo [Langley] is sittin' there and [Jim] Hurtubise is puttin' on his. Hurtubise is all burnt up and Elmo said, 'Boy, you want to be a racecar driver? Look at Crispy here.' [Raymond roars with laughter.] He called him 'Crispy.' 'Now that's what you're gonna get.'" [Raymond still laughing hard.]

Hurtubise received disfiguring burns in an Indy car crash at Milwaukee in 1964, but returned to drive and win for years. The 125-mile qualifying races for the 500 were Raymond's first.

"I'm standin' in line with Richard Petty, Bobby Allison, Cale Yarborough, David Pearson, and people. I was standin' in line with those people and I'm gonna tell ya what, I have never been so happy to be in any place in my life. I had dreamed about this. It was just

Courageous and cocky, Raymond Williams defied death right off the bat and NASCAR afterwards, competing at stock car's top level 93 times (Raymond Williams).

some kind of crazy dream. Somebody told me, 'You're gonna get killed,' and I said, 'This is worth dyin' for.' The first rush was sittin' out there for the first 125-miler that mornin'. Big John Sears knew. By then, they'd figured out I never been in a racecar, but I was out there practicin'. All you do is hold it wide open. It was a rush. I'm sittin' in the car getting buckled up and Big John leans in my window. I had out-qualified Big John. He said, 'Boy, what are you gonna do when you get down into number one?' I said, 'I'm goin' to the front. Come on with me.' Raymond laughs.

"That first time you drop off down in that corner with a pack of cars, now you'd been out there practicin' by yourself. That was the rude awakenin'. Unless somebody actually wants to be in one of those cars, I don't think nobody can make them. Ya gotta really want to do it. I had two flats. You had about five or six cars that was racin' for the win. I had a fairly good qualifyin' time, but the car I had was a '68 Galaxie. You talkin' about a sled? That thing weighed 4,000 pounds and we run two-inch drum brakes. We were runnin' treaded tires then. It was a long time before I ever ran a new set of tires."

The record shows Raymond started 13th, finished 21st and did not make the 500. His teammate Bill Seifert and a newfound fellow rookie friend were in the second 125-miler.

"Bobby Allison and Bobby Isaac gave me and Tab Prince rookie tests together. Me and Tab were the only rookies and he was the only person I knew. Everybody else knew everybody else. So nobody ever said that much. That morning of the 125-milers, T. Taylor Warren came in the coffee shop and me and Tab was there. T. Taylor asked me and Tab to go out. He took a picture of me in my car and then a picture of Tab. I said, 'Tab, smile. If you win

Raymond's pre-race portrait prior to his February 19, 1970, first start ever in Daytona qualifying race #1 in which he finished 21st, not making the 500 (Raymond Williams).

this race, you'll want a good picture in the paper.' That's the picture that was in the paper that afternoon because ... it was on the 18th lap. He blew an engine and spun. Seifert run into Tab and killed Tab. Seifert really felt bad about him dyin' and all. I said, 'You know somethin'? That boy died doin' somethin' he wanted to do. To me, if I died racin', I wanted to be there. When somebody is gone, they're gone. My idea is to live ya life. If you're afraid of dyin', you're too afraid to live."

Seifert didn't make the 500 either and both he and Raymond were off to a very bad start. "He's probably one of the most unheralded people in racin'. He just sold BSR [Bill Seifert Racing]. He's done real well and deserved it. If I'da bought a car from anybody else, I'da lasted maybe one or two races. I knew absolutely nothin'. Seifert was one of the smartest of the independents as far as technology and set up. Seifert was involved in the wreck when Tab got killed. Seifert enjoyed more workin' on racecars than drivin' them. Financially, he had to drive. He was a hell of a driver. It wasn't in his heart. He really didn't want to be racin'. That was his livin'. That's what amazed me when I got to racin'. Seifert ran Banjo's operation till he formed BSR."

In NASCAR in the early 1970s, "you had about five or six big teams. I remember Petty sayin', 'We need slower cars because we're not fast unless we're passin' somebody.' [Raymond

After missing Daytona, Raymond got his first start at Rockingham on March 8, 1970. He finished a solid 20th of 40, the last man running 49 laps behind (Raymond Williams).

laughs.] NASCAR was just comin' into its own in the '70s. That's when they were startin' to get TV and people were gettin' interested. What NASCAR wanted the most was control. They really kept the control."

In 1970, Raymond Williams ran 21 of 48 races in his rookie year with a best finish at Columbia, South Carolina, on April 13. He learned to go faster by slowing down.

"I was havin' a terrible time gettin' around that track. I was spinnin' the tires on the dirt and came into the pits. Earl Parker from Champion Spark Plugs came over and told me to open the hood. I did and he reached in and yanked one of the plug wires off and said, 'Try it now.' I went back out and picked up a couple of seconds and it ran great. I wasn't spinnin' the tires anymore."

The record shows the Columbia 200 was its penultimate Grand National dirt track race. Raymond started 27th of 36, finishing 12th. Talladega really got Raymond's attention.

"I remember drivin' in and lookin' at Talladega. That was unreal. I crashed! Yeah, blew a tire and backed it in the wall. It knocked me out. I was rattled. In '69, they had the walkout because of the tires. Hell, I can remember tires blowin', knockin' windshields out. Seifert went out to practice and a windshield blew in! That's when they started puttin' bars in the windshield. Everybody was scared to death. David Pearson said one time, 'The man that runs Talladega that ain't afraid is a damn fool.' Ya know Isaac got spooked."

The record reflects that on August 23, 1970, Raymond started 31st and finished 36th of 50, crashing after 128 laps in the Talladega 500. In 1971, Raymond competed in 20 of the 48 races with his second straight 31st in the first Winston Cup Point standings. Not bad considering 146 others finished behind him, including Spencer (34th), Brooks (36th), Glotzbach (42nd), Lorenzen (45th), and Lund (61st). Rockingham started off Raymond's second season with a crash.

"One of the hardest hits I ever took was at Rockingham. Marvelous Marv Acton! Marvelous Marv was in three and four. He spun and was goin' up the racetrack. I came in there, slide sideways with him and I could see down to the bottom of the track. We're right above the tunnel. I hit the accelerator and I'm slidin' sideways. I'm gonna drive out of it. All it did was goddamn shoot it right down into the damn ... when that 800 horsepower caught, it shot down the bank and I hit that inside damn wall, I mean a ton! I hit that concrete wall and that was a damn crash! I'm gonna tell you one thing, my nuts swelled up. I've had my body black from them seatbelts. I busted the damn wall at Rockingham."

The record shows that Raymond started 26th of 40 on March 14 and crashed after five laps for 40th and last. The first live flag to flag coverage of a Winston Cup race was at Greenville Pickens Speedway on April 10, 1971. Raymond started an outstanding 11th of 26, but made it only four laps again for last. The official reason out is 'Fender.'

"When you run into the wall, it bends the fender. [Raymond laughs.] They was bein' kind to me. I just ran into the damn wall."

The Winston 500 at Talladega was May 16. For the second time in his 26-race career, death hovered near Raymond Williams.

"That Talladega race was the one where Petty's brother-in-law got killed. I was settin' on pit road. They were workin' on my car and I looked down there and heard the *BOOM* above the noise of the racecars and seen a body go up in the air. I come down and seen Petty climb out as I went by. Found out later that Petty's car was overheatin' and they had a hot water heater core and were gonna change the water in Petty's car. His brother-in-law leaned over the tank, reached and got an oxygen line instead of an air line, plugged it in and blew the top off the water tank and killed him. David Sisco's mother got killed there. She was walkin' down back of pit road and a truck come with a rear view mirror, hit her behind the head, and killed her like a rabbit. That's when Sisco quit racin'."

After their seventh race of 1971 at Dover, Raymond and Bill parted ways as a team. "I formed my own team. Your racecar was like your baby. You wanted to bring it home. I raced a Winston Cup team out of a one bay Esso station in Carrboro [North Carolina]. I never really tried to learn anything on engines. Hell, I couldn't set the timin' on a car right now. Basically what I knew was the most important thing on a racecar was handlin'. You had to make the racecar handle. I can't say I ever learned much, but whatever I learned was from Bill Seifert. And too, I was really, really interested in partyin' and havin' fun."

Raymond told an all too familiar tale of the independents.

"Ted Mann was athletic director for Duke University and owned the Blue Ribbon distributorship for Durham. I wanted to cut a deal with Blue Ribbon. I got all the students to buy Blue Ribbon for him. Years later, Ted was gonna help me get a Blue Ribbon sponsor. I had Black Label on my car in '71 and Bill France [Jr.] contacted Black Label and said, 'You don't want to sponsor him.' So they gave the sponsorship to Larry Smith. France used to do that to everybody's sponsor. James Hylton will verify this. James had a couple of

Raymond pits during 1971 sporting sponsorship from Bali Hai Wine. Being a barkeeper, his marriage of adult beverages and racing was a natural (Raymond Williams).

sponsors that he could have got. Hylton was a hell of a racer. France wanted total power. I don't think he could control James. If James would get a sponsor, France would call and say, 'I've got somebody else that you need to sponsor.' That was the kind of control that France had over everybody. The Old Man was not near as bad. When Billy, Jr., come in, it really *was* bad."

He described the weekly plight of the independent.

"The rest of us was just racin' each other. There was two races. There was one thing about NASCAR then that I loved. If you done a good job with whatever equipment you had, they respected you. They accepted you. That's the way it was. Everyone back in the field was racin' with each other. I don't think I ever had a brand new set of tires except one time. We was at Martinsville. I didn't think I'd be able to qualify. Ted Lobinger was with Goodyear and told me to go down and get a new set of tires. I run really good enough to qualify. I had picked up a second and a half from the time I practiced. Cheater tires. [Raymond laughs.] It was a hell of a long time before I ever ran a brand new set of tires. Many a time I'd run like hell for half a race and then park 'cause I didn't have enough tires to finish. I was not racin' there like everybody else. That was their livin'. Me? I was there havin' a hell of a lot of fun. I got to watchin' how Seifert, Cecil Gordon, Hylton, everybody was tryin' to make a livin'.

"If you finished in the top ten, to an independent like me it was just like winnin'. We would start the race knowin' we didn't have enough tires to finish the damn race unless somebody down the pit road would crash. Then we would borrow tires from them. Everybody respected you by how you done with what equipment you had. Nowadays, people say, 'What did you ever do? Did you ever win a race?' 'No, I *didn't* win a race.' We was racin' for tenth place because you had Petty cars, Buddy Baker, Cale, Pearson, whoever was in Bud Moore's cars. You was racin' for tenth. You was proud of yourself if you finished in the top twenty. When I first got in the car, I had expectations that all you had to do was have the nerve. It was a rude awakenin' that what you don't need is nerve, what you need is skill. What I tried to do a lot of times was to over-nerve it and crashed. It hurt me because I was a crashman."

So Raymond adapted a flat-out attitude and style to become a death-defying qualifier.

"I was the one that termed the thing 'kamikaze.' I used to be able to qualify cars. It was '71 at Charlotte. There was a hundred cars there for 40 positions. We qualified 12 on Wednesday, 12 on Thursday, 12 on Friday. I remember that morning there was about 40 cars settin' on the line to qualify for four positions. I was drivin' Seifert's car 45. My car wouldn't run. I was settin' on pit road and said, 'Seifert, do you think this thing will make it around here if I don't back out of the throttle?' He looked at me, laughed, and said, 'You gotta be crazy.' I said, 'That's the only way we gonna do it. The rpms. Can I try?' He said, 'Yeah. Hell, go for it.' So when I took the green, I went into number one and never cracked the throttle. I was mashin' the brake as hard as I was mashin' the throttle. I got through one no problem. [Raymond chuckles.] Went into three and come off four and slapped the shit out of the wall. *BAM!* Never backed off. Went back into one ... I didn't even get on the brake as hard. Come off four again, slapped the wall, but had the fastest time of the 40 cars that was on the line that mornin'. I was first, I believe Dick Brooks was second, Larry Smith, and Tiny Lund and the first alternate was Ray Elder in a new Petty Dodge. Elder had just won Riverside and Dodge had furnished him a Petty car."

He described some northern overexposure. "We were at Michigan. Chuck Blanchard and NASCAR official Lin Kuchler was sittin' by the pool with their wives. Me and Glotzbach was up in my room and we had some honey up there and some stripper. I got her to put on an STP t-shirt and walk out on the balcony, nothin' but an STP t-shirt on. 'Hey Chuckie!' and pulled that STP shirt up."

Raymond laughed heartily and launched into another tale of mischief.

"I reckon about 400 miles into the damn [Michigan] race a tornado comes by. They park the cars and cover 'em up. You could see the tornado goin' by the back of the grandstand. It rained like hell. Me and Seifert get out of our cars. I thought of Bill Seifert as much as my brother. I really respect that man. We went along pit road and they had a wire fence and a bunch of girls in a Ford station wagon. We go through the gate and get in that car with these girls to get out of the rain. Them girls had been to a rock concert that was the trial market for Boone's Farm Apple Wine. They had a cooler full. 'Ya'll want a drink of somethin'?' 'Whatcha got in there?' 'We got some Boone's Farm here.' Seifert drank a fifth and I drank a fifth. Man, they said [over the P.A. system], 'Drivers back to your cars.' Hot like that *and* a fifth of Boone's Farm Apple Wine ... we were plastered! We get back in the cars, I mean that was drivin' drunk. [Raymond laughs long and hard.] Johnny Bruner, Jr., gave five laps to go and I see Seifert behind me. Seifert peels off and goes down pit road. I wonder, 'What in the hell,' 'cause I know he's got enough gas. Frog [Fagan] and them's down there cleanin' up the pits and Seifert pulls in and Frog says, 'What the hell do *you* want?' 'I need some gas.' Frog says, 'The goddamn race is over!'" Raymond laughs loud.

Pre-race preparation was different for some independents.

"I can see Bill Champion now. He had that big ol' Ford truck and he'd climb up in there and put his uniform right over the top of his clothes. Pull it through his street shoes and all. He'd open the dash board up. He'd take him a couple of them ol' black beauties, damn bennies. He'd take that fifth of Early Times, take him a big hit on that thing. [Raymond claps his hands.] Put it back in there and go get in that racecar."

After another laugh, Raymond told how Elmo Langley got a surprise after going home.

"We was in Riverside and the race was rained out. Elmo took all his dirty clothes and put them in a laundry bag and threw 'em in his truck to carry home. I was bored as hell, so I go down to this lingerie shop and buy a pair of panties that goddamn big. [Raymond holds his hands as far apart as he can.] I mean, they were *giant* panties. I took a cigarette and blow nicotine-like hash marks in the thing and put 'em in Elmo's laundry bag. [Raymond laughs.] He carries it home to his wife. *Oh Lord!* Me and Elmo was always pickin' at each other about some shit."

Raymond stirred it up with NASCAR, too. "At Darlington they called me in the office and said they weren't gonna let me race because I was tryin' to form a union 'cause I was in the PDA [Professional Drivers Association]. When I joined the PDA, we had a meetin' at the Holiday Inn across from the racetrack at Daytona. I had never, ever got in a racecar and practiced the first time. Bobby Allison come to me and said they were havin' a meetin'. I went over there and it could have been the Klan, I would have joined. Hell, they were formin' the PDA and I wanted to be part of it. I had about half the University of North Carolina Law School workin' for me. My brother was in law school. They had a story one time that my pit crew consisted of one doctor and four lawyers. I remember them sayin' that none of them knew how to change a tire. [Raymond laughs real hard.] But John Green got me involved. I told John, 'Don't worry about lawyers. I've got the whole the University of North Carolina Law School.' That's when Bill France [Sr.] first got on my case because my brother was gonna be the lawyer and furnish lawyers for the PDA. They told the media that I had threatened to burn some racecars if they didn't join a union. I believe it was Gerald Martin and we was settin' there lookin' down through the garage area. I said 'Gerald, come here. You look at Elmo. You look at John Sears. You look at that bunch down there. Do you think I'm a goddamn idiot to threaten them with somethin'? Shit! You don't threaten this bunch, I'm tellin' ya.' [Raymond laughs.] These are some of the toughest son of a bitches I ever seen in my life. You ain't gonna threaten them with nothin'. That's just NASCAR's bullshit.' And it was. Bill France, Sr., seen that I was gonna be trouble from the start. Then when Billy, Jr., came in, Billy, Jr., hated me with a damn passion because of the deal there. The Old Man was pretty good. Billy, Jr., come in and was just rotten to the core. Every rule they've ever made was for power that they could control. Ya see, Billy, Jr., never called it 'a race.' He called it 'a show.' I remember Earnhardt lapped the field at Atlanta and they called him in the office and Billy said, 'You ain't gonna fuck up another one of my shows!'"

Even Raymond's hair was a problem, as was his overall appearance. "NASCAR said it was a fire hazard. 'Bout that time Lorenzen comes back. Lorenzen's got hair longer than mine. I never had hair that long. I told Freddy, 'I sure am glad you're back.' [Raymond laughs.] See, I was a racin' hippie. I was in Chapel Hill with all the hippies. Hell, I had

With the air hose flying, Raymond hustles through a pit stop on May 28, 1972, in Charlotte's World 600. He blew on lap 211 for a dismal 31st of 40 (Raymond Williams).

hair down to my ears and always wore Indian headbands. My great-grandmother was a full-blooded Cherokowa-Apache. I always had a real dark suntan, long hair, whatever. I was the racin' hippie. Everybody said, 'The only reason you're racin' is 'cause all these groupies and girls around the racetrack.' I said, 'I'm gonna tell ya what. You come to Chapel Hill and get on Franklin Street in any bars and the girls there, Lord God.' The Fourth of July race at Daytona. This little girl had a body on her in a bathin' suit and wanted my autograph. I gave her my autograph. She said, 'Where you goin'?' I said, 'Back to the motel.' 'Can I go?' 'No, my wife and kids are there.' Lobinger used to bring his wife and kids. LeeRoy and Gloria [Yarbrough] was there. I remember Gloria was there and one of them pelicans come over and shit on her. This little girl says, 'I want to go.' 'Why?' 'I want to sleep with you tonight. If you get killed tomorrow, I want to be the last one.' [Raymond laughs.] The next day when I got over 50 miles an hour I thought about it.' [Raymond laughs hard.] The race started and I come off four and there's [where] Tiny crashed."

A tale from Texas followed. "Richard Childress was there at an ol' Texas barn dance in College Station. They had big signs on the wall, '$250 Fine for Fighting.' This boy from Louisiana, we're all settin' at a table and he's drunk. He reached up and pulled one of them Texan's hat off and put it on his head and said, 'There wouldn't have been a goddamn Texas if the Alamo had a backdoor!' [Raymond laughs hard and slaps his hands.] Somebody knocked him out from under that goddamn hat and me and Childress just set there. I wasn't about to stand up."

The Captain America theme appeared before the Daytona race.

"We had a boy that painted, Pinto Bean. He was the damndest painter. He could take a paint gun and do anything. He was paintin' the car over in the shop. We left and come back and it was red, white, and blue. Pinto wanted to fix it up. He put red, white, and blue stars on it. I believe it was Norman [Raymond's brother] that walked in and said, 'Damn, that looks like Captain America!' I didn't think nothin' about it. We loaded the car up and I think maybe we was goin' to Daytona. We got there and pulled the cover off and it had 'Captain America.' I never run a racecar again with my name on it." Raymond laughed.

The 1972 campaign was the year that Raymond Williams went for it. He competed in 28 of 31 races with five top tens and ended with a very respectable 14th in the standings, a mere 76 points out of 11th. He bested the likes of Marcis (15th), McDuffie (18th), Isaac (19th), Pearson (20th), Rookie of the Year Larry Smith (23rd), and Buddy Baker (24th). Captain America was full-time and a force to be reckoned with among the independents. He started the season where you're supposed to, Riverside, starting 33rd and finishing a fine 15th in the only road race of his career.

"I loved Riverside. That was just like drivin' drunk," he said with another raucous laugh.

On Thursday, February 17, 1972, Raymond danced again with death on the backstretch during a 125-mile qualifier for the Daytona 500.

"Friday [Hassler] and all of us traveled together and partied out there [at Riverside]. Me and Friday were sharin' pits. Everybody used to share pits because nobody had a full crew. We were stayin' at the Casa Linda Motel. Friday and Cotton, we called him 'Grandpa,' an older guy that worked for Friday, and Watts that worked for me, [rode] to the racetrack that mornin'. We had a bad crash and Friday was killed. I think David Boggs blew a tire. I came off of two, went high, and got in the loose stuff. When I go up in the marbles, I slapped the damn wall right at the orange Union 76 thing. I slid the whole length of the back straightaway and the car was stuck to the wall and was totaled. When I'm slidin' down the wall, every time I'd pass them iron gates, you go to the concrete and go to the gates, you could hear it go by. I finally had just come to a stop, I heard Friday get hit. That was a *BOOM*, I mean, *unbelievable!* They put me in the ambulance and went to the hospital and that's when they brought Friday in. Friday was dead. I come out and Ken Squier interviewed me. That was one of Ken Squier's first interviews when Friday got killed. They televised that on *Wide World of Sports*. My car was a total damn loss."

With amazing determination and a little help from his friends, Raymond finally started the Daytona 500.

"I had a fast enough time to start. Harold Fagan, Bill Seifert, [and] two boys from Durham had a body shop, Bobby and Doody Matthews. They were in the stands. They come over and asked to help. I said, 'Man yeah you can help! From Thursday until Sunday morning we worked and rebuilt. We put a whole front clip on it, back clip, Seifert had gone to Orlando and got all new sheet metal. We built that car back from Thursday to Sunday and I started the Daytona 500. It had no inner panels. I knew I couldn't race it. You couldn't have kept it in a 40-acre field. I started for the money. Larry Smith wanted to buy my position because he failed to qualify. He was runnin' for Rookie of the Year. Well STP for me to start paid $2,500. I wouldn't sell him the position and he got mad a little bit. Later he understood. I had to do what I did. I started, but was the first one out. I run a few laps

In a Herculean effort, Raymond's friends and other strangers worked for three days to rebuild the Ford to start 40th, run four laps, and park for 40th (Raymond Williams).

With Captain America on the door, Raymond gets a sip of water. He started 22nd and finished 35th in the Carolina 500 at Rockingham on March 12, 1972 (Raymond Williams).

and parked. Got the startin' money. Watts, after we fixed the racecar and came back home, wouldn't work on the racecar no more. He was real close to Friday."

Raymond's best season had a nice streak in the spring with 14th at Darlington, 12th at North Wilkesboro his first top ten at Martinsville, and a 13th in the World 600.

He finished '72 with a ninth at Talladega, 11th at Richmond, 13th at Martinsville, tenth at North Wilkesboro, and a 13th at Charlotte. It all added up to 14th in The Winston Cup standings.

"Here was my problem. I had been away from my business from '70. Absentee from the business, I was goin' belly up financially to race. Racin' was definitely on hard times. Everybody was havin' a hard time."

Raymond talked about Wendell Scott.

"Wendell was my buddy. Up the road about five miles is a weigh station. Wendell called me one night; was in the Hillsborough jail. They got Wendell at the weigh station and I had to go get Wendell out of jail. [Raymond chuckles.] He didn't have no license, no fire extinguisher, nothin'. I really liked Wendell. Me and Wendell were good. When they'd have the NASCAR banquet, I'd go. Me and Wendell's wife used to dance all the time. I was really upset when they made the movie about Wendell. They were makin' a thing about Wendell was black.... I didn't a bit more think of Wendell bein' black.... I remember at Talladega we was goin' to the driver introduction at the start finish line. They put us on an Alabama school bus. Me and Donnie Allison was sittin' up front. Wendell come through and I said, 'Wendell, us blacks got to go to the back.' [Raymond laughs hard.] Wendell laughed like hell. A lot of the redneck fans didn't like it."

Raymond commented on the racing community as he knew it.

"I've never met a finer group of people in my life. Junior Johnson, Hoss Ellington, Seifert, Cecil Gordon, Buddy Arrington, I call him 'Harvey' Hylton, and those people. I'm gonna tell ya one thing, they were amazing. I was in Chapel Hill and campaign manager for Jim Gardner when he got elected to Congress. I went to a congressional breakfast and watched politicians and was not impressed at all. But when I went racin', guys like Pearson and Cale were good. Richard Petty was hell in a car. I thought the world of Richard. I had a boy when I quit racin' wanted a job. I called Richard and said, 'You remember Billy Biscoe? Billy wants a job in the shop. He don't want to travel. He's tired of travelin'. He started with me when he was about 16 years old.' Petty said, 'Yeah, you just tell him to forget everything you ever taught him and send him on over.'" Raymond had a good laugh with that story, too.

"One time at Charlotte, we used to run 427 Fords. They was some damn good engines. I had a damn engine in my car that we had close to 3,000 racin' miles on. Racin' and practicing. The 427 was really losin' horsepower, gettin' real tired. Bobby Unser [Indianapolis 500 winner] came to Charlotte and I have never driven so hard in my life just to pass him on the racetrack."

The record shows that on October 8, 1972, Raymond had an outstanding 13th in the National 500 while Unser finished 43rd in Ray Nichels' Dodge. It was time for some serious talk.

"What kept me alive with no experience? What kept me alive runnin' Talladega and Daytona? The tires, no brakes. What kept me alive durin' those first races amazed me. Hell, I remember standin' in the drivers' meetin' and look around and say, 'Wonder who ain't gonna be here when this shit's over?' [Raymond laughs.] By the end of the '72 season, I got to where I really felt like I could drive a car if I could get in a good car."

Raymond also raced other racers' racers. "The best finish I ever had was in Ben Arnold's car. Ben run maybe 30, 40 laps and I got in his. I believe it was Nashville. I relieved G.C. Spencer at Bristol one time. That's the first time I ever drove a Dodge. Joe Frasson, his pit crew come down, got me, and wanted me to relieve Joe. I get in Joe's car and goddamn, his seat's like a sofa! Big son of a bitch. [Raymond chuckles.] Shoulder harnesses or nothin' wouldn't fit. I was lucky to get off pit road. I come back and I'm beatin' on my helmet, 'Get somebody else in this thing!' I come down and who's gettin' in the car, Buck Baker. Buck got in and set sail. He was drivin' the shit outta that thing. When the race was over, I asked Buck, 'How in the hell did you drive that thing?' He said, 'I was just tryin' to crash.' [Raymond laughs.] That Buck could drive a damn race car."

Raymond had one more season in 1973 where he put forth an effort to race regularly on the tour. He competed in 22 of 38 races with three top tens and 25th in the final standings. His fifth race of the season was his best at Darlington in the Jet Way Wax Ford.

"I was proud of that because I had so much trouble with Darlington when I first started. Seifert could get a car around Darlington. Seifert was talented as a driver, but didn't want to drive. Hell, when I got in, if I'da had the talent of Seifert, I coulda made him a team driver. That '73 Ford had a big ol' body on it. It was like the Monte Carlos. That son of a bitch handled unbelievable. All these races I run were pre-power steerin' and pre-disc

In the 1972 Carolina 500, Big Joe Frasson watched as Raymond strapped in for relief. He said the seat felt like a sofa and quickly got back out for Buck Baker (Raymond Williams).

brakes. You had to *drive* the car then. Five hundred miles at Rockingham, 500 miles at Darlington, I mean, it would wear your ass out."

The record shows that on May 15, 1973, Raymond started 33rd, finishing a solid tenth of 40 in the Rebel 500. On May 6, Raymond timed 44th in a monstrous field of 60 in the Winston 500 at Talladega. Nine laps into the race, Ramo Stott, running at the front, blew an engine on the backstretch. A massive crash involving at least a third of the field ensued.

"I come down the backstretch when the heat waves were comin' up and you couldn't see the cars through the heat waves. I'm in a pack, I mean, you're just packed up in cars wide open. [Raymond makes a racecar noise.] I saw Cale's car up in the air. I read the number on Cale's car above the field. When somethin' like that happens, it's absolutely like layin' a blanket over your windshield. There was a boy from California [Ronnie Daniels] and this was his first race. He started 60th; I think [actually 57th]. His car shut off and he was coastin' down the back straightaway. Cale was leadin' the race drivin' in his rearview mirror and that heat waves [were] comin' up. Cale never seen him and hit him in the ass about 200 and somethin' miles an hour. [Raymond chuckles.] It was unbelievable! That boy from California, it broke his car in half and they said he slid out on the racetrack in his seat, got up, and climbed the fence. Nobody's ever seen him around again. I remember comin' back down through there and they wouldn't stop the race. We run under the caution for 45 goddamn minutes. I'd come in and have flat tires. They wouldn't stop the race because

Captain America was in his prime with Jet Way Products on the sides of a new Ford for his first nine races of 1973. They failed to pay him a dime (Raymond Williams).

they knew if we got out of the cars, we'd never get back in. NASCAR was afraid to stop because everyone was skittish as shit about the tires."

Through all the carnage that ended Wendell Scott's career, Raymond steered clear and raced until lap 84 before retiring with engine trouble for 28th. He beat over half the field that day. After six lackluster races through the summer of '73, Raymond scored a fine seventh at Bristol on July 8 in a field of 30. On August 12, he returned to Talladega, started dead last of 50, and dodged the Grim Reaper yet again.

"Me and Larry Smith was both in '71 Fords. John Green was Larry's crew chief and we was stayin' at the Holiday Inn in Anniston. John rode to the motel with me and had Larry's helmet to work on that night. Larry had already gone back because he said he had a headache. I gave Billy Biscoe and Benny Freeland the keys to the truck. We had a rent-a-car and I said, 'I'm goin' to the motel, y'all just come on in in the truck.' I'm back at the motel and I'll be damned. They drive under the awning and knocked the front off the Holiday Inn." [Raymond laughs.]

"Me and Larry had practiced together and the next day we could keep up a little bit if we drafted. We would draft and switch back and forth. You could run five of six laps, but then you had to switch because the car behind would heat up so bad. Couldn't get any air. We went down the back straightaway and Larry motioned. I went real high in three, Larry went on, and I fell right behind him. We come through the tri-oval, Larry backed out of the throttle, and I bumped him. When I got out of the throttle, he got back in and run off maybe 20, 30 car lengths. So he goes down into number one and goes up into the wall ... *BAM!* He hit it early goin' in the corner. It wasn't that he went in and lost it. Somethin' broke. I don't think it was a flat tire. I seen him and knew he wasn't gonna stick. When they hit that outside wall, they gonna come off. I just stayed right next to the wall, but it knocked his back bumper off and I run over his bumper. I looked at my oil pressure gauge. I coasted around and come in. Had the hospital right there next to the end of the garage area. We carried our trailer in there and was loadin' the car. The ambulance come in and the attendant said, 'He's dead.' Another one bit the dust. He really didn't hit the wall that hard."

The record shows that Smith's Carling Black Label 92 was a 1971 Mercury and finished 49th after 13 laps and Raymond was credited with 46th. he offered another reason for the death of 1972 Rookie of the Year Larry Smith and wondered again.

"We used to have in some of the cars — I never run one, hell, it cost too damn much — but you had a lever on the side of your seat. The lever run a cable that ya hook your shoulder harnesses to. On a caution, you could knock your lever forward and move around in the seat. [It relieved the pressure of the belts.] Then you would pull back and lock your lever and shoulder harnesses in. Larry had one of those and maybe it gave way and he hit his head on the roll bar. The crash wasn't that bad. I've seen a hell of a lot worse. Hell, I was an old man in the car. I didn't know shit from shinola. [Raymond chuckles.] What amazes me the most about it, all the people that got killed in them years, most of them were real experienced drivers. What in the hell kept me alive?"

Car painter and artist extraordinaire Alan "Pinto" Bean sketched a caricature of Raymond Williams precisely illustrating the spirit of Captain America (Raymond Williams).

Talladega wasn't all bad.

"The best race I ever had was the consolation race. I hadn't qualified. I got there late. I had engine problems, so I run the consolation. I believe I had the fastest time. That was Neil Bonnett's first try and he was outside. They had about 20 cars in the race. I never cracked the throttle the whole time. Just run wide open. Comin' off three, Neil blew an engine, crashed, and me and Charlie Roberts were leadin'. Charlie got under me and I ran Charlie all the way in the damn dirt. He beat me by about six inches. The first two cars in the consolation got to start the race. To have a chance to win a race at Talladega ... that was as good to me."

Raymond brought on some more stories about race scoring and the gas shortage.

"You had two scorers in the stand and a clock that flipped. At Bristol one time we started the race and run about ten laps. Walter Ballard's wife, Katie, scored him and it snowed. We come back the next week and they gathered all the cards and Katie had Walter leadin' the race. [Raymond chuckles.] I remember one time at Texas the gas pump failed. I come down pit road, didn't have no gas in the pits. I knew I couldn't go back in the race. I drove around to the garage area and over to the gas pump. [Raymond laughs.] I figured I'd get gas quicker then, but my scorer quit scorin'. Hell, I missed a couple of laps gettin' gas, but everybody was missin' gas. The only ones they was givin' gas to were the ones that were leadin'. We had a big to-do at the end about the scorers. Morris Metcalf, that son of a bitch, could score a whole race in his head. You'd go in there and argue with him. We was always in there arguin' about scorin'. Morris was hell."

In '73, Raymond was sponsored by 'Jug.'

"It was wine. I was in the bar and restaurant business and these people would give you all the wine you could drink. I'd put decals on the car, but never got any money out of it. I think it was Bally Hai Wine on some and Jet Way Wax. Jet Way went belly up. They were gonna pay me so much at halfway of the season and so much at the end. I never got a penny."

After a tenth at Richmond on September 9, Raymond closed 1973 with four lackluster races and that was it for four years with one start in 1977 and the finale in 1978. The Independent 250 in 1973 was promoted by Raymond Williams and held at Trico Speedway in Rougemont, North Carolina.

"That was the end of the season in '73. I done the independent race so somebody would have money for Christmas. I done that not so much to protest against NASCAR as it was for somebody to make money. The head of the AFL-CIO in Durham come in. He was the one that done the posters and wanted to meet. That's when Childress told Bill France I was tryin' to form a union. I really wasn't. All I was tryin' to do was make it where somebody would make money for Christmas. Everybody was broke. Guys were racin' and they gave their whole life to build that sport. When I done that, Bobby Allison said, 'Boy, you gotta find some place else to race.' I run a few more races, tried everything to get back into it. Hell, I even went to Costa Rica and played mercenary for a year to try to make enough to get back into racin'. We was flyin' into Zimbabwe when they was havin' a revolution. *That* will get your attention.

"But that was a damn good race. It was a cloudy November day. Trico never had crowds. Financially, it was a great race. Everybody there could have won. You had Elmo, Bill Dennis, Hylton, Childress, myself, Buddy Arrington, Wendell, McDuffie, Bill Champion, Cecil Gordon, Marcis, it was a hell of a field. There was passin' goin' on. We had about 25 cars and 23 of them finished on the same lap. We took out expenses. I had leased the race track from Fred Daniels. Every bit of the money other than expenses went into the purse. The night before at a bar I had in Chapel Hill, we had a big party and everybody was about half tore down the next day or had a bad hangover."

Where did you go Captain America?

"Hell, Bill France told me I was gonna have to find somewhere else to race. That's when I left and went down to Costa Rica. Ya see, the velocity in my cash flow had gone." Raymond laughs.

Dover was the site of Raymond's penultimate start on May 15, 1977, in Bill Champion's Ford. He started 35th, finishing 36th and completing no laps.

"I was the 'Bonsai Man.' I qualified a lot of cars at different racetracks for people and never started. I could get a car in the field. When I went up there with Champ, I was just a damn spectator. We'd been out in the infield drinkin' beer. Hell, I'd gotten [NASCAR chaplain] Brother Bill Frazier drunk. Champ come over and asked me to get that car in the field. He wanted the startin' money. I put the car in the field for him. I could get one in the field."

Captain America's final curtain came down in 1978, but with more than the one race it shows in the records. Raymond had a beautiful, swift Thundercraft Boats Buick Regal 16. You might call it a "Funny Car."

"That was one hell of a nice car. I hung the sheet metal and done everything at a shop

Fittingly, Captain America's last ride was July 4, 1978, at Daytona in this gorgeous Buick. It was so fast the clear coat blew off. He finished 29th (Raymond Williams).

I built over on 86. Pinto painted that car. Pinto Bean was the damndest you ever seen paintin'. That was a beautiful paint job and he clear-coated it. The first race we carried that car to was the Daytona Fourth of July race. I didn't get there for first day qualifying. We got there, unloaded, and went out to practice. The clear coat blew off. Everybody got the damndest laugh at me with that clear coat blowin' off. I run two practice laps. This was the second day. You had to make it then or not make it. Carol Hutchins [Raymond's scorer] was on pit road and bet a guy that I'd make the race. I come off of four and had that son of a bitch sideways. We'da qualified in the top ten if we'da qualified the first day. Janet Guthrie was there and she didn't qualify the first day because she wanted the newspaper articles so she could be second day fastest. I beat her and *I* was the second day fastest."

The record shows that Buick 16 started 21st and finished 29th in Raymond Williams' final Winston Cup start. Next came a reprieve, a last trip west, and a wager.

"We worked a deal with Mel Larson that run Circus Circus. Dr. Ted Rodgers owned the car. He ended up getting killed in an ultralight. We kept the car at Banjo's and Seifert was working for Banjo. This was at Ontario Motor Speedway. It was a TV race and Mel wanted in. So Mel worked a deal. Dr. Ted would pay for the thing and all. John Rawl was a motorcycle racer. Didn't know shit. John loaded that racecar on a truck and we're goin' to California. We get with Childress and Earnhardt who had just started drivin' for Childress. We stopped at College Station, Texas, for a USAC race. Hell, I see me an opportunity to make some beer money. We unload the car and qualified fifth or sixth, but all I'm gonna do is run a couple of laps and park. On the first lap they had a hell of a crash. I snuck by. You talk about Seifert and Dr. Ted; those would have been some mad sons of bitches [if Raymond had crashed in a USAC race on the way to Ontario]. We loaded the car and went to Ontario. Me an Earnhardt bet who was gonna out qualify each other. I qualified ninth and Earnhardt qualified 11th. Mel knew he couldn't qualify the car. He wanted me to qualify and he'd start the car and run the race. He paid the expenses. I don't think he run but a couple of laps and parked it."

Raymond gave his view of where racing has gone.

"It was a show. Now, they're payin' the price because you've got four or five teams that control the whole thing. Hendrick's Stewart-Haas thing? That's just a front. That's still Hendrick. Childress is money, money, money, money, money. That's all he cares about. Childress is not spendin' any of that sponsor's money. He ain't doin' nothin'. It takes money to run up front. Joe Gibbs, Roush, and them people? Junior Johnson, Bud Moore, the Wood Brothers, those people really [clap] loved [clap] racing [clap]. Roush, Childress, and those people love the power and the money. The Money Pump? We called him [Penske] 'The Money Pump.' Lobinger and Penske were good buddies. Penske had the Goodyear deal up north. When we'd go up north, Penske would furnish the tires. If you're out of NASCAR and they don't control you, they don't want you back around the racetrack. All these announcers. Everybody that's involved's got to say what NASCAR wants to protect their little jobs. There's nobody with the balls to come out and tell the story because it's all about greed. In '70, I noticed the stands when Tab got killed. We go back to Daytona and Friday gets killed. Go to Talladega Larry Smith gets killed. I made the statement then, 'Nothin' sells tickets like a funeral.' One of the things that's taken the mystique out of racin' is you got safer barriers, HANS devices, spotters. The guys don't have to drive. Twenty years later, J.D. McDuffie's lawyers were gonna subpoena me because NASCAR talked about all the safety features they had. They were gonna get me to testify that NASCAR let me race and I'd never been in the window of one."

Raymond Williams sums it all up.

"If I'da kept my mouth shut, by the end of '73, if I hadn't had the protest race, I'da got me a ride and I'da been able to make it. I was broke at the end. I did that [Independent 250] more to help the guys to have money than I did to protest NASCAR. Every decision they made they say is for racin'? Every decision they have made is to protect their power. Everybody understood that Earnhardt was drivin' the 'company car.' You can't tell a NASCAR fan that. What about this deal where you gotta be in the top 35 to qualify, top 12 [to make The Chase]? Five or six people own 80 percent of the cars? One time they were interviewing me at Darlington about fighting with NASCAR. I said, 'I feel like Don Quixote, but no NASCAR fans know who Don Quixote is.' I used to pull their chain. I was pullin' their chain, but they were pullin' my head off."

To say that Raymond Williams went about his racing career in an unconventional manner is an understatement. He was a 30-year-old saloonkeeper and didn't have time for convention. To go big time racing, Raymond cut out the steps where one works his way up through the ranks. He bought a Grand National stocker having only seen one race and headed for Daytona. He was told that he was going to be killed, a fellow rookie friend immediately paid that price. Raymond made sure he had a good time as injury and death surrounded him. He gained experience, competitors' respect, and was a few decent breaks from a top ten point standings finish in 1973. Raymond became an outspoken thorn in the side of NASCAR, which made his path most difficult. Who was this man that started at the top, laughed aloud while questioning his own mortality, and thumbed his nose at authority? Captain America, who else.

Still the life of the party in September 2009, Raymond Williams is hard to beat as storyteller, NASCAR critic, and representative of independents.

11

D. K. Ulrich

The Wild Westerner

Donald Keith Ulrich was born on April 10, 1944, in Woodbury, New Jersey. He said he was just passing through that day. D.K., as he came to bill himself early on, started 273 Winston Cup events from 1971 through 1992 with his best finish being fourth in 1981 at Dover, Delaware. He managed 16 top tens and led a lap in 1978 at Michigan. As a car owner, his drivers are legendary. But D.K. was a racer, a scrapper, a jokester, a cheater, and most of all, a survivor from an age when a shot of whiskey was as common as a shot of nitrous oxide. D.K. Ulrich was a revolutionary then and rides the cutting edge of technology today with his business coordinating charter travel arrangements for NASCAR teams and others around the country through his fleets of jet aircraft, helicopters, and ground transportation. At his writing, he is age 65 going on 21. He began by giving his perspective of the independents traveling the circuit in his era.

"Our guys, my group that I ran with, almost felt like the old west when we went to town. We would go somewhere, drank their whiskey, jumped their women, took their money, and went out of town. That's what it felt like. It was like the old west. We just went from town to town. We didn't go back and fix our cars and come to the next race. We lived in the truck. Once in a while we got a hotel and many times we run out without paying the bill. You'd go in and sign up. At check out time, take your suitcases, push them out the window, walk by the counter, 'How's it goin', and leave. Not because we wanted to cheat anybody, but because we didn't have any money. The money was difficult to get from one place to another and hotels were only when you got in the top ten. You'd have enough money the next week for that. We went from one place to another to another to another. We had a garage, but we hardly ever got to it. We had all kinds of places, friends everywhere. Our m.o. was that we would come into town on Wednesday, go to the bar, find some chicks, find some guys. If the girl had a husband, bring your husband. If the girl had a boyfriend, bring your boyfriend. If you didn't have anybody, she now has a boyfriend for the weekend. We would take a group like that in a bar and take the guys and they would be our pit crew. Carl whatever his name was would give six or eight or ten pit passes, whatever I needed. We'd bring the guys in and they'd work on the car, the girls cook the food, and the others cheering you on. [D.K. laughs.] We'd take the new guys and show them how to change tires, how to use the tools, work in the garage, and on race day they'd be your pit crew.

You'd leave the car at the track after the race and go party Sunday night, then get rid of all them. Hug the girls, shake the guys' hands, we didn't pay them any money, we just had fun.

"The next morning we'd work on the car at the track. Monday you'd get it ready to go. Tuesday you hit the road. Wednesday night you'd be into the next town and the same program all over again. When you go back the second time around, the girls that had husbands, some would be divorced. Some that were free, they'd have new boyfriends or husbands. We put our crews together that way. The second time around and after that, you go in and the same people would show up at the bar. They know you're comin' and the bar, the Red Fox Lounge, would be on that car at Riverside. They'd give us food and drinks and let everybody know we were comin' and everybody showed up and auditioned."

Donald Keith Ulrich details how he got his direction in life.

"I was actually born in New Jersey. I was three days there. I'm not really a New Jersey boy. I moved to California early. My dad was working with the government during the war in 1944 and bouncing around. I got raised in California from the time I was six. My mom and dad were very religious and very strict. I couldn't do a lot of things. They had five children and liked to have a night alone. My mom's lucky night was Saturday. My three brothers and I had to do something and we discovered the midget races. We wound up doing that every Saturday night. We stayed at a daycare in the afternoon on Saturday and went to the races and came back. There was one of the midgets that was the slowest and always finished last every race. The worst guy was Harry Stockman and he was six feet tall and stuck out the top of the midget. One day a young kid came from Texas that needed a car so they put him in that car. The guy won the trophy dash, the heat race, and the main event. He won all three races in that sled. We got together with some people that knew the guy and I got his autograph. It's the only autograph I ever got in my life. His name was A.J. Foyt. He come in from Houston. That was 1956.

At the beginning of this career, D.K. looked the part of the hard-partying race driver from California.

"He went to Indianapolis in '58 and was always a hero for me. I felt I might like to be like him and that's maybe why I use my initials, too. The funny thing is we went separate ways. He went to Indianapolis, I went to NASCAR. Indianapolis runs the same day as the 600 and my whole 25 years, I could never go to the Indianapolis 500. But in 1994 when NASCAR went there, he called me for a ride. A.J. needed a car in that first stock car race. He was kinda old at the time. I told him to put a sponsorship together and I would do it. I got another deal going, so it never worked. It was like a whole 360 deal. It came all the way back around. He was my hero, then he's looking for a ride from me."

His dream as a young boy was to race.

"I remember in 1956, my dad took us to the beach for Memorial Day weekend. I sat in the friggin' car and had the radio goin' listening to the 500 with Sid Collins and the guy in the second turn, Howdy Bell. I remember all those guys. If you listen close, they didn't have to tell you what turn they're in, you could tell whose voice was where. I knew where they were at all times. In 1955, I cried when Bill Vukovich got killed. Drivers got killed every week back in that time. That's how I got started. My mom and dad's situation and I said, [clap] 'That's it. I wanna be a racecar driver.'

"I wanted to race and had no money. No sponsor, no money, no nothin'. That's how I'm goin' to race anyway. I went to a Ford dealership and bought a 1970 Ford Torino, four speed, 427. I got the whole package. I financed it with Ford Motor Credit for $144 a month for four years. Lit it off and drove to the house. That was the end of it. Took it all apart right there. I got eight miles on it and my buddies come and we took everything out. Made it into a shell. Sold all that stuff. The motor I could use and some of the transmission stuff. Some of the rear end stuff I could use, but I had to put a different housing. Me and my buddy took off in a pick up and took it to Holman and Moody [from San Bernardino, California] and left it. A month later when they finished, we picked it up. They had done a roll cage and front clip on it. I had to keep it insured for the bank. About $6,000 is what it cost me. They used to have a kit car at that time that you could buy for ten. It was 9999, but I didn't have that much money. I managed to scrape together the money to do the deal and had it coming from everywhere. I had a couple of little sponsors that put in $500 a piece. You know they used to have Ford written like that on the back when they had factory support? [D.K. refers to my photo of that car in the pits at Columbia.] I put it on there because I wanted it to look like that."

D.K. set out on his quest for the inaugural Winston Cup Championship in 1971.

"A guy named Bob Brown in San Bernardino had a muffler shop and was my biggest supporter. He had a 1945 Ford flat-nosed city bus and give it to me to use. We gutted it and used two by fours to build some bunks and that was our motor home. On the back, it was too weak to pull the car so we took a pick up with an open trailer and a car on the back and headed for Atlanta. We painted that bus canary yellow with a black vinyl top. It was a city bus geared for 30 knots or something. We were doin' 55 runnin' wide open. It was a six cylinder, flat-head, 1945 Ford motor and blew up. We weren't 155 miles out of town and dropped a rod alongside the road on the other side Needles, almost to the border. We didn't get out of California. We couldn't find parts for it and it's a '45 Ford bus and you ain't gonna find parts. We were riding along in Needles when I saw a fire truck outside a fire station. It wasn't one they used. It was a monument or something like 'Here's this old fire truck sittin' here.' We went over and looked in it and it had the right engine. The guys are not gonna let me take the parts out of that thing. So ... we called in a fire on the other side of town and those guys left. We had a cutting torch in the back of that pick up and we cut the pan off, dropped the crankshaft down, pulled the rod out, and hit the bricks. That old engine you could pull them out the bottom, but you had to move the crankshaft. I don't know if they ever knew it or not. It was just sittin' out there lookin' pretty. We didn't hurt nothin', but you know we didn't have time to unbolt the pan. [D.K. chuckles.] It was fun. We had to do what we had to do."

Easy money appeared on the way east. "We got to Mesquite, Texas, and ran out of money. There was a track there, the Devil's Bowl maybe? We convinced them that we were a Grand National team and they paid us a couple of hundred dollars to come in and run that car around the track and let people look at it, a real Grand National racer! It hadn't even seen a Grand National race yet and I hadn't either. [D.K. laughs.] We did that for a few hundred dollars and made it on in. We missed Atlanta, but got to Columbia."

Team Ulrich tests the Winston Cup waters for the very first time on April 8, 1971, in Columbia, South Carolina, and the author was there.

"We made an attempt to qualify and I'm tellin' ya, we didn't know our ass from centerfield. We were the first guy to miss and there was probably 45 or 50 cars trying to make a 30-car field. I wanted to sit on the pole. I was goin' there to sit on the pole. I wasn't goin' there to miss the race and it was very discouraging when we did. They gave me first alternate. They used to have first and second alternate. I got to put the helmet on, sit in the car, and line up right behind the 30 guys that was startin', or 36, whatever it was [actually 26]. The rule book states, 'You must start under your own power. If you don't start under your own power, you don't race.' Well, two guys didn't start; Earl Brooks and E.J. Trivette. I got the car fired up ready to go in case somebody don't start. Everybody pulls away and those two guys are still settin' there. So I say, 'I'm in the race, man. I'm outta here!'

"I lit it off down pit road and got in line with the rest of them. When I came around they black flagged me. I looked over there on pit road and both of them cars were gone. Pretty soon they come up in my mirror. They got in line and I come in, shut the car off, disappointed as hell. The race started, and I asked my brother, 'I guess them guys got started, didn't they?' He said, 'Them tow trucks come in and pushed 'em off.' I said, 'That ain't the way this works. I know the rule book. I got it right here.' A fellow named Bill Gazaway was runnin' the show, so we went over and he's busy runnin' the race. My brother's not real long-tempered and he's pissed now because we come all the way out there. I mean, we had an ordeal.

I tried to talk to Gazaway. He had a headset on. I'm talking' to him and he's making hand signals to me. [D.K. gesticulates.] I said, 'Look man, I need to talk to you now! I want to race now.' I still want to get in it. [D.K. laughs.] My brother got so mad at him, he went up and pulled his headset off like this [D.K. shows the earpieces being pulled wide apart] and said, 'Look, you need to talk now!' then let 'em go. It popped him in the head, you know. [D.K. laughs.] He took his headset off and started pointing his finger and started tellin' me they were gonna, well anyway, we never did get to talk to him during the race. After the race, he was a very slow talking guy and says, 'Son, that's not the way you handle yourself here. You're brand new over here in NASCAR and that's not the way you handle yourself here and we're gonna fine you,' and I'm goin', 'Wait, wait, we don't have any money.' We got through all that and I don't think NASCAR ever liked me after that and that was the first race. I got off on the wrong foot big time."

D.K. had a post race adventure his first night out.

"After the race, I was trying to get some appearance money just because I'd been there. I was trying to get a few hundred dollars so I could get up the road. The promoter, I can't remember his name, didn't have a lot of people come in for the show and he kinda disappeared after the race. Neil Castles, Ed Negre, myself, Earl Brooks was there. We decided we were going to burn the grandstands down. So we always took the gas that was left over and put it in cans and in the truck till we could get down the road with it. We took the gas cans and headed up in the grandstands and started pourin' gas on the guy's seats. We didn't light it. [D.K. laughs.] Neil had a gun. We poured the gas a little bit and a couple of shots up in the air and the guy come right out with the cash. 'I just had to get the cash.'

This is the showroom Ford Torino on April 8, 1971, at Columbia Speedway before it ever hit the track. D.K. was "Don Ulrich," according to the roof.

We got his attention and got a couple of hundred bucks and headed down the road. [D.K. laughs hard.] That's just one race. Now I got 375 others."

On July 15, 1971, Islip, New York, was start number seven for Team Ulrich.

"There was a fellow that came there. It's the first race that I'd ever seen him. His name was Richard Childress. He pulled up next to me and we were rookies and he had 96. It's like we had practice and qualifying one day and raced the next. On that Northern Tour, we did Malta [New York] on Wednesday, Islip on Friday, whatever it was every couple of days. When we would ride into town, we'd take their money, drink their whiskey, jump their women, and hit the bricks. [D.K. laughs.] At that race, Richard and I took a subway down to New York City lookin' for hookers. They got 'em and we were lookin'. We didn't have enough money, but we were still lookin' anyway. Somehow I picked up a roll of tickets that says, 'Admit One' on it. I picked them up somewhere along the line and had this idea. We went into the city and started goin' bar to bar pickin' up chicks and givin' them tickets to the race. 'How many tickets ya need? Bring your friends. Tear off six or eight tickets and give 'em to 'em, buy 'em a drink, take 'em in a car for a little bit. We had a great time. We were up to 2:30 in the morning givin' tickets away. We had to haul ass out of town when that race was over. A bunch of women [were] standin' outside at the gate with their husbands tryin' to get in. Got their husbands and boyfriends out there. [D.K. laughs.] We already took advantage of them. That was kinda fun and Richard and I been friends ever since. Richard's a great guy. We split and went different ways. He'll go out of his way to find me. If we're walking down pit road and he's way over here, he'll go out of his way to come over and say hey and see what's going on. In Kansas City, he got some friends of mine on his truck to watch the race. He's one that don't forget stuff when he gets famous."

The record reflects that this was actually the seventh Winston Cup race for both. As far as their first race together, that was in South Boston, Virginia, on May 9, which was both drivers' second race ever. At Islip after a night of handing out "free tickets" in New York City, D.K. copped 12th and Childress was 31st of 33 on a .2 mile track. The Talladega 500 on August 12, 1973, found him riding alongside Larry Smith on lap 13.

"We're between turns one and two and I'm right next to him and he disappeared. When I come back around, the car was down in the infield. We never touched or anything, but he was above me. He was passing me. Something happened to him. That was the year after he won rookie of the year." Larry Smith died in the crash.

D.K. discussed his feeling about running Talladega.

"I'm a smart man and a young man at that time. We used to run 170, 175 then. It got faster after that. I've qualified at over 200 at Talladega. Those brakes, when you needed 'em? That's why that 60-car wreck happened over there. You might as well step on the clutch or step on anything. They just didn't work. So for Talladega and Daytona, I realized that's a good spot to get killed. With the brakes the way they are, you really need to drive up the road a little bit. Drafting wasn't nearly as important then. You had open carburetors and you could catch up. You could do a lot of things. I was very careful there and quite frankly, they were not my favorite tracks. I did not like it. I went and did it."

To his immense credit, D.K. competed at Talladega and Daytona 22 times from 1973 to 1982 and never crashed. He made the first of 20 career visits to the famed Darlington International Raceway in the 1973 Southern 500 finishing 18th of 40, running at the finish. He relishes describing the skill of negotiating the tricky layout and jousting with others.

"My favorite track. It was good. The driver could make a difference. Talladega ... the driver didn't mean shit. Charlotte, if you didn't have the horsepower.... Darlington? You could take a marginal car and move right along with it. I remember a lot of good days down there and it was fun. The third turn was fun. You could sail in there and just touch the left wheel on the bottom of the track, burp it, and the car would roll right up there against the wall and you can handle it as long as there wasn't nobody beside ya. You know you had to use the whole track. You come right down in the fourth turn and touch the bottom, go on out and bang the wall a little bit, and go on down. It was really a fun track. If you timed it just right, you could pass the best of 'em in one of them turns. They'd be fumblin' around doin' somethin' and once you got next to 'em ... if you could take it a little harder into three than the guy in front of you, when he backs off and goes against the wall, you just go down beside him. He can't do shit comin' off the fourth turn. He's done. If he can't come down ... you have to come down at that time. You had to drop down and touch the bottom to make it ... to not crash into the fourth turn wall. It's OK to bump it, but if you couldn't come down, you'd crash into it. So he'd have to back off and you'd get him. The percentages are up when you have a track like Darlington. The percentages are up for a guy like me. Darlington was always my favorite track."

The record shows that Darlington was one of D.K.'s most frequented speedways. And save for his horrendous 1978 crash, he was accident-free on the South Carolina oval, arguably the circuit's most storied and difficult to drive course. The last year D.K. campaigned his original, reskinned 1971 Ford was 1973, and he has some not so savory memories.

"That first car there. That's the door that came with the car. I never got going until I got my Chevrolets. I kept trying to get Holman Moody to give me parts, you know, something that would run. I remember going in to talk to John Holman one time.... He sat behind his desk and I wanted a pair of hemispherical heads. They used to have a Ford hemi for a while. It was a real strange bird, but it was quick. It was aluminum heads. I needed a set of aluminum heads. Eddie Pagan worked there before he started Hutcherson-Pagan. I went to him first because Eddie's the guy I talked to to help me build that car. [His first car.] I got to John Holman and he set back in his chair and I'm over there beggin'. *I'm beggin'.* I need a set of fuckin' cylinder heads. He said, 'Ford won't let me sell them to ya.' I said, 'I'm talkin' about the used ones you got layin' over here that you're going to scrap. I need those. I'll fix 'em. I'll make 'em work.' He said, 'Ford won't let me do that.' I said, 'I've seen James Hylton go out of here with a set of cylinder heads. I've seen him. I know James.' I finally talked him into letting me buy a set of heads. Old, beat up ones. Whatever they had layin' around. I said, 'Now how much are they?' He said, 'Just as much as the traffic will bear.' I emptied my pockets on his desk. 'This is what I have. Will you take that for 'em?' He said, 'Hell no!' I walked out. He could have said, 'I'll take what you got and you can pay me some later.' We broke in and stole 'em, but he caused it. I'm not a thief. My boys went over and got me a set of cylinder heads. We didn't know much about what we were doin' anyway. It worked better than what I had.

"You will find a car of mine at Daytona. You will see a scale model with all those decals on it. Across the back I had F-F-A-H-T written on it after I had that run in with John Holman. I ran it in Daytona and it [meant] "FUCK FORD AND HOLMAN TOO." That was when Ford, or Holman, wouldn't give me what I needed. So I just put it on there. People asked me and I'd tell 'em. [D.K. laughs heartily.] That's when I changed to Chevrolet."

In 1975, D.K. Ulrich was a tad more frequent on the tour, racing in 16 of 30 events and finishing a career high 27th in the standings. On August 17, Tiny Lund lost his life on the backstretch in the Talladega 500 and D.K. was there.

"I remember seeing that car. It was really bowed up and he was really big. He was hunched in there and I drove by and said "Good-bye" to Tiny. [D.K. salutes.] I didn't have to ask anybody what happened. He got hit right in the door by Terry Link in a Pontiac. That car was just bowed up like a horseshoe. The top was bowed up. He was graveyard dead immediately."

The record reflects that D.K. was the last car running at the finish that tragic Sunday in 25th place, 20 laps behind. On September 14, 1975, D.K. got down with friends and came home 10th at Dover in the Delaware 500.

"Dover was party time. It [the circuit] was all local, drivable. Dover was the first one where [it wasn't]. We'd go to Dover, Michigan, Riverside, Texas sometimes, this whole swing on the road. When we took off, Dover was our first stop where we'd just grab the queens, drink the whiskey, hit the road. It was always party time. We had a group of people there. There's still one of those girls that called me a few days ago that wanted to know if I was going to Dover. I probably will. [D.K. chuckles.] We've been good friends forever. We used to run with 'em. We used to do anything with them. But we've all grown older and become good friends. They're really good people. We called them 'The Deuces' at that time." D.K. laughs.

The first time D.K. legitimately went for the Winston Cup title was 1976, when he ran all 30 races and finished 14th in the standings, his high-water mark to that point.

"I ran 'em all. I got a deal. I'd been around a few years and started getting some money. I ran into Rudy [J.R. DeLotto]. He had a body shop in Paterson, New Jersey [Garden State Auto]. Somewhere in there, I had to fix that car and had to really scramble. He and his wife put us up in their house and we worked in his body shop. We got it back together for the next race and went. He decided he wanted to have a NASCAR license and I said, "'Let's make you the owner.' We'd put his body shop name on there and he'd give us a few dollars to help with tires. When that started, that's when I started runnin' better."

On August 22, 1976, D.K. scored a seventh in the Champion Spark Plug 400 at Michigan.

"I remember the day. The car was right for a change. I think it was the first time I had a radio that worked. I remember there was a green light and you'd let off by that light. You'd get down in the corner, you know, big wide turn. That car was so good, I let that green light go by and I just kept hammerin' all the way down to the bottom that day. Just hammer it all the way to the bottom and I was never able to do that before. I remember yellin' in the car, '*Yahoo!!!*' I'd punch the button a couple of times so they could hear me I was havin' so much fun."

In 1976, D.K. tried to level the playing field.

"In the day, independents didn't have shit to run with. Even if we had money, we couldn't get the parts. The factories only gave parts to the factory cars. We're cheatin' by then, too. We started playin' with tires. Started playin' with nitrous oxide just for qualifying. We'd never use that stuff in the race."

In 1977, D.K. ran the entire season for the second straight year in his Chevrolet 40

D.K. sits out a long pit stop in the 1975 Talladega 500 on August 17. He was 25th of 50, the last man running the day Tiny Lund died.

Top: Limping in after his involvement in the Waltrip-Yarborough crash in the 1976 Rebel 500. D.K. salvaged 16th and Cale nicknamed Darrell "Jaws." *Bottom:* On March 19, 1978, in the Atlanta 500, D.K. passes Bill Elliott (9) and Chuck Bown (77) for a solid 11th. Bill and Chuck finished 38th and 30th.

and slipped to a still very respectable 15th in the standings. It is notable that 116 racers finished behind D.K. Sponsors were an interesting assortment. Two trips to Riverside were sponsored by the Red Fox Lounge.

"That's where we dragged them queens out of there," D.K. laughs. The Hair Shack was sponsor at Daytona, where in July he started and finished 41st of 41. "That was some girls that we found. We were busy playin'. That's all we were doin'," he said, still laughing. Howard Johnson came through in Atlanta. "See, they gave us rooms. It was always in Atlanta and it was the same kinda deal. It was a hotel we went to and they give us rooms, food, and the girls were all over us. That's what it was all about."

The following year, he missed the last eight of thirty races and fell to 22nd in the rankings. It was the best of times and the worst of times for 34-year-old D.K. and Chevrolet 40. He stayed glued to the top ten or eleven in the standings the whole season and coming down the stretch was a few good races from finishing there or higher. On July 30, 1978, D.K. joined the ranks of the haves if only for a brief time, and had a ball.

"There's one race at Pocono where I started about tenth or eighth. I made a set of tires there. They were so frickin' fast. What I would do was take a tire from a different racetrack or softer compound and the numbers on the side, the compound number, would be like 1330 or 2550, four numbers. It stuck out a little bit from the tire. I'd take a grinder and grind that whole number off the rubber. Take the tire number that you want, put Bondo on that tire, and when that dries you take it off and you've got a mold. Then you spray this with Pam like you put in your fryin' pan and fill it up with black silicon, stick it on the tire, line it up just perfect, let 'er dry overnight, peel that thing off the next morning, and perfect! I mean they'd look right at 'em and it had the other compound written on this tire. So at Pocono I qualified in the top ten. I had to start on those tires because I was in the top ten and they used to take your tires. If you qualified 11th, you could put whatever tires you wanted on there and I didn't plan on being in the top ten. I just wanted to get in the race. So I wound up in the top ten and they took my tires. I'm sweatin' the whole time because they got 'em stacked by the NASCAR trailer. When it comes time to start, you put the tires on. Now I've got these soft tires on at the start of the race. I'm goin', 'What'll I do now 'cause they ain't gonna last long.' I had regular tires sittin' in the pits. Donnie, Bobby, and The King, we're all goin' down into turn one. I took off and everybody goes down into turn one and I didn't have no horsepower, but these tires were just superior to everybody. I go down to turn one and 'boom, boom, boom,' pick three guys off. We go down the straightaway and they're pullin' me back in and we go into the tunnel turn and 'boom' got one in the tunnel turn, couple of them go by me in the short chute, and I go right back by 'em in the turn. After the race, Donnie Allison come over and said, 'Just what the fuck did you do to that car? Man, I'm doin' all I can and you're goin' in there pickin' us off like we ain't doin' nothin'.' I said, 'Well, you see it stopped after about eight laps and I had to get tires. I was chopped liver after that.'"

The record shows that D.K. started tenth and retired with engine woes with 34 laps to go for 25th. He started tenth at Michigan on August 20 and led the 38th lap, the only lap led of his career. At Bristol on August 26 he followed up with a ninth. "That's my tires."

A nice supplemental income was created as D.K. went into the underground tire business.

"I was makin' tires every day. [D.K. laughs.] They used to have an award for who sat on the pole the most and we won that award. When I say we, I mean me and Harry Hyde won the award with my tires. I made tires for him for money and he had Lennie Pond as his driver. He was my next door neighbor at Charlotte Motor Speedway and I showed him these tires one day and he said, 'I gotta have a set of those.' The first ones I got for him he set on the pole at Bristol and they won the most poles that year. That was on my tire and I got paid for that. Harry, he's dead, so we don't have to worry about pissin' him off or anything. He was the worst cheater of them all anyways.

"Nitrous oxide we used strictly for qualifying. We had a cylinder that was in the framework in the front and it came up and blew nitrous oxide into the air cleaner. It worked good qualifying. We just needed a little boost now and again because we didn't have horsepower. We used it once at Rockingham. I usually do good at Rockingham, but I goofed up in one of the turns and I said, 'If I'm gonna make this race, I need a little help.' I'm comin' off four and punched the button and that car went completely sideways. You don't do it in four. You do it comin' out of two down the straightaway. The reason I ran marginal for the first three or four years and then started pickin' up a little better was because we learned how to cheat. The cheatin', they look at it quite differently today than they did then. It was gettin' competitive is all that was. Everybody cheated and the guys that had the engineers and the technology, they cheated a lot. We tried to cheat as hard as we could to keep up with 'em. It was all about that. Gary Nelson was a crew chief at that time. He wasn't an inspector. He did a lot [of] that stuff."

Debris flies on lap 166 of the Southern 500 at Darlington on September 4, 1978, as D.K. (left), Grant Adcox, and David Pearson (right) crash violently in turn two.

Track workers cover the remains of the car that "killed" D.K. Ulrich. Contrary to reports, it was not covered due to illegal nitrous oxide on board.

Fresh off that season-best ninth at Bristol, D.K.'s fall from the upper reaches of the Winston Cup heap was sudden and painful. It happened on Labor Day, September 4, 1978, in Darlington.

"I got killed. I was on the lead lap, Pearson behind me and comin' to get me, comin' to lap me. I ran good enough to where I felt like I had a good chance at a top ten finish. I don't remember what position we were in, but Grant Adcox got in the wall and bumpin' the wall. I look in the mirror and see Pearson comin' and he [Adcox] was stayin' up there. I had a choice; back off, let the wreck happen, and pick my way through or go down or up, one or the other. You know, the track's only two lanes wide anyway and I took down and it was wrong. I had to make a decision. Am I gonna chance getting lapped or am I gonna try to get through this and let him wreck. I made a choice to try to get through and it was wrong. Pearson came right in behind us."

I [the author] photographed the grinding crash as it unfolded in front of me. Adcox hit the wall in turn one and scraped along for hundreds of feet. That should have been the end of it, but with high-speed traffic boring in, he dropped down and was blasted by Coo Coo Marlin. Adcox was immediately drilled by D.K. The leader, Pearson, piled into the melee. It was a spectacular and extremely destructive crash with all the cars coming to rest on the apron of turn two. D.K. continued.

"I got killed and lived through it. All my stuff was unhooked inside. You know what I mean? You know, that quick stop. He [Adcox] looked just like me in the hospital. We looked like twins. We were black and blue all down one side. We hit like right front to right front and just stopped dead. And the nitrous oxide, you could see a line going through the roll bars on the right front of the car. There used to be a loop that went up the front and it broke apart and there was a braided line. They went in there and found all that. When I said I got killed, I went from a waist size of 36 to 52 in one day. I swoll up that bad. All my stuff came loose inside. Everything in my body changed positions a little bit. Ya know my heart was somewhere else; liver was over here, everything was just kinda moved around. I was totally black and blue all the way down one side. *Completely* black and blue. I bumped my head and was kinda tweeting around. I was revived in the ambulance. They brought me back from wherever I was 'cause I was headed for Saint Pete. [D.K. chuckles.] *Saint Peter.* That's why they covered my car up 'cause when they took me out of it, they had no signs of ... that's why they were coverin' it up. They just threw the body in the ambulance. It was covered up out there. It was covered comin' in.

"I talked to the ambulance driver next time I went down there and I bought 'em dinner. I appreciated them saving my ass. They said when they threw me in there, there was no signs of ... they did the thing with the paddles. It was hot and I was beat up. All my stuff was goin' in all directions. I can't tell you physically what was wrong, but everything changed positions because of the quick stop. It all came out ... it all went back. I hit so hard that the roll bar I could touch like this when I was strapped in the seat [an arm's length away] my helmet hit. That came this way ... I went that way. Stretched and everything. There's a definite mark on my helmet and a definite mark where my head hit. I just remember the big pop and that was the end of the story.

"Next thing I knew is I felt like I had flopped over railroad tracks in the ambulance on a buckboard. I felt like I went up in the air and down. I think it was just the paddles that made me feel that way. I woke up for a second. Just a brief memory of that and the next thing I know it's the next day in the hospital. I'm dead and I don't know if I'm gonna see another day I hurt so bad. If I moved my finger, I could feel it in my nuts. It was just bad. Caroline [my wife] was with me and the kids had got home. She had taken care of all the details. The phone rings and its Bill Gazaway. Old Bill Gazaway is a slow-talkin' guy and he says, 'Son, what did you have in that car there? We found some strange stuff in the front of that car there.' I hardly could talk. She had to hold the phone up to my ear. I said, 'Talk to my crew chief.' He said, 'We have, we have, and I'll tell ya that you're suspended for the rest of the year and there's a $5,000 fine.' I'm going like, 'Why would you call a man dyin' and tell him that?' [D.K. chuckles.] Why would you do that? That guy is really the bottom of the barrel. I never did like him much up to then. I got to know him and he straightened things out with me before he died."

D.K. was done for 1978, and when his year ended, he sat 11th in the Winston Cup standings 134 points behind Richard Childress with eight races to go. Relaxed, locked, and loaded for 1979, D.K. Ulrich with Chevrolets and Buicks competed in all 31 events, finishing 26 while placing a career high 12th in the final standings. More precisely, he was 81 points behind Buddy Arrington for 11th, 107 points behind Terry Labonte in tenth, and 134 behind Ricky Rudd in ninth. D.K. pocketed $113,457 and was poised for even better results in the future.

"When I came back, I was a determined son of a bitch. Yeah, '79 was fun. You'll find that many sponsors you see today, I was the first guy to bring them into racing; M&M Mars, U.S. Army. I was my own PR guy. My whole career was about trying to get enough money to do somethin'. I never really did have enough. In '79, I was motivated because it pissed me off after that Darlington deal, ya know. Midwestern Farm Lines was the sponsor on most of 'em. He was a character named Bob Wagner and he liked me and had a little bit of money. I went to Buick. There was a reason. There was a club at Darlington [the Pure–Darlington Record Club for the fastest qualifier in each make] and nobody ran a Buick. My chance of making that club was better running Buick than Chevrolet. None of the big guys were runnin' Buick. There was a lot of Oldsmobiles, a lot of Chevrolets. The Army was a local deal that the track arranged.

"When I first came here, I was a hippie from California and nobody would even talk to me. Pretty soon I got to where I understood everything and they understood me. I knew where I was and I knew what I had to do. I was dealin' at the time with Junior Johnson. His guys all liked me and I kept a pocket full of $100 bills. Whenever I needed tires, whenever I needed somethin', they'd get me somethin' somehow. I called him Ivan. His name is Tim Brewer. Tim was crew chief there for a while and I needed a set of tires. He'd call their car in to change tires so I could get the ones that came off. I mean he would make a pit stop on my behalf. [D.K. laughs.] Nobody knew it. He knew it. Shorty Edwards, he was a tire guy for them and during the races, I had a guy that worked for me. I gave him the $100 bills while I was racing. He'd go up and down pit road and find a set that we could use. We weren't buyin' from the team. We were buyin' from *the guy*. Ya know the team's out

Head on with D.K.'s Airport Howard Johnson Buick at Atlanta on March 18, 1979. He started 24th and finished 14th of 40, a respectable seven laps behind.

there racin' and he'd go, 'Here's a stack of tires.' Give a hundred bucks and roll 'em right down and put 'em on at the next stop. We didn't have the money. I don't think I ever had a new set of tires. I've had to borrow them to qualify."

Good tires are not worth much without the power to make them turn.

"We'd run a motor 15 races. We had one motor I called 'The All Day Unit.' It was a low-keyed engine. Never quit. I bet I got 100 races on that thing. A small block Chevrolet. We had one good qualifying engine. Stick it in, get it in the race, take it out, put the other in, and run the race. With a tall gear, we'd run in the back. We couldn't run up front. It wasn't we didn't want to, we had to. I never had horsepower. Everybody beat me on the straightaway all the time."

Through smoke, mirrors, and sleight of hand, a top notch engine became available.

"In Daytona, they used to qualify on Saturday for the pole. Sunday they'd have the ARCA race. Then you had Monday, Tuesday, and Wednesday, three more days of qualifying. That's four rounds. Then you had the qualifying races. The whole ticket is get a good time. You get a good time and you're in the race. My figuring was about 21st. If you could get about 21st in time, you would always make it no matter what happened in the qualifying race. The first Saturday, we weren't close to a good time and on the pole is a Junior Johnson car. Cale was drivin' 200 miles an hour. They pulled that engine out and put their practice engine in. I make a deal with Shorty for the engine and qualify with it only. I told Shorty, 'Look, I don't know how good our car is, so I need the engine for Monday, Tuesday, and

D.K. was 11th, 15 points from ninth in the standings in the American 500 on October 21, 1979. He is being passed by the first three finishers in order.

Wednesday. He told me I could have it for $2,000. That was a ton of money for me. 'I'll do it.'

"So what I did, on Monday, I let J.D. McDuffie use it for $500. [D.K. laughs hard.] I'm subletting. I sublet the motor out for two days. Checked the weather to make sure I'd be able to go on the last day. On the last day, I put the motor in my car and hauled ass and had a good time. I was like 15th or something. Guaranteed in the race. They couldn't roll the motor over to me. Shorty would go in the back door of the truck with it and out the side door into his pickup and meet me at the motel. We'd back the pickup trucks together, slide the motor over, and I'd go in the next morning lookin' like I'm bringin' my own motor. Drive in, back it up, stick it in the car, and away we go. We had to do that every night. [D.K. laughs.] I made money on the deal; $500 just to use it and $1,000 if you get in the race. All of them got in. That engine got four cars in the race; the pole-sitter, me, J.D., and I forget the other.

"One time at Wilkesboro, I was strugglin' and Tim Brewer said, 'Take that new set of tires over there and stick 'em on. What shocks ya got? Put this shock on and that shock over there and put that set of tires on and go out and run.' Tim will tell you today, 'No one ever has gone that far into the corner at North Wilkesboro on the gas.' Cale was his driver. But, it would stick and I didn't have the power those guys have so I could go a little further. I went way down in the corner. I got in the race. Fast time second round." D.K. laughs.

When 1980 rolled around, D.K. Ulrich cut back as driver to 11 races in a 31-race season. However, he had a baker's dozen drivers, including Tim Richmond's first five Winston Cup starts, three of which were 12ths in the UNO 40. There were some good runs like tenth at Bristol and 13th in the Southern 500. There was an occasion once at Riverside where D.K. asked for and received much needed help from a fan.

"I always ran good at Riverside. We were out there about the early '80s and my car broke down right off the bat way out on the backside about as far away as I could get from the pits. The engine was dead and I rolled to a stop up near a fence and out of the way where lots of spectators were with their cars and motor homes. I wanted to figure out what was wrong with the motor and get goin' again. I needed to pop the distributor cap to see if it was turnin' in there. That way I might get an idea if it was terminal. I had gathered a pretty good crowd and asked, 'Can anybody get me a screwdriver?' I kept messin' around under the hood and awhile later somebody yelled, 'Here's a screwdriver.' I came out from under the hood and walked over to the fence and here's this old guy standin' there holdin' out a glass of vodka and orange juice. 'Here's you a screwdriver' he said and about 50 people died laughin' includin' me. [D.K. laughs.] He'd gone to his motor home and mixed me a cocktail, then invited me over for more. Seein' as how he had a lovely young female companion who turned out to be his daughter, I hopped the fence helmet in hand and that was the end of my Riverside race."

The record shows that on June 8, 1980, D.K. parked after no laps completed, finishing 36th and dead last in the Warner G. Hodgden 400. Ontario, California, was the final race of 1980 with the 4 sponsored by Juarez Racing.

"See, I had two cars in that race. [D.K. laughs.] That was me and Stan Barrett. Not Stanton, his father. Stan was drivin' 40. I put him in there because it had a guaranteed spot and I qualified the 4 car. I had to bring some boys out of jail in Juarez on the way in. Some of L.G. DeWitt and Pete Wright who is still hanging out. He works for Red Bull. Barry Dotson, some of those names all got on the wrong side of the law in Juarez and I bailed them out in exchange for a qualifyin' motor for the 4 car at Ontario. [D.K. laughs loudly.] We were just makin' a few dollars with that. Stan was payin' for the ride. What I started durin' 1980 was rentin' rides. As a driver, I just couldn't afford it anymore and I had to have some outside stuff."

The record reflects that on November 15, 1980, Stan brought the 40 home a decent 13th while D.K. DNF'd for 37th. In 1981, D.K. competed in 15 of 31 races and scored the only top five of his career, a fourth at Dover on May 17.

"The story on that was simple. Richmond was my driver. Richmond in 1981 drove the first several races and I hadn't run. I was rentin' myself out to qualify cars for guys that couldn't get 'em in. I'm runnin' 99 now as my primary car. I was just startin' anything and still owned the 40. Anyway, 99 was my primary car and Tim was my driver. He had to go to Indianapolis for the 500. For those two races of Dover and Charlotte, he was gonna be missing. So I decided to drive Dover and Chuck Bown drove at Charlotte. That's the best finish of the year was fourth. Had nothing to do with the equipment or the driver or anything. We were on that day. I had some money for the first time and could run with some of these guys. You'll find Earnhardt, Rudd, a lot of guys fell out, but we beat a lot of guys, too. The track got tore up and you had to run right up against the wall. It was another issue where I could make a difference. The other guys didn't have the set up that they always had. That's why we run good there. The circumstances just fell in our favor. Plus, I had

Tim Richmond is in D.K.'s 99 beside James Hylton in the 1981 Coca-Cola 500 at Atlanta on March 15. Tim crashed for 26th and James blew for 25th.

tires and a sponsor. That was fun. You had to run the whole rim of the racetrack. I'd got around the rim and they were tryin' to run down and I'd go right around them. It worked good even though I was ten laps down or whatever."

In 1983, D.K. had 22 starts and another 24th in the final rundown with the high point being a tenth in the spring at Darlington. He had six other drivers including Mark Martin. There was also a number change. "There's a reason for that. I gave up the 40 when I went to 99 for Richmond and the reason we went to 99 was because they [UNO] wanted two cars. They wanted Buddy Baker and they wanted me or Tim Richmond. So we had the 1, which was Hoss Ellington with Buddy drivin', and the other end of the numbers, 99. We had the numbers 1 and 99. During that year I had money with the UNO deal so I had a shit load of decals. They wanted to take 99 and do somethin' with it so I said, 'Why not turn this decal over and make a 6 out of it and 6 was open. So that's why I took 6. Worked. [D.K. laughs.] I had plenty of them."

D.K had ten starts in 1986 with six drivers, including Richard Petty, and Finky's Tonight, a beer joint in Daytona, as a part-time sponsor. The record shows that The King started 37th and finished 38th for D.K. in the World 600. After skipping a couple of seasons at the controls, D.K. drove along with nine others in 1990 and ran the 2 at Richmond.

"Two, The Deuce. I moved over to The Deuce when I took Ernie Irvan. The Deuce.

D.K. and one of his charter jets at the Concord, North Carolina, Airport in May 2009. He moves thousands of racing personnel countrywide during the season.

I owned that until Rusty Wallace approached me at Talladega. He was gonna drive for Penske and they wanted the 2. I think he was drivin' for Raymond Beadle at the time. I had just learned how to fly and had a Bonanza I bought and paid $115,000 for, but I financed $90,000 of it. They told me they wanted my number 2. I told them no problem. You need to pay off my airplane. [D.K. laughs.] He didn't like the idea and he don't claim it now, but he did. I got the check. [D.K. laughs heartily.] I think Rusty was tryin' to get this deal done and didn't want to own up to the fact. We did make a deal and they got the 2."

On May 31, 1992, D.K. strapped in for the last time at Dover Downs, having timed last in the Aroneck Racing Pontiac 85, and quit after 21 laps for 39th. "It wasn't even a start and park. It was worse. They had a short field and NASCAR needed a car to fill it. All I did was find a driving suit, get the thing in the race, run a couple of laps, and hit the road."

They say, "What goes around, comes around." Nothing could be truer for D.K. Ulrich's career. In his first attempt to start a Winston Cup race, D.K. was black flagged by NASCAR and not allowed to race when two others were pushed off contrary to the rules. At Dover 21 years and 273 races later, the field was a little light and NASCAR asked him to drive and he did. At first, D.K. wanted to race and NASCAR denied him. At the end, NASCAR asked him to race when he did not want to. He came full circle. He worked hard and played harder. When the driver could make a difference in a race, D.K. did. When money was scarce and he was backed in a corner, he did whatever it took to survive. He only had one bad crash and it killed him. He was wild and wooly, profane and profound, and damn good. D.K. Ulrich is self-described hippie who came east from the Wild West in a converted city bus. Today he owns ETA Logistics USA, a massive charter transportation network encompassing every mode of travel. He has been on the move his whole life. The day he was born, he was just passing through.

12

James Hylton

Ageless Wonder

James Harvey Hylton was born on August 26, 1934, in Floyd County, Virginia. He was a farm boy sliding tractors around the steep hillsides. A Curtis Turner fan, he followed his dream of racing on the crews of Frankie Schneider, Rex White, Tommy Irwin, Ned Jarrett, and Dick Hutcherson. He relocated in Spartanburg County, South Carolina, next door to legendary independent G.C. Spencer and went Grand National racing with his own team in 1966. He not only won Rookie of the Year, but finished second to David Pearson in the point standings. From there, James Hylton's stock car racing journey went from improbable to incredible to unbelievable with his next nine consecutive point standings finishes of second, seventh, third, third, second, third, fourth, eleventh, and third. No stock car driver has even approached a record such as that to start. To top it all off, *he is not finished.*

In June of 2009, James stood 16th in ARCA points with every intention of winning races and notching a top ten points finish. He has not run a Cup race since 1993, but came within a whisker of making the grid for the 2007 Daytona 500. In NASCAR's premier stock car series now known as the Sprint Cup, he totals 601 starts, 301 top tens, 140 top fives, and 2 impressive victories. He has over 700 starts in major series including NASCAR, ARCA, IMSA, and USAC. The man is ageless and talks with the spirit of someone 50 years younger.

"I've been a racer all my life. I was raised on a farm in Roanoke, Virginia. My father also worked for the state. He was a foreman on a road gang of prisoners. He would take me there and have the utmost respect of the prisoners. They'd call him 'Captain.' My middle name is Harvey after a warden. I remember the farmhouse we lived in. My brothers and I slept in one bed. The room in a log cabin was built on the back. I remember snow blowin' through the cracks. You wake and shake the snow off your blanket. You thought everybody lived that way. I had a good life. I never remember goin' hungry."

James got his first seat time behind the wheel of a tractor.

"I was drivin' a tractor when I was eleven. I was there everyday with the hired hands runnin' machinery. That's what got me right off the bat interested in anything that ran. The first thing I ever drove was a T-Model Ford. I attribute my drivin' skills from tractor days. Even though you're runnin' two mile an hour up on the sides of the hills, you'd actually have this tractor in a four-wheel drift pullin' a hay baler or a hay rake. You had to gauge how much room you had to slide or you'd slide off the edge of the mountain. One of my brothers died runnin' a bulldozer. Got too close to the edge and the thing caved in. I didn't realize how dangerous it was. They did a movie about me tryin' to qualify the number 58 in Cup two years ago. *Retirement Living* made a movie and I got to drive on the backroads where I learned to drive at speed. Got to run around those mountain roads that are not built up. With the tractor help, I learned how to drive."

Floyd County, Virginia, also home to Curtis Turner, was fertile moonshining territory and James knew the ropes. He witnessed the dawning of a new sport.

"If you lived in that area, if you didn't have a connection one way or the other, you just wasn't *in* that area. I'm not gonna say I did it for a livin' or did it for fun, but I did have connections. I did have a '36 Ford that we updated and made a racecar out of for the highway. It had heavy springs. I had a '48 Ford with a flathead and three carburetors. This car would haul the mail. There was many a chase with the county police and once in a while state troopers. When the police first started getting those overhead cars, a flathead was a hundred horsepower. With three carburetors and headers, it *was* a racecar. I believe if you check your history, that's how racing started. You built up your car. You put heavy springs in it, shocks, carburetors, and the thing was fast. I was around moonshine people. I was around moonshine garages, I call 'em, 'cause that's where the cars were built. I didn't haul myself, but I was around it. I was just interested in out runnin' the cops. That's where I got my road racin' experience."

James risked it all to see Curtis race.

"I really believe I was born to race. That's all I lived for in Virginia. Curtis Turner was my hero. Me and my buddies built a raft and the raft sank and we wound up swimmin' the Roanoke River to get to Victory Stadium 'cause I wanted to see that Curtis Turner Ford beat that Petty Dodge.

"My childhood sweetheart and I went to school together. They moved to Tampa, Florida. She was the love of my life and only 16 years old. I was four years older. We stayed connected by phone and I wound up talkin' her dad into lettin' me marry her. She was 17 when we got married. We got a house right across the street from a guy called Frankie Schneider, a modified driver in Lambertville, New Jersey. He raced down there in the wintertime and had a little shack. His old car sat outside. I'd go over there and help him work on it, then I brought my car down. He helped me work on my car and I got to where I could win races. Rex White and Schneider were good friends. Rex had worked for Schneider. I learned the knowledge from Rex and Frankie on chassis set up.

"One winter I was helping Schneider on a regular basis. Out of 32 feature races in Lakeland and around Tampa, he won 30, had a second, and a DNF. Rex out of the blue asked me if I wanted to go Grand National racing. I told him, 'I don't know. I'll have to think about it.' He said, 'Well ya got to hurry. I need somebody.' I said, 'If I'm up there [in Spartanburg] tomorrow by three o'clock, would that be quick enough?' So I moved my family, my son was maybe a year old [1959], when I moved with Rex down on White Avenue with the understanding that I wanted to be a racecar driver."

James was associated with the best in Grand National racing.

"I worked for Rex. He was Grand National Champion [1960], then in '64 went to work for Ned Jarrett and Bondy Long. Rex was one of the greatest drivers ever. Rex could have been a full-blown engineer without any problem. Rex was the man that invented these weight-jackers the springs set on and you raise and lower the car. Holman-Moody copied it from Rex. I was there when it happened. [Louis] Clements was also a great mechanical guy. Rex give him an idea, Clements built it right there on White Avenue. After Holman-Moody seen it, they started mass-producing it. I got the basic trainin' and that's what got me prepared early on. In '64, I was crew chief on the Bondy Long car with Ned and won the championship in '65. I moved to Inman [South Carolina] in 1965 after I worked for Ned. The last part of '65, I worked with Dick Hutcherson at Holman-Moody in the engine room with Robert Yates and Waddell Wilson. We were all three there. They were wantin' me to stay and I said, 'No, I want to be a race driver.' Ya see what happened? They went on to make millions, retire with lots of money, and I'm still out here diggin'." And doing exactly what he wants.

Finally, for three straight races beginning July 8, 1964, James drove his dream.

"I was doing start and park. That's when we were makin' the tour and they didn't have enough cars. It wasn't like I didn't know how to drive. One race, I was supposed to do a couple of laps and come in, but I kept runnin'. It was time to pit for gas, but old Ned outsmarted me. [James laughs.] Ned put a locked cap on it, so he knew what I was thinking. [James chuckles.] Ned was runnin' fifth or somethin' and blowed up."

The records show that took place on July 12, 1964, at Bridgehampton, New York. Ned retired Long's 11 with engine trouble and James fell out for 14th in Long's 71. Obviously, a little tape can make an 11 into a 71. Inman has a solid Grand National heritage of its own. Tommy Irwin also raced cars out of that Spartanburg County town.

"He was down the street. I was workin' for him as crew chief. After he wrecked [at the Spartanburg Fairgrounds in 1963], he was history."

James needed a number and got it from another Inman neighbor. "Next door was G.C. Spencer. He had 48 and 49. I was wantin' 4, but John Sears got that. Ol' G.C. liked to play poker and was over there one night. I said, 'Boy, I gotta find me a number.' He said, 'Well, take 48. I'm not usin' that number.' That's where I got it. That's where he had his shop, the buildin' right next to me."

James Hylton hit the Grand National circuit full time with phenomenal success in 1966 piloting the yellow '65 Dodge with the white roof sporting black 48s. "I drove for Bud Hartje in Tampa. He came up with the money. He told me to find a racecar, so I went to Cotton Owens. Owens had the toughest cars that were ever built. We were runnin' a lot of dirt races and they had to be. Nothing broke on Cotton's cars. I bought that car for $5,500 ... turnkey. Big old hemi, just like David stepped out of the car. Everything Cotton said, he lived up to. I bought a flat-bed truck from Hutcherson and our total when we left to California was $18,000. We had one car, one engine, one everything. My first race was Riverside. I qualified good, ran good, and took that same car to Daytona. I think we finished third at Daytona with that dirt car. That's when they was all runnin' windows. It was optional. This thing was a square back; wasn't fastback, no windows. I run that car 187 races before a fender bender. Run the whole season and finished second [in the standings]. Same engine, same everything. I was pretty good with engines. Every fifth race we'd pull it down, overhaul it, rings and stuff, put it back together, and go racin'."

The record reflects that in his incredible 1966 season, James started 17th, finishing 21st in his debut at Riverside followed by 23rd on the grid and ninth the 500. The year's statistics all in the same racecar; 41 starts, 20 top fives, 31 top tens, a pole, 155 laps led, second in points behind Pearson, and Rookie of the Year honors. Astounding! It is hard to believe James didn't win a race.

"I actually had a couple won my rookie year. In Virginia, I was outrunnin' everybody. Pearson was second and I outrun him. Made a pit stop and they left my gas cap off. I had to stop under the green. In Greenville [South Carolina], Pearson was leadin', I was second, but could outrun him. Just couldn't get by. On the restart, they said I jumped him. Of course, he was the hero, so again I lost. There was about three or four races I shoulda won. Islip, New York, we run that series [Northern Tour]. Bobby Allison and I was teamin' up with our guys. The race before Islip [Fonda, New York], Bobby totaled his Chevrolet and had some cousins up there with a body shop. Actually rebuilt a car in less than a week to go to Islip. My crew helped him work on his car 'cause my car was in good shape, except the gas tank. You made your own gas tank and it was leakin' at the top of the neck. We got to Islip, a real high-banked track. We're settin' there ready to race and it was drippin' fuel. There was no way we could fix it. So we just drained a couple a gallons off till it stopped and they let us race. With seven laps to go, I run out of fuel leadin' with a straightaway on Allison. I was out runnin' Bobby with that Dodge. I still finished second. You help your buddy, it bites ya in the butt. That one bit me bad. But I don't regret it. We did the best we could do with what we had."

The record shows that on July 16, 1966, James' Dodge finished second two laps back to Allison's J.D. Bracken Chevelle 2.

With the '65 Dodge showing the battle scars of three seasons, James is eager to go at Trenton, New Jersey, on July 9, 1967. He started sixth and finished tenth (James Hylton).

On October 29, 1967, James had the worst crash of his career in the American 500 at Rockingham. He did sheet time with the racer destroyed (Jeff Droke).

"I wasn't interested in politics. I didn't see the importance of messin' with the factory. I didn't call 'em, beg 'em, ask 'em, anything. Anything I needed to know, Cotton was there for me. I bought the car set up for Pearson. I run that same car in '66 and '67. That's where I shot myself in the foot. I had a car that ran second in points two times in a row. In their rookie year, nobody has finished second other than me. Ain't even close. I give that car away. I'm busy racin', it's in the way. The car that I won Richmond with, a Holman-Moody car, I should have kept. How 'bout the one I won Talladega with? A Mercury. Wood Brothers built three of them. I got one and I won the race. It was mine."

The record shows that in 1967, James finished behind Petty, running two less races and scoring 26 top fives, 39 top tens, a pole, and 109 laps led in consecutive runner up point standings finishes. James has been remarkably free from disastrous crashes, but not completely. "I been in some bad wrecks. One in Cup at Rockingham. I was unconscious I don't know how long. I was in the hospital for, I think, eight days. I was goin' for the lead, Bobby Isaac blew an engine, and I was right underneath him. That's when they run five gallon oil pans. It dumped all that oil and it was history. While I was in the hospital, my wife had what was left baled up and hauled off to the junkyard. I never did see the car. It had the engine knocked out of it. If you had the seats in the cars then like you have now, I wouldn't have got hurt. Back of my head hit the roll cage 'cause ya didn't have a headrest. We used to have a seat out of a Ford Econoline van. That was Banjo Matthews' official racecar seat. Ol' dadgone Earnhardt run that seat. He liked it because it had springs in the bottom. Wasn't so hard on ya. Now you sit on the floor on that piece of metal. The shocks that ya run beat ya to death."

The record shows that during the American 500 on October 29, 1967, James was involved in a lap 56 crash with G.C. Spencer, Wayne Smith, and others, finishing 38th. Isaac's reason for retiring 36th is listed as 'Timing Chain.' The walkout of the Professional

James and the crew look sharp all decked out in yellow with the Dodge Charger 48 in the pits in 1968 (Don Smyle).

Drivers Association [PDA] the day before the inaugural Talladega 500 on September 14, 1969, is a landmark of stock car racing history.

"It was the same old greed, misunderstanding. After everybody left, they brought in the rest of the gang. Whatever looked like it would run. If he'd [France] have told me, 'We're gonna run ten laps and change tires,' I woulda stayed. I just didn't wanna die like a bunch of other people. After we left, he come up with that idea, 'We'll just run ten laps.' That's all the tires were good for. That's when Glotzbach and all them guys had factory cars. Chrysler offered, 'Take your pick.' I said, 'No, I'm gonna stick with the guys.' I was the first car outta there. I had my little pickup and my open trailer. I happened to be parked on the end of the garage and I really believed backin' up what you said. We had a final vote on it and said, 'We're leavin'. I says, 'OK,' got in my truck and left. I was the first one out the gate. Then the rest of them followed. So I got credit for being the instigator and everybody followed me. People don't know I turned down a factory ride just to stick to my word. If I had to do over, I probably would have jumped into one of them cars, to tell you the truth.

"Soon as we left and things settled down, the Allisons, the Pettys, and the Yarboroughs; Mr. Goodyear was over there makin' a deal with them for the rest of the year. They abandoned ship right away and left the independents out in the cold, which I happened to be."

On February 19, 1970, Talmadge Prince drove a Dodge Daytona purchased from James in the second 125-mile qualifier at Daytona. James reflects on death on the speedway. "It was a winged Dodge. I sold him that car. Had zero experience. He blew an engine and

In 1969, James was a Mopar winged warrior with a third in the point standings. He scored an amazing 27 top fives and 39 top tens in 52 starts (Jeff Droke).

wound up crossways, door facing traffic and Bill Seifert T-boned him. I don't care if you put four-inch thick roll bars around, the impact, if it's hit right, will kill ya. It don't necessarily have to cave in on ya, just the impact, the trauma, will shake everything in a human bein' out. It's just like Earnhardt. The wreck didn't look that bad. It's just the way he got hit. That's somethin' that the racer knows can happen."

The next day, Friday, February 20, 1970, James dominated the Citrus 250 Grand American race on the Daytona road course.

"That was a fun race. My car was so fast it was scary. I'm leadin' and I'm comfortable. Come down off the track and go around the esses. That rotten Tiny turned me around. I did a 360 and took a short cut and he got the lead. I come out about a quarter mile behind. My car was runnin' so good that I run him down. By the time we got back to where you turn down to the road course, I had him. He backed off and turned down in there and I turned underneath him. I turned *him* around. [James chuckles.] He backed across a sandy area and got stuck. I was leadin' the race and come back around and he was still there. He tore his transmission up tryin' to get out. So I win. After the race, here comes Tiny. He's a giant! Big man! I never could tell the mood he was in. I said, 'Oh hell, here he comes!' He wasn't sayin' nothin'. He was just lookin' at me and comin'. I said to myself, 'Well, I guess this is the time you get your ass whipped.' [James laughs.] I didn't know whether to run or get a jackhandle or what. I just stood there. He come up and grabbed me, lifts me way up in the air, squeezed me real hard, set me down, and said, 'That was a good race, wasn't it?' [James laughs harder.] 'It sure was.'"

Daytona Speedweeks 1970 brought mixed results for James Hylton. He was 11th as Jabe Thomas' teammate in the first 125-mile qualifier, witnessed Tab Prince's death in his old car in the second qualifier, both on Thursday, had a rousing win the next day in the Citrus 250, capped off with a lackluster 21st in the 500 on Sunday. James shelled out for a new ride and by the following Sunday was ready to take Richmond. "I had just bought a Holman-Moody Ford, an ex–David Pearson car. I run it under Pearson's colors. It was pretty. We just had time to put 48 decals on it. Went racin'. Picked it up at Holman-Moody, Ralph Moody set the car up, took it up to Richmond, unloaded it, qualified either second or third [third], and wound up winnin' the race. Petty had the hotrod. He was the fastest car there. He was factory backed, I was independent. Havin' a Holman-Moody car kinda put us on an equal basis temporarily anyway. Richard had trouble early with his ignition. They lost several laps gettin' his car runnin' again. He was unlappin' himself to the point where at the end I won the race by 15 seconds, which on a track of that size was a good half a lap. He was within 15 seconds of havin' a shootout. I set a track record that still stands today until they changed the configuration [500 laps, 271 miles on a .542 mile paved at that time. It was changed to .750 miles and 400 laps in 1988]. That and $1.19 will buy you a cup of coffee. [James laughs.] That's the hardest race I probably ever drove in my life. That was before we had power steering. And 500 laps! It wasn't no 300 or 400, it was 500 laps. At the end of the race, you had to pry my hands off the steerin' wheel. Had gloves on, of course, and blisters through the blisters. My hands were like raw steak or somethin'. That's how much determination that a driver, when he gets in a trance of tryin' to win, will go to the extreme to win a race.

"The third place man was five laps behind. [Elmo Langley was actually nine laps back.] In the end, it was Petty and myself and was, without question, the best race I ever drove. Just got lucky, had a good car. Being an Independent, it was like 15 minutes of fame because without financial backing and stuff you're done. It didn't really change anything. The pay was $4,700. [Actually $5,195.] It did boost our morale for our whole team. We had a good run that year. You just can't compete with the factory boys."

The red-hot Camaro that James took to Victory Lane on February 20, 1970, in the Citrus 250 at Daytona. He won a terrific battle with Tiny Lund (Jeff Droke).

The record reflects that in the 500 lap race with one caution for seven laps, Petty led the first 303 laps, Isaac took over for 37, then James brought it home ahead of the ever-closing Richard Petty by staying out front the final 160 laps for his first Grand National win. The Hylton Ford team went on to a very solid third in the last Grand National standings. In 1971, James' Ford chased The King and made it close.

"I was second in '71 against Petty and that's when Petty had 'em change the rules on points. I don't remember exactly how they was figurin', but the system I was workin' in was tearin' him a new one. He whined and whined and moaned and groaned till NASCAR changed the rules. Changed them at Talladega in the middle of the year before the race. After that, it was kinda downhill chasin' Petty."

James qualified fourth and parked after one lap for 17th and last on May 21, 1971, in the Asheville 300 at New Asheville Speedway. Sacrificing points for his beliefs, Petty won the race and six other independents joined James in protest. James' withdrawing while in a tight points duel with Petty is a display of enormous integrity.

"I was raised that way in Virginia. Parents raised their kids by the Good Book that you were honest, you treated everybody like you needed to be treated, you didn't lie, and whatever you stood for, you stood for it. That handicapped me through my racin' career just like the walkout at Talladega."

James' second and arguably most famous Cup win was August 6, 1972, in the Talladega 500. Starting 22nd in the Pop Kola 1971 Mercury 48, he dominated the 50-car field leading a decisive 106 of 188 laps. There was no massive crash or incident that can remotely diminish the scope of victory by a car length over Ramo Stott in Junie Donleavy's Ford. It was as solid as any win by anyone ever.

James notched his first Cup win on March 1, 1970, at Richmond in a converted David Pearson Holman-Moody Ford, seen here later in the year (Jeff Droke).

On August 6, 1972, James fought his heart out in the Talladega 500, nipping Ramo Stott at the wire. James totally dominated the race, leading 106 laps (Jeff Droke).

"The do-gooders say all the big guys blew tires and I had the tire deal. I started 24th, I think it was. In about five laps, I was fifth. What the public don't know was I *did* dominate the race. I could handle Ramo. In another lap, I'da had him lapped. Caution come out. Oh yeah. I slow down lookin' for debris. There was no debris. That put Ramo right behind me. Well, that was all right. I wasn't worried. On the restart, I think it was about 30 laps to go. I went down in the third corner and I'd been able to run right around the bottom. All the sudden, my car started slidin' up a lane. Just move up a lane on me. Ramo drove right underneath. I drafted back by. We got back over there again, I was already past him. Same thing. I said, 'Well, this ain't good.' Unknown to me, the Fords' and Mercurys' hemis, instead of having a solid cross member, it was a bolted-in cross member 'cause you couldn't get that big engine in the hole without takin' the cross member out. What had happened is my cross member cracked where it was bolted up. My car was flexin' makin' me loose and slide up the hill. I figured this ain't good. He couldn't pass me on the outside, but he could get underneath. I said, 'Self, I gotta work on somethin' here.' Instead of goin' in like I been, I went in with my wheel almost on the flat below the line. I'd drift up half a lane and he couldn't get under. He didn't have enough stuff to do it out here [outside]. We got to the end of the race and I remember very distinctly, white flag and he's right there. I said to myself, 'Self, if he wins this race, he's gonna do it over the top. He ain't gettin' by. I done run too long, too much sweat, too much blood to just give it away or make a gentleman's deal.'

"Anyway, I used the racetrack up that white flag lap. Every time he'd make a move, I'd block him. Comin' for the flag, I pretty well knew his pattern. He was gonna try the outside thing. I went right up there. He had to get out of it or hit me and as soon as he got out of it, I just dropped back down and beat him by about a car length. Ol' Ramo was a real gentleman about it. Even to this day we're best buddies. He told me flat out, 'I'da probably done worse.' I don't know that he even could have got by me, but I wasn't goin' to take the chance. Why take the chance? I wasn't goin' to. Buddy Baker, I never will forget, was tellin' me, 'Man, I'm glad you won, but you used up and awful lot of racetrack.' He said, 'Y'ain't s'pose to block people like that.' I told him. 'I drove too long too hard and I wasn't lettin' him by unless he went over the top and that's the only road he had.' I don't remember exactly where it was, but it wasn't long after that Buddy won. He used up the racetrack and made me look like an amateur. Ever who was runnin' second, he run 'em up here and down there. I said, 'What was that Buddy? What do you call what you was doin'?' He said, 'I ... I ... I....'"

Exactly what was Pop Kola?

"That was the dadgonedest thing ever. They was a subdivision of Coca-Cola out of Atlanta and had this shyster manager. Ya know, we was rockin' and rollin'. Won the race for Pop Kola. Cale Yarborough was comin' off the Indy deal. They wanted me to hire Cale and have two cars. I gave Cale the choice of the Ford or the Mercury. He wanted the Mercury. We go to Michigan and I'm fourth and Cale's fifth. Cale was a master drafting and he drafted by me at the finish line and the Mercury run fourth and the Ford fifth. We was gonna run Cale the rest of the year and before we could even have another race, the shyster run off with the money. I believe it was about $250,000. He bought a big house in Miami. Sued 'em. Won the suit. My first part of the deal was $40,000. So the judge let 'em pay $2,500 a month till they paid off the $40,000. They made one payment. The thing disappeared. No more Pop Kola. They had Pop Kola trucks runnin' around here sellin' drinks in stores. The guy just ripped it off and Coke did away with it. Gone. Kaboom! [James claps his hands.] That's all we got left. [James presents an empty Pop Kola bottle.] I still got on my Ford, the 48. I still run that number like that from the Pop Kola days. [The black 48 inside a white circle.] I'm the only car out there that's got that circle. It's a little different."

James and ten passengers roll down pit road after his second Cup win. The Mercury was from the Wood Brothers (Jeff Droke).

James is surrounded by one happy bunch in the Talladega Victory Lane. With his jubilant crew are his son James Jr. on his right and beautiful wife Evelyn on his left (Jeff Droke).

With Cale Yarborough in the Mercury and James in the Torino, they ran fifth and sixth respectively on August 20, 1972, in Michigan's Yankee 400 (Jeff Droke).

The records show that in the Yankee 400 on August 20, 1972, Cale finished fifth in the Pop Kola Mercury 98 and James sixth in the Pop Kola Ford 48.

In 1974, James picked up a sponsor that ended abruptly. "I had a potential good sponsor in Nashville, Tennessee, Nitro 9. Nitro 9 was kickin'. What happens then? The sucker dies! I got shorted again. Spent all this money. I had a little money at one time, but I spent it all back into the cars with the promises. "We're gonna do this and we're gonna do that. That cat just died."

James Hylton lost many friends racing. He finished seventh the day Tiny Lund lost his life on August 17, 1975.

"I was fortunate. I wound up in the middle of the pack stopped on the backstretch. I spun and didn't get any damage. That was sad. It was a big pile up. I don't know if it's fate, life, I don't know what. Tiny saved a driver at Daytona. Pulled Panch out of a burnin' car and then loses his life in a racecar. It makes you think."

James wasn't beyond playing a gag to break the tension of a deadly sport.

"Old Elmo Langley at North Wilkesboro had a big box truck he hauled his racecar in. You'd go on a Tuesday and were there till Sunday. A lot of time to play. Elmo was underneath his truck takin' a nap. Somehow, I got a hold of a military smoke bomb and I rolled that underneath that truck. He's there snorin' away. I started beatin' on the truck. '*Fire! Fire!*' He wakes up and can't see nothin' but smoke. He 'bout killed hisself bumpin' his head tryin' to get out from underneath the truck. [James laughs hard.] The things we used to pull. Childress was the one that you really liked to get somethin' on. He was a prankster, really. He might have been second. Jabe Thomas was the prankster of all times. There ain't nobody ever raced that didn't get pranksterized by Jabe. That was fun days. Now all the drivers, mechanics, and stuff are not like you used to be. It's all business and we ain't got time to talk to ya. We ain't got time to look at ya! We don't even have time to make eye contact with ya. That's the one thing about ARCA right now. There's hardly a driver or crew member or official that I don't know by first name and they don't know me by first name."

James Hylton and Darlington Raceway started a relationship in 1966 when the Southern 500 was on Labor Day morning and the turns had steel rails.

"I wasn't scared of Darlington, I respected Darlington. There wasn't no way to keep the right side off the guardrail. You'd run the rail if you were runnin' at all. That's one of those things where you just grit your teeth and do it. I can drive Darlington fairly well. I won the Fireball Roberts Trophy for independents. Pearson was probably the best driver that ever drove that racetrack. I didn't fear it, but I sure respected it. One crash I remember, Mr. Earnhardt was in his early days. I was actually out-runnin' him. We're comin' for the checkered flag and he was tryin' one of them intimidatin' moves that he became famous for. He was very clever about it. He didn't run into the back of ya ... *BOOM!* Or run into your quarter panel and turn ya sideways. He'd just get against ya, loosin' ya up comin' off the corners. You'll spin out and he'll drive on by. I had a picture around here. It shows me and Earnhardt walkin' up pit road, him carryin' his helmet, and he'd done that deal on me. I knew what he was doin' and figured about the time he was goin' to loosin' me up. I got on the brakes comin' off four. Brake checked him! It took us both out, but he went out with me." James laughs.

"You're drivin' down the backstretch and there's what I call a swag where, at that time, would be turn three. You automatically went into a four-wheel drift and if you timed it just right, you'd kiss the rail a little bit. If you really misjudged it, you slammed the rail. That was back when you had real racecars. They had bumpers, real steel sheet metal, not

The loaded remains of James' Nitro 9 car after another driver took him out on lap 72 of the 1976 Rebel 500 on April 11. He finished a rare 32nd that day.

In the 1977 Southern 500 on September 5, James comes up to speed from the pits as D.K. Ulrich roars by. James took 13th while D.K. finished 27th.

this thirty-thousandths stuff we got on 'em now. You could do that and get away with it. It was kindly a badge of honor that ya leave and had the guardrail on the side of your racecar. You were a racer! I didn't particularly like it, but I lived with it. I had a guy take me out. It might have been that Nitro 9 car. It becomes a game of idiots. I was lappin' him for the umpteenth time goin' into three. You swept down in there. The guys bein' lapped or that you're racin' with, you're trustin'. The guy takes the inside 'cause that's the only choice he's got. You drive on the outside 'cause you got no choice either. This particular guy, I drove in on the outside of him like normal. He just pile drives straight in the door and stuck me in the wall. Nothin' you can do. That was the most hazardous part of that racetrack and I ain't so sure it still isn't. Halfway down the backstretch as it was, you had to start makin' plans what you were gonna do when you got to three. Who was in front of ya or beside ya or who was catchin' you. That was a real game of chess. It's the most stressful racetrack on the circuit, without a doubt, 'cause you're not gaugin' feet, you're gaugin' inches."

The record shows that at Darlington, James Hylton raced 38 times with three top fives and ten top tens with a highest finish of fourth in the 1970 Rebel 400. James remembered Wendell Scott.

Here is a tight shot of James at the office in the 1979 Carolina 500 on March 4. He drove the Palatine Auto Parts Monte Carlo to a solid seventh place.

"Wendell was a great driver. We never had no race issue with Wendell. He came to the racetrack and ran his race and we came to the racetrack and ran our race. There never was any, 'Hey, you a black man, we don't like ya.' I never seen it. *Nobody* didn't like Wendell. A lot of the big drivers, big teams, would help him out with parts and do what they could. But Wendell ... he had the heart and guts of a grizzly. It didn't get too tough for him. One thing that stands out in my mind was Riverside. Here come Wendell towin' a racecar. Just imagine that. Flat towin' a racecar to California with I don't remember what year Packard. Had his whole crew, his whole family in that old Packard with all his stuff he was gonna race with. It never got too tough and he could fix anything. He built his own engine right there at the racetrack. Ordinary man couldn't have done it. I was at the racetrack when he won his race. It was one of them good ol' boy things. The word was out that Wendell told Buck, 'I won the race. You can kiss the beauty queen. All I want's my trophy.' Wendell got out there and run a steady race. Everybody was havin' trouble and beatin' on each other tearin' up cars. Wendell's old car lasted. That was good for the sport."

James reflected on the lost art of flat towing.

"They ran another circuit in Virginia. I was flat towing and that sucker went off some mountain curve. I heard some noise and looked over and there went the thing over the side of some mountain. [James chuckles.] He [Frankie Schneider] was the one that built the tow bar. It was his fault. [James laughs.] He just blamed me. We dug it out of the mountain. It about totaled the car. Fixed it up and went on."

At the Cracker Barrel Country Store 420 on May 8, 1982, James pulled a gag for the ages.

"I had two sponsors; Suzuki and Kawasaki. A friend of mine in Hendersonville [North Carolina] had a dealership. Both motorbikes. We painted half with Kawasaki color and half with Suzuki color. Nashville is where I brought the car. You go up the frontstretch it had Kawasaki color and go down the backstretch it was a different color. [James chuckles.] It confused the scorers and NASCAR thought they were lookin' at two different cars. They weren't smart enough to figure out, 'Hey, that's the same car. It has 48 on it.' They didn't read the number, they were goin' by color. Before I could bring it back, I had to do away with that. Yeah, that was pretty."

The record reflects that James started the Dal-Kawa Cycle Pontiac Grand Prix 26th finishing 17th in an otherwise forgettable race. The car was Suzuki yellow on the driver's side and Kawasaki green on the right with red 48s on both. The hood, roof, and deck were red. He talked about cheating then and now.

"What they call it these days is 'engineerin'. I did quite a bit of 'engineerin'. We used to have fun with carburetor plates. It wasn't policed as it is now and we had all kinds of tricks. I had boxes full of stuff we did. We had tricks where it would slide back. Turn a bolt on a carburetor and move stuff around to get air. Ain't nowhere close to bein' over with. I never did use nitrous. That stuff will put it to walkin' if you can get by with it. I *have* run fuel. Put some stuff in the tank. There's all kinds of stuff like they put in go-karts to hop it up. Even today, you can get away with it occasionally. Nitro 9 in there, yeah." [James laughs.]

Inspection was a constant deal. "[Bill] Gazaway was pretty good to me. It was his stupid brother Joe. [James chuckles.] What Joe did was at Dover, Delaware. We was runnin' an old beat up car we'd been runnin' all year. It was in the '70s because it was a Ford. They didn't have 700 templates yet, but they had the one that goes over the top. The roof on that car was about a half inch low. Joe Gazaway said we wasn't goin' to run the car with the roof that low. So how you gonna fix the roof at the racetrack? He made it very plain we wasn't goin' nowhere. I said, 'Joe, if I cut this roof off, it's gonna look awful.' 'I don't care. You can't race it with the roof till you move it up.' 'OK.' He got my nerves pretty good. Took a torch and cut it off. It's not a clean cut by any means. Raised it up a half inch. Took one inch metal strips, welded it back. The roof fit the template. He was happy. I told him, 'I'll not paint the car the rest of this year.' And I didn't! [James grins broadly.] Here's this thing where the roof was cut off with a torch all raggedy, dirty lookin'. Old weldin' had rusted after a race or two. We run that car the rest of the year. I didn't paint no part of the car. You can't get by with that now, but back then ya could. But there at Dover we had to cut the roof off."

Bill Senior, as far as James was concerned, was an honest man.

"He cared about his racers; took care of his racers pretty good. Whatever he said, you could take it to the bank. I liked the old man. The old man would do exactly what he said he'd do. I can't say the same for his son."

High noon came at stock car racing's OK Corral in Martinsville, Virginia. It was James Hylton and the independents versus William H.G. France, Jr., and NASCAR.

"I was head of what NASCAR calls 'Plan 1.' We rebelled. I was elected leader of the independent group and went head to toe with Bill, Jr. We was ready to walk. This had been goin' on for about three months. With Jr., all we wanted to do was have a meetin' with him as a group. He'd talk to ya one on one. But as a group of two or three, he wouldn't hold a meetin'. It boiled down to a shootout. I was lookin' at Jr., face to face in [promoter] Clay Earle's office. What brought that on, the promoters were helpin' us independents and France cut it out. Made the promoters not help us anymore. We didn't even have enough money to get *to* the race. I told Bill, Jr., 'You do this plan, it'll be good for you, it'll be good for NASCAR, it'll be good for the fans, it'll be good for the racer. We'll have better cars. We can't afford to paint the damn things.' The deadline was twelve o'clock. At twelve o'clock, I said, 'Boys, he won't talk to us. Let's load up.' We had actually loaded up and were ready to pull out when they opened the gate at one o'clock. Jr. sent for me. I went up to the office and we set there and looked each other in the eye for about 15 minutes. All he did was say, 'Hey, come in.' I didn't even shake hands with him. I'm settin' here and he's settin' there and I'm lookin' at him and he's lookin' me. Ain't sayin' nothin'. Seemed like 15 hours. He said, 'Go get 'em.' 'OK.' So I went down, 'Come on, guys.' He had a motor home parked behind the office. We got in that motor home and went on the four lane and that's where everybody had their say. That's when Plan 1 was born. Of course, the Pettys and Allisons, big guys, Yarboroughs, came. They had to start givin' the big boys show money. I think then it was $10,000 for a Petty and so forth. It was such a bad idea, just look at the payoff now.

"That plan is still in effect when they don't need it. We got a little money so we could upgrade and it worked. We upgraded, we run harder, we could buy tires. Big boys were happy. Course they got credit for doin' it. They didn't have a damn thing to do with it. That was an independent deal. We started somethin' with that plan forcin' Bill, Jr., and NASCAR to help us. Old Bill, last thing he told me was, 'Ain't never gonna work.' Years later, I said, 'Ya know, everything's pretty good now. Let's put the money back in the purse and run for the money.' 'Nah.' It's still there today. You see a guy that runs tenth in Cup and look down and there's a guy that finished 32nd. He made more money than the guy tenth! That's Plan 1(c). I feel proud 'cause it wasn't all my idea. It was part my idea, but I was spokesman for the independents. That's the hard-core reason I had from my daddy in Virginia. You do the right thing, believe in what you believe in, and stick to it. Just like Talladega. I believed in it and I believed in the guys. After it's all said and done, ya see the big boys sneakin' around. They gettin' the free tires and we're gettin' ... the weenie. That right there made me lose a lot of respect for guys like Petty. I'm not sayin' anything about Petty I won't say to his face. Or Allison. Or Yarborough. Or any of the rest of them 'cause it's fact. They threw us in the river like a big ol' wet rag. That's one thing I can say the independents accomplished. I was proud of it and I'm still proud of it 'cause if it wasn't worth a hoot for NASCAR, why are they still usin' it? There's definitely enough money now that these guys don't need a cent. The drivers're makin' five million dollar salaries. Whoever said that NASCAR's 100 percent good guys anyway?"

James nearly made the 2007 Daytona 500 via a 125-mile qualifying race on February 15. Millions were watching on television that Thursday afternoon pulling as hard as they could for James to hold on.

"Jimmy Johnson was leadin' the second pack and we were pullin' away. I was runnin' eighth in a nine-car draft. Wasn't no way I was gonna come out of that draft. Of all the times for one of the big teams, I think is was Red Bull, to blow an engine with eight laps to go. That screwed me. I had a rookie spotter. That was one big mistake. What he did ... they bought off the ninth-place car, whatever his name ... I should remember it real good.

He got paid $10,000 to do what he did. He was back there draftin' with me and we were in good shape. I found out later from the spotters he made a deal to line up like he was gonna go with me. When we took off, he whipped out and had the whole train back there pushin' him by me. I couldn't get goin'. The slave cylinder on the transmission quit. You know, the clutch. It was like drivin' a four-speed without a clutch. Every time you shift, you lose a half a car length. I'm back here strugglin' and that give him just enough stuff to push him up on me. If I could have got goin' and stayed with the lead cars, the seven cars in front of me, I'da been all right. I've had a lot of hard knocks like that through my career for whatever reason. I think sometimes God gets even with me. Maybe I get too greedy, want to do too good. It's just like my rookie year. I should have won three or four races. Gas cap, black flag, flat tire, this, that, the other. Couldn't *buy* a race! I'm surprised at Talladega somethin' strange didn't happen, but it didn't. I guess it all evens out."

James spoke out on the Car of Tomorrow [COT].

"I'm not so sure that's not the worst mistake NASCAR's ever made. We started out back in the '50s when you outrun the law with your '36 Ford. You're haulin' liquor and you build your car up so you go fast. It's your Ford against the Chevrolet, or your Chevrolet against a Plymouth. People could go out and buy a car off a showroom and they *were* stock. They really had bumpers on 'em, everything just like real. The good ol' days is gone forever. I try to put myself in the fans' place. I'm goin' to a NASCAR race and see this Ford run. What makes it a Ford, a paper decal on the nose? If they're gonna run Toyota, run a real Toyota. Make them go back to the real bodies, then people would probably pay more interest. NASCAR has taken initiative out of the deal. I don't think ARCA's gonna be that dumb. They still got enough of these cars. If they do that little trick [COT], then they'll put theirselves outta business. I got a new car we're buildin'. It's a Dodge. This time tomorrow, it'll be a Ford. We changed the nose, the tail, different hood, and it's a Ford. Even with these cars you can't actually say it's a Ford. It's a big hunka iron that's got a Ford engine. These cars ain't legit. Everybody's got a Ford housin' and rear end. Chevrolet truck arms is what holds the rear end. You build them yourself, but they're Chevrolet designed. You got a Chevelle-designed suspension for the front. Now you make your own chassis. You can't call it a stock car.

Next year in ARCA, we gotta put the eighth-inch steel in between the roll cage and make that all one panel. There's no reason we can't put the same thing that's in the COT in these and make the car safer. We can move the driver over a couple of inches. We already got transmissions where we can do that. The COT roll center is way high; it takes a magician to drive 'em. It takes engineers to work on 'em. A fifty-thousandths washer on the shock makes the difference on whether you can or can't drive the car. I don't like nothin' about 'em. I think they're a joke. They're playin' on the intelligence of the fan. Fans are not stupid. Fans are payin' the bill; should be able to see the car that's on the highway. These cars, there ain't nothin' stock. Nothin'! Where's IROC now? You couldn't pay people to go see 'em. That's what's happened to Cup. Big, fat IROC cars and you can't tell one from another. Ford makes an engine, Dodge makes an engine, Chevrolet makes an engine. There's *some* difference there. You put it in the same body where all are IROC cars. I don't dig it and a lot of fans don't dig it either."

On April 24, 2009, James Harvey Hylton ran the ARCA Re/Max 250 at Talladega and provides an amazing tale of guts and fortitude.

"I run Talladega hammerin' on cars tryin' to get to the front. I'm not tryin' to be a martyr or super hero. I'm doin' what I love. I'm 74 years old and'll be 75 in August. I have no problem with it. This car had windows and we didn't put up enough preparation. Some of them guys got mini-air conditioners and fans. I didn't have any fans. I didn't have anything in the car, but car. Didn't have time to put a water bottle in it like it should have been. They tie-strapped a little water jug beside the seat. With the race going on, this thing got floppin' around and I tried to get a drink. I pulled the tube out of the jug. So, done! No water. I didn't even get a taste and got dehydrated. I was dehydrated before we went there ... workin' day and night.

"I was leadin' the race. [James points to a photo of the scoring pylon showing 48 leading at 87 laps.] They had a crash and I took the northern route. I was runnin' about 12th and they went down pit road. I went through the wreck, made it, and come out leading. Well, that confused the hell out of ARCA. For 20 minutes we set over there on the backstretch. They're tryin' to figure out what happened. The electronics showed I come out ahead. I passed all them guys. It was a wreck happening. Caution came after I crossed the finish line. They couldn't figure it out for 20 minutes. We were settin' over there cookin' sure enough. That was a hot day. Normally, NASCAR, when they park the cars, have rescue people bring a bottle of water around to the drivers. Didn't happen. Nobody got water. It was ten laps to go. They couldn't figure out what happened. They didn't believe their electronics. So what did they do? They put me in 16th place. I got to 15th at the end. It's one of them deals like NASCAR. When it's over, it's over. You can argue all ya want. I learned that a long time ago with NASCAR. You're better off to keep your mouth shut and go on about your business 'cause that was their decision. They wasn't about to let me lead the race under the green, so they just put me back."

The 2009 Talladega ARCA/Remax 250 was over and James finished 15th. The fun had only just begun.

"I was dehydrated, plain and simple. I got out under my own power. I wasn't dizzy, ready to pass out. I was just feelin' bad and wanted somethin' to drink. I hadn't had anything to drink all day. They were pourin' water on me and I was startin' to come around. They talked me into goin' to the infield hospital. I rode there on the back of one of them little carts. I thought it would be a good chance to rest. The minute I went in that hospital, I said, 'Uh oh! You done messed up big boy.' That was a NASCAR probe there. They were treatin' me for a heart attack. I didn't have no heart attack. I been that way before in my young days. I been hot in a racecar. I kept tellin' these people, '*No.*' 'Does your chest hurt?' '*No.*' 'Got any pain?' '*No.* I just need somethin' to drink.' When I went in that hospital, there were two NASCAR nurses and they're as cute as they can be. [James chuckles.] I had fun with 'em. They're just standard NASCAR. They also got an official NASCAR doctor. Once I got in there, they pounced on me. This doctor's over there puttin' all this stuff on me. They put an IV in and give me fluid. This doctor said, 'Well you look OK.' This other NASCAR doctor said, 'Everything's showin' all right, but ... you need to go to the hospital.' 'For what?' He said, 'Well, we gotta check ya out.' There was a place about as big as my hand that ... I still got the scars on the right side of my toes. I fried my toes. At Talladega, your foot is on the floor and you don't think about liftin'. If you lift, you'll go to the back. You stay right there on the throttle the whole time. If you get in trouble, you tap the brake or somethin' to slow down a little bit, but you do not let the throttle off 'cause it takes another lap or two before the engine picks back up. I set there and cooked my toes, the whole side of my foot, and it was really hurtin'. 'Anything hurt ya?' I said, 'Yeah, my foot's killin' me.' By then, blisters were startin' to come up and they wouldn't even look at my foot.

"I ride in the ambulance to Birmingham, police escort, the whole deal. They got all this stuff monitorin' me in the ambulance. I keep tellin' this guy, 'Man, I ain't got no heart attack.' [James laughs.] They had the hospital set up when I come in. Don't have to sign no papers, no nothin'. They got a room waitin'. Here comes the doctor. He checks me out. He draws blood. They put it through the lab. They had a blood test to tell whether you had a heart attack. The second doctor comes in and says, 'Well, you didn't have no heart attack.' I said, *'That's what I been tryin' to tell you people!'* [James claps his hands loudly and laughs heartily.] I drove a 250-mile race competitive. Could have won the race. The third doctor comes in. Yep, the third doctor is a full-blown heart man. They say he's the best in the south. Even though the blood test was such and such, he was convinced somethin' was wrong with my heart. After 250 miles, they give me six IVs, that's how dried out I was. They put me through all this bull. They insisted I stay the night. They're in there all durin' the night takin' blood, doin' this, doin' that.

"Next mornin', I had to go do a stress test. You know, after drivin' the race and goin'

Going strong in June 2009, James Harvey Hylton is with a Ford that took him to 15th in ARCA points.

through what I had to go through, now I gotta take a stress test! They got a series of two different kinds. You walk a treadmill and blah, blah, blah. This is what I call an atomic deal. They put the stuff in your veins, big-time radioactive junk that's supposed to make you pass out. Oddly enough, it didn't bother me at all. They got to doin' this stuff and watchin' the meters and nothin' happened. They put me in these things and spin me around. X-rays. They got my heart up here showin' my heart beatin'. The nurse, she's tellin' what this does and that does. They drug that thing out and the doctor all the time tellin' me I needed to do this and that. Well, there wasn't nothin' wrong. So they finally give up and I come back home. [James laughs.]

"NASCAR's done called two or three times askin' me how I felt; Jim Hunter and John Casey. ARCA called me two or three times. They insisted I go to a doctor here in Spartanburg and get another physical. I'd already had three physicals this year. One for drivin' my tow truck. You gotta have a medical card so DOT don't getcha. One for NASCAR. One for ARCA. Then I had to get another for ARCA before they let me go racin' again. I don't see what's so unusual. Ya notice I don't have glasses and contacts. [More laughter as James claps his hands.] Far away I got 20–20. I'm havin' fun with it, ya know. Why can't a 74-year old man drive a racecar? We're not all built the same. Not only did they do all this heart stuff, they put stuff in my veins and checked my arteries. I figured, 'They gonna do four or five roddin' out of the arteries. They ain't nothin' to rod out. I'll quit when I get ready. The one thing NASCAR won't touch with a ten-foot pole is ... they won't dare say, 'You're too old.' [James laughs.] They'll do everything else, but NASCAR ... whoa! They'll not tackle that! Just like now. I'm 16th in driver points with ARCA. Been to all the races. Just run a top 15 at Talladega where we run 200 mile an hour. That was a case where they were gonna give me a heart attack whether I wanted one or not. I hate to disappoint them."

On June 12, 2009, James Hylton reached a milestone in his spectacular stock car racing career.

"Michigan was my 700th race in a national series countin' The Cup 601. I got it in the record book. I ran USAC, IMSA, ARCA, major series."

On October 11, 2009, James completed the ARCA season with hard, leg-breaking crash at Rockingham, his 714th major-series race. James Hylton's 714th major event enabled him to finish a solid and amazing 15th in ARCA points out of 116 racers.

James Hylton is not finished. Parked in his Inman garage is a blue Dodge Charger, a red Ford Fusion, and a bare metal car under

On January 5, 2010, James Hylton was honored with a special resolution by the Spartanburg, South Carolina, City Council in recognition of his lifetime of achievements in auto racing and citizenship.

construction that was some make in between. He has not run Cup since 1993, but came within a whisker of making the 2007 Daytona 500. In 601 big time NASCAR starts over 27 seasons, he won twice, captured four poles, finished in the top five 23 percent of the time, and came home in the top ten in over half of those races. James loaded up and split or parked after a lap when he felt things were not safe or fair, even if it hurt him in a tight championship race. He went eyeball to eyeball with Bill France, Jr., and James didn't blink. He is a leader, a winner, and at 75 years old, the doctors can't even slow him down. This Babe Ruth of stock car racing believes he was born to race. He does not believe he was born to stop.

Bibliography

Books

Fielden, Greg. *Forty Years of Stock Car Racing, Volume One: The Beginning, 1949–1958.* Surfside Beach, SC: Galfield Press, 1987.

_____. *Forty Years of Stock Car Racing, Volume Two: The Superspeedway Boom, 1959–1964.* Surfside Beach, SC: Galfield Press, 1988.

_____. *Forty Years of Stock Car Racing, Volume Three: Big Bucks and Boycotts, 1965–1971.* Surfside Beach, SC: Galfield Press, 1989.

Films

Thunder in Carolina. Howco International Pictures, 1960
1957 Southern 500. Rare Sportsfilms, Inc., n.d.
1960 Southern 500. Rare Sportsfilms, Inc., n.d.
1960 World 600. Racing Legends, Inc., 1988
1961 Rebel 300. Racing Legends Productions, n.d.
1961 Southern 500, Racing Legends Productions, n.d.
1962 Southern 500. Rare Sportsfilm, Inc., 2003

Newspapers

The Spartanburg Herald-Journal (3/3/63)

Web Sites

www.jameshylton.com, James Hylton's website.
www.raceplace.zoomshare.com, racing information.
www.racersreunion.ning.com, racing information.
www.racing-reference.com, racing information.

Index

AAA 5, 6
ABC 24, 25; *Wide World of Sports* 24, 25, 193
Activated Angels 123
Acton, Marvelous Marv 187
Adams, Buddy 103
Adcock, Marvin 128
Adcox, Grant 213, 214
AFL-CIO 199
Airlift 8
Alabama 57, 173; Anniston 197; ARCA/ReMax 250 240; Birmingham 57, 59, 94, 129, 194, 242; Montgomery 124; Talladega 7, 165, 167, 169, 170, 172–174, 187, 194–198, 201, 208, 221, 226, 227, 230, 233, 239–241; Talladega 500 187, 209, 210, 230, 231; Talladega International Speedway 165; Winston 500 169, 172, 187, 196
Alaska 81, 92
Allen, Johnny 86, 100
Allen, Tim ix
Allison, Bobby 4, 6, 77, 103, 124, 164, 165, 180, 183, 184, 190, 199, 212, 225, 227, 239
Allison, Davy 180
Allison, Donnie 6, 194, 212, 227, 239
Allison, Judy 164, 165
Anders, Bob 103
Anderson, John 129
Andretti, Mario 160
Anheuser-Busch (Budweiser/Busch) 6, 171, 172, 178
ARCA (ReMax) 146, 217, 222, 235, 240–243
Ard, Sam 4
Arizona 56
Arkansas 9, 11; Lehi 9; Memphis-Arkansas Speedway 9, 11, 29
Arnold, Ben 195
Aronek Racing 221
Arrington, Buddy 128, 133, 140, 146, 167, 195, 199, 215
Austin, L.D. 76
Autolite 85

Bacon, Bruce 95, 96, 103
Bailey, Don 14, 16–19
Bailey, H.B. 140
Baker, Buck 5, 6, 9, 12, 22, 28, 33, 35, 36, 52, 53, 56, 58, 59, 65, 73, 78, 95, 97, 120, 128, 130–132, 137, 143–148, 150–152, 158, 159, 195, 196, 237

Baker, Buddy 6, 22, 59–62, 77, 95, 96, 101, 128, 131, 132, 137, 139, 141, 145–147, 149, 189, 192, 220, 231, 232
Baldwin, Tommy 36
Bali Hai Wine 188, 199
Ballard, Katy 199
Ballard, Walter 199
Barker, Bill 183
Barrett, Stan 218, 219
Barrett, Stanton 218
Barron, Bob 89
Beadle, Raymond 221
Beam, Alex 4
Beam, Herman "The Turtle" 76, 85, 89, 91, 111–113, 115, 117–119, 121, 127
Bean, Alan "Pinto" 192, 198, 201
Bearden, Homer 67, 68, 70, 74
Beauchamp, Johnny 19, 83
Bedford, Lucie 42
Bell, Howdy 205
Bennett, John 128
Bettenhausen, Tony 5
Biscoe, Billy 195, 197
Black, Gene 158
Black Label Beer (Carling) 188, 198
Blackburn, Bunkie 183
Blackwell, Pete 78
Blackwell, Tom 78
Blair, Bill, Jr. 3
Blanchard, Chuck 190
Blue Ribbon Beer 183, 188
Boggs, David 192
Boland, Pete 62
Bonanza (Beechcraft) 221
Bonnett, Neil 199
Boone's Farm Apple Wine 190
Bown, Chuck 211, 219
Bracken, J.D. 124, 225
Bradley, Melvin 39
Braun Plywood Company 16, 18
Brewer, Tim (Ivan) 216, 218
Brooks, Dick 187, 189
Brooks, Earl 206
Brown, Bob 205
Bruner, Johnny, Jr. 95, 112, 190
Bryant, Darrell 127

Buick 133, 143, 200, 201, 215, 216
Burdick, Bob 33, 85
Burns, Gov. Haydon 102
Burton and Robinson 39
Busch, Kyle 39
Byron, Red 5

Cadillac 26, 104
California 8, 26, 66, 77, 99, 111, 120, 121, 183, 189, 190, 196, 201, 203–205, 216, 224, 237; Bellflower 99; Hollywood 115; Los Angeles 8; Needles 205; Ontario 218, 219; Ontario Motor Speedway 201; Red Fox Lounge 204, 212; Riverside 28, 56, 160, 161, 183, 192, 204, 209, 212, 218, 224, 237; San Bernardino 205; Warner G. Hodgden 400 218
Canada 48
Car of Tomorrow (COT) 240
Carrier, Larry 106, 111, 119, 139
Casey, John 243
Caspolich, Joe 103
Castles, Neil 3, 4, 48, 97, 135, 143–148, 150, 206
Champion, Bill 190, 199, 200
Champion (Spark Plugs) 85, 168, 187
Chapman, Charlie 77
Chapman, Walt 5
Cheeseburg, Bill 16
Chester, Ted 5, 6
Chevrolet (Camaro/Chevelle/Chevy/Corvette/ El Camino/Impala/Monte Carlo) 14, 16–19, 22, 37–41, 67, 68, 70, 72, 104, 105, 107–110, 112–114, 124, 145, 156, 160, 170, 171, 173, 209, 210, 212, 215–217, 225, 237, 240
Childress, Richard 6, 192, 199, 201, 207, 208, 215, 234
Christian, Frank 5
Chrysler 5, 9, 10, 12, 28, 63, 64, 114, 120, 121, 143, 144, 146, 147, 159, 161, 162; Hemi 63, 121, 147, 163, 174, 209, 227; Mopar 5, 113, 147, 150, 151, 162, 169, 170, 228
Circus Circus 201
Clayton, Paul 79–81
Clements, Crawford 22–24, 26, 78, 167, 168, 170, 171, 173, 174
Clements, Louis 67, 70, 224
Coca-Cola 6, 103, 219, 232
Cole, Dr. Eric v
Collins, Sid 205
Colorado 92
Colvin, Bob 54, 111, 149
Commonwealth Ford 26
Connecticut 41, 42, 46; Fairfield Firestone 42
Cooke, Ed 83
Cooper, Bob 146
Cooper, Doug 132–134
Costa Rica 199, 200
Cowart, Delma 178, 179
Cox, Marion (Preacher) 178
Crawford, Spook 9–13
Crider, Curtis 22, 76, 92, 126, 127, 139
Crider, Ike 50
Crider, Mary Frances 59, 126
Cunningham, Briggs, III (Briggsy) 41, 42, 44

Dal-Kawa Cycle 238
Daniels, Fred 200
Daniels, Tom 37, 38
Daniels, Ronnie 196
Deese, Sonny 49
Deese's Garage 49
Delaware 203, 238; Delaware 500 209; Dover 188, 200, 203, 209, 219, 238; Dover Downs 221
DeLotto, J.R. (Rudy) 210; Garden State Auto 210
Derrington, Bob 138, 140, 151–153
Derrington, Junior 151, 156
DeSoto 10, 52, 53
DeWitt, Horace 129
DeWitt, L.G. 129, 219
Dieringer, Darel 91, 101, 132, 134, 137, 148
District of Columbia (D.C./Washington) 26, 60, 104; Café Burgundy 26, 60
Dodge (Charger/Daytona/Petty) 5, 6, 62, 63, 71, 89, 116, 122, 123, 127, 128, 133–137, 141, 145, 146, 161, 162, 165–167, 173, 189, 195, 223–225, 227, 240, 243
Don Quixote 202
Donahue, Mark 168
Donleavy, Junie 230
Dorton, Keith 157
Dotson, Barry 219
Dow Chemicals 6
Droke, Jeff ix, 228–233
Duke University 183, 188
Dunbar, Budgy 79

Eargle, Eugene "Pop" 89, 91, 110
Earle, Clay 239
Early Times 190
Earnhardt, Dale 155, 201, 219, 226, 228, 235
Earnhardt, Ralph 92, 158
Economacki, Chris 24
Edwards, Carl 136, 142
Edwards, Shorty 216, 218
Elder, Ray 189
Ellington, Hoss 195, 220
Elliott, Bill 6, 211
Elliott, Stick 63
England 48, 49; London 49
Epton, Joe 164
Esso 67, 188
ETA Logistics USA 221
Eubanks, Joe 5, 10, 11, 15, 66, 67, 75, 86

Fagan, Harold "Frog" 190, 193
Farmer, Red 85
Fielden, Greg L. ix, 13, 15, 16, 34, 38, 111, 118
Firestone 12, 17, 80
Flat towing 52, 74, 89, 105, 106, 138, 145, 237
Flock, Bob 158
Flock, Fonty 10, 13, 158
Flock, Francis 3
Flock, Tim 3, 5, 10, 77, 158
Florida 11, 28, 38, 83, 89, 92, 99, 100, 102, 126, 127; Bradenton 89; Casa Linda Motel 192; Citrus 250 228, 229; Daytona (Beach) 5, 7, 10, 14, 16, 22, 27–30, 33, 37, 39, 42, 46, 50, 51, 61, 64, 68,

69, 72, 75, 77, 79, 80, 83, 84, 86, 87, 95, 96, 101, 104, 115, 117, 118, 122, 126, 143, 144, 147, 150–152, 154, 158, 161, 163, 165, 170, 171, 175, 178, 179, 183, 184, 186, 190, 192, 195, 200–202, 208, 209, 212, 220, 224, 227, 229, 234; Daytona 500 14, 15, 34, 42, 67, 69–72, 83–85, 92, 96, 103, 104, 122, 134, 146, 147, 155, 175, 183, 185, 192, 193, 217, 222, 229, 239; Daytona International Speedway 14, 64, 70, 183; Ed Cooke Motor Company 83; Finky's Tonight 220; Firecracker 250/400 14, 23, 50, 51, 54, 83, 87, 94, 96, 126, 147, 151; Florida Boat Racer of the Year 101; Florida Dirt Track Champion 65; Golden Gate Speedway 91; The Hair Shack 212; Hialeah Racetrack 102; Hollywood 11; Jacksonville 28, 38, 79; Lake Lloyd 30, 34; Lakeland 223; Long Boat Key 83; Lynhurst Hotel 126; Miami 85, 95; Orlando 193; Palm Beach 99; Permatex 300 178; Pompano Beach 127, 129; Sarasota 83; Speedweeks 16, 20, 33, 61, 79, 80, 84, 183, 229; Tampa 91, 223; Volusia County Speedway 65
Fogle, Sam 64, 134
Foley, Dick 15
Ford (Econoline/F-100/Fairlane/Fastback/Fusion/Galaxie/Model T/Torino/WT9000) 5, 6, 8, 10, 19, 26, 28, 30, 36, 41–43, 45, 49–51, 53, 60, 62–64, 66–68, 74, 75, 77, 79, 81, 95–98, 101, 109, 112, 113, 124, 126, 127, 132, 134, 138, 140, 145, 146, 148, 150, 152, 156–158, 165, 178, 184, 190, 193, 195, 197, 205, 207, 209, 222, 223, 226, 229–232, 234, 240, 243; Banana Boat 157; Hemi 209; Motor Credit 205
Forty Years of Stock Car Racing ix
Fox, Ray 59, 62, 67, 72, 146
Foyt, A.J. 92, 95, 97, 147, 151, 152, 160, 161, 204
France, Bill, Jr. (Billy/William H.G.) 164, 171, 180, 181, 188, 189, 191, 238, 239, 244
France, Bill, Sr. (Big Bill, The Old Man) 28, 112, 120, 164, 166, 170, 171, 189, 191, 199, 238
Franchitti, Dario 6
Frank, Larry 26, 60, 77
Frasson, Joe 195, 196
Frasson Racing Enterprises 171; Excuse Lounge Chevy 172, 175
Frazier, Brother Bill 200
Freeland, Benny 197
Friel, Norris 14, 58, 88, 97, 102, 107, 108, 110, 137, 146, 147, 150, 152, 154, 156

Ganassi, Chip 6
Gardner, James 160
Gardner, Jim (Congressman) 195
Gatorade 6
Gavaway, Joe 164, 167, 238
Gazaway, Bill 85, 117, 139, 160, 161, 163–169, 171, 206, 215, 238
General Motors 170
Georgia 63, 71, 95, 103, 126, 131, 151; Airport Howard Johnson 212, 216; Atlanta 7, 11, 14, 16, 26, 27, 30, 37, 38, 58, 59, 77, 78, 93, 94, 96, 102, 121, 126, 143, 147, 155, 161, 162, 170, 205, 211, 216, 219, 232; Atlanta 500 19, 26, 29, 58, 112, 121, 162, 168, 174, 206, 211; Atlanta International Raceway 27, 85; Augusta 57, 132, 133, 154; Augusta International Raceway (A.I.R.) 28, 57, 59; Cartersville 95; Dixie 300/400/500 26, 59, 85, 96, 156; Georgia Racing Hall of Fame 49; Griffin 27; Lakewood 29, 30, 32; North Georgia 50; Novelty Machine Company 5; Savannah 49, 54, 132, 143, 148, 149; Valdosta 103, 129, 131, 151
Gibbs, Joe 39, 201
Gilder, Jeff 125
Gill, Billy 92, 103
Glotzbach, Charlie 170, 187, 190, 227
Goldsmith, Paul 13, 56, 67, 162
Goodyear 11, 12, 75, 85, 147, 151, 156, 189, 201, 227
Gordon, Cecil 183, 189, 195, 200
Gordon, Robbie 6
Grace National Bank 21
Grace Steamship Lines 21
Graham, Frank 59, 60
Granger, Gene 178
Gray, Henley 155
Great Northwest 83
Green, George 90, 104
Green, John 163, 190, 191, 197
Grey Rock 147
Greyhound Bus 24
Griffith, Andy 104
Gurney, Dan 160
Guthrie, Janet 177, 201

Hanks, Aunt Erma 51
Hanks, Uncle Harry 51
Hanks, Jerry 52
Hansen, Swede 157
Harn, Rock 153, 154
Hartje, Bud 224
Hassler, Friday 164, 170, 192; Cotton "Grandpa" 192, 193
Hawaii 126
Hawk, Rip 157
Hawkins, Hawkshaw 158
Helms, Jimmy 64, 137
Henderson, Betty 71, 82
Henderson, Kim 71
Hendick, Rick 6, 201
Hendrick, Ray 90
Herbert, Tommy 85
Hernandez, Fran 58
Hinesley, Ronald 128
Hirschfield, Dave 160
Hobby, Christy 141, 142
Hobby, Gene 3, 4
Hobby, Gina 141, 142
Holder, Joe 128, 141
Holiday Inn 131, 162, 178, 190, 197
Holley Carburetors 168
Holloway, B.G. 21
Holloway, Lynne 21
Holly Farms 6, 22, 23, 26, 39, 78, 120
Holman, John 97, 113, 114, 209
Holman-Moody 26, 35, 36, 41, 95–97, 113, 124, 132, 148, 205, 209, 224, 226, 229, 230

Hood, Odell 103
Householder, Ronnie 12, 120, 121, 161–163
Howard, Richard 154
Hudson Hornet (Teaguemobiles) 5
Hudson River 52
Huggins, Ross 151
Hull, Dr. Gerald v
Humphries, Barney 128
Hunter, Jim 243
Hurtubise, Jim 56, 161, 183
Hutcherson, Dick (Hutch) 113, 222, 224
Hutcherson-Pagan 209
Hutchins, Carol 201
Hutchins, Sonny 153
Hutelin, Don 27
Hyde, Harry 165, 213
Hylton, James ix, 161, 188, 189, 195, 199, 219, 228

IMSA 222, 243
Independent 250 199, 202
Indian 192; Cherokowa-Apache 192
Indiana 14, 77, 78, 92; Highland 92; Indianapolis 204; Indianapolis 500 (Indy) 6, 195, 204, 232; Indianapolis Raceway Park 92; Indy Racing League 6; Yankee 300 92
Interstate Batteries 39
Into, Bubba 132, 133
Iowa 83, 121; Sioux City 121
IROC (International Race of Champions) 240
Irvan, Ernie 220
Irwin, Tommy 31, 222, 224
Isaac, Bobby 123, 184, 187, 192, 226

Jack Kochman's Hell Drivers Show 136
Jarrett, Ned 6, 7, 21, 22, 28, 38, 57, 62, 78, 86, 91, 129, 131, 132, 144, 147, 152, 172, 222–224
Jeffords, Steve ix
Jet Way Wax Products 195, 197, 199
Jim Beam 6
Johns, Bobby 20, 23, 33, 37, 38, 59, 72, 74, 76, 77, 88, 95, 102, 132, 133, 146
Johns, Papa (Shorty) 59, 73, 74, 95
Johnson, Jimmy 239
Johnson, Joe Lee 19, 26, 74, 76, 77, 85, 86, 88, 106, 130
Johnson, Junior 22, 23, 34, 38, 39, 56, 72, 73, 77, 78, 86, 87, 106, 111, 112, 120, 134, 137, 144, 150, 157, 158, 168, 170, 195, 201, 216
Jones, Lewis "Possum" 48–50, 87
Jones, Parnelli 56, 85, 161
Juarez, Mexico 218, 219
Juarez Racing 218
Judd, Ashley 6

Kaiser 9
Kawasaki 238
Keck, Bobby 3
Kiekhaefer, Carl 5, 6, 8, 10, 12
King, A.J. 122, 123, 173, 174
King, Bob 128
King, Brownie 104
King Kong 129

Kite, Harold 140, 153, 154, 176
The Klan 190
Kodak 171; Camera Days 171
Korean Conflict (Korea) 104, 182
Kuchler, Lin 190

Labonte, Terry 215
Lamphear, Sonny 157
Langley, Elmo 85, 139, 146, 149, 157, 182, 183, 190, 191, 199, 229, 234
Larson, Mel 201
Las Vegas 16
Lebanon 126
Lewis, Paul 2, 4
Lilly, Betty 103
Link, Terry 174, 209
Liquori, Ralph 9, 11
Little, Marty ix
Littlejohn, Joe 78
Lobinger, Ted 189, 192, 201
Locks, John 17
Long, Bondy 223, 224
Lorenzen, Fred 6, 21, 26, 29, 53, 56, 86, 120, 134, 153, 157, 187, 191
Louisburg College 182
Lovette, Fred 22
Lowe, Ted 92
Lund, Betty 126
Lund, Ma 174
Lund, Tiny 10, 57, 85, 93, 94, 110, 111, 126, 132, 139, 146, 150, 155, 172–174, 187, 189, 192, 209, 210, 228, 234
Lund, Wanda 174
Lynn, Loretta 64

M&M Mars 215
Mann, Ted 183, 188
Manning, Skip 175–177
Mantz, Johnny 10
Marcis, Dave 4, 192, 200
Marlin, Coo Coo 170, 214
Martin, Gerald 191
Martin, Mark 220
Maryland 26, 27
Massey, Jimmy 3
Matador 165, 168
Matthews, Banjo 23, 71, 77, 201, 226
Matthews, Bobby 193
Matthews, Doody 193
McCarthy, Skip 163–165
McCluskey, Roger 16
McDonald, Dave 28
McDuffie, Paul 14, 19, 74, 76, 88, 141, 164, 192, 199, 201, 218
McHugh, Clint 11
McKinney, Stewart 41, 42
McMillan, Allen 183
McQuagg, Sam 122, 146
Mercury (Comet) 6, 54, 55, 57–60, 62–65, 81, 99, 126, 134, 178, 198, 226, 230–232, 234
Mercury Outboard Chrysler 10
Metcalf, Morris 22, 32, 199

Michigan 92, 167, 190, 203, 209, 210, 212, 234, 243; Champion Spark Plug 400 210; Dearborn 113, Detroit 5, 6, 7, 12, 31, 49, 58, 63, 163, 171; Jackson 167; Lake Michigan 92; Michigan State Fairgrounds 5; Motor City 250 5; Yankee 400 234
Miller Beer 172
Milwaukee 14, 92, 161, 162, 172, 183
Mims, Buzz ix
Minnesota 160; Golden Valley 160; Minneapolis 160
Mississippi 103; Jackson 103
Missouri 177; Kansas City 208; Odessa 177; Rolla 177; St. Louis 171
Moody, Ralph 26, 53, 96, 113, 114
moonshine (liquor/shine/whiskey) 50, 89, 91, 92
Moore, Bud 5, 6, 38, 79, 81, 89, 134, 153, 172, 189, 201
Moore, Don 79–81
Moore, Little Bud 4, 135, 150
Morgan, Bill 79
Morrison, Pat 103
Morton, Bill 90
Muhlman, Max 149
Mundy, Frank 5, 11
Musgrave, Ted 4
Myers, Bob (sportswriter) 149
Myers, Bobby 11, 13, 21, 48
Myler, Kenny 21

Nabb, Herb 137
NASCAR 1, 5, 6, 9, 16, 26, 30, 33, 36, 38, 39, 41, 43, 47, 48, 57–59, 63, 66, 73, 74, 82, 83, 85, 88, 89, 92, 97, 99–101, 104, 106, 107, 113, 120, 121, 125, 128, 130, 139–141, 143, 147, 156, 160, 163–167, 169–171, 174, 178, 181, 184, 186, 187, 189–191, 194, 197, 199, 201, 202, 204, 206, 212, 221, 222, 238, 239–242, 244; Busch Series 178; The Chase 202; Dash 142; Grand American 228; Grand National 6, 7, 9, 11, 14, 20, 21, 22, 28, 30, 33, 36, 39, 41, 43, 46–48, 50, 56, 63–67, 71, 72, 77, 79, 82, 91, 97, 101, 103–105, 109, 116, 124, 127, 131, 134, 137, 140–143, 145, 146, 149, 154, 155, 158, 182, 187, 202, 205, 206, 222, 223, 230; Nationwide Series 178; Rookie of the Year 2, 30, 33, 47, 49, 73, 88, 175–177, 192, 193, 198, 222, 225; Sprint Cup 6, 36, 222; Strictly Stock 5; Winston Cup (Cup) 2, 6, 129, 160, 176, 178, 182, 187, 188, 194, 201, 203, 205, 206, 208, 209, 215, 218, 221–223, 226, 230, 232, 233, 240, 243, 244
National Motorsports Press Association Stock Car Hall of Fame 53
Negre, Ed 206
Nelson, Gary 213
Nelson, Norm 5, 10
New Jersey 12, 203, 204, 210; Lambertville 223; Old Bridge 12; Paterson 210; Trenton 225; Woodbury 203
New York 52, 60, 61, 207, 224, 225; Bridgehampton 7, 60–62, 155, 224; Fonda 225; Islip 61, 62, 207, 225; Long Island 60; Malta 207; New York (City) 104, 207, 208; Sag Harbor 60; Watkins Glen 12, 29, 155

Nichels, Ray 67, 72, 73, 92, 94, 161–163, 195; "Minnie" 163
Nitro 9 234–236, 238
Nitrous oxide 167, 214, 215, 238
Norman, Whitey 13
North Carolina (N.C.) 3, 48–50, 52, 53, 89–91, 100, 104, 105, 125–129, 138, 142, 146, 148, 155, 174, 178, 182, 183, 188, 199, 238; American 500 121, 122, 217, 226; Apex 126, 127; Apex High School 126; Archdale 100; Asheville 89, 183; Asheville 300 230; Asheville-Weaverville 11, 89, 95, 109; Bowman-Gray Stadium 22, 29, 38, 105, 131, 138, 139; Camp Lejeune 126; Carolina 500 175, 194, 196, 237; Carrboro 188; Chapel Hill 48, 52, 183, 191, 192, 195, 200; Charlotte 7, 18–20, 27, 38, 54, 57, 63, 79, 85, 88, 95, 100, 114, 121, 138, 140, 143, 145, 147, 149, 150, 154, 155, 158, 162, 163, 170, 172, 189, 191, 194, 195, 208, 219; Charlotte Fairgrounds (Speedway) 66, 158; Charlotte Motor Speedway 73, 85, 153, 183, 213; Concord 220; Denton 140; Dog Track 140; Durham 182, 193, 199; Durham High School 182; East Carolina University 126; Fayetteville 11; Folger Buick 143; Ft. Bragg 182; Franklinton 141; Gastonia 143; Greensboro 49, 52; Gwen-Staley 160/400 90, 104; Harris 113; Henderson 127, 132, 133; Hendersonville 238; Hickory 105, 138, 146, 174; Hickory 250 156; Hillsborough 2, 4, 52, 64, 125, 128, 134–137, 142, 155, 182, 194; Hillsborough Historic Speedway Group 142; Hob Nob Restaurant/Team 149, 151, 158; Hoskins 158; Jacksonville 146; Jonas' Ridge Mountain 105; King's Mountain 178; Lacy's Alignment 143; Lake Wylie 158; Memory Lane Museum 4; Monroe 143; Mooresville 4; Mount Airy 104; Moyock 140; Myers Brothers 200 22; National 400/500 19, 79, 88, 111, 112, 114, 153, 195; New Asheville Speedway 230; North Wilkesboro (Wilkesboro) 13, 26, 89, 90, 92, 95, 101, 104, 120, 141, 194, 218, 234; Occoneechee Speedway 7, 125, 142; Orange County 135; Prince's Auto Service 127; Raleigh 141; Robinwood Speedway 143; Rockingham 121, 122, 141, 175, 186, 187, 194, 196, 213, 226, 243; Rougemont 199; Shelby 154; Statesville 148; Surry County 104; Trico Speedway 199; Trinity 127; University of North Carolina (Law School) 100, 190, 191; Weaverville 105, 108, 111, 115, 134; West Mecklenburg High School 143; Western North Carolina 500 108, 109; Wilkes County (Moonshine Capital of the World) 91, 92; Wilson 105; Winston-Salem 22, 56, 105, 140; World 600 18, 19, 27, 29, 38, 65, 73, 85, 88, 106, 124, 144, 150, 155, 162, 170, 191, 194, 220
Northern Tour 12, 51, 60, 141, 207, 225
NUCAR Series 139

O'Dell, Homer 157, 158
Ohio 137, 141; Akron 141; Cincinnati 112; New Bremen 160
Oklahoma City 11
Oldsmobile (Olds) 5, 6, 31, 66, 75, 83–86, 88–91, 97, 103, 145, 216

Oliver, Jackie 164, 178
Oregon 83; Newberg 83
Osborne Brothers (Lewis and Roy) 28, 111, 112
Owens, Cotton 3, 11, 18, 19, 35, 37, 59, 66, 67, 70, 72, 73, 82, 85, 86, 88, 128, 132, 133, 136, 137, 224, 226
Owens, Dewey 70

Packard 237
Pagan, Eddie 56, 66, 209
Page, Lenny 106
Palatine Auto Parts 237
Panagra Airlines 21
Panch, Marvin 11, 24, 26, 33, 57, 61, 62, 85, 126, 128, 129, 132, 151, 234; Marvin Panch's Four Wheel Brake Service 151
Pardue, Jimmy 22, 28, 63, 73, 89, 91, 92, 131, 132
Parker, Earl 168, 187
Parker, J.C. 145
Parks, Raymond 5, 6
Parsons, Benny 7, 129, 146, 147
Paschal, Jim 20, 22, 56, 77, 78
Passino, Jacque 113, 114
Pearson, David 6, 56, 66, 68–70, 73, 75, 78, 81, 88, 92, 120, 131, 132, 171, 174, 181, 183, 187, 189, 192, 195, 213, 214, 222, 225, 226, 228–230, 235
Pennsylvania 12, 51; Heidelburg 51; Langhorne 12, 13, 29; Philadelphia 104; Pittsburgh 104; Pocono 212
Penske, Roger 6, 201, 221
Peterson, Pete ix
Petty, Lee 6, 9, 11, 13, 30–33, 36, 38, 51, 52, 57, 62, 73, 75, 83, 86, 105, 106, 130
Petty, Maurice 6, 78, 122
Petty, Richard (The King) 6, 22, 26, 30–32, 56, 57, 64, 78, 86, 89, 101, 106, 109, 116, 120–122, 128, 129, 131, 132, 141, 149, 156, 163–165, 169, 171, 174, 175, 181, 183, 186–189, 195, 212, 220, 226, 227, 229, 230, 239
Pettys of Gaffney 178
Piedmont Carolinas 66
Pierce Tractors 72
Piggins, Vince 40
Pironi, Jimmy 83, 103
Pistone, "Tiger" Tom 4, 19, 21, 34, 86, 132, 138, 146, 148–151, 156
Plantation Club 18
Plymouth (Fury/Petty) 6, 9–14, 20, 28, 31, 118, 119, 121, 122, 130, 133, 147–149, 152, 158, 160, 161, 240
Pontiac (Grand Am/Grand Prix/LeMans) 6, 13, 14, 19, 21–23, 37, 38, 66–70, 72, 73, 75, 78, 79, 80, 82, 88, 92, 94, 95, 101, 106, 126, 146, 169, 170, 171, 174, 209, 221, 238
Pop Kola 230, 232, 234
Pops Racing Team 75
Porter, Marvin 75, 79, 111
Porter, Tommy 132, 133
Potter, Jess 104, 105, 109, 115
Poulos, George 149, 158
Powell, Floyd 66
Presley, Elvis 142
Priddy, Cotton 11

Prince, Tab 161, 184, 186, 201, 224, 227, 228
Proctor, Clem 76
Professional Drivers Association (PDA) 190, 191, 227
Prout, Warren 60
Pruitt, Gerald 69
Purcell, Pat 16
Pure Oil 71
Purolator 6
Purser, Jack 66–68, 70, 71, 74, 75, 77
Putney, J.T. 131, 135, 140, 141

RacersReunion.com 125
Rawl, John 201
Red Bull 219, 239
Redline 7000 115
Reed, Jim 10, 11, 22, 33, 86
Retirement Living 223
Richmond, Tim 218–220
Ritter, Ron 127
RJ Reynolds (Winston) 6, 171
Roach, Dr. 150, 155
Robbins, Bert 97
Robbins, Marty 156, 158
Roberts, Cherlie 199
Roberts, Fireball 3, 9, 11, 13, 14, 17, 22, 27, 28, 53, 63, 65, 76, 79, 85–88, 91, 92, 95, 126, 128, 129, 144; Fireball Roberts Trophy 235
Roberts, Pam 3
Rodgers, Dr. Ted 201
Rollins, Shorty 76
Rose, Gene 9
Roush, Jack 6, 201
Rudd, Ricky 215, 219
Rupert Safety Belts 10
Rutherford, Johnny 92

Sachs, Eddie 92
Schneider, Frankie 223, 237
Scott, Frank 128
Scott, Sybil 3
Scott, Wendell 3, 7, 22, 28, 29, 56, 57, 115, 128, 129, 137–139, 145, 146, 150, 194, 195, 197, 199, 236, 237
Sears, Earl 128
Sears, John 184, 191, 224
Second World War 182; Battle of the Bulge 182; Guadalcanal 182
Seifert, Bill 183, 184, 186, 188, 193, 201, 228; Bill Seifert Racing (BSR) 186, 189, 190, 185
Shaw, Reid 140
Shook, Monroe 39, 40
Silent Speedways of the Carolinas 3
Simpson, Bill 175
Sisco, David 188
Skeen, Belinda 100
Skeen, Buren 97–101, 139, 140, 152, 153, 155, 176
Skeen, Chris 100
Skeen, Eric 100
Smith, Bruton 22
Smith, Frank 100
Smith, Freddie 178

Smith, Jack 11, 14, 21–23, 27–29, 53, 68, 78, 79, 92, 106
Smith, Larry 188, 189, 192, 193, 197, 198, 201, 208
Smith, Wayne 139, 140, 226
Smyle, Don 15, 17, 19, 20, 23, 24, 157, 227
South America 81
South Carolina (Palmetto State) ix, 26, 30, 39, 41, 48, 50, 52, 64, 66, 126, 142, 173, 174, 180, 187, 206, 208, 222, 224, 225; Abbeville 50, 54; Aiken 50; Charleston 48–50, 52, 54, 58–60, 62, 139; Cherokee County 66; Coastal Speedway 12; Columbia 32, 126, 147, 187, 205, 206; Columbia Speedway 74, 207; Columbia 200 187; Cross 173; Darlington 7, 11, 12, 17, 21, 23, 27, 29, 33, 34, 53, 59, 67, 74, 75, 80, 86–88, 93, 95, 97, 98, 100, 107, 111, 123, 124, 143, 144, 149, 150, 152–154, 157, 158, 160, 170, 171, 190, 194–196, 202, 208, 213, 214, 216, 220, 235, 236; Darlington Historic Racing Festival 102, 142; Darlington International Raceway (The Lady in Black) 54, 111, 146, 149, 208; Darlington Museum 169; Darlington Stripe (Third Turn) 21, 53, 54, 76, 77, 87, 97, 98, 124, 150, 208, 236; Florence 50, 88, 98, 140; Greenville 26, 72, 73, 78, 107, 225; Greenville-Pickens (Speedway) 29, 66, 70, 73, 78, 145, 158, 187; Greenwood 50; Inman 30, 39, 41, 42, 224, 243; Jimmy's Restaurant 45; Jonesville 74; Lake Moultrie 126; Little Rebs 93; Monks Corner 64, 126, 174; Myrtle Beach ix, 12, 36, 40, 55, 127, 138, 139, 151, 158; North Charleston 126; Parris Island 126; Piedmont Interstate Fairgrounds (The Fairgrounds) 43, 77, 78, 224; P.J.'s Bar and Grill 68; Pure–Darlington Record Club 216; Rebel 300/400/500 15, 17, 21, 29, 93, 124, 143, 150, 171, 196, 211, 235, 236; Rogers' Esso 68; Southern 500 12, 13, 19, 20, 23, 26, 33, 53, 59, 60, 62, 65, 66, 72, 74–76, 79, 83, 86, 88, 97, 103, 107, 110, 111, 139, 140, 146, 147, 152–155, 175, 176, 208, 213, 218, 235, 236; Spartanburg (County) ix, 19, 20, 26, 43, 48, 63, 66, 68, 70, 72, 74, 77, 79, 81, 129, 131, 133, 134, 142, 145, 157, 173, 178, 180, 223, 224, 243; Spartanburg City Council 243; Spartanburg General Hospital 44, 47; *Spartanburg Herald-Journal* 66; Tinsley's 67; Union 74; Village Supper Club 72; Whitmire 74
Southern Motorsports Journal 135
Spencer, G.C. 22, 76, 91, 113, 140, 147, 148, 150, 187, 195, 222, 224, 226
Spikes, Ken 140
Squire, Ken 193
Stacy, Nelson 26, 27, 41, 53, 57, 77, 112
Stairs, Carl 151
Staley, Enoch 141
Staley, Gwen 10, 13
Standard Oil 42
Starr, Tommy 18
Stelter, Lyle 126
Stevenson, Chuck 10
Stewart-Haas 201
Stockman, Harry 204
Stott, Ramo 196, 230, 231
STP 6, 190, 193

Stroppe, Bill 77, 99
Styrofoam 7
Sutton, Len 56, 92, 94, 96
Suzuki 238
Sweatlund, Charles 88

Tanner, Frank 62
Tarlton, Angela v
Tate, Joe 67
Taylor, Joe 88
Teague, Marshall 5
Tennessee ix, 63, 116, 124, 142, 158, 234; Boyd Speedway 131; Bristol 21, 22, 27, 29, 90, 93, 94, 97, 104, 111, 116, 122, 129, 139, 148, 155, 158, 181, 195, 197, 199, 212, 213, 218; Bristol International Speedway 119, 137; Chattanooga 129, 130; Confederate 300 131; Cracker Barrel Country Store 420 237; Johnson City 104; Knoxville 158; Maryville 2, 116; Memphis ix; Nashville 23, 130, 156, 234, 238; Nashville 300 31, 106, 195; Shelbyville 142; Smoky Mountain 250 116; Southeastern 500 90, 123, 148; Volunteer 500 21, 22
Texas 9, 21, 56, 164, 192, 199, 201, 204, 205, 209; Alamo 192; Alamo 500 164; College Station 160, 192, 201; Corpus Christi 9–11, 28; Devil's Bowl 205; Houston 9, 203; Mesquite 205; Texas World Speedway 164
Thomas, Herb 5
Thomas, Jabe 2, 229, 234
Thomas, Larry 28, 63, 91, 127, 128, 131
Thomas, Ronnie 2
Thompson, Jimmy 77
Thompson, Speedy 10, 11, 12, 85, 143
Thompson, Tommy 5
Thornburg, Wade 127
Thunder Craft Boats 200
Thunder in Carolina 66
Thunderbird (T-Bird) 31, 33, 34, 36, 38, 77, 83, 85
Toyota 5, 36, 240
Trickle, Dick 176, 177
Trivette, E.J. 206
Tunis, Parker 83, 103
Turner, Curtis 3, 6, 10, 11, 21, 29, 65, 73, 77, 86, 119, 120, 156, 222, 223
Tyner, Roy 14, 88, 126, 128, 129, 143, 146, 150, 157

Ulrich, Caroline 215
Ulrich, D.K. 236
Underwood, Ray 95, 98
Union 76 193, 233
USAC 8, 14, 16, 92, 160–163, 201, 222, 243
U.S. Air Force 48
U.S. Army 215
U.S. Marine Corps 126; Operation Blue Bat 126
U.S. Navy 8, 66, 143
U.S. Senate 42
University of South Carolina 175
UNO 218, 220
Unser, Al 161
Unser, Bobby 195

Vaughn, Linda (Miss Pure Firebird) 91
Vietnam War 126; Viet Cong (VC) Hunting Club 126, 139
Virginia 26, 30, 39, 48, 56, 60, 115, 138, 150, 208, 225, 230, 237–239; Alexandria 39, Arlington 39; Capital City 300 140, 141; Columbia Furnace 30; Danville 48, 49, 56, 65, 115; Floyd County 222, 223; Hampton 138, 150; Keysville 39; Langley Field 138, 150; Manassas 130; Martinsville 17, 64, 72, 74, 95, 117, 120, 128, 129, 132, 135, 137, 154, 157, 189, 194, 238; Martinsville 500 136; Richmond 26, 64, 118, 134, 140, 141, 145, 158, 194, 199, 220, 226, 229, 230; Roanoke 222; Roanoke River 223; Ron's Ford 139; Schoolfield 48; South Boston 129, 208; Victory Stadium 223; Virginia 500 128, 157; Winchester 30
Vogt, Red 5, 22, 28
Vukovich, Bill 205

Wade, Billy 28, 62, 63, 131, 152
Wagner, Bob 216; Midwestern Farm Lines 216
Walker, Jack ix, 40, 42, 55, 59, 70
Wallace, Rusty 177, 221
Walters, Ratus 26, 27, 60, 62
Waltrip, Darrell 164, 165, 211
Warren, David 64, 148, 150, 151, 155–157, 159
Warren, Frank 153, 154
Warren, T. Taylor 184
Watson, W.H. 67, 70
Watts (Raymond Williams crewman) 192
Wayne Heads 67
Weatherly, Joe 10, 11, 14, 22, 28, 33, 39, 56, 63, 65, 73, 78, 85, 86, 134
Welborn, Bob 11, 56, 65, 73, 78, 86, 106
West Marine 158
West Virginia 57; Huntington 57, 95; Mountaineer 300 57
Whataburger 51
Wheeler, Humpy 177
White, Don (Snuggy) 161, 163
White, Gene 19, 80
White, Rex 3, 11, 19, 20, 22, 23, 28, 29, 70, 73, 74, 78, 82, 88, 222–224

Whitmore, M.E. (Mickey) 128, 133, 136, 137
Wickersham, Butch 103
Wickersham, Frank 103
Wickersham, Gail 103
Wickersham, Reb (Charles/Johnny Reb/Johnny Yuma) 51, 84, 110, 140, 152, 155; *The Flying Rebel* 84; Flying Rebel Racing Team 83, 84, 102, 103; *Rebel a Go Go* 101; Reb's Sport Shop 92
Williams, Dr. Clifton v
Williams, Don 180
Williams, Norman 192
Wilson, Waddell 224
Wilson, Woodie 111
Windsor (heads) 169
Wolford, Johnny 18, 19
Wood, Glen 38, 168
Wood Brothers 6, 59, 163, 201, 226, 232
Woods, Bob 83
Woods, Earnest 5, 6
Woods, Snooker 70
World Book Encyclopedia 174
World Stock Car Racing Championship 48
Wright, Margaret Sue Turner 3
Wright, Pete 219

Yarborough, Cale 5, 50, 112–114, 118, 131, 137, 139, 152, 165, 166, 183, 189, 195, 196, 211, 217, 218, 227, 232, 234, 239
Yarborough, Gloria 192
Yarbrough, LeeRoy 24, 131, 132, 141, 162, 192
Yates, Doug 150
Yates, Ollie, Sr. 128
Yates, Robert 224
Yon, Cecil 50
Yon Brothers 48, 49, 50
York, Les 66
Young, Bill 103
Yunick, Henry "Smokey" 5, 14, 39, 72, 79, 126, 156

Zervakis, Emanuel 39, 78, 86
Zimbabwe 199

www.ingramcontent.com/pod-product-compliance
Ingram Content Group UK Ltd.
Pitfield, Milton Keynes, MK11 3LW, UK
UKHW050537150426
5217IPUK00026B/1967